Human Capital Analytics

Scrivener Publishing
100 Cummings Center, Suite 541J
Beverly, MA 01915-6106

Publishers at Scrivener
Martin Scrivener (martin@scrivenerpublishing.com)
Phillip Carmical (pcarmical@scrivenerpublishing.com)

Human Capital Analytics

Exploring the HR Spectrum in Industry 5.0

Edited by

Deepa Gupta
GL Bajaj Institute of Management, Greater Noida, India

Mukul Gupta
GL Bajaj Institute of Management, Greater Noida, India

Pawan Budhwar
International Human Resource Management, Aston University, UK

Jim Westerman
Department of Management, Appalachian State University, Boone, NC, USA

Rajesh Kumar Dhanaraj
Symbiosis International Deemed University, Pune, India

and

Balamurugan Balusamy
Shiv Nadar University, Delhi-NCR Campus, Noida, India

Scrivener Publishing

WILEY

This edition first published 2025 by John Wiley & Sons, Inc., 111 River Street, Hoboken, NJ 07030, USA and Scrivener Publishing LLC, 100 Cummings Center, Suite 541J, Beverly, MA 01915, USA

For more information about Scrivener publications please visit www.scrivenerpublishing.com.

Wiley Global Headquarters
111 River Street, Hoboken, NJ 07030, USA

For details of our global editorial offices, customer services, and more information about Wiley products visit us at www.wiley.com.

Library of Congress Cataloging-in-Publication Data

ISBN 978-1-394-23832-3

Front cover images courtesy of Adobe Firefly
Cover design by Russell Richardson

Set in size of 11pt and Minion Pro by Manila Typesetting Company, Makati, Philippines

Printed in the USA

10 9 8 7 6 5 4 3 2 1

Contents

Preface **xvii**

Part 1: Foundation and Strategic Framework of Human Capital Analytics in Industry 5.0 **1**

1 Human Capital Analytics in Industry 5.0: Opportunities and Challenges **3**

Veena Grover, Manju Nandal, Divya Sahu and Mahima Dogra

Abbreviations 4
1.1 Introduction 4
1.2 Evolution of Industry 5.0 6
1.3 Concept and Definition of Human Capital Analytics 7
1.4 Features of Human Capital Analytics 9
1.5 Advantages and Disadvantages of Human Capital Analytics 10
1.6 Uses of Human Capital Analytics 11
1.7 How Human Capital Analytics Help in Industry 5.0? 13
1.8 Difference Between Industry 4.0 and Industry 5.0 14
1.8.1 The Pillars of Industry 4.0 14
1.8.2 The Pillars of Industry 5.0 15
1.9 Human Capital Analytics Enabled in Different Sectors 16
1.10 Challenges and Opportunities of Human Capital Analytics 18
1.10.1 Challenges of Human Capital Analytics 18
1.10.2 Opportunities of Human Capital Analytics 18
1.11 HR Analytics and Artificial Intelligence 19
1.12 HR Analytics and Blockchain 20
1.13 HR Analytics and the Internet of Things 21
1.14 Level of Analytics Used in Human Capital Analytics 22
1.15 The Shift of People Analytics 23
1.15.1 People Analytics 23
1.15.2 Why People Analytics More Effective at Driving Value 25

1.15.3 Example of How People Analytics Can Improve Business Value 26
1.16 Conclusion and Future Direction 26
References 28

2 Human Capital Analytics and Emerging Technologies in Industry 5.0 31
Harpreet Kaur Channi and Surinder Kaur
2.1 Introduction 32
2.1.1 Background and Motivation 33
2.2 Industry 5.0 and the Role of Human Capital 35
2.2.1 Evolution of Industrial Revolutions: From Industry 4.0 to Industry 5.0 36
2.2.2 The Significance of Human Capital in the Modern Industrial Landscape 37
2.2.3 Synergy Between Technology and Human Expertise in Industry 5.0 39
2.3 Emerging Technologies Shaping Human Capital 40
2.3.1 Emerging Technologies' Revolutionary Effect on Workforce Management 42
2.3.2 Integrating Human and Technological Capabilities for Optimal Outcomes 43
2.4 Human Capital Analytics: Enhancing Workforce Management 44
2.4.1 Role of Data Analytics in Human Capital Management 46
2.4.2 Data-Driven Insights for Employee Performance and Skill Assessment 47
2.4.3 Predictive Analytics for Workforce Planning and Employee Retention 47
2.4.4 Harnessing Data to Optimize Resource Allocation and Training Strategies 48
2.4.5 Case Studies 48
2.5 Challenges and Ethical Considerations 51
2.5.1 Data Privacy and Security Concerns in Human Capital Analytics 51
2.5.2 Fairness, Bias, and Transparency in AI-Driven Workforce Management 52
2.5.3 Ethical Guidelines and Governance 53
2.5.4 Bus Automation with Human Empowerment 53
2.6 Recommendations for Organizations 54
2.6.1 Building a Data-Driven Culture 56

2.6.2 Developing a Comprehensive Human Capital Analytics Strategy 56
2.6.3 Investing in Continuous Learning and Development 56
2.6.4 Balancing Technology with Human-Centric Approaches 57
2.7 Conclusion 57
References 59

3 Fifth Industrial Revolution and an Overview of its Impact on Human Resources 65
Aduku Alex Akubo, Okpanachi Linus Odiji and Muhammed Bature Muhammed
3.1 Introduction 66
3.2 Trajectory of Industrial Revolutions 67
3.3 An Overview of the Fifth Industrial Revolution 70
3.4 The Fifth Industrial Revolution and Human Resource Management of the Organizations 71
3.5 Fifth Industrial Revolution: Implications of the Technological Advancements on the Workforce 76
3.6 The Fifth Industrial Revolution: Opportunities and Challenges 77
3.7 Conclusion 78
References 78

4 Human Capital Transformation - Revolutionizing HR Practices with Advanced Technologies and Ethical Insights 81
Vijeyata, Chitra Jha and Sunil Tegwal
4.1 Introduction 82
4.2 Systematic Review 82
4.2.1 The Industrial Revolution 82
4.2.2 What are the Key Technologies Driving the Development of Industry 5.0? 84
4.2.3 Different Industrial Revolutions' Effects on Human Resource Functions 85
4.2.4 Industry 5.0 Technologies 88
4.2.5 A Summary of Journal Search Results 91
4.3 Its Impact on HR 91
4.3.1 How these Technologies are Transforming Industries 91
4.3.2 Changing Workforce Dynamics 94
4.3.3 Talent Acquisition and Recruitment Activities 94
4.3.4 Challenges in Industry 5.0 Revolution 95
4.3.5 Limitations of Industry 5.0 97

4.4 Conclusion 97
References 98

5 HR 5.0 Strategic Planning and Evolution of HR Functions in the Business Environment 101
M. Bharathi, K. Praveena, M. Dharani, V. Madhurima, Krithikaa Mohanarangam, G. Sandhya Kumari and Saleha Tabassum
5.1 Introduction 102
5.2 Evolution Cycle of HR Functions 103
5.2.1 Analytics for HR and HR Driven by Data 103
5.2.2 Digital HR and Employee Experience 103
5.2.3 Future of Work and Agile HR 104
5.3 Factors Influencing the Business Environment and its Connection to Strategic Planning 104
5.3.1 Economic Factors 104
5.3.2 Political and Legal Considerations 105
5.3.3 Social and Cultural Factors 105
5.3.4 Challenging Factors 105
5.3.5 Environmental Factors 105
5.3.6 Scientific Advances 106
5.4 Three Steps to Strategic Planning in HR 5.0 106
5.4.1 Environmental Assessment 106
5.4.2 Goal Setting 107
5.4.3 Strategic Planning 107
5.5 Summary and Conclusion 108
5.5.1 Future Perspective 108
References 109

Part 2: Analytical Techniques and Applications in Workforce Management 111

6 Investigating the Transformative Effects of AI, Machine Learning, and Robotics on Human Capital Analytics - An Empirical Study 113
Gagandeep, Jyoti Verma and Deepa Gupta
6.1 Introduction 114
6.1.1 Background and Significance of the Study 114
6.1.2 Research Problem and Research Questions 115
6.1.3 Objectives of the Study 115
6.1.4 Contribution and Value-Add of the Study 116
6.2 Literature Review 116

6.2.1 Overview of AI, Machine Learning, and Robotics in the Context of Human Capital Analytics 116
6.2.2 Theoretical Frameworks and Models 117
6.2.3 Previous Empirical Studies on the Impact of AI, Machine Learning, and Robotics on Human Capital Analytics 118
6.2.4 Conceptual Framework and Hypotheses 119
6.3 Research Design and Methodology 120
6.4 Data Analysis 122
6.4.1 Descriptive Analysis 122
6.4.2 Inferential Analysis 125
6.4.2.1 Structural Equation Modeling (SEM) 125
6.4.2.2 Hypothesis Testing 127
6.5 Practical/Managerial Implications 131
6.5.1 Implications of the Study for Business Practitioners and Managers 131
6.5.2 Recommendations for Implementing AI, Machine Learning, and Robotics in Human Capital Analytics 132
6.6 Limitations of the Study 133
6.7 Future Research 134
6.8 Conclusion 135
References 136
Appendices (if applicable) 138

7 Unleashing Human Capital Analytics for Data-Driven Workforce Management 143
Princi Gupta, Deepa Gupta and Mukul Gupta
7.1 Introduction 144
7.2 Theoretical Background 145
7.2.1 From Metrics to Strategy: The Evolution of Human Capital Analytics 145
7.2.2 Dissecting HR Analytics: Exploring Different Types and Applications 146
7.3 Illustrative Case Studies: Transforming HR with Data-Driven Strategies 148
7.4 Strategic Integration: Deploying Data Analytics and Technology Solutions in HR Operations 151
7.5 Optimizing Talent Acquisition Through Data-Driven Human Capital Analytics 152
7.6 Data-Driven Strategies for Optimal Workforce Performance in Industry 5.0 153

7.7 Engage and Retain: Data-Driven Success 155
7.8 Navigating Complexities: Challenges and Strategic Solutions in Deploying Human Capital Analytics 156
7.9 Emerging Technological Solutions: AI and Machine Learning in HR Optimization 157
7.10 Conclusion 159
References 160

8 Mastering the Art of HR Data Collection and Management Techniques 165
Deepa Gupta, Mukul Gupta, Priti Rai, Karishma Sharma and Parth Mukul Gupta
Introduction 166
Importance of HR Data in Modern Organizations 167
Overview of HR Data Collection and Management 169
Data Collection Techniques 169
Data Management Systems 170
Leveraging HR Data for Decision-Making 171
Future Trends 171
Objectives and Benefits of Mastering HR Data Techniques 172
Fundamentals of HR Data 174
Data Privacy and Compliance Considerations 176
Data Collection Techniques 177
Manual Data Collection Methods 177
Computerized Data Collection Strategies 178
Best Practices for Accurate and Reliable Data Collection 179
Integrating HRIS with Other Business Systems 181
Data Quality and Accuracy 183
Best Practices for Data Storing 185
Analyzing HR Data 189
Techniques for Data Examination 191
Using HR Data for Free Course 192
Using Data to Enlighten HR Game Plans and Strategies 192
Case Studies of Data-Driven HR Decision Making 193
Future Trends in HR Data Management 195
The Occupation of HR in the Time of Cutting-Edge Change 196
Assumptions for the Inevitable Destiny of HR Data Collection and Management 196
References 197

9 Communicating Human Capital Analytics Insights to Decision-Makers Effectively **201**
Sandeep Singh Chandel, Astha Shukla, Sakshi Shukla and Shivansu Sachan
Introduction of Analytics for Human Capital Analysis 202
Role of Retention in Analytics for Human Capital Analysis 205
Analytics for Human Capital Analysis 205
Human Capital Analysis Analytics Framework 207
Factors Affecting Human Capital Analysis (HCA) Analytics 207
Understanding the Needs and Inclinations of Choice Makers 208
Human Capital Analysis Calculations 209
Employee Turnover 209
New Contract Turnover Rate 209
Retention Rate 210
Offer Acceptance Rate 210
Cost per Hire 210
Time to Productivity 210
Types of HR Analytics 210
Training and Development Work Metrics 215
Conclusion 216
References 217

10 Predictive Analytics - Next Chapter in Talent Management **219**
Swati Rai, Rakesh Kumar Yadav and Rajesh Kumar Dhanaraj
10.1 Introduction 220
10.1.1 Role of Predictive Analytics in Talent Management 221
10.1.1.1 Recruitment and Selection 221
10.1.1.2 Candidate Assessment 222
10.1.1.3 Retention and Employee Engagement 223
10.1.1.4 Succession Planning 225
10.1.1.5 Performance Management 226
10.1.1.6 Human Resource Planning 226
10.1.1.7 Learning and Development 227
10.1.1.8 Continuous Feedback and Improvement 228
10.2 Predictive Analysis - A Game Changer 228
10.3 Challenges in Predictive Analytics 229
10.3.1 Quality and Availability of Data 229
10.3.2 Privacy and Security of Data 230

10.3.3 Complexity of Models 230
10.3.4 Overfitting and Underfitting 230
10.3.5 Lack of Domain Expertise 231
10.3.6 Scalability Issues 231
10.3.7 Changing Data Patterns 231
10.3.8 Interpretable Models 231
Conclusion 235
References 236

11 Employee Engagement and Performance Management - Critical Role of Employee Potentials 237
Asma Bano and Ayesha Khatun
11.1 Introduction 238
11.1.1 Human Resource Analytics (HR Analytics) 238
11.2 Literature Review and Theoretical Concepts of the Study 240
11.2.1 Literature Review on Theoretical Concepts of Employee Potential 240
11.2.1.1 Factors of Employee Potential 241
11.2.1.2 Ways to Unlock the Employee Potential 242
11.2.2 Literature Review on Theoretical Concepts of Employee Engagement 243
11.2.2.1 Definitions of Employee Engagement 243
11.2.2.2 Factors of Employee Engagement 244
11.2.2.3 Methods of Attaining Employee Engagement 244
11.2.2.4 Outcomes of Employee Engagement 245
11.2.3 Literature Review on Theoretical Concepts of Organizational Performance 245
11.2.3.1 Factors of Organizational Performance 246
11.2.3.2 Steps to Achieve Organizational Performance 247
11.2.3.3 Outcomes of Organizational Performance 247
11.3 Conceptual Framework 248
11.3.1 Employee Potential 248
11.3.2 Employee Engagement 249
11.3.3 Organizational Performance 249
11.4 Research Objectives 250
11.5 Research Methodology 250
11.5.1 Research Method and Design 250
11.6 Findings and Discussions 251
11.7 Practical Implications 253

11.8 Limitations and Future Directions 254
11.9 Conclusions 255
References 256

12 Performance Evaluation and Measurement of Human Capital Analytics in the Information Technology (IT) Sector in India 261
Manoj Kumar, Pratibha Maurya and Rinki Verma
12.1 Introduction 262
12.2 Literature Review 263
12.2.1 Need for Evaluation of Human Capital 264
12.3 Objective of the Study 266
12.4 Methodology Adopted 267
12.4.1 Human Capital Return on Investment (HCROI) 267
12.4.2 Human Capital Value Added (HCVA) 267
12.4.3 Human Economic Value Added (HEVA) 267
12.5 Data Analysis 270
12.5.1 Objective 1 270
12.5.2 Objective 2 273
12.5.3 Objective 3 274
12.6 Discussion 276
12.7 Conclusion 277
12.8 Implications 277
References 278

13 Data-Driven Strategies to Improve Workplace Diversity, Equality and Inclusion (DEI) 283
Arkja Singh, Rakesh Kumar Yadav and Deepa Gupta
13.1 Introduction 284
13.1.1 Data-Driven Strategies in Workplace 284
13.1.1.1 Demographic Analysis 285
13.1.1.2 Sentiment Analysis 285
13.1.1.3 Network Analysis 286
13.1.2 DEI Initiatives within the Workplace 286
13.2 The Coalesce 288
13.2.1 Data-Driven Strategies and DEI 288
13.3 The Contraption 290
13.3.1 Data-Driven Mindset among the HR and Technology Leaders 290
13.3.1.1 Diversity 292
13.3.1.2 Equality 292
13.3.1.3 Inclusion 292
13.3.2 DEI Software 293

13.4 Challenges and Deliberations 296
13.4.1 Data Precision 297
13.4.2 Data Confidentiality 297
13.4.3 Steer Clear of Tokenism 297
13.4.4 Persistent Loyalty 297
13.5 Conclusion 298
13.5.1 Attracting Apex Talent 299
13.5.2 Driving Employee Retention and Loyalty 299
13.5.3 Nurturing Belonging and Inclusion 299
13.5.4 Identifying Gaps in Employee Representation 299
13.5.5 Tracking Progress Alongside Representation Goals 299
13.5.6 Furnishing Teams for Victory 300
13.5.7 Gaining an All-Inclusive View of DEI Experience 300
References 301

Part 3: Future Trends, Challenges, and Sustainable Development in HR Practices 303

14 Role of Human Capital Analytics and Industry 5.0 in Advancing the United Nations' Sustainable Development Goals 305
Agagu A. A., Odiji O. L. and Akubo A. A.
14.1 Introduction 306
14.2 Review of Extant Literature 307
14.3 Conceptual Clarification 308
14.3.1 Human Capital Analytics 308
14.3.2 Fifth Industrial Revolution 309
14.4 The UN SDGs 311
14.4.1 Nexuses Between HCA, Industry 5.0, and the SDGs 312
14.5 Inherent and Emerging Challenges 319
14.5.1 Measures to Address the Challenges which Bedevils HCA and Industry 5.0 from Advancing UN SDGs 320
14.6 Concluding Remarks 322
References 323

15 Transforming Workplaces with Human-Robot Collaboration 325
B. Swathi
15.1 Introduction 326
15.2 Sustainability and Industry 5.0 326
15.2.1 Human-Robot Co-Working (HRC) 326
15.2.2 Literature Review 327
15.2.3 Objectives and Methodology 328

15.3 Industry 5.0, Human Resources, and Robots 328
15.3.1 Human and Robot Interaction 329
15.3.2 Industry 5.0 - Advantages 330
15.3.3 Concerns in Industry 5.0 330
15.4 Conclusion 332
References 333

16 Human Capital Analytics in Industry 5.0 for Sustainable Growth 337
Channi Sachdeva, Veena Grover and Veer P. Gangwar
16.1 Introduction of SDGs and the Role of Humans in Organization 338
16.2 Human Capital Analytics: Concepts and Applications 338
16.3 Literature Review 339
16.4 Integrating SDGs with Human Capital Strategies 340
16.5 Utilizing Data Analysis for Managing Talent and Development 341
16.6 Industry 5.0 Principles for Sustainable Value Creation 342
16.7 Challenges and Opportunities for Promoting Sustainable Development via Insights and Industry 5.0 343
16.8 Future Directions 344
References 345

17 HR 5.0 – Demystifying the Way Forward 347
Ritu Saxena, Priyanshi Jindal and Harshit Gouri
17.1 Introduction 348
17.2 Literature Review 349
17.2.1 Challenges in Implementing in HR 5.0 351
17.2.2 Opportunities in Implementing HR 5.0 353
17.3 Recommendations for Solving the Challenges Faced in HR 5.0 355
17.4 Conclusion 356
References 357

18 The Digital Transformation of HRM: Comparing Traditional and Technology-Based Practices 359
Pardeep Kaur
18.1 Introduction 359
18.2 Background of HRM and Related Work 361
18.2.1 Literature Review 361
18.3 Research Methodology 363
18.3.1 Research Objectives 363

18.3.2 Limitations of the Study 364
18.4 Data Analysis and Interpretation 364
Conclusion 370
References 371

19 Technological Implementation of Industry 5.0 at Kinara Capital – A People's Welfare Organization 373
Kala Raja Mohan, R. Narmada Devi, Nagadevi Bala Nagaram, Sathish Kumar Kumaravel and Regan Murugesan
19.1 Introduction 374
19.2 Kinara Capital 375
19.3 HR Team Responsibility 376
19.3.1 Growth of the Organization 376
19.3.2 Employee Growth 376
19.3.3 Industry 5.0 376
19.3.4 Predix 377
19.4 Highlights of HR in Employee Welfare 377
19.4.1 Newsletter 377
19.4.2 Mental Wellness Stories 379
19.4.3 Health Tips 379
19.4.4 Birthday and Work Anniversary Wishes 379
19.4.5 Children's Day Celebration 379
19.4.6 Annual Day Celebration 380
19.5 Kinara and Industry 5.0 380
19.6 Conclusion 380
References 381

Index 383

Preface

The role of human capital is evolving due to advancements in technology in a world rapidly transitioning to the Fifth Industrial Revolution. In the era of Industry 5.0, the collaboration between humans and technology is more integrated than ever. Understanding the implications of these changes for human resources has never been more crucial. *Human Capital Analytics: Exploring the HR Spectrum in Industry 5.0* delves deeply into how human capital analytics is revolutionizing HR practices in this new age. The book provides insights into the future of work, workforce management, and talent enhancement.

The structure of this book provides a comprehensive view of how HR is transforming in Industry 5.0. Initially, it addresses the primary opportunities and challenges presented by human capital analytics today. It also examines how emerging technologies like artificial intelligence (AI), machine learning, and robotics are significantly impacting HR functions. As organizations embrace these technologies, the strategic role of HR is shifting, necessitating new approaches to data-driven decision-making, workforce optimization, and people management.

A key focus of the book is the alignment of human capital analytics with global goals for sustainable development. Industry 5.0 is not solely about technological advancement but also about creating a future that benefits all, where human capabilities and technology converge to achieve global objectives. The book discusses how HR 5.0 strategies are crucial for fostering workplace diversity, equity, and inclusion, highlighting the need for comprehensive, ethical, and progressive approaches.

The chapters further explore the practical application of human capital analytics. They detail methods for collecting and managing HR data, employing predictive analytics in talent management, and assessing performance in India's IT sector. These examples illustrate the growing importance of data and analytics in enhancing employee engagement, maximizing workforce potential, and ensuring organizational success.

As you read through this book, you will gain a deeper understanding of how Industry 5.0 is reshaping the HR landscape. It equips HR professionals, leaders, decision-makers, and students with the knowledge and tools necessary to thrive in a rapidly changing business environment, covering everything from strategic planning to the impact of AI and robotics. This book demystifies HR 5.0 concepts and techniques, enabling you to fully leverage human capital in this new era.

Human Capital Analytics: Exploring the HR Spectrum in Industry 5.0 offers a wealth of valuable insights and intelligent perspectives worth exploring. It represents a journey into the future of human resources, where technology and people collaboratively strive to create a better, more sustainable world.

We hope that this book will inspire further research and innovation in this exciting field and contribute to the development of practical solutions that can be implemented on a global scale. Finally, our gratitude goes to Martin Scrivener and the team at Scrivener Publishing for their support in bringing this volume to light.

February 2025

Part 1

FOUNDATION AND STRATEGIC FRAMEWORK OF HUMAN CAPITAL ANALYTICS IN INDUSTRY 5.0

1

Human Capital Analytics in Industry 5.0: Opportunities and Challenges

Veena Grover[1*], Manju Nandal[2], Divya Sahu[1] and Mahima Dogra[1]

[1]*Department of School of Management, Noida Institute of Engineering & Technology, Greater Noida, Uttar Pradesh, India*
[2]*Department of Management, Chandigarh University, Chandigarh, India*

Abstract

For the past 10 years, the industry has been provided with Industry 4.0 to address the challenges and shortcomings; ultimately, the time has come for Industry 5.0. It is concerned with augmenting the digital shift with more effective and efficient collaboration between humans, machines, and systems within their digital ecosystem. Human capital analytics (HCA) incorporates this technology to make the most efficient use of a limited but valuable part of resources. The HCA is a traditional method for analyzing and effectively utilizing people's data by shifting from viewing HR as an organization's supporting arm to viewing HR as a source of revenue. The objective of this chapter is to describe the most significant potential for HC analytics in Industry 5.0 using the fundamental concepts of key technologies, such as artificial intelligence (AI), the Internet of Things (IoT), and big data analytics. This article discusses a few essential aspects and difficulties that every firm may encounter when it comes to Industry 5.0. There is also a discussion of the benefits and drawbacks of Industry 5.0, as well as future research prospects and applications made obtainable by Industry 5.0. Finally, this chapter discusses the difficulty in recognizing the connected concerns, as well as how HCA has run its course and people analytics is emerging as a preferable strategy for using human capital.

***Keywords*:** Human capital analytics (HCA), human-centered, technologies, robotics, digitalization, 6G systems

**Corresponding author*: Veena.grovere@gmail.com

Deepa Gupta, Mukul Gupta, Pawan Budhwar, Jim Westerman, Rajesh Kumar Dhanaraj and Balamurugan Balusamy (eds.) Human Capital Analytics: Exploring the HR Spectrum in Industry 5.0, (3–30) © 2025 Scrivener Publishing LLC

Abbreviations

- **HCA** Human capital analytics
- **IOT** Internet of Things
- **AI** Artificial intelligence
- **KPI** Key performance indicators
- **ROI** Return on investment
- **IT** Information technology
- **HR** Human resource
- **CV** Curriculum vitae
- **GDP** Gross domestic product
- **R&D** Research and development
- **CSTI** Council for Science, Technology, and Innovation

1.1 Introduction

Human capital has become more important than ever in this era of Industry 5.0, which revolves around the integration of today's technologies like cyber-physical systems, artificial intelligence (AI), and the Internet of Things (IoT). HCA is included as a critical technique in any organization that is willing to optimize its workforce and use the whole efficiency of its human resources (HRs). HCA utilizes analytics and data-driven insights to improve different HR practices such as employee engagement, workforce management, talent acquisition, and performance management in decision-making processes. As we make a shift toward Industry 5.0, using HCA becomes important for businesses wanting to prosper where humans and intelligent machines are more linked. Integrating HCA as organizations traverse the intricacies of Industry 5.0 gives both possibilities for growth and obstacles to overcome. Success in this endeavor necessitates a strategic and ethical approach, with an emphasis on optimizing human-technology collaboration for a more productive and sustainable future.

Many HR managers today deal with greater complexity and difficult questions than their predecessors. These new inquiries, rather than focusing on traditional "personnel" issues, address essential business issues: Where should we locate our plant? Which M&A target will provide the necessary skills? Where should we put a new R&D facility? Why is our turnover rate so high in China [1]? Answering questions like this necessitates new information and new ideas. Today's HR executive must think like an economist, someone who studies and oversees the allocation of limited resources. One of the rare resources in the global economy is talent. Embracing that perspective is half the battle. The other half is gathering relevant information. Companies are accustomed to monitoring internal "leading indicators," but the economist-minded HR chief must also look outward [1]. Macroeconomic metrics such as GDP (gross domestic product), employment movements, and public infrastructure spending are crucial in guiding corporate decisions. By calibrating the limited talent expenditures that organizations can make, these leaders want to make their workforce more responsive to their organization's current and future demands. Finally, HR decisions are like many other business decisions. Humanity is going through the Fourth Industrial Revolution, commonly known as "Industry 4.0," which is based on the broad adoption of information technology (IT) in various domains of industry, process automation, and the spread of AI technologies [2].

Each decade, the magnitude of humanity's economic, environmental, and social challenges grows. Industry 5.0 is a novel approach, and there is significant doubt regarding what it will offer and how it will impact business and manufacturing. People must prepare for changes that will be more complicated than those that humanity has previously encountered. Before moving on to Industry 5.0, it is important to understand what is wrong with Industry 4.0 and why it needs to be replaced. The need to boost industrial efficiency while simultaneously lowering production costs has resulted in the active implementation of automation in all its forms. The integration of physical, network, and computational processes inside a shared cyber-physical system is, by definition, complex [2]. We can conclude that several modifications are required, which will ultimately free us of most, if not all, of the difficulties. Primarily, it will enhance the significance of mankind, diminishing a substantial quantity of risks and dissatisfaction. Ultimately, he is the focal point of the cosmos; without his existence, there would be a void, therefore we cannot just exclude him from any future advancement. There should be a strong correlation between humans and machines, along with a widespread growth in trust in technology. These objectives can be achieved during the upcoming Industrial Revolution. Industry 5.0 refers to the fifth generation of development of industry, characterized by advanced technologies and automation [2]. At the April 2021 "international scientific conference on economic and social development problems", the concept of Industry 5.0 was introduced. This word suggests a combination of human intelligence and the advanced capabilities of machines, resulting in a collective intelligence that will drive technological advancements, enhance human capabilities, and prevent technological singularity.

During the Aveva World digital event on June 17, 2021, a comparable perspective was shared. It emphasized the ability to merge Industry 4.0 technologies with the human-centric concepts of Industry 5.0. These changes over time aim to facilitate the seamless connection between human intelligence and cognitive computing [2]. Industry 5.0 and HC analytics should be merged to succeed in a dynamic, world-class, and cutthroat competition. Industry 5.0 reflects a transition from a focus on value to the economy to a focus on social worth, as well as a transition from a focus on welfare to a focus on well-being. The concept of Industry 5.0 is not limited to only industry but is also being used in the organization and different sectors of the market. Industry 5.0 presents itself as a plan that fixes the worker's well-being at the place of production, along with more resilient and environment-friendly production systems. Industry 5.0 is necessary for obtaining economic growth for the factory and competitive advantages in today's business environment characterized by paid advancements in technology. It discusses analyzing the prospective applications and benefits of Industry 5.0 for organizations to increase their return on investment (ROI). The seismic shift of Industry 5.0 indicates the human and machine collaboration to increase the production efficacy of industrial goods. Leveraging HCA as organizations traverse the intricacies of Industry 5.0 gives both possibilities for growth and obstacles to overcome. Success in this endeavor necessitates a strategic and ethical approach, with an emphasis on optimizing human-technology collaboration for a more productive and sustainable future.

1.2 Evolution of Industry 5.0

The very first revolution in the industry was Industry 1.0, which took place in the 18th century. It comprised of utilization of machines to invent and create products or items with the help of tools and techniques. In 1760, the Industrial Revolution started in England and eventually reached America by the late 18th century. The arrival of Industry 1.0 noted a transition from a manual labor–based economy to one filled with the usage of equipment. This modification influenced various sectors like textile, mining, glass, agriculture, etc. [3]. The shift from 1871 to 1914 to the manufacturing industries is usually known as Industry 2.0 because it ensures faster transportation of persons and the introduction of new ideas. The present revolution is marked by economic growth, corporate efficiency, and a rush in unemployment rates due to the replacement of factory workers by machines.

By the 1970s, the commencement of Industry 3.0 took place, also generally regarded as the period of the digital revolution with the introduction of memory-programmable controls and computers for automation. The era is characterized by the large-scale production and utilization of integrated circuit chips and digital age technology. It encompasses technologies like digital cellular phones, computers, and Internet [4]. The progress of technology is changing both conventional objects and business procedures. Technology is undergoing a transformation into a digital format as a component of the digital revolution. Industry 4.0 refers to the integration of assets with current technologies like AI, cloud computing, robots, IoT, 3D printing, and other similar innovations [5]. Organizations that have implemented Industry 4.0 are very flexible and prepared to make decisions based on data. Industry 5.0 is the upcoming iteration of previous technological advancements, focused on enhancing the efficiency and intelligence of machines. The Industry 5.0 revolution signifies the collaboration between machines and humans to enhance the efficiency of industrial production. The productivity of production is growing due to the collaboration between human workers and universal robots [6]. Every executive team in the manufacturing company has the responsibility of establishing the production line, overseeing important performance measures, and assuring the smooth functioning of the activities. The production of robots and industrial is the future trajectory of Industry 5.0. The implementation of AI and computing technologies is expediting progress in the manufacturing business and augmenting operational efficiency within corporations [7]. Emphasizing the advantages of the manufacturing sector, Industry 5.0 also fosters sustainability by aiming to develop a renewable energy-powered system that operates in a sustainable manner. To implement Industry 5.0 in organizations, it is crucial for the staff to establish effective machine-to-machine and operator-to-machine interactions. Proficiency in fields such as robotics and AI is required [8]. The primary objective of a business organization is to generate profit. Decisions are based on sophisticated variables. To reduce costs, virtual schooling is essential for enterprises, as production is not required. Employee training should be discontinued.

1.3 Concept and Definition of Human Capital Analytics

HCA is a data-driven technique for managing as well as optimizing an organization's workforce. It involves the use of data analytics, data mining, and other quantitative methods to extract meaningful insights from HR and other relevant data sources [9]. The aim of HCA is to make strategic decision-making in areas such as employee engagement, talent acquisition, workforce planning, and complete organizational effectiveness. HCA enhances statistical analysis and data to understand many aspects of human capital management within an organization. It comprises activities like retention, recruitment, training and development, and overall workforce productivity. Some of the components of HCA are as follows:

- **Data Collection:** Combining the important data from various sources within the organization, like employee surveys, records, performance reviews, and other workforce-related processes.
- **Data Analysis:** With the help of statistical methods and analytical tools, the collected data are analyzed. It comprises finding out trends, and patterns that can show valuable insights into workplace performance.
- **Visualization and Reporting:** With the help of visualizations like charts and graphs, it allows the outcomes to come in a clear and better format to help in decision-making by leaders and HR professionals.
- **Benchmarking:** For assessing performance and identifying areas for improvement, the organization's human capital metrics are compared with internal historical data or industry benchmarks.
- **Strategic Decision-Making:** Applying the insights gained from analytics to making effective decisions about organizational development, and other HR strategies. This assists in aligning the workforce with the overall organizational goal.
- **Predictive Modeling:** Making use of predictive analytics to predict trends and results of human capital like forecasting employee turnover or forecasting skill gaps in the organization.

The objective is to enhance the effectiveness of HR management by making it more data-driven. By knowing the drivers and patterns of workforce performance, organizations can utilize their talent management strategies, allocate resources, and generate a more productive workforce [10]. It is necessary to note that successful implementation of HCA needs a mixture of technology infrastructure, analytical skills, and a powerful understanding of both HR practices and the organization's business aims. Furthermore, ethical considerations, transparency, and data privacy are important features when working with HCA data.

1.4 Features of Human Capital Analytics

HCA involves using analytics and data to understand, manage, and utilize the organization's human capital. Some of the features are as follows:

- **Talent Acquisition and Recruitment Analytics:** Analyzing the data related to talent acquisition and recruitment helps organizations find out the effective sources of talent, streamline the hiring process, and make data-driven decisions to attract and retain the right persons.
- **Employee Performance Analytics:** It analyzes data related to the performance of employees including key performance indicators (KPIs), performance reviews, and goals. It helps to identify areas of improvement, high-performing employees, and factors influencing performance.
- **Benchmarking Analytics:** Organizations get help by comparing human capital metrics against industry benchmarks by understanding how they stand against their peers. This is valuable for setting realistic goals for continuous improvement.
- **Workforce Planning:** It helps in forecasting and planning for future needs of the workforce in an organization. It assists the organizations in understanding their current workforce, finding the skill gaps, and planning for the development of the talent to meet the objectives of the organization.
- **Predictive Analytics:** This involves predictive modeling to forecast turnover, identify high-performing employees, and anticipate skill needs, future trends, and outcomes related to human capital.
- **Technology Integration:** HCA often integrates with HR systems and other technology platforms to collect and analyze relevant data efficiently. This streamlines the process and improves overall HR effectiveness.
- **Retention Analytics:** It helps organizations to understand the causes for employees leaving and identify strategies to improve retention rate by analyzing data related to turnover.

1.5 Advantages and Disadvantages of Human Capital Analytics

HCA has several advantages for organizations wanting to optimize their HR and workforce management. Some of them are as follows:

- **Efficient Recruitment Process:** Recruitment analytics helps in improving the efficiency of the hiring process by finding out the effective source channels, evaluating candidates, and streamlining the overall cycle of recruitment.
- **Effective Learning and Development Programs:** HCA assists organizations in assessing the training and development programs by analyzing data on skill development and impact on training, which, in turn, optimizes their initiatives to meet the needs of the employees and the organizations.
- **Cost Saving:** With the help of predictive analytics, organizations can estimate workforce trends and address potential issues proactively which helps in cost savings.
- **Strategic Workforce Planning:** It allows organizations to predict and plan for the future of workforce needs based on analytics and data. This ensures aligning the right talent at the right place to facilitate business goals and objectives.
- **Employee Engagement:** HCA measures and analyzes employee engagement, helping to find the areas for improvement and deploying strategies to enhance employee satisfaction.
- **Adaptive HR Strategies:** The HR department can adapt quickly to the changing dynamics of the workforce with the use of real-time data and analytics. This allows organizations to react effectively to shifts in markets, advancing technologies, and other external factors.
- **Better Productivity:** It contributes to overall productivity by identifying the factors that affect employee performance and engagement.

Now, while HCA has many advantages, there are also potential challenges related to its implementation. Some of them are as follows:

- **Lack of Standardization:** Most of the time, there is a lack of standardization in the tools used for HCA across organizations. It becomes challenging to measure performance and analyze data effectively.

- **Data Biases:** Another issue arises in the arena of biases in data which can affect the outcomes of HCA. For example, performance evaluations or promotion decisions that are biased can lead to biased data, contributing to existing inequalities within organizations.
- **Limited Predictive Accuracy:** When involving human behaviors, predictive analytics are not usually accurate even though they might provide valuable insights.
- **Data Quality and Integrity:** Outdated, incomplete, or inaccurate data can lead to flawed analyzes and inappropriate insights despite HCA being highly dependent on the accuracy and quality of the data being used.
- **Employee Resistance:** Resistance among employees due to constant monitoring of their performance and analyzing of their behavior can cause mistrust and negatively impact the atmosphere of the organization.
- **Cost of Implementation:** There is always a cost attached to technology investments and resources required for training and upgrading the staff to be able to use the newly implemented systems.

1.6 Uses of Human Capital Analytics

HCA is used in multiple facets of HR management to enhance decision-making, improve workforce performance, and align organizational strategy with human capital goals. Here are some major applications of HCA:

- **Talent Acquisition and Recruitment:** HCA helps in making neutral selections for hire by accessing data on candidate abilities, competencies, and efficiency during the recruitment process. Organizations can improve their employee attraction strategies by analyzing data to determine the most effective talent acquisition areas.
- **Workforce Planning:** HCA enables organizations to recognize existing skill gaps and prepare for future workforce demands through the examination of data concerning staff capabilities, qualifications, and training demands. Predictive

analytics may lead to planning for succession by identifying workers with high potential and preparing for significant leadership changes.

- **Employee Performance Management:** For the purpose of giving information on team and individual performances, HCA focuses on employee performance statistics, including key performance markers. To create effective feedback and recognition programs, data analysis can be used for tracking and analyzing employee feedback.
- **Employee Well-being:** By analyzing data pertaining to employee welfare, healthcare usage, and absence from work, HCA may determine how successful health and wellness initiatives perform. Developing a welcoming workplace for workers involves an examination of factors impacting work-life balance.
- **Success Standards for HR Initiatives:** HCA performs the evaluation of many HR strategies such as engagement programs, compensation packages, and workmen training. Organizations can adjust their processes and guidelines to streamline the goals of the organization by evaluating the effects of HR policy.
- **Compliance and Risk Management:** HCA helps monitor and ensure compliance with labor rules, limiting the potential for legal complications in human capital management. Reviewing data may assist in identifying feasible personnel management risks, allowing organizations to act on preventive actions.
- **Learning and Development:** HCA inspects training programs by checking the data associated with improving skills, knowledge acquisition, and its impact on workforce performance.
- **Employee Engagement Satisfaction:** HCA undertakes an analysis of employee survey data to evaluate engagement levels, highlight issues impacting job satisfaction, and design plans for improvements. Predictive models can assist in identifying employees who will probably leave the organization, providing proactive approaches to retention.

1.7 How Human Capital Analytics Help in Industry 5.0?

HCA plays a vital role in Industry 5.0 by employing data-driven insights and analytics to optimize HR utilization in an increasingly integrated and technologically advanced industrial context. While the concept of Industry 5.0 may not be widely established as of my last knowledge update in January 2022, it can be speculated that it builds upon the foundation of Industry 4.0, emphasizing a more collaborative and holistic integration of human intelligence with advanced technologies [11]. HCA is poised to play a crucial role in Industry 5.0 by addressing the evolving dynamics between human workers and intelligent technologies. In Industry 5.0, where machine and human collaboration is likely to be more intricate, HCA becomes instrumental in optimizing this collaboration. Organizations can gain a vision of how effectively humans can work with each other and able to interact with new technologies. This information helps in improving training initiatives, ensuring that the workforce is equipped to work in a highly sophisticated technological atmosphere [13]. With the evolving technological landscapes, the skill requirements of the workforce also follow. HCA allows organizations to utilize the present skill sets of their employees, identify gaps in skills, and create customized training programs to hone the skills wanted for successful collaboration with new technologies. This adaptability is important in Industry 5.0, especially where some instant growth of current technologies is required for a workforce with a versatile skill set. Workforce planning is a central point in Industry 5.0 where the integration of emerging technologies is an ongoing process. HCA helps organizations in predicting workforce needs by analyzing the skill demand and identifying areas for upskilling or reskilling for the workforce. This approach helps to ensure that the workforce stays aligned with technological advancements. Employee well-being is considered most important in high-tech environments. HCA gives measures to monitor and assess factors like job satisfaction, stress, etc. Knowing the impact of technology on employee well-being allows organizations to implement procedures to maintain a stable and healthy workforce in Industry 5.0 [12].

Additionally, HCA contributes to helping organizations guide the cultural shifts linked with the integration of new technologies by changing management strategies in Industry 5.0. With the help of knowing potential resistance to change and knowing the implications for employees, organizations can create better change management initiatives that help to smooth the transitions, fostering an effective organizational culture [14]. HCA acts as a guiding force in Industry 5.0 that ensures the seamless merging of human intelligence and new technologies. It empowers organizations to guide the complex evolving industrial sphere while helping the human element remain at the peak of technological advancements.

1.8 Difference Between Industry 4.0 and Industry 5.0

The Fourth Industrial Revolution or Industry 4.0 remains a novel concept for many companies. Importantly, it entails using cutting-edge technology to improve productivity and efficiency. This comprises the integration of technologies like IoT, robotics, AI, sensor utilization, and system automation. There exists a new player known as Industry 5.0 beyond the realm of Industry 4.0 which shows a subsequent stage in industrial evolution. This recent development has been characterized by the incorporation of the human element into every phase of industrial operations [14].

With the adoption of Industry 4.0, organizations harness technology, increasing market competitiveness, efficiency, and productivity. Yet, it is inevitable to consider additional areas beyond the pursuit of technologically driven factories by AI and other technologies. This philosophy of Industry 5.0 is the foundation of today's world. This method accepts the importance of technological advancements as well as the creative potential of human beings. The companies, that have made this shift like Tesla Motors, Apple, and Boeing, are recognized for the collaboration of personalization, technology, and innovation brought by human presence. The focus on big companies like Apple, Tesla Motors, and Boeing is not whimsical. Unlike smaller corporations struggling with the utilization of technology of Industry 4.0, these big corporations have transcended these limitations. They studied them and invested in the processes and values of the human factor which is important for business growth.

1.8.1 The Pillars of Industry 4.0

- Data Analysis entails collecting and analyzing data from numerous sources to make better decisions and analyzes.
- Autonomous Robots: Intelligent robots that can perform monotonous jobs that people previously accomplished.

They can comprehend information and make decisions while completing their tasks.

- Simulation: Simulating the performance of an industrial product or process using real-world data.
- System integration: The organized and centralized merging of data from several departments within a corporation.
- IoT: Physical devices linked together by sensors, software, and technologies that enable interaction.
- Cybersecurity: Guaranteeing data security is critical, and this is accomplished through secure systems.
- Cloud computing: Data and analysis are saved in the cloud for real-time access from anywhere in the world.
- Additive manufacturing: By using 3D printing, it is feasible to make systems and components that are both stronger and lighter.
- Augmented reality: When a product or physical item is combined with virtual reality to improve industrial operations.

1.8.2 The Pillars of Industry 5.0

This industry possesses immense possibilities to revolutionize the current operational practices of enterprises. The Japanese Council for Science, Technology, and Innovation (CSTI) has characterized the pillars of Industry 5.0 as follows:

- Encourage initiatives that create new value for the future development of industry and social reform.
- Address economic and social concerns.
- Strengthen the pillars of scientific and technological innovation.
- Create a virtuous systemic cycle of human capital, knowledge, and capital for innovation.

The distinction between Industry 4.0 and 5.0 is therefore evident. The first is concerned with technology and automation. The second step entails examining technology foundations and encouraging social transformation and HR actions. Industry 4.0 places a significant emphasis on machine connectivity, fostering increased automation in processes. In contrast, Industry 5.0 takes a dedicated approach to customer experience, often necessitating individualized and personalized considerations. A notable distinction between Industry 4.0 and 5.0 lies in the former's focus on intelligent products with seamless traceability throughout the production process, while the latter prioritizes products designed to enhance the consumer experience through the integration of technology.

1.9 Human Capital Analytics Enabled in Different Sectors

HCA is utilized in different sectors as organizations recognize the benefit of implementing data-driven insights to enhance their employee resources. Here are some different key industries where HCA is typically utilized:

- **Corporate Enterprises:** Large organizations in different fields use HCA to improve their workforce, promote employee engagement, and make well-informed decisions concerning personnel management, training, and advancement.
- **IT and Technology Services:** HCA helps in talent acquiring, skill mapping, and discovering areas in continuing learning and development in the growing technological industry.
- **Healthcare:** Healthcare organizations implement HCA to supervise and improve the performance of healthcare employees, like doctors, nurses, and executives. It assists in employee planning, training, and enhancing overall treatment.
- **Finance and Banking:** HCA helps in recruiting employees, risk control, and compliance inside the financial sector. It serves as a requirement for identifying top-performing individuals and making sure the workforce may meet evolving regulatory needs.
- **Manufacturing and Industry:** HCA is used in manufacturing to maximize employee productivity, promote safety, and improve total operational efficiency. It helps by assessing skills, conducting training, and developing the workforce for the challenges of the Industrial Revolution.
- **Retail:** Retail businesses implement HCA for personnel management, boosting customer service, and predicting

hiring needs during excessive seasons. It assists in comprehending consumer behavior and combining employee abilities with consumer demands.

- **Education:** HCA is used in the education sector for managing staff and educators, analyzing student success, and improving institutional performance. It helps in identifying productive methods of instruction and maximizing educational results.
- **Telecommunications:** Telecommunication organizations utilize HCA to effectively monitor their workers, integrate abilities with new technologies, and improve customer service. It supports hiring individuals for positions in network leadership, cybersecurity, and interaction with customers.
- **Energy and Utilities:** HCA has been utilized in the energy industry to simplify the labor engaged in producing energy, transportation, and service. It assists in recognizing inadequacies in abilities overseeing talent, and ensuring a proficient workforce for a shifting energy environment.
- **Government and Public Sector:** Government agencies implement HCA for workforce planning, boosting public service delivery, and ensuring employees possess the necessary abilities for the digital evolution of government services.
- **Transportation and Logistics:** HCA assists in optimizing labor scheduling, strengthening safety measures, and ensuring that the workforce is well-equipped to manage the intricate details of contemporary transportation and logistics systems in this sector.
- **Hospitality and Tourism:** HCA has been used in the hospitality sector to regulate varied workforce, optimize guest experiences through involving employees, and optimize employment based on seasonal needs.

HCA is a strong and powerful technology that can be used in many fields. The fact that it can offer statistical information for decision-making makes it crucial for organizations aiming to enhance their HR while managing the complexity of the modern business environment.

1.10 Challenges and Opportunities of Human Capital Analytics

1.10.1 Challenges of Human Capital Analytics

Some of the Challenges of HCA are as follows:

- **Privacy and Ethical Concerns:** It is always impossible to find the right proportion between the need for data and the rights of individuals. To manage these issues and boost trust in the workplace, effective privacy policies, gaining informed consent, and following ethical rules can be established in place.
- **Data Quality and Integration:** HCA can be less accurate and helpful if the data are compromised in their quality or if it is difficult to blend data from various sources.
- **Skills Gap in Analytics:** There are not sufficient skilled workers in various industries that can fully utilize and comprehend HCA. To make sure that data efforts are successful, the organization must invest money into training programs and hiring strategies to fill the skills gap.
- **Change Management:** When organizations use HCA, they often need to change their culture. Employees and supervisors who do not want to change can make it harder to use data-driven decision-making. Using effective interaction and change management plans, in addition to showing the real-life advantages of HCA, may help to overcome reluctance and encourage an environment of analytics.
- **Complexity of Models and Algorithms:** Complex sophisticated statistical models and formulas can make individuals hard to comprehend and apply, especially for people who are not technical. HCA can be made better by making the interfaces more user-friendly, teaching non-technical users, and motivating the HR and data science teams to work together.

1.10.2 Opportunities of Human Capital Analytics

Here are some of the Opportunities that come with HCA:

- **Strategic Workforce Planning:** HCA helps businesses estimate which abilities their employees will need in the future, search skill gaps, and make sure their employees are contributing toward identical strategic business goals. This proactive technique makes the organization more adaptable and competitive.

- **Talent Acquisition and Retention:** Organizations can make better decisions about attracting and retaining employees when utilizing predictive analytics. HCA helps firms find potential employees and put systems in place to keep key workers.
- **Employee Engagement and Well-being:** HCA offers details about how involved, happy, and healthy its employees are. The organizations can use this information to make efficient programs that may boost the workforce culture, working experience, and overall well-being.
- **Productivity and Performance Optimization:** Performance analytics are found to be located in the field of improvement, workflow enhancement, and upgrade overall productivity. Finally, it finishes by making an organization's workings more efficient.
- **Flexible Learning and Development:** HCA provides altered learning and development programs that will allow employees to learn new things and create the requisite skills to perform their past and future work.
- **Diversity and Inclusion:** HCA assists in diversity and inclusion by providing relevant information on how to hiring procedures, looking for reasonable biases, and providing an improved working atmosphere.
- **Improving Human-Machine Duo:** With Industry 5.0, HCA makes it extra easy for humans and machines to work together without any issues. It utilizes both strengths and challenges to make the best collaboration possible, leading to total efficiency in the organization.

1.11 HR Analytics and Artificial Intelligence

HR analytics and AI integrate to construct a powerful synergy in the workforce. HR analytics advantages the data analysis to provide HR decision-making, while AI enriches the HR processes by using a machine learning approach and proper automation. These composites are transforming the way organizations hire, educate, and sustain, boosting the strategic and adaptive nature of HR to meet changing company needs. HR analytics and AI have a significant role in hiring and talent acquisition. Algorithms based on AI can rapidly analyze huge amounts of CVs, assessing candidates according to their set criteria. This will improve the recruitment process and enable a more reliable and unbiased initial selection. HR analytics provides insights on previous hiring data, permitting predictive analytics to fix the best applicants and anticipate their success for roles. AI may include processes like hiring, recruiting, and instruction for employees more personalized, which is advantageous for both the employer and the employee. Through the extensive use of AI, customized training, and onboarding personalization based on each worker's personality, companies can help important steps efficiently. On the other hand, HR analytics plays an important role in identifying skill gaps in the workforce and importantly making sure that training programs are very precious and in accordance with strategic goals. When it applies to performance management, AI's anticipating skills notify the company's assessment of how well the workers will do. Machine learning algorithms assess past performance data, the outcomes of training, and other factors that are important in finding out how well a concept will be suited in the future. This capacity is to predict future goals that help HR analytics make options about succession planning, individualized job development, and advertisements that promote a culture of continually getting better.

1.12 HR Analytics and Blockchain

HR analytics and blockchain-based technologies are two distinct technologies that may combine collectively to change the numerous elements of HR management by including more open, secure, and efficient technology. HR analytics uses data and analytics to help employers make smart choices regarding the workforce. On the other hand, blockchain is a decentralized and dispersed technology that keeps records secure, open, safe, and not changeable. When it comes to HR analytics, using blockchain may make data precise and confidential. Security and the integrity of data are uses often issues with traditional HR tools. Data that have been kept are incapable of being changed or messed with the time it has been saved. Being not able to be changed can be particularly useful for making an accurate record of employee information, details, credentials, and performance metrics. HR analytics may use this safe and reliable data to find useful information that can assist them in generating smart decisions.

1.13 HR Analytics and the Internet of Things

The powerful duo of HCA and IoT, when worked together, can do wonders in improving the workforce by giving the benefits of real-time data from many interconnected devices. HR analytics uses data analysis to appraise HR decision-making, while IoT uses interconnected networks to share data. When they are mixed, they emerge into creating a dynamic environment where HR professionals gain deeper data about employees. HRA processes these data to gain insight into employee engagement, collaborations, and overall efficiency of the workplace. Another important application of this lies in employee health monitoring and well-being. With the help of wearable IoT devices, we can track employee's physical activities, sleeping patterns, and stress levels. Then, HR analytics can analyze this data to find out the correlations with the parameters like work hours, job roles, etc. This gained information allows HR professionals to execute targeted programs, address potential burnouts, and create a better and healthier work atmosphere. IoT's influence expands its wings to talent acquisition and management. IoT data can be used by smart recruitment tools to assess candidate's digital footprints, determine their online presence, etc. In addition to that, IoT-enabled devices can give real-time performance metrics. For example, the sensors found in manufacturing environments can track production efficiency, allowing HR analytics to assess employee performance, know the areas for betterment, and create data-driven decisions for training and development.

Collaboration and employee engagement are other areas that are pretty much influenced by the combination of HR analytics and IoT. IoT sensors found in smart meeting rooms can track data on meeting durations, employee interactions, and participation levels. HR analytics analyzes these data to use collaboration patterns, utilize team dynamics, and identify communication strategies. These obtained data contribute to building a collaborative and engaged workplace culture. However, the amalgamation of HR analytics and IoT sometimes raises concerns about data related to privacy and security. Since sensitive data are gathered on IoT devices, organizations should impose tight security measures to protect the employees' information. Employees must be clearly communicated regarding the aim and advantages of IoT data collection which is primarily crucial for building trust and ensuring compliance with privacy measures. There lies the vast potential for transforming workforce management with the dynamic combination of HR analytics and IoT. By utilizing real-time data from IoT devices, HR professionals can obtain valuable insights into employee performance, well-being, and behavior, allowing them to make better and informed decisions that enhance workforce efficiency, employee satisfaction, and overall organizational success. As technology continues to advance, the integration of HR analytics and IoT is likely to become increasingly sophisticated, offering new opportunities for innovation in HR management.

1.14 Level of Analytics Used in Human Capital Analytics

HCA encompasses understanding and development of the workforce of company management through the application of data and analytics. The degree of analytics utilized for HCA may differ, with organizations choosing varying degrees of complexity in accordance with their objectives, current assets, and data capabilities. Various levels of analytics are implemented within the domain of HCA which are as follows:

- **Descriptive Analytics:** At this stage, key documentation and descriptions of historical data are contained. It serves as an answer to the inquiry "What happened?" and gives perspectives on previous changes and patterns in the workforce. Data on employee turnover, trends in employees, time, and attendance are a few examples.
- **Diagnostics Analytics:** The objective of diagnostic analytics is to ascertain the roots of past incidences. It includes an analysis of past data to figure out the elements that have influenced specific results in the workforce. Analyzing the factors that contribute to high employee attrition and identifying factors that enhance employee engagement are two examples.
- **Predictive Analytics:** By applying machine learning models and statistical algorithms, predictive analytics can predict future workforce patterns or outcomes. It facilitates organizations in making proactive decisions and predicting potential problems, such as identifying high-potential employees, calculating workforce demand, and estimating employee turnover.
- **Prescriptive Analytics:** In addition to predicting the outcome, prescriptive analytics gives guidance on the specific

actions that need to be executed to attain the desired outcome. It requires the application of training and optimization techniques. Examples: Requesting training initiatives to rectify deficiencies in skills, therefore optimizing the allocation of employees for optimal efficiency.

- **Advanced Analytics and Machine Learning:** By applying advanced machine learning algorithms, people can discover patterns, correlations, and valuable insights within tremendous and elaborate datasets. This may involve sentiment analysis, natural language processing, or anything more. Implementing machine learning to employee sentiment analysis derived from survey responses with the goal of identifying performance-influencing factors.

Many organizations initiate their analytics implementation with fundamental descriptive and diagnostic analytics, then advance to more sophisticated forecasting factors, directive, and strategic analytics. The level of complexity in analytics tends to be dependent upon the data maturity, technological framework, and analytical capabilities of the organization.

1.15 The Shift of People Analytics

1.15.1 People Analytics

People analytics, commonly referred to as HR analytics or workforce analytics, is a data-driven approach to managing people at work. It indulges the usage of statistical analysis, data mining, or other analytical techniques to extract meaningful insights from data related to HR. The primary goal of people analytics is to inform and improve decision-making processes in areas such as workforce planning, employee engagement, talent acquisition, and performance management. The human-centered approach prioritizes fundamental human interests and needs. Rather than modifying individuals' talents, we leverage technology to adapt procedures to their requirements. Workers' rights, autonomy, and human dignity are also protected. Technological advancements do not allow for the full provision of a sufficient degree of customers' expected customization. Production workers continue to play an important role in this process, allowing technology to be used and improved [14]. After all, only people who exist can come up with unique concepts that can lead to product development. With the emergence of Industry 5.0, the individual is thrust into a new role within the organization. There are some key concepts which are as follows:

- **Data-Driven Decision-Making:** People analytics relies on data to make informed decisions regarding human capital management. This includes analyzing, collecting, and interpreting data connected to employees to derive actionable insights.
- **Talent Acquisition and Recruitment:** In the context of people analytics, organizations use data to optimize their talent acquisition processes. It involves analyzing recruitment channels, forecasting candidate success, and finding areas for improvement in the recruitment process.
- **Performance Management:** People analytics helps to analyze performance metrics, identify high-performing employees, improve team and individual performances, and guide performance improvement programs to be initiated.
- **Workforce Planning:** People analytics is used for strategic workforce planning in organizations. This comprises predicting talent requirements, scrutinizing skill gaps, and ensuring the right combination of skills to obtain business goals.
- **Diversity and Inclusion:** People analytics promotes diversity and inclusion among organizations. With the help of data, hiring procedures, and employee experiences, organizations can know the areas requiring change and eventually implement procedures to facilitate an inclusive workplace.
- **Employee Well-being:** Organizations use people analytics to enhance employee well-being. Well-being means analyzing data on the overall well-being programs of the employee and implementing decisions related to helping employees to their wellness and health.
- **Ethical Consideration:** Ethical consideration problems like data privacy, security, and different needs consideration by HCA. They play a vital role in fostering belief and maintaining data transparency in organizations.

Therefore, HCA gives a transformation from intuition-based decision-making to evidence-based decision-making through HR in any organization.

By developing data analytics, employers can achieve deep insights into their workforce that can lead to efficiency and growing employee experience with alignment in business objectives.

1.15.2 Why People Analytics More Effective at Driving Value

HCA is very effective in different aspects of the HR decision-making process due to several reasons which are given as follows:

- **Patterns and Trends Identification:** The analytics outline the offering trends and patterns within big datasets. This ability will help organizations to discover insights about employee engagement, and other HR metrics decisions.
- **Talent Acquisition Optimization:** The HCA grows with the talent acquisition by enriching the hiring processes which is done by the HR in any organization. The companies that can use recruitment channels effectively, assess hiring policies, and create data-driven strategies to gasp and retain good talent from the aspirants.
- **Strategic Workforce Planning:** It can help workforce planning by providing such insights as present and future workforce composition. It involves identifying succession planning and critical competencies, as well as ensuring that organizations are ready for the future perspective.
- **Efficient Resource Allocation:** It enables employees to allocate resources in a sufficient way. With the help of workforce trends and patterns, organizations can understand the methods of optimizing staffing levels, identifying areas for skill development, and aligning resources with business goals.
- **Enhancing Diversity and Inclusion:** People analytics adds to diversity and inclusion programs by giving valuable insights into recruitment processes, knowing potential biases, and promoting an inclusive workplace environment.
- **Continuous Improvement:** People analytics supports a culture of continuous improvement in HR management. Organizations can figure out the areas for enhancement, improve the impact of interventions, and modify strategies for continuous success.

1.15.3 Example of How People Analytics Can Improve Business Value

People analytics is tested crucial in delivering commercial value for some well-known companies like Google and IBM. Some of the reasons why these companies use people analytics are as follows:

- **Strategic Decision-Making:** People analytics allows organizations to make strategic decisions related to human capital. For example, it helps in understanding the competencies and capabilities of the workforce to align their talent with business strategies and industry trends.
- **Employee Retention Strategies:** People analytics enables organizations to know the elements that impact employee turnover. Organizations can then implement targeted retention strategies, such as personalized development plans, to keep high-potential employees engaged and satisfied.
- **Cost Saving:** Organizations use people analytics to find out places to improve and utilize workforce deployment ensuring cost savings. Companies allocate resources more efficiently by understanding workforce trends and patterns and ultimately, stay ahead in the game.

In summary, both Google and IBM, along with other forward-thinking companies, demonstrate how people analytics can drive business value across various HR functions. By leveraging data-driven insights, these organizations optimize talent management, enhance employee experiences, and align their workforce with strategic business objectives.

1.16 Conclusion and Future Direction

The limitations of this study in terms of research approach are connected with the restricted amount of real situations from the industry application of Industry 5.0 principles and philosophies. Furthermore, the importance of the human-centricity theme and urgency, it is critical that the data of the research not be limited to English exclusively. As a result, using articles in multiple languages to generate fresh and significant insights in this study would be critical in the future. On the contrary, studies in laboratories set up to speed the process of research will be a future problem. It would be notified, however, that the tests can provide findings that are not in line with the current situation of the world. From a social, technological, and ethical standpoint, there are various problems, restrictions, and opportunities in advancing toward human-centric production and manufacturing. Concerning ethical considerations, ethical concerns arose early in Industry 4.0. However, just as Industry 5.0 builds on and coexists with Industry 4.0, ethical issues do as well. In this situation, humans are often faced with ethical dilemmas that are increasingly relevant due to human centralization. Ethical, health, and safety issues are particularly significant in industrial and automated contexts using digital technologies, and this is a hot topic for future research [12].

To transition from an Industry 4.0 high-performance industrial strategy to an Industry 5.0 human-centric strategy, it will be necessary to achieve a harmonious balance between digitalization technologies, performance, and well-being. Although humans have limitations, there exists a chance for growth and progress by making use of interactions between humans and machines to enhance skills and competencies in preparation for the upcoming digital era. Gaining people's trust and appreciation of technology is a difficult task. In workplaces where people are valued most, it is crucial to employ technologies that are reliable, intelligent, and user-friendly while consistently upholding privacy limits. In the future, robot-human interaction poses a challenge and obstacle that is a requirement for cooperative technologies and collaborative support instead of replacing them. However, by surmounting the challenges presented by the human-centric era, such as shifts in work dynamics and the need for continuous learning, individuals can seize opportunities and adapt to emerging technological advancements. An additional formidable obstacle in conducting studies inside industrial settings is the challenge posed by operators' and higher management's resistance to embracing and implementing novel technologies and ideas.

To establish a future research agenda, it is important to make sure to strongly seek out and develop feasible and achievable goals approaches and techniques that prioritize the human element in production. This should be done while considering the human aspect and incorporating the concepts of Industry 5.0. Discussing Industry 6.0 at this point may be premature, considering that Industry 5.0 is still in its nascent phase of advancement. It is crucial to emphasize that, as stated by the European Commission, sustainability is a fundamental component of Industry 5.0. This encompasses the environmental and ecological considerations related to the limitations of our planet. Nevertheless, since Industry 5.0 prioritizes human-centric approaches, can we expect Industry 6.0 to prioritize environmental considerations? Currently, the objective of Industry 5.0 is to prioritize the welfare of workers in many industries.

References

1. Little, G., Deloitte human capital trends in perspective: The science of organization design and operation, 2017, Available at SSRN 2937125.
2. Lykov, D. and Razumowsky, A., Industry 5.0 and human capital. *E3S Web Conf.*, 376, p. 05053, EDP Sciences, 2023.
3. Longo, F., Padovano, A., Umbrello, S., Value-oriented and ethical technology engineering in industry 5.0: A human-centric perspective for the design of the factory of the future. *Appl. Sci.*, 10, 12, 4182, 2020.
4. Pathak, A., Kothari, R., Vinoba, M., Habibi, N., Tyagi, V.V., Fungal bioleaching of metals from refinery spent catalysts: A critical review of current research, challenges, and future directions. *J. Environ. Manage.*, 280, 111789, 2021.
5. He, D., Ma, M., Zeadally, S., Kumar, N., Liang, K., Certificateless public key authenticated encryption with keyword search for industrial internet of things. *IEEE Trans. Ind. Inf.*, 14, 8, 3618–3627, 2017.
6. Majumdar, A., Garg, H., Jain, R., Managing the barriers of Industry 4.0 adoption and implementation in textile and clothing industry: Interpretive structural model and triple helix framework. *Comput. Ind.*, 125, 103372, 2021.
7. Chen, H., Simoska, O., Lim, K., Grattieri, M., Yuan, M., Dong, F., Lee, Y.S., *et al.*, Fundamentals, applications, and future directions of bioelectrocatalysis. *Chem. Rev.*, 120, 23, 12903–12993, 2020.
8. Zhang, C. and Chen, Y., A review of research relevant to the emerging industry trends: Industry 4.0, IoT, blockchain, and business analytics. *J. Ind. Integr. Manage.*, 5, 01, 165–180, 2020.
9. Chowdhury, M.Z., Shahjalal, M., Ahmed, S., Jang, Y.M., 6G wireless communication systems: Applications, requirements, technologies, challenges, and research directions. *IEEE Open J. Commun. Soc.*, 1, 957–975, 2020.
10. Adel, A., Future of industry 5.0 in society: Human-centric solutions, challenges and prospective research areas. *J. Cloud Comput.*, 11, 1, 1–15, 2022.
11. Isson, J.P. and Harriott, J.S., *People analytics in the era of big data: Changing the way you attract, acquire, develop, and retain talent*, John Wiley & Sons, 2016.
12. Andronie, M., Lăzăroiu, G., Iatagan, M., Uță, C., Ștefănescu, R., Cocoșatu, M., Artificial intelligence-based decision-making algorithms, internet of things sensing networks, and deep learning-assisted smart process management in cyber-physical production systems. *Electronics*, 10, 20, 2497, 2021.

13. Varma, C. and Chavan, C., A Case of HR Analytics–to Understand Effect on Employee Turnover. *J. Emerging Technol. Innov. Res.*, 6, 6, 2019.
14. Banholzer, V.M., From „Industry 4.0 "to „Society 5.0 "and „Industry 5.0 ": Value- and Mission-Oriented Policies. *Techn. and Soc. Inno. –Aspects of Sys. Trans.*, IKOM WP 3, no. 2, 2022, 2022.

2

Human Capital Analytics and Emerging Technologies in Industry 5.0

Harpreet Kaur Channi[1]* **and Surinder Kaur**[2]

[1]*Department of Electrical Engineering, Guru Nanak Dev Engineering College, Ludhiana, Punjab, India*
[2]*Guru Nanak Girls College, Ludhiana, Punjab, India*

Abstract
Industry 5.0, the newest phase of industrial growth, integrates modern technology with human-centric methods. Human capital—worker skills, knowledge, and abilities—drives innovation and production today. Human capital analytics (HCA) helps companies harness their people resources and link them with technology. This chapter examines HCA and upcoming technologies in Industry 5.0. It examines how data analytics might improve human capital strategy and performance. Companies may make educated decisions by using predictive analytics, machine learning, and artificial intelligence to understand workforce trends, skill shortages, and employee engagement. The chapter also examines how AR, VR, and robots might change conventional workplaces. These technologies boost productivity and efficiency and change employment responsibilities, requiring ongoing upskilling and reskilling. Additionally, the abstract discusses the ethical issues and limitations of using HCA and current technologies to manage human capital. It stresses openness, privacy, and justice in data-driven decision-making and addresses employment displacement and digital divide issues. This chapter concludes that new technologies and human capital analytics are essential for navigating Industry 5.0. In the ever-changing industrial world, businesses may unleash fresh development, sustainability, and competitiveness by establishing a symbiotic link between human inventiveness and technical innovation.

***Keywords*:** Industrial growth, machine learning, artificial intelligence, sustainability, ethical issues

**Corresponding author*: harpreetchanni@yahoo.in

Deepa Gupta, Mukul Gupta, Pawan Budhwar, Jim Westerman, Rajesh Kumar Dhanaraj and Balamurugan Balusamy (eds.) Human Capital Analytics: Exploring the HR Spectrum in Industry 5.0, (31–64) © 2025 Scrivener Publishing LLC

2.1 Introduction

As new technologies revolutionize business operations in the dynamic era of Industry 5.0, human capital analytics is essential to achieving organizational success. Modern technology and human skills are more valuable when industries aim for unprecedented levels of productivity, creativity, and competitiveness. With its focus on the integration of humans and machines, Industry 5.0 represents a drastic departure from Industry 4.0. This change makes it more crucial than ever to understand how digitally enabled human capital analytics may lead companies into the future [1]. The goal of human capital analytics is to help businesses make better decisions about hiring, developing, and retaining top people by methodically analyzing workforce data.

With the integration of cutting-edge technologies like blockchain, augmented reality, artificial intelligence (AI), and machine learning (ML), this analytical technique has entered a new phase. The combination of these state-of-the-art technologies with human capital analytics is going to usher in a completely new age of workplace dynamics. Real-time performance tracking, predictive workforce planning, and customized learning experiences are just a few of the ways that analytics and technology have come together to help firms navigate the challenges of Industry 5.0 [2].

It is conceivable that issues will arise with this upgrade. Important challenges that firms must overcome include data security, ethical concerns, and the requirement to teach staff about new technology. Notwithstanding these concerns, workers may benefit much from training to succeed in an increasingly digital and connected society. In our examination of Industry 5.0's emerging technologies and human capital analytics, we examine the tactics, suggestions, and case studies that demonstrate how fusing technology know-how with human intelligence may be a game changer [54, 56].

Our mission, as we embark on this journey, is to learn, using data-driven insights and cutting-edge technology, how to optimize human resources and rethink business processes for the era of Industry 5.0 [3]. The most recent stage of industrial development, Industry 5.0, expands upon the concepts introduced in earlier ones, such as Industry 1.0, which involved mechanization powered by water and steam, Industry 2.0, which involved mass production powered by electric power, Industry 3.0, which involved automation powered by computerization, and Industry 4.0, which involved the integration of cyber-physical systems. Industry

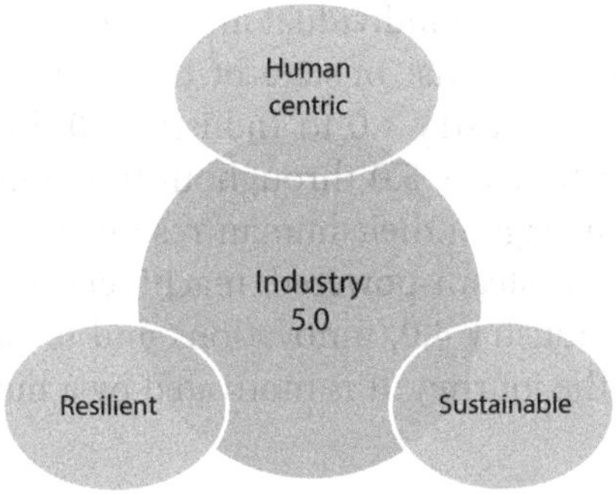

Figure 2.1 Pillars of Industry 5.0.

5.0 is different from its forerunners in that it places a premium on human-centric methods alongside technical breakthroughs and automation as shown in Figure 2.1. It acknowledges that innovation, problem-solving, and customer-centricity are driven by human intellect, creativity, and emotional intelligence.

2.1.1 Background and Motivation

The ever-evolving character of industry and the methods by which businesses operate and thrive have evolved with each new Industrial Revolution. The focus has shifted from individual innovation to group efforts in the collaborative and integrated use of state-of-the-art technologies, marking a dramatic shift from Industry 4.0 to Industry 5.0. During this shift, companies looking to maximize Industry 5.0 should concentrate on managing their people resources. Innovations and technical advancements have shaped the Industrial Revolution, from the steam-powered machinery of the First Industrial Revolution to the digitization and automation of Industry 4.0. Industry 5.0 emphasizes the mutually beneficial relationship between humans and machines more than Industry 4.0, which only focuses on automation. In today's networked and technology-dependent business, human capital's ability to promote innovation, creativity, and adaptation is crucial [4]. Technology's rapid advancement has frequently had a negative impact on human capital, or the skills, knowledge, and creativity of the labor force. With each successive Industrial Revolution, the nature of industry and the means by which companies function and prosper have changed.

The focus has shifted from individual innovation to group efforts in the collaborative and integrated use of state-of-the-art technologies, marking a dramatic shift from Industry 4.0 to Industry 5.0. Businesses that want to make the most of Industry 5.0 throughout this transition should center their efforts on managing their human resources [56]. From the First Industrial Revolution's steam-powered machinery to the digitalization and automation of Industry 4.0, innovations and technological developments have defined the journey. It is motivated by a number of important factors [5]:

- **Optimizing Workforce Performance:** Understanding how human capital analytics can be leveraged alongside emerging technologies to enhance individual and collective performance is a key motivator. This involves exploring how data-driven insights can be translated into actionable strategies for workforce optimization [57, 59].
- **Navigating Ethical Challenges:** Concerns about privacy, prejudice, and justice rise to the surface as HR practices increasingly include technology. By delving into these questions, we want to shed light on how to make ethical and responsible use of new technology in HRM.
- **Preparing for the Future Workforce:** The skills needed by workers will likewise alter as a result of the technological shifts brought about by Industry 5.0. To be successful in the digital era, companies must proactively address the need for reskilling and upskilling their personnel. This is where motivation comes from [56, 58].
- **Showcasing Best Practices and Innovations:** In order to shed light on the best practices and creative techniques used by businesses leading the charge in integrating human capital analytics with new technology, this inquiry will analyze real-world case studies and success stories. If other firms are also on a path of transformation, these insights may help them along the way [6].

Essentially, firms are driven to explore human capital analytics and emerging technologies in Industry 5.0 in order to get insights that will enable them to harness the full potential of their workforce even in the face of technological disruption. This investigation seeks to provide a thorough comprehension of the tactics and procedures that may enable the integration of human intelligence with technological progress, which offers a one-of-a-kind chance for firms to prosper in the era of Industry 5.0. Investigating human capital analytics and emerging technologies in Industry 5.0 covers a lot of ground and takes a lot of factors into account. Within the framework of Industry 5.0, this investigation seeks to probe the many facets of human capital management and its incorporation with developing technology [7]. This chapter primarily aims to accomplish three main objectives:

- Implement human capital analytics and emerging technologies to streamline HR processes, from talent acquisition to performance management, aiming for increased operational efficiency and resource optimization.
- Establish ethical guidelines and practices for the integration of emerging technologies in human capital analytics, addressing concerns related to data privacy, bias, and fairness in decision-making.
- Develop strategies for continuous learning and upskilling initiatives, ensuring the workforce remains adaptable and possesses the necessary skills to thrive in the evolving landscape of Industry 5.0.

2.2 Industry 5.0 and the Role of Human Capital

The interaction between people and machines in manufacturing is being redefined in the age of Industry 5.0, which is characterized by a dramatic change in thinking. Industry 5.0 prioritizes collaborative human-machine interaction, in contrast to its predecessor, Industry 4.0, which prioritized complete automation. In this regard, human capital's function becomes crucial in propelling the revolutionary power of the modern industrial age. Human intelligence, with its special set of talents like imagination, empathy, and the capacity to make nuanced decisions, is front and center in this cooperative setting. Industry 5.0 acknowledges that robots are great at processing data and doing repetitive activities, but that humans are essential for creative problem-solving, flexibility, and understanding complex circumstances. Human capital drives the merger of human inventiveness with cutting-edge technology [8]. Human capital is crucial since it not only helps with technical operations but also encourages creativity and new ideas.

Human capital becomes the source of new insights and concepts as Industry 5.0 highlights ongoing innovation as a critical competitive advantage. When workers regularly generate fresh concepts and cultivate a culture that encourages innovation, businesses are better equipped to adjust to changing market conditions. A workforce that is both creative and adaptive is also necessary in the dynamic environment of Industry 5.0. In order to keep a workforce adaptable and ready to employ new technology, upskilling and reskilling efforts rely heavily on human capital [9]. The necessity of taking ethical considerations into account when making judgments is further heightened by Industry 5.0's growing sectoral interconnection.

Organizations implement sustainable and ethical practices with the help of human capital, which encompasses moral judgment and civic duty. Incorporating human insights increases the likelihood that decisions will consider values, ethics, and social concerns. With Industry 5.0's customized and customer-focused approaches, human capital's knowledge of a broad variety of client requirements becomes a competitive advantage. Workers who are skilled at developing a personal rapport with customers are more likely to devise creative solutions that satisfy the market's ever-evolving requirements. At the end of the day, in this age of mutually beneficial cooperation between machines and people, human capital is what really matters when it comes to combining human intellect with technological progress; this is what defines Industry 5.0 and how it will succeed [10].

2.2.1 Evolution of Industrial Revolutions: From Industry 4.0 to Industry 5.0

Going from Industry 4.0 to the new Industry 5.0 is an incredible voyage across revolutionary technology landscapes in the history of Industrial Revolutions as shown in Figure 2.2. The Fourth Industrial Revolution, or Industry 4.0, revolutionized production by integrating the Internet of Things (IoT), AI, and big data into industrial operations. In this stage, smart factories were born, where machines could talk to each other without a hitch, paving the way for massive amounts of personalization and decentralized decision-making. But it was not the end of evolution [53]. The cutting-edge innovation, Industry 5.0, ushers in a new era by placing an emphasis on teamwork and people. A future where people and robots collaborate together is the ideal of Industry 5.0, in contrast to the entirely automated procedures of Industry 4.0. Modern times are defined by an emphasis on human-machine cooperation, augmented reality, and sophisticated robots. The Fifth Industrial Revolution, or Industry 5.0, acknowledges the indispensability of human intellect by incorporating elements

Industry 1.0

- **The Era of Mechanization**
- *Late 18th to early 19th century*
- Water and steam power, mechanization of textile production

Industry 2.0

- **The Age of Mass Production**
- *Late 19th to early 20th century*
- Electricity, assembly lines, and the introduction of the concept of interchangeable parts.

Industry 3.0

- **The Digital Revolution**
- *Late 20th century*
- Electronics, computers, and automation.

Industry 4.0

- **The Fourth Industrial Revolution**
- *Early 21st century*
- Internet of Things (IoT), Artificial Intelligence (AI), Big Data, and Cyber-Physical Systems.

Industry 5.0

- **The Era of Human-Centric Collaboration**
- *Ongoing, emerging concept*
- Advanced robotics, augmented reality, and symbiotic human-machine collaboration.

Figure 2.2 Evolution of Industry 4.0 to Industry 5.0.

such as emotional intelligence, intuition, and creativity into manufacturing processes. It sums up a future in which people and machines work together in perfect harmony, playing to each other's strengths in a highly automated and linked industrial setting to promote creativity, flexibility, and moral decision-making. Industry 5.0 ushers us into a new age where technical progress and human inventiveness work hand in hand to write the next chapter in the continuous tale of industrial revolutions [11, 17].

2.2.2 The Significance of Human Capital in the Modern Industrial Landscape

Human capital is an essential factor in the performance and longevity of enterprises in today's industrial world. Human capital provides a pool of future employees as well as a repository for the information, expertise, and experience that drive advancement and innovation. Even in our highly technologically advanced civilization, innovation is primarily driven by the human brain. As a result, industries continue to lead. Furthermore, human capital's capacity for learning and flexibility is essential for negotiating the complex landscape of developing technologies. Robotics and AI are examples of disruptive technology that can be successfully integrated with a resilient workforce and utilized to their fullest potential. Technical skills are only one aspect of human capital; it also includes teamwork, healthy work environments, and increased creativity.

An edge in customer-centric approaches is the capacity to recognize and satisfy human demands. Incorporating ethical and social responsibility into decision-making processes is another way that human capital pushes corporations to prioritize the welfare of society and individuals. Human capital is the key to overcoming obstacles and achieving better business results since it facilitates efficient cooperation and teamwork. In the current industrial landscape, where human ingenuity and technical advancements constantly intersect, businesses must recognize the value of human capital and make investments in its potential as a fundamental approach. Human capital has never been more valuable in the modern corporate environment [12]. It determines a company's level of creativity, success, and longevity. Figure 2.3 lists the several ways in which a company's human capital—which includes the knowledge, experience, and creativity of its employees—may be a useful asset.

Figure 2.3 Human capital in the modern industrial landscape.

2.2.3 Synergy Between Technology and Human Expertise in Industry 5.0

A creative and cooperative future for industry is at the center of the Industry 5.0 concept. The key component of this scenario is the fusion of human expertise and technology. This age, in contrast to others, celebrates the harmonious coexistence of state-of-the-art technology with the singular powers of the human mind. By fusing ethical concerns, human intuition, and contextual information, Industry 5.0 enables both humans and robots to make decisions based on a greater understanding of complicated instances. This collaboration is ushering in a new era of people-centered invention, where technology complements human creativity rather than replaces it. Resilience and adaptability are fundamental human abilities in a society where unforeseen circumstances and shifting market conditions are commonplace.

People are capable of comprehending complicated communication and efficiently managing interpersonal relationships, according to the synergy between emotional intelligence and industrial operations [13]. In an ever-evolving world where people and technology are always changing, it is imperative that the workforce be flexible enough to adjust to changing conditions and quickly pick up new skills. The incorporation of augmented reality into Industry 5.0 is a prime illustration of how these two ideas complement one another to boost output. Augmented reality increases productivity by combining human expertise and technological precision by superimposing digital data on top of the physical world. Above all, the collaboration ensures that technology is used in a moral and responsible manner. Human knowledge adds moral judgment, ethics, and responsibility to the rollout of technology, ensuring that it advances in a way that is compatible with societal values and unbiased. Seeing the convergence of tools as more than just technology and human abilities working together, Industry 5.0 is paving the way for a more efficient, imaginative, and human-centric industrial environment. They are working together strategically, playing to each other's strengths. Industry 5.0 redefines the future of industrial processes via the intentional integration of human knowledge and technology. It goes beyond just bringing together different tools. Leaving behind the fully automated systems of Industry 4.0, this new era prioritizes the complementary strengths of state-of-the-art technology and human intelligence [14]. Figure 2.4 shows the relevance and dynamics of this synergy, which are shown by the following points.

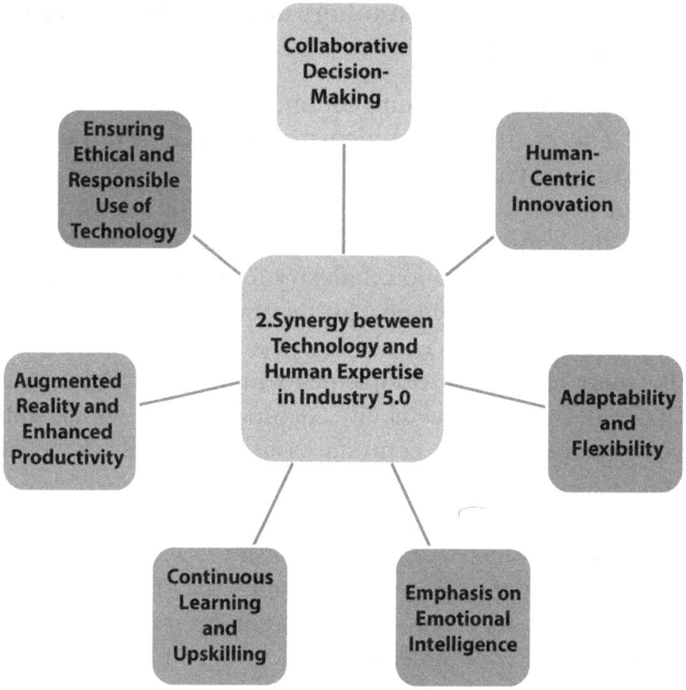

Figure 2.4 Synergy between technology and human expertise in Industry 5.0.

2.3 Emerging Technologies Shaping Human Capital

In order to optimize the workforce, nurture talent, and achieve organizational success, human capital management is being transformed by a number of new technologies. Improving strategic HR management and meeting modern problems both depend on integrating these tools [15]. The following are examples of significant new technologies that are having an impact on human capital:

- **Virtual and Augmented Reality (VR/AR) for Training:** Professional development is changing as a result of advances in augmented and virtual reality. Immersion learning environments are provided via apps for augmented reality and virtual simulations. This is especially true for positions that value having real-world experience. Increased skill development, lower training expenses, and better retention are the results of these technological advancements.

- **Chatbots and Virtual Assistants:** Natural language processing-capable chatbots and virtual assistants may offer a scalable and useful solution for HR-related activities. They aid with onboarding, promptly offer information to employees, and address often requested questions, allowing HR to concentrate on other important tasks.
- **Artificial Intelligence (AI) and Machine Learning:** AI and ML algorithms are changing the game in human capital analytics by taking over repetitive HR tasks, predicting talent trends, and providing insights into employee performance. Personnel development, workforce planning, and talent acquisition are all made more successful with the use of data-driven choices made possible by these technologies.
- **Gamification in Learning and Development:** Gamification techniques, of which game-based learning platforms are a part, are transforming training and professional development initiatives. Organizations may augment professional development and boost engagement, pleasure, and retention by including gaming aspects. Using these new technologies in HR practices results in an information-age workforce that is more adaptable, agile, and self-sufficient, which boosts morale [16, 18].
- **Data Analytics and Predictive Analytics:** Businesses may use big data for improved HRM decision-making with the help of sophisticated data analytics tools like predictive analytics. Utilizing predictive analytics, talent acquisition strategies can be fine-tuned, high-potential people can be identified, and workforce trends can be forecasted.
- **Human Resource Information Systems (HRIS):** Payroll, benefits, KPIs, and employee data management are all made easier with the help of HR information systems. These systems are always evolving and incorporating fresh technologies. Since a cloud-based HRIS offers real-time data accessibility, it boosts employee and HR management productivity and satisfaction.
- **Blockchain in HR:** Payroll, credential verification, talent management, and other HR-related processes may all profit from blockchain technology's enhanced security and transparency.
- **Employee Engagement Platforms:** Through the use of data and AI, platforms are redefining what constitutes a

motivated workforce. These mood monitoring and evaluation tools may help HR managers improve workplace satisfaction, productivity, and problem-solving abilities.

- **Continuous Performance Management Tools:** Modern performance management systems enable performance to be continually regulated with features like goal tracking, data analytics, and real-time feedback. These tools, which keep everyone informed, foster growth and assist employees in aligning their professional and personal objectives with the organization's long-term goals.

2.3.1 Emerging Technologies' Revolutionary Effect on Workforce Management

With the integration of cutting-edge technology into workforce management, our knowledge of talent acquisition, development, and retention is undergoing a significant transformation. The effects are manifold and diverse; they include anything from the hiring process being accelerated by ML and AI to the immersive experiences that VR and AR provide during the onboarding phase. AI-driven continuous learning systems allow for the personalization of training for each individual worker, while data analytics reveal patterns in worker productivity and predicted skill shortages. This shakes up performance management. With the use of workforce analytics tools, organizations may make data-driven decisions that impact succession plans and strategic workforce planning. With the advent of several mobile and collaborative applications, remote work has become more common, allowing for more flexible work hours, improved work-life balance, and access to a bigger pool of competent applicants. While blockchain ensures transparency and equality in recognition programs, AI-powered sentiment analysis tools assess employee pleasure and engagement [19]. To top it all off, AI and predictive analytics help with proactive labor planning by revealing talent shortages and directing businesses to anticipate and meet future demands. This change is more than just a technical one; it influences the whole fabric of the company, making it more open, flexible, and responsive. Businesses that are quick to embrace new technology are preparing themselves for the future of work by creating an engaged and productive staff. How companies find, train, and keep employees is changing as a result of a new technological revolution that is sweeping across labor management. Efficiency, insights, and better employee experiences are just a few ways in which these technologies are changing the face of HR

Figure 2.5 Impact of emerging technologies on workforce management.

as we know it. See Figure 2.5 for a high-level picture of how new technology is revolutionizing worker management [20].

2.3.2 Integrating Human and Technological Capabilities for Optimal Outcomes

Where human inventiveness and technology mastery meet is where the best results in today's world may be found. A growing number of companies are rethinking their approaches in light of the fact that human and technical talents complement one another. Instead of aiming to supplant one another, the goal of integration is to build a cooperative environment in which technological advancements and human intellect work hand in hand. Precision, efficiency, and scalability of technology create a formidable partnership with human emotional intelligence, flexibility, and creativity. Simplified decision-making is a product of this partnership as human insights supplement data-driven decisions with subtlety and ethical concerns. For example, in Industry 5.0, high-tech robots and AR do not replace humans but rather complement them, forging a mutually beneficial partnership that maximizes output and creativity. In order for employees to be able to adjust to and make use of new technology, it is necessary to cultivate a culture that supports lifelong learning and welcomes change. In addition to improving operational efficiency, organizations that effectively integrate human and technological capabilities foster an environment where innovation thrives and the full potential of both is realized for optimal and sustainable outcomes [21].

2.4 Human Capital Analytics: Enhancing Workforce Management

By capitalizing on data-driven insights, human capital analytics is changing the face of labor management. This fresh method goes above and beyond standard HR procedures, providing businesses with a detailed picture of the dynamics inside their staff. Human capital analytics allows for targeted talent acquisition strategies by analyzing large amounts of data to determine the best routes for acquiring new talent, as well as to forecast the performance of individual candidates. Its influence grows into continuous performance management, allowing for the continual assessment of team and individual productivity measures. Organizations may use sentiment analysis and feedback data to improve workplace culture and employee happiness, which in turn helps with employee engagement and retention. Learning and development are pushed to the next level when analytics are used to detect skill gaps and give individualized learning pathways [22]. This assists in aligning personal achievements with organizational objectives. The idea behind succession planning is to find existing workers with a lot of potential and help them grow so that you do not have to hire as many new people. Analytics power initiatives to diversify and include the workforce by revealing program effectiveness and guiding improvements. Working with predictive modeling allows for proactive preparation for future skill needs and industry changes while also ensuring workforce planning. Human capital analytics provides a holistic view of the workforce and enables data-driven decisions, which organizations may utilize to maximize talent, foster innovation, and enhance overall workforce management performance. Organizations are finding that human capital analytics is a powerful tool for personnel management and driving strategic decision-making. The new approach uses analytics and data to maximize the workforce's performance, potential, and overall impact [23]. Human capital analytics mines a company's mountain of data for useful insights applicable to a wide range of HR functions:

- **Workforce Diversity and Inclusion**
  Initiatives to promote diversity and inclusion in the workplace may be tracked and promoted thanks to analytics. Organizations may evaluate diversity programs, pinpoint areas for development, and promote an inclusive and egalitarian work environment by examining demographic data.
- **Employee Engagement and Retention**
  Human capital analytics assesses team and individual performance via ongoing observation and evaluation. By matching employee goals with company objectives, businesses may identify their finest workers, address their shortcomings, and boost productivity.
- **Talent Acquisition and Recruitment**
  By analyzing historical data to forecast how applicants will perform and identifying the most effective methods to advertise for new hires, human capital analytics streamlines the recruiting process. Consequently, recruitment drives provide better results.
- **Employee Performance and Productivity**
  By continuously monitoring and assessing, human capital analytics analyzes the performance of both teams and individuals. Companies can find their best employees, fix their weak spots, and increase production by aligning employee goals with corporate objectives.
- **Learning and Development**
  HRM uses analytics to pinpoint skill gaps in employees, evaluate the success of training programs, and determine the best ways to support their further education. This data-driven strategy guarantees the accomplishment of company objectives through learning activities.
- **Succession Planning**
  Being able to identify potential candidates and assess their suitability for leadership positions makes HR analytics a crucial tool for succession planning. Developing and training internal staff members can help businesses minimize their reliance on outside assistance and facilitate a seamless transition in critical positions.

- **Cost Management and ROI**
  Human capital analytics allows businesses to measure the ROI of HR projects by analyzing their costs. In order to contribute to more strategic budget allocations, it is necessary to evaluate the cost-effectiveness of various recruiting channels, training programs, and employee perks. Workforce management practices that incorporate human capital analytics help organizations better understand their human resources. This, in turn, allows for data-driven decision-making, promotes a growth mindset, and boosts the workforce's overall effectiveness and competitiveness.
- **Predictive Workforce Planning**
  Through the application of predictive modeling in human capital analytics, businesses may anticipate future talent requirements and take proactive measures to solve skill gaps, adjust to changing market conditions, and maximize staff planning and development [24–26].

2.4.1 Role of Data Analytics in Human Capital Management

Organizations may greatly benefit from data analytics in their efforts to turn human capital management into a data-driven, strategic function. Using advanced analytical tools and approaches, human resources managers may glean useful information from massive workforce databases. These findings have implications for many areas of human resources, including but not limited to talent development, employee engagement, and performance management. Through the identification of trends in successful hires and the prediction of applicant success, data analytics improves the efficiency of sourcing, screening, and recruiting procedures in talent acquisition. Analytics allows for data-driven decision-making and focused interventions for improvement in performance management by continuously assessing individual and team productivity. Sentiment analysis and surveys measure employee engagement, which helps HR tactics improve workplace satisfaction and culture. The use of analytics in learning and development helps to fill skill shortages, monitor the efficacy of training, and guarantee that development activities are in line with corporate objectives. By identifying and evaluating workers with high potential for leadership positions, analytics improve succession planning. When it comes down to it, data analytics gives HR professionals the tools they need to maximize workforce strategies, make smart choices, and help their organizations succeed by bringing out the best in their employees [27].

2.4.2 Data-Driven Insights for Employee Performance and Skill Assessment

In today's world, data-driven insights are crucial for evaluating performance and skills. In order to discover trends in the massive amounts of data generated by workers, modern firms utilize sophisticated analytics tools. Key performance indicators (KPIs), project outcomes, and task completion rates are a few examples of performance measures that firms may use to assess staff productivity, both individually and collectively. Results like this provide a more complex picture of workers' current efforts than what is achievable with traditional performance reviews. Also, data-driven approaches let you go deep into skill assessments, which is great for identifying your strengths and areas for improvement. Constantly evaluating and adapting people's skill sets to match their individual needs may foster a culture of lifelong learning. In addition to facilitating more objective and knowledgeable performance evaluations, this data-centric approach helps influence strategic choices on talent development, succession planning, and training. As businesses grow to appreciate the value of data-driven insights, aligning worker capacity with corporate goals becomes a proactive, adaptable, and future-focused endeavor. This includes evaluations of workers' abilities and performance [28].

2.4.3 Predictive Analytics for Workforce Planning and Employee Retention

Predictive analytics has allowed businesses to develop a people management strategy that is ready for the future. The use of these technologies in workforce management and staff retention is growing. By using ML algorithms, statistical modeling, and historical data more effectively to foresee workforce trends, challenges, and choices, businesses may benefit from predictive analytics. If organizations are aware of the skills that will be in demand in the future, then they may be able to better prepare for their personnel needs. Predictive analytics is useful in some situations, such as this one. This facilitates hiring and guarantees that the right people are accessible and available when needed. Employers may use predictive analytics to estimate the likelihood that a worker would depart based on a variety of factors, including job happiness, engagement, and performance metrics [29]. Using these data helps employers establish a more engaged workforce and better plans for employee retention, preventing issues from growing worse [30].

2.4.4 Harnessing Data to Optimize Resource Allocation and Training Strategies

Businesses are using data more and more to enhance their training programs and allocate resources as efficiently as possible. By doing in-depth data analysis, businesses may get a great deal of insight into how to manage resources like time, money, and human capital. Through the analysis of operational data, employee input, and performance measures, companies may gain an important understanding of their areas of strength and growth. They could thus distribute funds in a way that encourages development and innovation. Data-derived information is also frequently utilized in the creation of training programs [53]. Companies may better meet their training needs if they assess the workforce's skill gaps, learning styles, and program outcomes. This guarantees that training supports skill development and is in line with business objectives. Data integration into training and resource allocation methodologies can lead to improved decision-making, resource usage, and staff training to meet the changing demands of modern business [31].

2.4.5 Case Studies

- **Global Manufacturing Corporation Optimizing Workforce with Analytics**
A famous manufacturing business was able to optimize production per person through the application of cutting-edge analytics within the context of the Industry 5.0 paradigm. The business improved talent acquisition, streamlined performance management, and responded to changing market demands by utilizing human capital analytics. The organization was able to allocate resources, hire more employees, and provide training thanks to insights gleaned from analytics. This transformation showed the strong link between labor optimization and analytics in the context of global production, and better equipped the company to meet the difficulties of the modern industrial environment. It also enhanced operational efficiency. Learn how one multinational manufacturing company adapted to Industry 5.0 standards, improved labor management, and increased productivity with the use of human capital analytics and new technology [32].

- **Tech Giants Leading the Way in Human Capital Innovation**
Tech companies are revolutionizing labor management with innovative human capital strategies that use state-of-the-art technology. For talent

recruiting, employee engagement, and skill development, companies like Google, Amazon, and Microsoft were early adopters of analytics, ML, and AI. Personalized learning, data-driven decision-making, and the development of vibrant, welcoming workplace environments are some of their novel methods. By placing a strong emphasis on human capital innovation, these tech titans successfully recruit top personnel and establish new standards for the industry. They demonstrate how cutting-edge technology can revolutionize HR processes, help businesses adapt to Industry 5.0, and drive ongoing development in the dynamic digital world. Learn from the successes and failures of IT giants who were early adopters of new HR software by perusing their case studies. Possible topics covered include how they plan to acquire talent, how they will train their employees, and how analytics and AI will influence their workforce plans [33].

- **Financial Services Industry Embracing Human Capital Analytics**
Financial institutions and insurance companies are using human capital analytics to prepare for the game-changing innovations of Industry 5.0. Powerhouses in the banking and financial sector are enhancing labor management via the use of state-of-the-art analytics and innovation. Included in this are the following: enhancing overall performance via data-driven insights, using predictive analytics for talent acquisition, and using AI-driven solutions for personalized employee development. Strategically integrating human capital analytics allows financial institutions to maximize operational efficiency while also keeping up with the constantly changing demands of the market. This new outlook positions the industry for success at a time when technology advancement and human capital are complementary. Examine how leading financial institutions are using human capital analytics and cutting-edge tech to deal with the challenges brought up by Industry 5.0. Some of these challenges include getting employees more invested, getting ready for remote work, and changing to a workforce with higher skills [34].

- **Healthcare Sector Utilizing Analytics for Workforce Planning**
The healthcare business is preparing for Industry 5.0 by using data strategically for workforce planning, which is causing a drastic shift in human capital management techniques. By using current analytics, healthcare organizations are able to optimize labor productivity, enhance people levels, and anticipate talent needs. Predictive modeling allows for the proactive adjustment of people and skill deployment in order to anticipate patient demand. This data-driven approach ensures effective resource allocation while optimizing patient care by aligning workforce levels with healthcare

demands. By establishing a foundation for efficient and adaptable human capital management, analytics-driven workforce planning ensures that the healthcare sector is ready to tackle new challenges as they emerge. Find examples from the healthcare sector that use the 5.0 framework to show how HR analytics and tech have enhanced workforce planning, talent retention, and patient care [35].

- **Global Retail Chains Transforming HR Practices**
All throughout the globe, businesses are rethinking their HR practices to align with the principles of Industry 5.0. By using human capital analytics and cutting-edge innovation, these supply chains are reimagining training programs, boosting employee engagement, and streamlining talent acquisition. Performance evaluations that are data-driven, recruitment processes that are AI-driven, and individualized learning modules are causing a revolution in human resources. This change improves operational efficiency and consumer experience while also responding to the ever-changing retail industry. Positioning themselves to prosper in the digital era, multinational retail chains are establishing norms for personnel management in a fast-altering industrial environment by embracing technology and smart HR strategies. Adapt to the needs of Industry 5.0, improve the customer experience, and transform HR procedures with the help of new technology and human capital analytics. Find out how international retail chains are doing it [36].

- **Cross-Industry Collaboration in Implementing Advanced Technologies**
Collaboration across industries is revolutionizing the way cutting-edge technology is being used in Industry 5.0. Diverse industries are banding together to learn more about human capital analytics and cutting-edge IT. This collaborative approach facilitates the dynamic sharing of workforce optimization best practices, innovative solutions, and lessons learned. When companies combine their knowledge, they may be better able to understand the opportunities and risks presented by innovative technologies. If we band together, we can cultivate an infinitely intelligent collective and hasten the acceptance of new methods. As a result, workers across all sectors will be more equipped to use technology to their advantage, and they will be able to adapt more quickly to new situations. Look at cases when companies from different industries collaborate to share knowledge and insights on human capital analytics and cutting-edge tech. When we pool our resources, we can observe how different industries are affected and how to fix them. You may find the most recent and applicable case

studies by searching for them in industry-specific journals, consulting firm papers, and publications from organizations that focus on human resources and workforce management. Attending Industry 5.0–related conferences, seminars, and forums may provide you with access to practical case studies and valuable insights about human capital analytics [37].

2.5 Challenges and Ethical Considerations

Many problems and ethical questions arise with the use of human capital analytics and other new technologies in the context of Industry 5.0. Prospects for data abuse and privacy breaches pose a serious problem. Protecting sensitive information is becoming more important for firms to maintain trust and stay in compliance with privacy requirements as they gather and analyze massive volumes of employee data. Another issue brought about by the quick pace of technological change is the need to upskill the workforce so that people can use new technology to their advantage. In the context of AI and ML implementations, ethical concerns naturally rise to the surface. It is crucial to give serious consideration to concerns like algorithmic biases, decision-making fairness, and openness in automated procedures. To keep morale and productivity high, businesses must find a way to use technology to their advantage while also being ethically responsible employers [38]. Also, many are worried about how automation will affect jobs in society because of the possibility of job loss. Ethical workforce transformation strategies, such as reskilling programs and assistance for laid-off employees, should be seriously considered by organizations. The development of a reasonable and long-term strategy for integrating human capital analytics with new technology depends on our ability to resolve these issues and ethical concerns. To successfully manage these challenges and establish a work environment that conforms to digital age ethical norms, organizations must place a premium on openness, ethical decision-making, and the welfare of their employees [39, 60].

2.5.1 Data Privacy and Security Concerns in Human Capital Analytics

With the rise of human capital analytics, companies now face serious challenges with data privacy and security. As businesses collect and analyze more and more data on their workers, safeguarding that data is becoming an increasingly critical concern. It is reasonable that workers would be concerned about the potential misuse of sensitive information pertaining to their health records and performance reviews. If there is a data breach, then the safety of confidential employee information might be compromised. Human capital analytics systems may include security flaws that allow hackers to steal personal information or conduct other forms of cybercrime [40]. Avoiding legal consequences and keeping the confidence of the workforce requires compliance with data protection rules like GDPR or HIPAA. Strong cybersecurity measures, such as encryption, safe data storage, and access restrictions, should be prioritized by firms that use human capital analytics to address these problems. Employee confidence must be earned via open and honest communication about data collection methods, intended uses, and security measures. To reap the advantages of human capital analytics without jeopardizing personal information or company security, ethical data governance policies must be put into place [41].

2.5.2 Fairness, Bias, and Transparency in AI-Driven Workforce Management

Concerns of bias, openness, and fairness are paramount in AI-driven labor management. Ensuring fairness and eliminating biases becomes crucial as businesses depend more and more on AI to make choices about recruiting, performance appraisal, and talent development [42].

- **Fairness**
  In order to maintain fair AI practices, all workers must be treated with respect and dignity. To be fair, AI systems should not give or take advantage of people depending on their gender, color, or age. In order to detect and address any potential biases, organizations should consistently monitor and evaluate their AI systems.
- **Inclusive Training Data**
  To minimize bias, AI systems should be trained on a range of sample datasets. If data from different demographic groups is included in the AI model, then it could be more egalitarian and less likely to worsen labor disparity.
- **Bias**
  Whether intentional or inadvertent, biases already present in the workplace may be amplified by AI systems. This might happen because the data used to train AI systems has

inherent biases. Businesses need to regularly check their AI systems for prejudice, fix it, or at least lessen its impact.

- **Transparency**
  Open AI systems might shed insight into how decisions are made. Employees should be aware of the rationale behind AI-generated hiring decisions. It may foster a sense of accountability and confidence in staff members when they understand the reasoning behind AI-generated suggestions or judgments.
- **Explainability**
  Transparency and explainability go hand in hand. When creating AI solutions, it should be the first concern to ensure that HR professionals and staff can comprehend the reasoning behind the system's suggestions or conclusions. This enhances credibility and protects people's ability to appeal unjust verdicts.
- **Regular Audits and Monitoring**
  Continuous auditing and monitoring are required to find and fix any potential biases in AI systems. Regular reviews are essential to ensure that the AI system adheres to the company's commitment to equality and does not inadvertently foster bias [43].

2.5.3 Ethical Guidelines and Governance

Transparent governance frameworks and moral standards must be created from the start for AI-driven workforce management. The policies of this organization should demonstrate a commitment to transparency, fairness, and unbiased decision-making. When developing and utilizing AI systems, governance mechanisms make sure that these requirements are fulfilled [44]. Organizations should give top priority to the following areas in order to overcome the challenges posed by AI-driven workforce management and establish a just and fair workplace: openness, equity, explainability, ongoing audits, ethics in governance, hiring transparency, and prejudice reduction [45].

2.5.4 Bus Automation with Human Empowerment

Success in Industry 5.0 requires finding the ideal balance between human agency and ML. Businesses that plan to integrate automation must be smart in identifying processes that may be mechanized but still require human ability in critical areas like creativity, emotional intelligence, and complex decision-making. To keep this balance, staff training expenses must be made on a regular basis to improve their ability to operate machinery. Prioritizing human-centered design, resolving ethical dilemmas, and fostering collaborative work cultures are crucial. While automation boosts productivity, ongoing feedback systems and a focus on employee well-being free up workers to concentrate on the high-value, creative components of their jobs [46].

2.6 Recommendations for Organizations

Businesses need to carefully balance automation with human empowerment in the age of Industry 5.0 to ensure sustainable development and a good work environment. First things first: make sure that automation projects are in line with long-term goals, with a focus on efficiency, innovation, and the company's overall objectives. Make training a top priority so that employees may grow professionally and help create a workforce that can work well with machines. Foster an environment of teamwork where technology is seen as an enhancing tool that may be used to complement human strengths, not a replacement for them. To make sure that automation plays to people's strengths and to provide interfaces that are easy for them to use, human-centric design principles should be followed. To address concerns about bias, lack of transparency, and unfairness, set up governance structures and ethical standards to direct responsible automation processes [47]. To understand how employees feel and what they think about automation, it is important to have a system in place that allows for continual input. This will help make educated modifications. Strive for a well-rounded approach to task allocation by recognizing duties that can be automated and freeing up individuals to concentrate on the strategic and creative parts of their jobs. Make use of automation to make work easier for employees by eliminating monotonous and unpleasant jobs. This will help create a more positive work atmosphere. To guarantee candor on the advantages and disadvantages of automation, top-down support and clear communication are essential. If you want to keep up with the latest innovations and market trends, then you need to adopt an agile attitude. In the end, it is important to become involved with the larger community, take on social issues, and do your part to promote social responsibility.

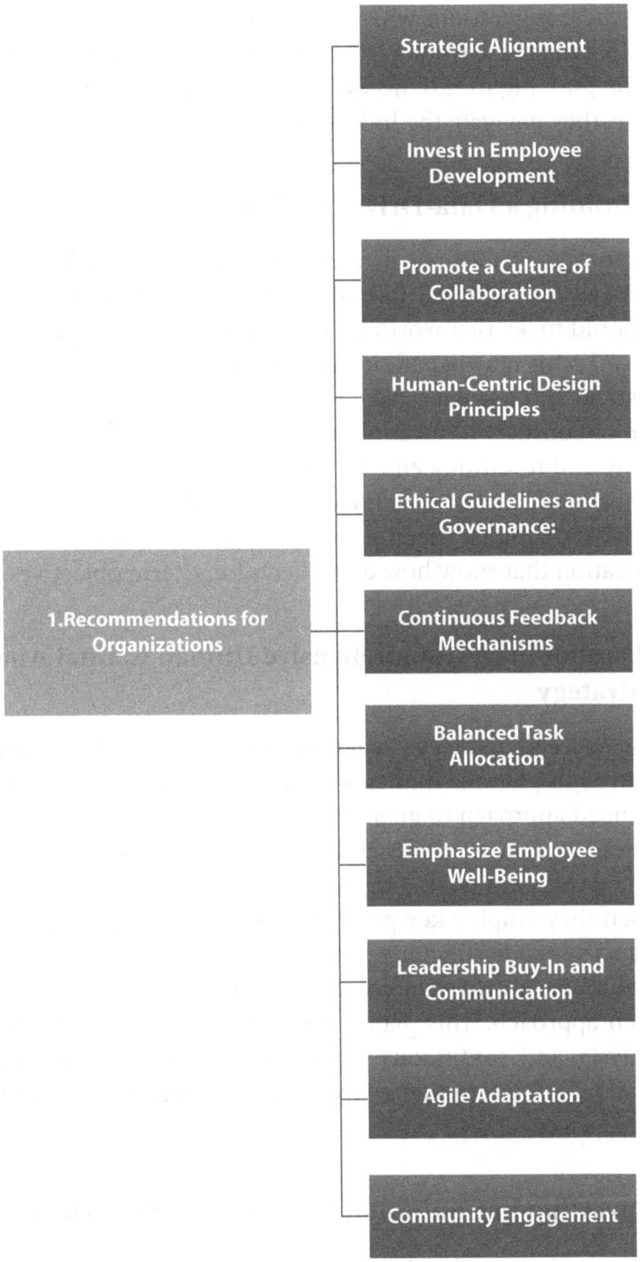

Figure 2.6 Recommendations for organizations.

Adopting these suggestions will help organizations succeed in the Industry 5.0 era by paving the way for a balance between human empowerment and automation [48]. Figure 2.6 shows some suggestions that organizations can consider as they navigate the Industrial Revolution.

2.6.1 Building a Data-Driven Culture

Organizations may foster a data-driven culture by teaching employees to see data as fundamental to making decisions. Data are valuable, and leaders should make that worth clear and promote its usage in day-to-day operations. Teams may benefit from increased data literacy and the ability to understand and use data insights if training programs are put in place. A culture of constant innovation and improvement may be nurtured by recognizing and rewarding efforts that are driven by data. The success and flexibility of an organization in the dynamic world of Industry 5.0 depends on data-driven choices, therefore it is important to set up clear lines of communication that show how data affects long-term objectives [49, 55].

2.6.2 Developing a Comprehensive Human Capital Analytics Strategy

In order to succeed in the ever-changing world of Industry 5.0, firms must have a thorough plan for human capital analytics. The initial step in this multi-pronged approach to guaranteeing reliable and easily accessible HR data is assessing data readiness and coordinating analytics objectives with more general company goals. Organizations demonstrate effort in resolving issues when they employ key performance indicators and predictive analytics to uncover staff difficulties. Fundamentally, a strong strategy should provide equal weight to data compliance and protection and promote a data-driven approach. This plan is strengthened further by cooperation, effect analysis, and continuous monitoring. We will create a framework that will allow human capital analytics to be a driver for innovation and institutional success [50].

2.6.3 Investing in Continuous Learning and Development

Businesses need to prioritize investing in learning and development if they want to successfully navigate the obstacles presented by Industry 5.0. In this day of fast technological innovation, a successful team requires members with up-to-date abilities. Comprehensive training programs should be put in place by organizations to meet present skill shortages and prepare for future ones. Together, in-person seminars, online resources, and mentoring programs should promote a development culture that emphasizes lifelong learning. Companies may assist staff adapt to new technology, improve as problem solvers, and ultimately increase the bottom line of the firm by encouraging them to never stop learning. The workforce's adaptability is guaranteed, and the company's dedication to the welfare and career advancement of its staff is reaffirmed by this investment, which serves two purposes. Organizations need to put continuous learning first if they want to prosper in the fast-paced world of Industry 5.0 [51]. They will eventually flourish as a result of being able to adapt to change and encourage innovation.

2.6.4 Balancing Technology with Human-Centric Approaches

Innovations in technology must coexist peacefully with human-centered approaches in the complex environment of Industry 5.0. Modern technology must be integrated with human-centered strategies to be successful in the long run. This combination allows for unmatched creativity and efficiency. Instead of seeing technology as a substitute for human abilities, we should see it as a supplement to them. Because of this, initiatives that train employees to be more flexible and tech-savvy need financial backing. Principles of human-centric design should guide the creation of technologies to ensure they are intuitive and meet human needs. Additionally, fostering an atmosphere of open communication, empathy, and support may help to fortify the human aspect of the workforce. By integrating human-centric strategies with technology, organizations may easily adjust to changing conditions. Innovation is promoted by this synergy, which prioritizes the health and potential of people resources [52].

2.7 Conclusion

Finally, the advent of Industry 5.0 heralds a new era in which state-of-the-art technology and human-centered approaches complement one another. Organizations need a well-thought-out strategy to integrate human initiative with AI and automation if they want to thrive in this new paradigm. A data-driven culture, a commitment to lifelong learning, and a comprehensive strategy for human capital analytics should be your top priorities. The true challenge is striking a balance between the indispensability of technical efficiency gains and the inestimable value of human empathy, imagination, and resourcefulness. Businesses that provide an atmosphere where flexibility, creativity, and wellness are valued by employees may find success in the fast-paced world of Industry 5.0. You must understand that the secret to success on this route is learning how to combine technological know-how with human qualities.

As businesses struggle to comprehend Industry 5.0, they are becoming more and more worried about the ethical implications of automation and AI. In order to be respected by the general public and staff, you need to find the right balance between doing what is right and what is practical. Any business should have transparency, equity, and responsibility in its technology usage policy. Success requires cooperation both inside and across the industry. A feeling of collective intelligence is fostered by employee discussion of objectives, concepts, and accomplishments. Realizing the full potential of new technologies and tackling shared issues need cross-industry collaboration. The final portion is not only a place to start but rather an impassioned cry to action. The paper stresses that companies should first weigh the social and ethical ramifications of Industry 5.0 before seizing the benefits it presents. When innovation, sustainability, and human happiness meet in unprecedented ways in the future, businesses that successfully combine technology with human values will set the standard. In Industry 5.0, human capital analytics is about to take a revolutionary turn that is both adaptable and strategically forward-thinking. The importance of human capital analytics is expanding as more companies employ cutting-edge tools for human resource management. By leveraging ML algorithms to better forecast and adapt to the changing needs of the modern workforce, this method outperforms earlier attempts at predictive analytics. The ongoing prominence of ethical problems highlights the critical necessity for the immediate development of transparent AI systems and robust regulatory frameworks. Businesses will soon be able to utilize data to improve the efficiency of their workforce, performance management, and talent acquisition procedures, thanks to the advent of real-time analytics. Human capital analytics can only progress if there is more communication and cooperation across different sectors. Organizations will succeed in the ever-changing world of Industry 5.0 if they are willing to learn, adapt, and integrate technology and human skills in a harmonic way.

References

1. Zhang, C., Wang, Z., Zhou, G., Chang, F., Ma, D., Jing, Y., Zhao, D., Towards new-generation human-centric smart manufacturing in Industry 5.0: A systematic review. *Adv. Eng. Inf.*, *57*, 102121, 2023.
2. Tiwari, S., Bahuguna, P.C., Walker, J., Industry 5.0: A macroperspective approach, in: *Handbook of Research on Innovative Management Using AI in Industry 5.0*, pp. 59–73, IGI Global, USA, 2022.
3. Aheleroff, S., Huang, H., Xu, X., Zhong, R.Y., Toward sustainability and resilience with Industry 4.0 and Industry 5.0. *Front. Manuf. Technol.*, *2*, 951643, 2022.
4. Maddikunta, P.K.R., Pham, Q.V., Prabadevi, B., Deepa, N., Dev, K., Gadekallu, T.R., Liyanage, M., Industry 5.0: A survey on enabling technologies and potential applications. *J. Ind. Inf. Integr.*, *26*, 100257, 2022.
5. Melnyk, L., Kubatko, O., Matsenko, O., Balatskyi, Y., Serdyukov, K., Transformation of the human capital reproduction in line with Industries 4.0 and 5.0, 2023.
6. Poláková, M., Suleimanová, J.H., Madzík, P., Copuš, L., Molnárová, I., Polednová, J., Soft skills and their importance in the labour market under the conditions of Industry 5.0. *Heliyon*, *9*, 8, 2023.
7. Wang, B., Zhou, H., Li, X., Yang, G., Zheng, P., Song, C., Wang, L., Human Digital Twin in the context of Industry 5.0. *Rob. Comput. Integr. Manuf.*, *85*, 102626, 2024.
8. Cillo, V., Gregori, G.L., Daniele, L.M., Caputo, F., Bitbol-Saba, N., Rethinking companies' culture through knowledge management lens during Industry 5.0 transition. *J. Knowl. Manage.*, *26*, 10, 2485–2498, 2022.
9. Saniuk, S., Grabowska, S., Straka, M., Identification of social and economic expectations: Contextual reasons for the transformation process of Industry 4.0 into the Industry 5.0 concept. *Sustainability*, *14*, 3, 1391, 2022.
10. Carayannis, E.G. and Morawska-Jancelewicz, J., The futures of Europe: Society 5.0 and Industry 5.0 as driving forces of future universities. *J. Knowl. Econ.*, *13*, 4, 3445–3471, 2022.
11. Ghobakhloo, M., Iranmanesh, M., Mubarak, M.F., Mubarik, M., Rejeb, A., Nilashi, M., Identifying industry 5.0 contributions to sustainable development: A strategy roadmap for delivering sustainability values. *Sustain. Prod. Consum.*, *33*, 716–737, 2022.
12. Huang, S., Wang, B., Li, X., Zheng, P., Mourtzis, D., Wang, L., Industry 5.0 and Society 5.0—Comparison, complementation and co-evolution. *J. Manuf. Syst.*, *64*, 424–428, 2022.
13. Pizoń, J. and Gola, A., Human–Machine Relationship—Perspective and Future Roadmap for Industry 5.0 Solutions. *Machines*, *11*, 2, 203, 2023.

14. Ghobakhloo, M., Iranmanesh, M., Foroughi, B., Tirkolaee, E.B., Asadi, S., Amran, A., Industry 5.0 implications for inclusive sustainable manufacturing: An evidence-knowledge-based strategic roadmap. *J. Clean. Prod.*, *417*, 138023, 2023.
15. Zhang, J., Patterns of innovation-driven tourism competitiveness: Insights from 270 Chinese cities. *Tourism Manag.*, 107, 105063, 2025.
16. Belizón, M.J. and Kieran, S., Human resources analytics: A legitimacy process. *Hum. Resour. Manage. J.*, *32*, 3, 603–630, 2022.
17. Parry, E. and Battista, V., The impact of emerging technologies on work: a review of the evidence and implications for the human resource function. *Emerald Open Res.*, *1*, 4, 1–14, 2023.
18. Ridgway, M., Oldridge, L. and Mavin, S., 'Leading'by example? Gendered language in Human Resource job adverts. *Human Res. Manag. J.*, 35, 1, 1–24, 2025.
19. van Dun, D.H. and Kumar, M., Social enablers of Industry 4.0 technology adoption: transformational leadership and emotional intelligence. *Int. J. Oper. Prod. Manage.*, *43*, 13, 152–182, 2023.
20. Yusuf, T. and Indrajaya, I.A.N., The Influence of Delegation Authority and Transformational Leadership on Individual Performance by The Existence of Individual Adaptability as Mediating Variable. Communication, Organization, Branding, Feasibility Analysis for Business Management: Inquiries with New Approaches in the Post-Pandemic Era, 5.
21. Tariq, S., Iftikhar, A., Chaudhary, P., Khurshid, K., Is the 'Technological Singularity Scenario' Possible: Can AI Parallel and Surpass All Human Mental Capabilities? *World Futures*, *79*, 2, 200–266, 2023.
22. Rajput, N., Das, G., Shivam, K., Nayak, C.K., Gaurav, K., Nagpal, P., An inclusive systematic investigation of human resource management practice in harnessing human capital. *Mater. Today Proc.*, *80*, 3686–3690, 2023.
23. Khor, L.K. and Tan, C.L., Workforce management in the post-pandemic era: Evidence from multinational companies using grounded theory. *Global Bus. Organ. Excell.*, *42*, 4, 93–104, 2023.
24. Zebua, S. and Chakim, M.H.R., Effect of Human Resources Quality, Performance Evaluation, and Incentives on Employee Productivity at Raharja High School. *APTISI Trans. Manage. (ATM)*, *7*, 1, 1–7, 2023.
25. Nyathi, M. and Kekwaletswe, R., Realizing employee and organizational performance gains through electronic human resource management use in developing countries. *Afr. J. Econ. Manage. Stud.*, *14*, 1, 121–134, 2023.
26. Khan, N. and Millner, D., *Introduction to people analytics: a practical guide to data-driven HR*, Kogan Page Publishers, London, 2023.
27. Shakir, M., Al Farsi, M.J., Al-Shamsi, I.R., Shannaq, B., Taufiq-Hail, G.A.M., The Influence of Mobile Information Systems Implementation on Enhancing Human Resource Performance Skills: An Applied Study in a Small Organization. *Int. J. Interact. Mob. Technol.*, 18, 13, 2024.

28. Karaboga, T., Zehir, C., Tatoglu, E., Karaboga, H.A., Bouguerra, A., Big data analytics management capability and firm performance: the mediating role of data-driven culture. *Rev. Manag. Sci.*, *17*, 8, 2655–2684, 2023.
29. Chung, D., Yun, J., Lee, J., Jeon, Y., Predictive model of employee attrition based on stacking ensemble learning. *Expert Syst. Appl.*, *215*, 119364, 2023.
30. Kanchana, L. and Jayathilaka, R., Factors impacting employee turnover intentions among professionals in Sri Lankan startups. *PLoS One*, *18*, 2, e0281729, 2023.
31. Olsson, A.K., Eriksson, K.M., Carlsson, L., Management toward Industry 5.0: a co-workership approach on digital transformation for future innovative manufacturing. *Eur. J. Innov. Manag.*, 28, 1, 65–84, 2025.
32. Kliestik, T., Nagy, M., Valaskova, K., Global value chains and industry 4.0 in the context of lean workplaces for enhancing company performance and its comprehension via the digital readiness and expertise of workforce in the V4 nations. *Mathematics*, *11*, 3, 601, 2023.
33. Costa, J., Pádua, M., Moreira, A.C., Leadership Styles and Innovation Management: What Is the Role of Human Capital? *Adm. Sci.*, *13*, 2, 47, 2023.
34. Cho, W., Choi, S., Choi, H., Human Resources Analytics for Public Personnel Management: Concepts, Cases, and Caveats. *Adm. Sci.*, *13*, 2, 41, 2023.
35. Piwowar-Sulej, K., Malik, S., Shobande, O.A., Singh, S., Dagar, V., A contribution to sustainable human resource development in the era of the COVID-19 pandemic. *J. Bus. Ethics*, 191, 2, 337–355, 2024.
36. Khang, A., Jadhav, B., Birajdar, S., Industry Revolution 4.0: workforce competency models and designs, in: *Designing Workforce Management Systems for Industry 4.0*, pp. 11–34, CRC Press, Boca Raton, 2023.
37. Dolgui, A., Gusikhin, O., Ivanov, D., Li, X., Stecke, K., A network-of-networks adaptation for cross-industry manufacturing repurposing. *IISE Trans.*, 56, 6, 666–682, 2024.
38. Siddiq, M., Exploring the Role of Machine Learning in Contact Tracing for Public Health: Benefits, Challenges, and Ethical Considerations. *Am. J. Econ. Manage. Bus. (AJEMB)*, *2*, 3, 99–110, 2023.
39. Dhiman, D.B., Ethical Issues and Challenges in Social Media: A Current Scenario, 2023, Available at SSRN 4406610.
40. Prastyaningtyas, E.W., Ausat, A.M.A., Muhamad, L.F., Wanof, M.I., Suherlan, S., The Role of Information Technology in Improving Human Resources Career Development. *J. Teknol. Sistem Inf. Bisnis*, *5*, 3, 266–275, 2023.
41. Valcik, N.A., Sabharwal, M., Benavides, T.J., Existing research on HRIS in public organizations, in: *Human Resources Information Systems: A guide for public administrators*, pp. 35–48, Springer International Publishing, Cham, 2023.
42. Burrell, D.N. and Mcandrew, I., Exploring the Ethical Dynamics of the Use of Artificial Intelligence (AI) in Hiring in Healthcare Organizations. *Land Forces Acad. Rev.*, *28*, 4, 309–321, 2023.

43. Rodgers, W., Murray, J.M., Stefanidis, A., Degbey, W.Y., Tarba, S.Y., An artificial intelligence algorithmic approach to ethical decision-making in human resource management processes. *Hum. Resour. Manage. Rev.*, *33*, 1, 100925, 2023.
44. Chen, Z., Ethics and discrimination in artificial intelligence-enabled recruitment practices. *Humanit. Social Sci. Commun.*, *10*, 1, 1–12, 2023.
45. Chowdhury, S., Joel-Edgar, S., Dey, P.K., Bhattacharya, S., Kharlamov, A., Embedding transparency in artificial intelligence machine learning models: managerial implications on predicting and explaining employee turnover. *Int. J. Hum. Resour. Manage.*, *34*, 14, 2732–2764, 2023.
46. Randhahn, A., Leitão, J., Foldesi, E., Dubbert, J., Pinto, A., Zachäus, C., Moertl, P., Automated Vehicles Empowering Mobility of Vulnerable Groups-and the Pathway to Achieve This, in: *Towards User-Centric Transport in Europe 3: Making Digital Mobility Inclusive and Accessible*, pp. 22–41, Springer International Publishing, Cham, 2023.
47. Van Eeghen, A.M., Stemkens, D., Fernández-Fructuoso, J.R., Maruani, A., Hadzsiev, K., Gaasterland, C.M.W., van Balkom, I.D.C., Consensus recommendations on organization of care for individuals with Phelan-McDermid syndrome. *Eur. J. Med. Genet.*, *66*, 7, 104747, 2023.
48. Tang, G., Ren, S., Wang, M., Li, Y., Zhang, S., Employee green behaviour: A review and recommendations for future research. *Int. J. Manage. Rev.*, *25*, 2, 297–317, 2023.
49. Nummela, P., Creating data-driven culture in a Finnish B2B software company's marketing department, 2023.
50. Chowdhury, S.R., Guha, S., Sanju, N.L. Artificial intelligence enabled human resource management: A review and future research avenues. *Arch. Bus. Res.*, 12, 6, 94–111, 2024.
51. Ulutaş, N.K. and Abuşka, A., Language Teachers' Investment in Digital Multimodal Composing (DMC) as a Manifold Application of Computer-Mediated Communication, in: *Multidisciplinary Applications of Computer-Mediated Communication*, pp. 17–30, IGI Global, USA, 2023.
52. Hu, W., Wang, S., Zhai, W., Human-centric vs. technology-centric approaches in a top-down smart city development regime: Evidence from 341 Chinese cities. *Cities*, *137*, 104271, 2023.
53. Singh, S., Gupta, D., Gupta, M., Optimized Task Allocation Technique using Mathematical Fuzzy Logic in heterogeneous Distributed Computational System. *2022 International Conference on Computational Intelligence and Sustainable Engineering Solutions (CISES)*, Greater Noida, India, pp. 37–45, 2022, doi: 10.1109/CISES54857.2022.9844410.
54. Agarwal, S. and Gupta, D., Digital analytics applications for sustainable training and education, in: *Digital analytics applications for sustainable training and education*, K. Sood, P. Kalia, S. Grima, A. Chaudhary (Eds.), p. 25, Apple Academic Press, United States, 2024, ISBN: 9781032713366.

55. Singh, S. and Gupta, D., Module Allocation Model in Distributed Computing System by Implementing Fuzzy C-means Clustering Technique, in: *International Conference on IoT, Intelligent Computing and Security*, Lecture Notes in Electrical Engineering, vol. 982, R. Agrawal, P. Mitra, A. Pal, M. Sharma Gaur (Eds.), Springer, Singapore, 2023, https://doi.org/10.1007/978-981-19-8136-4_14.
56. Agarwal, S., Gupta, D., Gupta, M., Techno Pedagogical Concept with Digital Skills, in: *Edutech Enabled Teaching*, pp. 129–152, Chapman and Hall/CRC, Academic Press, 2023.
57. Agarwal, S., Gupta, D., Verma, P., Impact of Employment on GDP Contribution of Various Sectors in India. *Global J. Enterp. Inf. Syst.*, *11*, 1, 47–53, 2019.
58. Gupta, D. and Agarwal, S., Skill Development Initiative-Literature Review. *Inspira-J. Mod. Manage. Entrepreneurship (JMME)*, *8*, 2, 319–322, 2018.
59. Gupta, D., Gupta, M., Tiwari, S., Singh, N., Motivation due to fear of failure is a key contributor in maximizing workers' productivity in today's competitive arena. *Int. J. Indian Cult. Bus. Manage.*, 23, 2, 193–217, 2021, doi: 10.1504/IJICBM.2021.115895.
60. Kumar, V., Gupta, M., Gaur, S., Intrusion detection for the Internet of Things, in: *Internet of Things and cyber physical systems security and forensics*, 1st ed., K. Kaushik, S. Dahiya, A. Bhardwaj, Y. Maleh (Eds.), p. 183, CRC Press, Boca Raton, 2023.

3

Fifth Industrial Revolution and an Overview of its Impact on Human Resources

Aduku Alex Akubo*, Okpanachi Linus Odiji and Muhammed Bature Muhammed

Department of Political Science, Kogi State University, Anyigba, Kogi State, Nigeria

Abstract

The integration of technology into the quest for our daily living and its implications for life itself has endured substantial growth and transformation. However, the emergence and innovation that culminated in the Fifth Industrial Revolution, necessitating and galvanizing profound visible positive outcomes in economies, society, and industries, have left no one in doubt. The study has provided an extensive assessment of the Fifth Industrial Revolution, and its implications for human resources is the anchor of this chapter. Industry 5.0 is concerned with the desire to adapt or fine-tune the current technologies to suit the changing world. Organizations must also adapt their HRM culture and outlook along with this evolution. The Internet of Things, automation, blockchain, robotics, and artificial intelligence are some of the driving forces galvanizing the revolution of these technologies. The chapter critically examines the evolving nature of these technologies and their impacts on traditional workforce structure. It equally appraises the implications of these technological developments on the workforce, not neglecting job roles, skill requirements, and workflows. It envisions the challenges and prospects of the Fifth Industrial Revolution for human resources, and its attendant possibility: for enhanced productivity, improved employee experiences, and the need for skill upgrading and retraining programs. Also, the chapter evaluates ethical issues and their effects on the application of Industry 5.0 in the workplace, with greater emphasis on employee well-being, regulations, and other practices while visualizing the future of work by comprehending the indeterminate influence of the Fifth Industrial Revolution on human resources. Ultimately, the chapter mirrors the consequences of Industry 5.0 for workforce, skills, and competencies, not

**Corresponding author*: akuboadukwu@gmail.com

Deepa Gupta, Mukul Gupta, Pawan Budhwar, Jim Westerman, Rajesh Kumar Dhanaraj and Balamurugan Balusamy (eds.) Human Capital Analytics: Exploring the HR Spectrum in Industry 5.0, (65–80) © 2025 Scrivener Publishing LLC

overlooking the need to implement it, keeping with the demands of the job market, reequipping, and skill development. Industry 5.0 represents a convergence of transitions toward environmental sustainability and digitalization, aiming to create a more efficient, effective, and sustainable society and economy.

Keywords: Industry 5.0, human resources management, industrial revolution, productivity, business environment, human capital

3.1 Introduction

Technology and science are ever-present in every facet of human life. There is a long history of connecting science and technology. These two elements are essential to the evolution of humanity since they are as old as human existence itself and have been vital to the development of prehistoric man. The past two centuries have seen a great deal of scientific and technological progress, which has had a huge impact on public policy, businesses, human resources, international relations, political institutions, and political struggle [1]. Improved knowledge of science and technology in earlier centuries has spurred substantial advancements in the world economy, leading to a shift away from traditional manufacturing methods. The Industrial Revolution is a shift in paradigms in science and technology, which are unified into different facets of our lives. It has gone through several stages of development. In essence, this shift has transformed enterprises, industries, economies, and communities. From the standpoint of development, science and technology have affected and interacted with economic domains including decreasing poverty, accelerating agricultural advancement, enhancing health, and boosting economic development. They unquestionably had a weighty influence on the development along with the administration of human resources, and they have been crucial in the growth of agriculture, energy security, environmental protection, and better lifestyles.

Economic prosperity and human situations have significantly improved as a result of scientific and technical advancements. The state of the market today suggests that entrepreneurship, innovation, and creativity are all overflowing with requests to digitize their business operations through the use of cloud computing and other cutting-edge technologies like artificial intelligence (AI), the Internet of Things (IoT), etc., so as to stimulate efficiency, engender productivity, fostering flexibility and agility. Some industrialists are concerned about the future and do not see existing business practices as they are, but rather how they could be in the future, despite the growing digital revolution inside Industry 4.0. We are approaching the Fifth Industrial Revolution. Without a doubt, technology is developing quickly, and Industry 5.0 is becoming more widely accepted and a crucial component of business.

The human-centric approach of the Fifth Industrial Revolution, the consequences of the interaction between humans and machines, and the effect on human resources are the main topics of this section. Specifically, the collaboration between the automated industrial environments of the future, IoT devices, and humans working alongside robots [2] is discussed. Combining mechanical and human labor opens up countless opportunities in manufacturing. The aim of the Fifth Industrial Revolution is to employ a strong, human-based, justified approach to effectively handle changes and difficulties. Since Industry 5.0 is still in its early phases, manufacturers need to actively think about how to join mechanical, human knowledge, and labor so as to engender the special benefits that will arise as the project develops [3]. Although the automation of production processes seems to be an irreversible phenomenon, a thorough investigation.

3.2 Trajectory of Industrial Revolutions

The history of science and technology can be traced through a number of eras and paths, including the Stone Age, Iron Age, Ancient Period, Medieval Period, Renaissance, and Age of Enlightenment, which flowed into the Industrial Revolution. An Industrial Renaissance is a changeover from one industrial technique to another one, frequently brought by developments in technology that began in Great Britain in the 1780s. Over the past 250 years, scholarly works have recognized five major technological revolutions. These revolutions are characterized as strong, conspicuous clusters of inventive, dynamic products, industries, and technologies that have the potential to seriously upend the entire system of economic relations.

The Industrial Revolution, which started in Britain in 1770, was the first of these revolutions. The second revolution, also known as the Age of Steam and Railways, began in Britain in 1830 and quickly extended to the USA and the rest of Europe. Which is known as the Age of Heavy Engineering, Electricity, and Steel. The third revolution began in 1875 and saw the United States and Germany overtake Great Britain. This was the Age of Mass Production, the Automobile and of oil. The fourth revolution started in the USA in 1910 and eventually spread to Europe. The Age of Telecommunications and that of Information and the last which is the fifth revolution finally began in the USA in 1970 and quickly extended to Europe and Asia.

While the third and fourth revolutions are generally known as "The Second Industrial Revolution," the first and second revolutions are frequently united under the title "The First Industrial Revolution." The conclusion of the Second Industrial Revolution, which occurred toward the end of the 20th century, particularly during World War I and the following years; the aftereffects of the First Industrial Revolution, which occurred in the other half of the 19th century; and finally, the Age of Information and Telecommunications, which emerged in the late twentieth century, clearly succeeded these three revolutionary periods. This latter time frame is regarded by many academics as the Third Industrial Revolution [1].

Tracing the trajectory of Industrial Revolutions 1 to 3 and their achievements [4] noted the following:

The 18th century saw the emergence of Industry 1.0, which was centered on the industries of mining, transportation, glass, paper, textiles, steam power, iron, tools, cement, chemicals, and gas. Transportation, employment, agricultural expansion, and steady growth are among the benefits of this revolution. Industry 1.0 is related to several downsides, such as pollution and implementation time required for associated processes. Geometry and linear programming were two mathematical tools used in Industry 1.0. Beginning in the 19th century, Industry 2.0 concentrated on the following areas: rubber, bicycles, vehicles, applied science, fertilizer, engines, turbines, telecommunications, paper, steel, rail, electricity, machine tools, paper, petroleum, chemical, and maritime technologies. The development of the electrical power grid, telephones, telegraph, and internal combustion engines are among the innovations of this revolution. The high cost of using electricity is Industry 2.0's main disadvantage. The mathematical tools of differential equations, linear equations, and geometry were used in Industry 2.0. Beginning in the 20th century, Industry 3.0 concentrated on the semiconductor industry, digital circuits, programmable integrated circuits, wireless communication, telecommunication, automation, and the renewable energy sector. Robots, automated industries, renewable energy, and telecommunication are among the innovations of this revolution. The main flaw in Industry 3.0 is that some scenarios would prevent automated systems from functioning. One of the main tenets of Industry 3.0, for instance, was the deployment of Flexible Manufacturing Systems (FMS).

Despite its seeming distance, Industry 4.0 is really a transitory phenomenon. When the Fourth Industrial Revolution's concept was uncovered in 2011 at the Munich Messe trade show in Germany, the phrase "Industry 4.0" became well-known [3]. Agile manufacturing was initially designed mainly for the smart manufacturing industries, German industrial automation, and for other EU member states following European law. Automation was once thought of as having a substantial effect on European business culture as well as legal systems, in spite of its rapid extension to other parts of the world [3]. Robotics, digitization, standardization, safe and dynamic networks, miniaturization, general modernization, and incremental mechanization are just a few of the many ideas that make up Industry 4.0.

The technological innovations that underpin the Fourth Industrial Revolution include blockchain, data analytics, cloud computing, robotics, the Internet of Things (IoT), cryptocurrencies, 3D printing, artificial intelligence, production line processing systems, and autonomous manufacturing with comprehensive process control. On the other hand, Industry 4.0 offers many benefits and has drawbacks, including the possibility that all data stored in the cloud are not protected and the lack of fully functional expert systems for various industries. Both optimization techniques and network theory are examples of mathematical tools used by Industry 4.0. Industry 5.0 is a nascent movement that advances technical modernization by emphasizing cost and resource optimization to meet particular social goals. Enhancing the standard of living, promoting environmentally friendly production methods that respect the constraints of the earth, and using technology to promote sustainable development are some of these goals. Research suggests that Industry 5.0 has German roots and first achieved international notice [3]. At the CeBIT 2017 trade show in Hannover, Japan shared its dream for the use of smart manufacturing technology, and robotics, which helped to shape Industry 5.0.

Formerly referred to as Society 5.0, this idea was stimulated by Japanese culture. It is a development of the innovative concept, highlighting the important role that people play in producing economic value in addition to robots. After the pandemic, Industry 5.0—where artificial intelligence, smart machines, robots, big data, and the Internet of Things will continue to be essential for economic success—is becoming more and more of a future goal for industrial automation. But with the help of increasingly intelligent and effective technology, there will be a stronger focus on human skills development, adaptation, and self-reliance [3]. The objective of the Fifth Industrial Revolution is to move the industry toward a resilient, human-centered, and sustainable paradigm that will benefit firms, employees, and the environment overall. The continuous paradigm changes highlight integrating production values for workers and the environment in addition to productivity and efficiency. Collaborative robots that help reduce risk are a fundamental component of Industry 5.0. These robots are able to recognize, understand, and feel empathy for human operators in addition to being able to comprehend the goals and requirements related to the jobs in question. The ultimate goal is for these robots to assist human operators in task performance by watching and learning from people performing tasks [4].

3.3 An Overview of the Fifth Industrial Revolution

The Fifth Industrial Revolution refers to a system whereby automated machines can improve human speed and efficiency through the use of cutting-edge instruments like big data and internet-connected items. Historically, industrial environments have used robots to carry out dangerous, repetitive, or physically taxing jobs like painting and welding in auto plants and offloading and loading big objects in warehouses. As offices get more sophisticated and networked, Industry 5.0 aims to fuse human intelligence and creativity with the cognitive computing powers of office equipment in coordinated tasks. This is not the same as Industry 4.0, which was mainly concerned with deploying intelligent machines and robotics to achieve high performance and maximum efficiency in manufacturing.

The European Commission has identified six key sectors as accelerators for Industry 5.0 technologies: 1) Personalized human-machine communication; 2) bio-inspired and intelligent materials; 3) digital twins and simulation; 4) data transportation, storage, and analysis technologies; 5) computerized intelligence (AI); and 6) energy-efficient, renewable energy, self-sufficient, and storage technologies [3].

Digital transformation, artificial intelligence, supply chain, Industrial Revolution, big data, machine learning, industry technology, digital twin, recent year, cloud computing, Internet of Things (IoT), sustainable development, future research, AI intelligence, smart manufacturing, digital technology, Fourth Industrial Revolution, manufacturing company, production techniques, and manufacturing system are among the highest 20 terms recognized by the Industry 5.0 database [4]. According to academics, Industry 5.0 will improve upon, not replace, the ideas of Industry 4.0. They see an office setting where humans and technology work together to create a more sustainable and inclusive work environment on a daily basis [5]. Many academics agree that the Fifth Industrial Revolution is a logical growth of Industry 4.0, with the goal of creating a more effective system to meet the social, ecological, and economic goals of green production. It is widely acknowledged that the Fifth Industrial Revolution should not be understood as an auxiliary for Industry 4.0, but rather as a step forward in time where businesses should take into account not only profits but also the welfare of people and the environment [5].

Industry 5.0 has been considered to be of great benefit to enterprises in various ways which include:

i. Enhancing human potential;
ii. Minimizing inefficiencies;
iii. Minimizing waste and promoting sustainability;
iv. Minimizing operational risk; and
v. Promoting creativity and innovation while minimizing operational risk
vi. Enhance the problem-solving abilities of human/robot partners [5].

3.4 The Fifth Industrial Revolution and Human Resource Management of the Organizations

Since the beginning of the First Industrial Revolution, technology's disruption has had a profound effect on people's lives and existence. This has led to a notable increase in productivity and job opportunities [6]. According to one school of thought, an organization's most valuable asset is its people, and the most successful organizations are those that effectively lead and leverage their human capital [7]. Human resources management is the collection of strategies and activities that are used to manage workers at all organizational units in an efficient manner so as to achieve the organization's goals and objectives [8]. In the end, human capital refers to the economic value that individuals within an organization bring and utilize. This value is mostly obtained from the education, training, experience, and information that each employee possesses and applies to the work environment. Organizations value these qualities, which include, but are not limited to, acumen, knowledge, readiness, promptness, talents, training, and well-being [6]. In the context of Industry 4.0 and 5.0, human resources management is crucial to processes that involve human-machine interaction. The degree to which humans and machines are involved can differ. The workplace has changed owing to the extensive use of digitalization [9].

Human resources management has become a crucial and highly valued role in today's enterprises in the age of globalization. It was created with the intention of managing employees in firms in an efficient manner. A new type of management is required as a result of technological improvements.

Human resources management has become more important at the same time that changes in the education and qualifications of the workforce have occurred. Workforce planning, recruiting, performance and wage management, coordination of training, protecting the health and safety of employees, and putting organizational improvement plans into action are just a few of the many responsibilities that fall under this umbrella [10]. The individual assigned to this position inside the company is in charge of human resources management. It covers a variety of themes as leasing, training, and pay.

Technologies and globalization like Industry 5.0 have made it necessary for human resources management to continuously monitor and oversee its operations. It is now possible to carry out the complete management procedure online [10].

Humans have always relied on technology, which has developed alongside society throughout history. The term "Industrial Revolution" refers to the change from one industrial method to another, usually caused by advances in technology. This trend started in the 1870s and lasted until it culminated in the Fourth Industrial Revolution, or Industry 4.0, which is the epoch we are presently living in. The primary emphasis on digitalization and AI-driven technology characterizes this revolution [6]. But this idea has been reassessed recently because it is no longer appropriate for dealing with urgent problems like the COVID-19 pandemic, the climate catastrophe, and the global emergency brought on by the overuse of resources.

Furthermore, when AI technologies are used more widely, fewer people are employed, which emphasizes the issue of unemployment and exacerbates societal tensions. In order to handle the new sociological and technological concerns that have evolved, the Fifth Industrial Revolution, or Industry 5.0, has to be introduced. There are many opportunities to address these difficulties more effectively with this new revolution. Industry 5.0 has made a home for itself in human resources, more especially in human resource management (HRM), much like other fields have. The application of artificial intelligence has demonstrated advantages in enhancing diverse facets of human resources, such as analytics and reporting from surveys, appointment and interview scheduling, workflow task execution, and assistance with talent acquisition, talent management, and succession planning [6].

Because of the emergence of digital technologies and AI-based solutions, the industrial sector and other enterprises are currently experiencing a rapid shift. The challenge facing manufacturers everywhere is to boost output while retaining human labor in the production process. As robots become more and more integrated into the manufacturing process, this duty gets even more complex because of technological breakthroughs like artificial intelligence and brain-machine interfaces. Industry 5.0, the next Industrial Revolution, suggests treating robots and people as partners rather than as rivals in order to overcome these obstacles [11]. By accomplishing societal goals and evolving into a sustainable engine of advancement, Industry 5.0 seeks to transcend beyond employment and growth. It respects environmental restrictions and integrates technical improvements while placing a higher priority on worker well-being and using nascent technology to generate riches above growth and employment. This revolution increases industry competitiveness, empowers workers, and draws top talent [5]. It also adjusts to the changing skill and training needs of the workforce.

Industry 5.0 is built on values like social benefit, environmental stewardship, and human-centricity rather than only technology. Human-centricity places a strong emphasis on the value of each participant's autonomy and sense of self-sovereignty. It stands for the freedom of individuals to make decisions free from compulsion or force [12]. The production process is centered on the basic needs and interests of people according to the human-centric approach. Technology is perceived as a tool that facilitates, supports, and adjusts production to the various needs of laborers, changing the paradigm from one that is technology-driven to one that is human-centric [13]. The objective of Industry 5.0 is to restore back human communication in the industrial sector, enhancing its sustainability, human-centeredness, and resilience. The development of a cooperative environment between people and robots, which results in the formation of a smart society, is one of the main trends of Industry 5.0 [5]. Establishing a secure and welcoming workplace that promotes employees' physical and emotional well-being and, in the end, protects their basic rights to privacy, autonomy, and human dignity is essential.

Three main advantages of applying the human-centric approach are listed in an industry paper from Europe. These advantages include giving industrial workers a new job, creating a compassionate and all-encompassing work environment, and encouraging skill development, upskilling, and reskilling. The industry worker [13] has brought attention to the growing part they play in encouraging a cooperative environment between people and machines. Businesses see employees as investments because they see them as assets. Adapting technology to the individual needs of the worker, encouraging inclusion, and boosting their talents are important components of this function. Workers are enthusiastically involved in the growth and application of nascent industrial technology, like artificial intelligence and robotics, in order to accomplish this goal. Humans are positioned at the center, with technology being used to optimize processes.

Creating a safer work environment is a central objective, and robots can be employed to replace human workers in tasks that are monotonous, hazardous, and physically demanding. Industry 5.0 is a human creation, more like humans creating less or superhuman tasks conducted by machines that act beyond the human capacity programmed to undertake the task; this will avert, eliminate, or reduce accidents in workplaces. This will translate to a mechanical process, leading to a safer and more serene work environment. Workers will have the leverage to perform more tasks that are less hazardous where professionalism, unique skills, and physical strength become the bane. As a result, individuals with restricted intellectual abilities or women can also contribute to the workforce. Making the workplace safer is one of the key objectives. In jobs that are physically taxing, hazardous, and repetitious, humans can be replaced by robots. Automating these tasks can reduce workplace accidents and create a more comprehensive and safe work environment. This enables the use of cutting-edge technologies to assist workers in doing highly specialized activities that typically need a certain set of skills and physical strength, such as augmented reality, virtual reality, and artificial intelligence. This means that people with limited mental capacity and women can both contribute to the workforce.

Employees can accommodate the potential dangers and impacts of an evolving work setting on their general and mental well-being with the use of digital technologies. For instance, wearable technology can notify staff members of critical situations that might jeopardize their physical or mental health. In the long run, this benefits firms by decreasing absenteeism and raising productivity by fostering a culture of well-being. The third benefit relates to skills and the workplace, particularly the importance of re- and upskilling workers in companies. The development and effective use of skills are critical to the success of businesses and the overall well-being of personnel. There is currently a glaring mismatch between the broad and specialized talents that people possess and those that are required. Workers no longer need to be technology experts or retrain themselves whenever new technologies are introduced because technology is so basic and easy to use.

The 10 pieces of expertise that will be most crucial for production in the future have been identified by the World Manufacturing Forum. These competencies include digital literacy, artificial intelligence, cybersecurity, data mindfulness, and data analytics. Additionally, stressed are cross-disciplinary skills including creativity, an entrepreneurial spirit, adaptability, and open-mindedness. Because they have access to the newest technology and knowledge, businesses are aware of the skills shortages and can fill them by giving people the required training and education. One of Industry 5.0's products is providing educational opportunities to allow human resources to specialize in enhanced digital abilities. This specialization aims to enhance creativity and advance IT.

This specialization aims to foster individuals' creativity and IT literacy in order to enable them to think independently and generate novel ideas when collaborating with others [14]. It is possible to foster a symbiotic interaction between humans and self-governing robots by offering comprehensive instruction and training concerning the concepts and proficiencies of Industry 5.0.

Two workshops' talks, captured in [15], identified that the various parts of Industry 5.0 were emphasized, which, in a specific sense, can be seen as follows:

i. The combination of technological and human skills and strengths benefits both industry and workers; technology enhances, not replaces, human abilities, allowing people to solve problems creatively, take on new tasks, and perform better in safer, more comfortable, and ergonomic work environments.
ii. The main idea behind Industry 5.0 is to choose technologies not only for their technical or commercial merits but also for how well they serve human values and needs.
iii. Technologies like human-machine interfaces, fusing AI with human brain capacities, and working with robots and machines are used to produce products and services. With the help of these goods and services, closed loops, energy independence, emission neutrality, and the circular economy can all be realized.

Human resource development under Industry 5.0 includes researching and establishing process improvements, implementing major change management in businesses and organizations, and examining, formulating, creating, executing, and evaluating learning and development activities. Industry 5.0's emphasis on artificial intelligence is changing everything, including social relationships, work settings, and daily routines. As such, it is crucial to human and technological advancement in this era of artificial intelligence and the Fifth Industrial Revolution. As opposed to routine, repetitive, and highly supervised jobs, Industry 5.0's collaborative work model requires the human workforce to provide high-quality work.

To facilitate these changes and guarantee successful operations, this work structure necessitates the deployment of an appropriate management strategy and the presence of specialized talents on-site [16]. Progress is inevitably accompanied by changes. Adopting new working practices requires careful thought through strategy and implementation choices, as well as strong change management procedures at every organizational level. These include top management support, project implementations involving financial planning, information technology, human resources, and enterprise security considerations.

3.5 Fifth Industrial Revolution: Implications of the Technological Advancements on the Workforce

i. Changes in Job Roles

The workforce has new demands as a result of the change, the reorganization of jobs, and the increased dependence on diverse technological competence. For example, new skills—including digital skills—are required. Employees in the sector might observe changes to their roles, or even hazards, [17]. To minimize the mismatch between job requirements and personnel capabilities, it is necessary to make efforts to attract and develop new talent, improve the skills of current employees through training programs, and adjust work procedures. Working together, humans and robots represent a paradigm shift that will surely alter the way that most people operate today. Supervisors and workers alike must face a variety of obstacles and adjust to a constant state of change. To address these, it is essential to manage company culture and human resources effectively.

ii. Skills Requirements

The following areas of skills were identified by [18]:
To encourage and maintain open innovation, give high-value co-creation more influence, the practical application of cobots is quick, accurate, inexpensive, and adaptable. Advantages over competitors for small and medium-sized businesses, Goals for both people and the environment, resources with a great degree of skill, flexibility, well-being, and safety. It is designed to support workforce efficiency, sustainability, and resilience in the face of major global problems like the pandemic.

Expanding on the argument, [18] pointed out that:
With an emphasis on mass personalization, resilience, and sustainability, the Fifth Industrial Revolution is human-centered and embraces a wide array of disciplines and companies, encompassing information technology, healthcare, finance, insurance, and manufacturing—an area that is dominated by Industry 4.0. However, utilizing cooperation between people, robots, and technology is where the Fifth Industrial Revolution's progress truly resides. It involves the cooperation of increasingly precise and potent machinery—like Smart CNCs and cobots—with leading-edge technology such as the Internet of Things and the uniquely creative.

iii Work Processes
Industry 5.0 advocates for efficient manufacturing with low waste, which supports resilient and sustainable development. The emergence of the digital age has resulted in notable changes due to the development of technology and how it is used. Examples of these changes include the widespread use of social media, smartphones, and video conferencing equipment during the COVID-19 pandemic [18]. The notion of Industry 5.0 was initially developed as a scalable and transportable industrial idea that goes beyond national implementations. It is not restricted to any one demographic, geographic area, or business. Rather, it seeks to ensure that technology gains are not reserved for industry pioneers, but rather promote justice and equality for current and future generations.

3.6 The Fifth Industrial Revolution: Opportunities and Challenges

The identification of issues within the current context involves multiple dimensions, such as the differences in proficiency with regard to technological innovations, the introduction of novel job prospects, moral considerations regarding human-machine interactions, and so on.

Moreover [18], these challenges can be condensed into the following categories:

The preservation of resources is one major issue that has emerged in the era of digitization. Concurrently, the technology-focused strategy intensifies worries about global challenges, negatively affecting the surroundings, exhausting resources, and underestimating the importance of human interaction in the place of work. The notion of human capital is used by economists and social scientists to determine the useful individual characteristics—such as abilities, knowledge, and well-being—that support the process of production. It is well known that employing human capital can promote sustainability, resilience, and economic growth through an innovative approach. These goals can be accomplished by converting human resources into extremely productive human capital that includes values, health, and education.

3.7 Conclusion

The human-centered approach of Industry 5.0, the relationships that arise in human-machine interaction, and the effects these have on human resources—that is, the cooperation of "individuals working alongside robots and IoT devices in automated work environments"—are the main topics of this chapter. The chapter explores how these technological developments have affected the workforce, including changes to employment positions, skill requirements, and work processes. The chapter brought to bear the benefits and challenges that the evolving Industry 5.0 has brought to human lives, particularly human resources which is pivotal in any organization. It is a key determinant factor in the building of any nation and prime to organizational development, growth, and transformation. It leverages the acquisition of new skills and enhances productivity and experience. There is a need for organizations to evolve a scheme where human welfare in the organization is made prominent and topmost on their agenda. The transformative influence of the Fifth Industrial Revolution becomes only significant when human resources become prime beneficiaries as organizations modify their strategies to suit the purpose of humans. It reflects on the admixture of impacts of skills and capabilities of the workers and how they can adapt to the technologically driven Fifth Industrial Revolution, expectedly meeting the requirements of the evolving skills which are the demands of the changing labor market.

References

1. Lindvall, J., Technology and Politics: A Research Agenda available @ https://www.johanneslindvall.org › uploads › te.. on 12/08/2021, p. 5, 2017.

2. Berg, C.H., Industry 5.0: Industrial revolution with a Soul, 2022, https://www.clarify.io/learn/industry-5-0.
3. Prakash, N., Sharma, S., Monu, B., Mukherji, R.K., Industry 5.0: A Paradigm Shift Towards Human Centric Industrial Revolution. *Elem. Educ.*, 20, 1, 6912–6922, 6913, 6915, 2021.
4. Akundi, A., Euresti, D., Luna, S., Ankobiah, W., Lopes, A., Edinbarough, I., State of Industry 5.0—Analysis and Identification of Current Research Trends. *Appl. Syst. Innov.*, 5, 27, 2022, https://doi.org/10.3390/asi5010027.
5. Savoretti, R. and Marinho Kitamura, T., Industry 5.0 A first step to find new balance in the market through MADE© being a master theisis submitted to Polytecnico Milano in partial fulfilment for the Award of Master's Degree in Management Engineering, 2022.
6. Burton, S.L., Grasping the Cyber-World: Artificial Intelligence and Human Capital meet to inform Leadership. *Int. J. Econ. Commer. Manage.*, 7, 12, 707–759, 2019.
7. Burrell, D., An exploration of the critical need for formal training in leadership for cybersecurity and technology management professionals. *Int. J. Hyperconnectivity Internet Things*, 2, 1, 52–67, 2018a.
8. Heathfield, S.M., What is human resource management? Beyond hiring and firing: What is human resource management? The Balance Careers. Retrieved from https://www.thebalancecareers.com/what-is-humanresourcemanagement, 2019.
9. Kemendi, A., HR process safety & security in the industry 4.0. era. *Bánki Közl.*, 4, 1, 55–60, 2021.
10. Ergen, S., Cloud system in digital human resources management in Turkey. *Secur. Def. Q.*, War Studies University, Poland, 29, 100, 97–107, 2020.
11. Østergaard, E.H., Welcome to Industry 5.0, Available online: https://info.universalrobots.com/hubfs/Enablers/White%20papers/Welcome%20to%20Industry%205.0_Esben%20%C3%98stergaard.pdf?submissionGuid=00c4d11f-80f2-4683-a12a-e821221793e3.
12. Lahteenoja, V., Flanagan, A.J., Warren, S., On the Importance of Human centricity and Data World available https://www3.weforum.org/docs/WEF_On_the_Importance_of_Human_Centricity_2021.pdf, 2021.
13. Breque, M., De Nul, L., Petridis, A., Industry 5.0 – Towards a sustainable, human centric and resilient European industry, Policy brief, Directorate-General for Research and Innovation, Electronic document available at https://op.europa.eu/en/publication-detail/-/publication/468a892a-5097-11eb-b59f-01aa75ed71a1/, 2021.
14. Japan Business Federation, Toward Realization of the New Economy and Society – Reform of the Economy and Society by the Deepening of Society 5.0, Keidanren Policy Action, Outline, April 2016, Electronic document available at https://www.keidanren.or.jp/en/policy/2016/029_outline.pdf, 2016.

15. Muller, J., Enabling Technologies for Industry 5.0 – Results of a workshop with Europe's technology leaders, European Commission – Research and Innovation, September 2020, Electronic document available at https://europeanunion.europa.eu/index_it, 2020.
16. Kemendi, A., Michelberger, P., Mesjasz-Lech, A., Industry 4.0 and 5.0 – Organizational and Competency Challenges of Enterprises. *Pol. J. Manage. Stud.*, 26, 2, 209, 228, 232, 2022.
17. European Commission, Industry 5.0. Towards a sustainable, human-centric and resilient European industry, Policy Brief, 2021.
18. Aheleroff, S., Huang, H., Xu, X., Zhong, R.Y., Toward sustainability and resilience with Industry 4.0 and Industry 5.0. *Front. Manuf. Technol.*, 8, 19, 2022.

4

Human Capital Transformation - Revolutionizing HR Practices with Advanced Technologies and Ethical Insights

Vijeyata[1*], Chitra Jha[1] and Sunil Tegwal[2]

[1]*G.L. Bajaj Institute of Technology and Management, Greater Noida, Uttar Pradesh, India*
[2]*Management Department, IIMT, Group of Colleges, Greater Noida, Uttar Pradesh, India*

Abstract

The current revolution that is replacing Industry 4.0 is called Industry 5.0. Industry 5.0 is centered on mass customization and ultra-automation of these already-existing technologies, whereas Industry 4.0 was characterized by technological advancements in the areas of data analytics, cyber-physical systems, and extensive exposure to AI, ML, IoT, etc. The existing human resource management (HRM) of the firms must undergo this change at the same time as the world. The current study examines a few variables that influence HRM practices throughout this phase. The idea of Industry 5.0 is to promote ideals of ethics, environmental effect, and equity in order to address societal issues.

This chapter describes HRM areas that have an impact on changes occurring in organizations. The main objective, techniques, and features of Industry 5.0 are analyzed. The key advantages are emphasized, which make it possible to increase the competitiveness of modern enterprises. Through this chapter, the authors have also covered the impact of AI technologies on human resource (HR) practices of various industries.

***Keywords*:** Industry 5.0, digital transformation, artificial intelligence, IoT, ultra-automation

**Corresponding author*: vijeyata.singh@gmail.com

Deepa Gupta, Mukul Gupta, Pawan Budhwar, Jim Westerman, Rajesh Kumar Dhanaraj and Balamurugan Balusamy (eds.) Human Capital Analytics: Exploring the HR Spectrum in Industry 5.0, (81–100) © 2025 Scrivener Publishing LLC

4.1 Introduction

The statement underscores the fact that the phrase "Industry 5.0" was initially used in "Productiveness 5.0 - from effective to physical," a 2015 LinkedIn article, which underlined the concept of Industrialized Upcycling [1]. The article's main goal was to convey to readers why it is imperative that we move from Industry 4.0 to Industry 5.0 and why robots should be seen as "Working with Us" rather than "Working for Us." Industry 5.0 imbues the technologies, machinery, and robotics that will play a significant role in this revolution with the human touch [2]. The organization's human resources management will face new difficulties as a result of these technologies or machines collaborating with people. Construction on the ideas of Productiveness 4.0, Productiveness 5.0 is a newly developed concept in the world of industrial and manufacturing technology [3]. It represents the next phase in the evolution of industry and production processes. Productiveness 5.0 goes beyond Productiveness 4.0 by highlighting the significance of human collaboration and interaction within these cutting-edge technological ecosystems. The goal of Productiveness 4.0 was to build more automated, connected, and efficient industrial systems by integrating digital technologies, data interchange, and the Internet of Things (IoT) [3]. After reviewing a number of articles, this exploration aims to demystify the assumption of Industry 5.0 and will also discuss the journey from Productiveness 4.0 to Productiveness 5.0 [3].

4.2 Systematic Review

4.2.1 The Industrial Revolution

Human resources (HR) have consistently advanced as a result of globalization and enormous evidence of technology revolutions, empowering it to surpass many hurdles that previously limited it to being regarded as a strictly administrative role exclusive the inventiveness (Rao, Mellam, and Mellam, 2015). This expansion may lead to ongoing variations in the concentrating HR-related tasks. The initial stage, which examined how HR procedures affected workers, became more regimented. In phase two, the HR department evaluated whole HR systems as opposed to specific HR practices, broadening its purview. In the last stage, HR practices changed from HR to strategic human resource management (SHRM) because it was determined that only HR could effectively unite the establishment's objectives with member goals (Wright & Ulrich 2017). However, taking on a strategic role is difficult because information and expertise are the most important components of any plan. Due to the necessity to satisfy information needs and adjust to the ever-changing demands of the profit-maximizing, cost-cutting business climate of today, HR has been compelled to go above and beyond. HR has evolved into a vocation that is greatly impacted by technology and the data that are often collected from employees in order to improve their strategic function [22, 31].

Consequently, E-HRM has developed, where HR now serves as a platform as opposed to an individual. Technology has advanced from a basic machine preordained to diminish human labor to additional complex organizations proficient in much more. Productions are now able to communicate with employees additional effectively because of a variety of skills, like information technology (IT), web-based apps, and reasonable reproductions (Oswal and Narayan Appa, 2015).

One of the most potent technologies with a common ancestry is artificial intelligence (AI). Because of AI's endless possibilities, HR departments all everywhere the world have embraced it. To find innovative solutions for employee HR problems, several of the largest companies in the world, like Google, Amazon, and IBM, are fusing AI with HR (Aspan, 2020). In HR, recruiting and selection, analytics and metrics, training and development, remuneration, and employee working hours and attendance are the areas where AI interventions show the most promise, according to a survey conducted by HR.com (HR.com, 2017). However, there appears to be resistance to investing and changing [27].

AI is now more common in HR operations than it is in other corporate functions like marketing, finance, and so forth in businesses all over the world (Brin, 2019). AI in HR has not advanced and become as integrated in India as it has in other commercial domains. Many HR professionals are skeptical of AI because they believe it will not be able to deliver satisfactory outcomes in fields that require intuition and empathy (PWC, 2017). Numerous Indian HR departments continue to maintain that a personal connection is necessary for effectively communicating with employees, even though many HR decisions are not solely based on statistics. The opposition seems to be strengthened by the emphasis on issues such as the morality of making judgments only based on AI and other technologies (Desai, 2019). Because of this, the majority of Indian HR departments have chosen to ignore the reality that a significant portion of the employee dataset is not being used effectively in this data-driven age, where data are significant to answering seemingly endless possibilities [25].

The concept of "Industry 5.0" is not widely recognized as of my last knowledge update in September 2021. However, it is possible that new developments and terminologies have emerged since then [4]. The two industrial revolutions that are most commonly referenced are the First and Second Industrialized Insurgencies, which acquired residence in the late 19th and early 20th periods (late 19th to early 20th century) [29].

4.2.2 What are the Key Technologies Driving the Development of Industry 5.0?

The growth of Industry 5.0 is being determined by the convergence of advanced technologies, each of which plays a key role in determining the upcoming engineering and industrial operations. At the heart of Industry 5.0 is the incorporation of AI and the IoT, which together form the basis for smarter, autonomous systems that can communicate and transmit data in real time [1]. Emerging technologies such as big data, virtual reality, cloud computing, and collaborative robots (cobots) are shaping the efficiency, security, and transparency of industrial networks by making them human-centric and resilient. It further enriches the Industry 5.0 landscape by enabling sustainable industrial practices [2, 18].

The importance of machine learning, robotics, and collaborative robots cannot be overestimated. These technologies will determine the future of production and business models by facilitating collaboration between humans and machines, thereby optimizing production processes [3].

Beyond 5G communications, the advent of artificial intelligence of things (AIoT) and collaborative robotics is expected to meet higher demands for data collection, processing, and communication in advanced manufacturing, diverting, and moving from Industry 4.0 to Industry 5.0 on average. Let us take it one step further [5].

The integration of advanced technologies such as edge computing, digital twins, interactive robots, blockchain, and 6G is poised to revolutionize various sectors by enhancing connectivity, efficiency, and Intelligence [6]. Industry 5.0 will integrate human knowledge with efficient, intelligent, and truthful devices to expand production capacity and create customized. We place great emphasis on providing products that are of the highest quality [7]. The IoT, including the Industrial IoT, plays a key role in regulating production development and expanding modern business models, supporting the core interests of Industry 5.0 [12]. Advances in electronic and optoelectronic technologies, such as nanocomposite sensors and mechatronic systems integrated with AI algorithms, are also contributing significantly to the advancement of Industry 5.0 applications, providing new research topics and business process modeling for manufacturing industries [8, 9]. Finally, human-machine collaboration, exemplified by the use of cobots in engineering processes, emphasizes the human-machine collaborative environment that is central to the Industry 5.0 concept, fostering innovation and optimizing solutions [10].

4.2.3 Different Industrial Revolutions' Effects on Human Resource Functions

Human resource management has advanced significantly over the past few centuries to meet the effects of dynamic market conditions, much like any other functional field. Along with capital and management strategy, one of the most significant factors affecting productivity is human resources. Human resource functions have also been impacted by developments in technology and management philosophy. The effective and efficient operation of human resource management has benefited from changes. However, the HR department has also faced a number of difficulties as a result. The purpose of this part is to provide some clarification on the four industrial revolutions and how they affect the function of human resource management [28].

The Fourth Industrial Revolution encompasses the latest wave of technological advancements that are reshaping our lives and workplaces. Many sectors and professions are undergoing significant alterations due to the summary of innovative technology such as automation, robotics, and synthetic astuteness. One area where these developments have had a big impact is human resources management.

We may better appreciate the Industrial Revolution's effects on life, work, and human resources if we are aware of their historical background. It is astounding not only how much has changed recently but also how quickly it has happened. From the 18th century to the contemporary, there have been several Industrial Revolutions that have significantly altered technology, the economy, and industry.

In Britain in the late 1700s, the Initial Industrial Revolution began with the shift from a manual to a machine labor industry. The textile industry was revolutionized by inventions like the steam engine and power loom, which resulted in a migration of people to cities for factory labor and subsequent urbanization and population expansion.

The Technological Revolution, which occurred during the late 19th and early 20th centuries, marked another industrial revolution. Steam power was superseded by electrical power, and communication was transformed by devices like the telephone and telegraph [30]. Mass production started with the assembly line and vehicle revolutionized manufacturing techniques [43].

The Digital Insurgency, the Third Industrial Insurgency, took place in the late 20th and timely 21st centuries. Our lives and work have been completely transformed by computers and the internet, which have made communication instantaneous and digitized operations possible. Additionally, globalization accelerated, promoting cross-border trade in products, services, and ideas [43].

Currently, the Fourth Industrialized Insurgency is defined by combining advanced technology like the Internet of Things, apparatus erudition, and AI. This revolution has the power to transform industries including energy, healthcare, and transportation, bringing sustainability and efficiency. But there are drawbacks as well, such as employment displacement.

HRM Practices with Advanced Technology

Informed decision-making also enables human resources to help achieve organizational goals [36]. You can also manage your employees through hiring, training, and assigning tasks based on job satisfaction, productivity, and qualifications. Additionally, it helps you identify the causes of turnover and pinpoint valuable talent who are retiring.

Several HR Practices Adapted by Industries:

Employee Experience and Engagement:

HR focuses on enhancing the digital employee experience by offering self-service tools, mobile apps, and online training platforms.

Surveys and feedback mechanisms are employed to measure and improve employee engagement.

Learning and Development:

HR facilitates online learning and development programs, including e-learning courses, webinars, and virtual classrooms. Continuous learning and upskilling are emphasized to keep employees competitive in a digital environment [9].

Remote Work and Flexibility:

HR policies and practices adapt to support remote work arrangements, which became more prevalent during the digital age. Virtual onboarding, collaboration tools, and performance management systems are implemented to manage remote teams effectively.

HR Automation and AI:
AI and automation are being used more and more by HR departments to manage regular administrative duties like resume screening, benefits administration, and payroll disbursement. HR procedures are streamlined and employee inquiries are promptly answered by chatbots and virtual assistants [17].

Cybersecurity and Data Privacy:
HR plays a role in ensuring employee data privacy and compliance with data protection regulations like GDPR. HR collaborates with IT to implement robust cybersecurity measures to protect sensitive HR data. Table 4.1 shows the approaches towards the comparison between Industry 4.0 and Industry 5.0 [17].

Table 4.1 A comparison between Industry 4.0 and Industry 5.0.

Industry 4.0	Industry 5.0
The objective is to ensure industrial development.	The objective is to strike a balance b/w machine and human engagement.
The significant element was technology.	This is one of the crucial collaborations between humans and machines.
The environment is computer-generated throughout.	The modification back to the real world.
Employment levels decreased when new, intelligent technologies were implemented.	An addition in the number of people who come into contact with machines.
Machines with intellect are more unified in the workplace.	Intelligent supercomputers and human minds are being combined.
Customization or personalization of the product was not possible.	Personalization and customization are available, allowing each product to be improved and tailored to the needs of the person.
B/w renewable and non-renewable energy sources, there is still constant back and forth.	It is more environmentally friendly since renewable energy sources will be used more often.

(Source: (IJACSA), 2021) [23].

Workforce Planning:
HR utilizes workforce planning tools to forecast future staffing needs and skills requirements. This helps organizations adapt to changing market conditions and technological advancements.

Agile HR Practices:
HR embraces agile methodologies to adapt quickly to changing business environments and customer demands. This includes iterative performance management, flexible organizational structures, and rapid response to market shifts [10].

Ethical AI and Automation:
HR ensures the responsible use of AI and automation technologies, addressing concerns related to bias, fairness, and ethics. It plays a role in developing guidelines for ethical AI deployment within the organization [40].

Industry 4.0 speaks to a critical move within the fabricating industry, driven by the integration of progressed innovations such as mechanization, fake insights, and the Web of Things (IoT). Industry 5.0 builds on these advances but centers on joining human creativity and instinct to make a more collaborative and flexible fabricating environment [38].

Whereas Industry 4.0 presented the notion of the circular economy, Industry 5.0 places indeed more prominent accentuation on feasible fabricating hones, with a center on minimizing squandering and advancing capable asset utilization (668 R. Wolniak) [16].

Industry 5.0 recognizes that the manufacturing industry has a significant impact on workers and communities and looks to make a more positive and steady working environment through advances like advanced colleagues and progressed security frameworks [37].

4.2.4 Industry 5.0 Technologies

If Industry 5.0 has become a recognized notion since then, it would likely expand upon the industrial underpinnings of 4.0 and continue to advance the integration of digital technologies in various industrial sectors. Any future industrial revolution should, in general, see a substantial impact from technology associated with automation, automation, big data analytics, AI, and the IoT [11]. To acquire the current information on Industry 5.0 and the specific technologies associated with it, I recommend checking recent industry reports, academic literature, and news sources since this is a field that is always changing and new things might have happened after I updated.

Shows a technological journey from Industry 1.0 to Industry 5.0 (Figure 4.1). Figure 4.2 shows the overview of key technologies (IoT, AI, Big Data, Robotics) and how these technologies are transforming industries.

A Technological Journey from Industry 1.0 to Industry 5.0

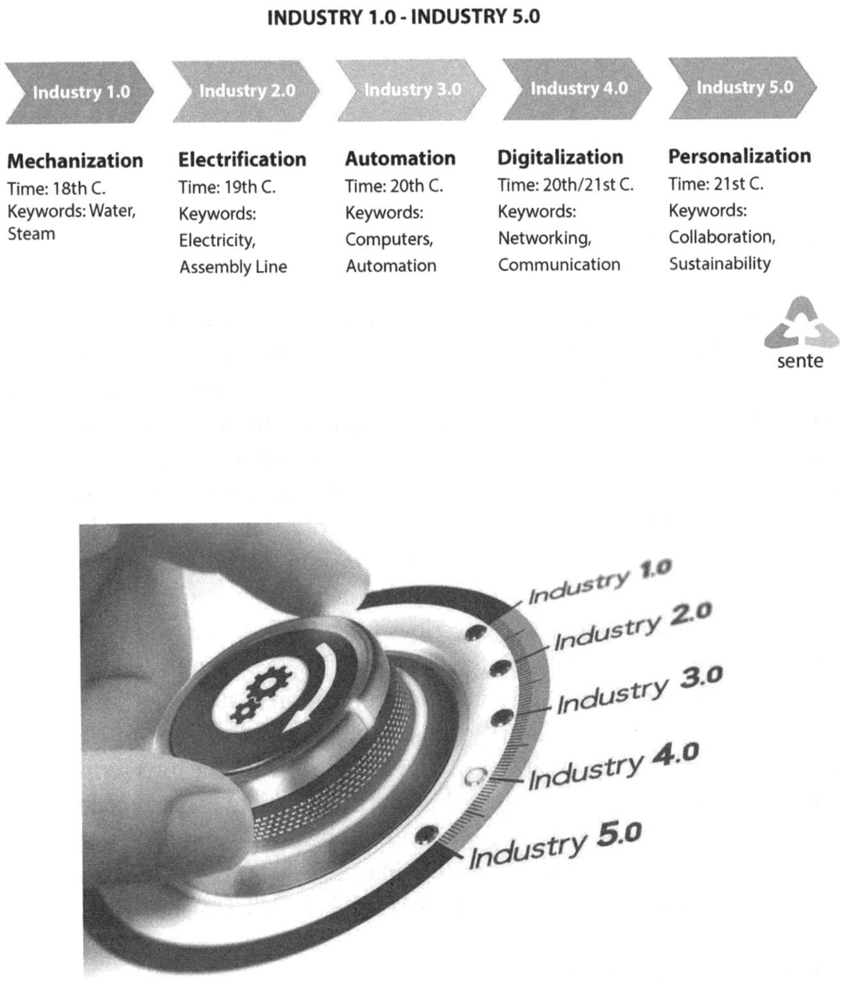

Figure 4.1 A journey from Industry 1.0 to Industry 5.0. (Source: Sente ventures).

Overview of Key Technologies (IoT, AI, Big Data, Robotics)
How These Technologies Are Transforming Industries:

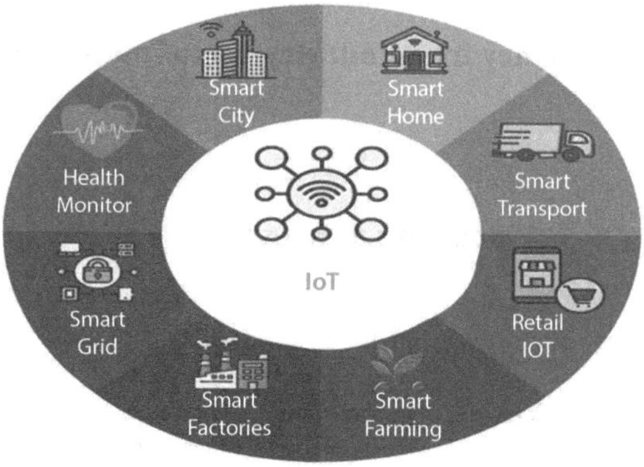

Figure 4.2 Key Technologies. (Source: Research gate)

The phrase "Internet of Things" (IoT) was first used in 1999, coined in response to the expansion of Internet-based technology in the 1990s. Madsen *et al.* [12] have focused on that major infrastructure and services are required to meet the essentials of the inhabitants living in megacities, as a result of the notable increase in population density in metropolitan areas. The world's population is expected to increase by more than 10 times over the next 30 years, reaching seventy million by 2050, with the majority of mature people living in urban areas. As a result, nations are considering how to get ready for the influx of wealth and the resulting pressure on their megacity structures [14, 15]. The term "Internet of Things" (IoT) describes how physical bias and objects are connected to each other through the Internet, allowing them to exchange and gather data. Detectors, selectors, and communication technologies are crucial factors in IoT systems. IoT allows for real-time observation, robotization, and remote management of bias and procedures. IoT refers to the interconnectedness of physical bias and objects via the Internet, enabling them to collect and change data. Detectors, selectors, and communication technologies are crucial factors in IoT systems. Robotization, inaccessible governor, and real-time checking of bias and processes are made possible by IoT [13, 41].

Artificial Intelligence (AI):
AI is the expansion of computer structures that can do tasks like learning, solving problems, and making decisions that often need human astuteness. AI comprehends countless subfields, with computer apparition, engine erudition, and natural philological dispensation. AI systems are capable of automating difficult activities, making predictions, and analyzing huge datasets.

4.2.5 A Summary of Journal Search Results

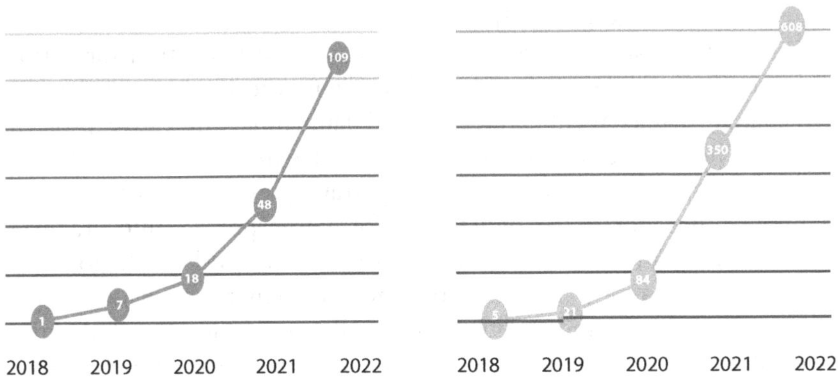

Figure 4.3 Number of citations (right) and journal articles (left) that Scopus has indexed for Industry 5.0 (2018–July 2022) [33].

4.3 Its Impact on HR

4.3.1 How these Technologies are Transforming Industries

Manufacturing:
IoT sensors monitor equipment conditions and supply chains, optimizing production processes. AI-driven predictive maintenance reduces downtime and increases efficiency. Robotics automates repetitive tasks, enhancing production speed and precision.

Using a digital transformation strategy, a company can gain a new competitive edge in utilizing and adapting to the newest digital technology. Without a doubt, new technologies like cloud computing, the IoT, Industry 5.0, Industry 4.0, and many more can transform how businesses operate. Business procedures are necessary to keep up with the swift advancement of technology, particularly in developing nations where there is a dearth of research in this area. When traditional and digital businesses are compared, the latter can expand their operations more quickly since they are more adaptable to customer demands and have embraced cutting-edge technologies at a faster rate. However, there are numerous obstacles and limitations to this transformation process that only affect huge organizations and smaller- and medium-sized businesses (SMEs). Depending on the industry, these difficulties could vary [28]. Furthermore, the severity of the same issues may vary across other industries. This part focuses on the difficulties that the manufacturing sector is encountering as it undergoes a digital transformation [43, 44].

The industrial sector presents several obstacles to digital transformation, including the lack of digital skills, embracing new technology, implementing change management strategies, and launching innovative projects. Different viewpoints and intensities characterize these difficulties [29].

It might address everything, including strategy and human issues as well as how to incorporate the digital transformation process into organizational culture. Furthermore, for this sector to efficaciously undergo digital transformation, a lot of support from the macroenvironment is required. At the national level, more initiatives in policy and innovation hubs must be created, and every action needs to be coordinated to support SMEs in the manufacturing sector as they embark on their journey of digital transformation. To successfully implement a digital transformation, manufacturers should share their success stories with training and mentorship programs [30].

Healthcare:

IoT devices monitor patient vitals and send information to medical professionals so they can monitor patients remotely. AI helps with drug development, medical diagnosis, and customized treatment regimens. Robotics assists in surgery, patient care, and drug dispensing.

AI helps with drug development, medical diagnosis, and customized treatment regimens. Robotics assists in surgery, patient care, and drug dispensing.

Data Science and IoMT:

The healthcare industry is undergoing a change thanks to data science and the Internet of Medical Things (IoMT). According to Reports Plus Data, the market for healthcare predictive analytics is expected to increase to $28.77 billion by 2027 from $3.74 billion in 2019. It can be challenging to manage and analyze the massive amounts of data generated by individuals through chronic diseases. However, advances in data science and predictive analytics provide doctors with a greater understanding of their patients' conditions, including risk assessment, family history, and more accurate diagnosis [29].

The IoMT market is anticipated to develop even faster, with a projected valuation of $1319 billion by 2026. For example, ever since the COVID-19 epidemic began, smart robot nurses have been monitoring patients' blood pressure and SpO2 values in Italian hospitals.

It is obvious that IoMT will continue to play an increasingly significant role in the healthcare business assuming its ability to enhance healthcare outcomes, boost efficiency, and lower costs.

Healthcare and AI:
Among numerous industries, the healthcare sector is one of the most notable for being at the forefront of implementing AI technology. It should come as no surprise that AI will continue to influence healthcare in 2023 and provide several advantages for medical practitioners [19].

For example, AI-assisted CT imaging was utilized in the USA in 2021 to treat COVID-19 patients and identify pneumonia. This study is only one illustration of how AI is used to improve the accuracy and timeliness of diagnosing patients with viruses.

The advent of generative AI in the AI era will hasten the use of AI, particularly in the healthcare sector. Recently, a search engine revealed AI tools to expedite the preauthorization process. These tools enable health plan administrators and providers to better utilize patient, diagnosis, procedure, and coverage data to promptly determine whether additional information is required and expedite the approval of prior authorization requests.

Transportation and AI:
IoT enables real-time tracking of vehicles and traffic conditions for efficient routing.

AI powers autonomous vehicles for safer and more efficient transportation. Robotics is used in warehouses for automated logistics [19].

Numerous new technologies, or technology clusters, are driving the advancement of smart mobility in a number of ways. The ones that will be most important up to 2030 include digital platforms, blockchain, smooth beams, AI, Internet of Possessions, and large information [31]. Applications built on these technologies are essential to comprehending how developing technologies are affecting the transportation industry. In the years leading up to 2030, the most promising (clusters of) terms "smart mobility" refer to the following: mobility as a service (MaaS), self-organizing logistics (SoL), supportive bright passage systems (S-BPS), and associated accommodating automated mobility (AAAM).

Every smart mobility application makes use of various new technologies, and every emerging technology supports several applications. Thus, an integrated strategy is beneficial for expanding and grabbing hold of smart mobility potential [34].

The examined developing technologies range widely in maturity. A few are already in extensive use. Others, who are frequently hailed as extremely promising, nevertheless need to demonstrate their worth in real-world situations. Though apps are just now beginning to combine 5G, AI, and blockchain, they have the potential to be revolutionary; they are learning what is already feasible and what still has to be developed [13, 24].

Smart mobility applications are associated with mobility transformation. A digital infrastructure that is also usable by C-ITS and CCAM is required for MaaS and SoL. For example, MaaS and SOL can accelerate the creation of providing the electronic framework for independent cars while C-ITS services can be utilized initially to lay the technological foundation.

Retail:
IoT enables inventory management and personalized shopping experiences. AI powers recommendation engines and chatbots for customer support. Robotics automates warehousing and delivery processes [14].

4.3.2 Changing Workforce Dynamics

The use of technology and software to modernize and improve different HR duties and functions is referred to as automation in HR (human resources) procedures [20].

HR professionals may focus on more strategic and value-added tasks with this strategy, which can also greatly increase efficiency and decrease mistakes. The following are some crucial areas in which HR automation is frequently used [21]:

Recruitment and Applicant Tracking:
Resume Screening: Automation can be used to scan the resumes and employment requests for keywords, qualifications, and experience, saving time and effort in the initial screening process.
Job Posting and Distribution: Tools can automate the posting of job beginnings to multiple job panels and social media platforms [35].

4.3.3 Talent Acquisition and Recruitment Activities

Industry 5.0: Transforming Talent Acquisition
The advent of Industry 5.0 brings forth exciting possibilities for various sectors, including the IT and IT-enabled services (ITES) industry. Let us

explore how Industry 5.0 is transforming talent acquisition in the IT and ITES sectors, highlighting the collaboration between humans and technology [32].

The organizations preferred to use media like radio (Saks, 1994), web announcements (Llorens and Kellough, 2007), newspapers (NP) (Breagh, 1981; Jones *et al.*, 2006), television advertisements (TA) (Taylor and Schmidt, 1983), and contract out (Ordaining and Silvestri, 2008; Shih and Chiang, 2011) in order to draw in the pool of potential candidates. (Shih and Chiang, 2011; Ordering and Silvestri, 2008).

Organizations also use the knowledge, attitude, skills, and habit (K.A.S.H.) model to acquire the right candidate for the right job. In recent years, the business has made substantial changes to its staff recruitment process. Organizations' recruitment departments use electronic channels all over the world, which are solely supported by ongoing technological advancement (Bondar Ouk *et al.*, 2017; Petrakov *et al.*, 2018; Van Esch *et al.*, 2019). Keeping abreast of evolving global conditions and addressing the ongoing pandemic, corporations have come to understand the importance of using social networking sites (SNWs) to find exceptional talent and foster innovation in order to attain sustainability.

Recruitment patterns have taken on a new dimension thanks to SNWs (Villeda *et al.*, 2019; Nikolaou, 2021; Rehman *et al.*, 2021). Social media sites are becoming more than simply a way to stay in contact with friends and family; according to Chang *et al.* (2022), social media recruiting technology (SMART) has made social networking sites a routine tool for hiring and selecting new employees.

HR teams must grasp a human-centric approach to talent acquisition, balance automation with personalization, and prioritize ethical considerations [30]. By adopting agile recruitment strategies, investing in upskilling initiatives, and fostering collaboration, HR professionals can lead the way in building a highly skilled, adaptable, and socially responsible workforce that thrives in the future of work [42].

4.3.4 Challenges in Industry 5.0 Revolution

The workforce is becoming more divided into two groups as a result of this trend: extremely competent and knowledgeable personnel, and low-skilled and untrained workers. Middle-skill employment is also declining. As a result, there may be a smaller divide in society between those with and those without competence [32].

Intelligent manufacturing systems require higher autonomy and sociability capabilities as key elements of self-organizing systems. The transition from the current situation to Industry 5.0 is difficult because current systems lack autonomy, such as integrated decision-making [39].

Highly automated manufacturing systems make skill development a difficult task. Train employees to adopt advanced, cutting-edge technology and bring about behavioral changes when interacting with employees.

- Collaborative robotics is an automation method that continues to pose significant risks in the workplace alongside human colleagues (Rossi, 2018).
- Maintaining high quality and integrity of data from manufacturing systems is difficult and accommodating different data storages (Thoben, 2017).
- Industry 5.0 business strategies require higher levels of dynamism to remain competitive due to different customer preferences.
- Because of the highly automated production processes, developing skills is a massive undertaking that involves changing employee behavior to engage with new and cutting-edge technology and educating the workforce to accept them.
- In addition to endangering human teammates, collaborative robotics is an automation technology that puts factory floor workers at serious risk.
- In smart industrial systems, more independence and sociality are necessary conditions for self-organized systems. The move from the present setting to Industry 5.0 is difficult because of the absence of independence in present systems, such as combined decision-making.
- Acquiring high-quality, reliable data from industrial systems is difficult, and accommodating different data sources is difficult.
- Critical industrial systems and production lines are weaker to cybersecurity breaches as a result of Industry 5.0's augmented connectedness and use of standard infrastructure rules.
- Industry 5.0 is exciting for businesses, particularly SMEs, to embrace as it requires a significant financial commitment to completely integrate all of its components [32].
- For occurrence, Industry 5.0 presents a lot of probables for the healthcare industry, but it also calls for a high degree of

precision and accuracy. Since this field of study is still in its infancy, substantial infrastructure and financial contributions are needed [31].

- Because of the increasing levels of mechanization in the various businesses, the current business models and strategies need to be reformed and customized to meet the expectations of Productiveness 5.0. Because of mass personalization, businesses will be focusing more on operations that are centered on the client. Over time, customer subjectivity might shift, making it difficult to consistently adjust business strategies and models.
- Due to varying client preferences, 5.0 needs a higher level of dynamism to maintain competition.

Massive personalization will force business strategies to focus extra on operations that prioritize customers. Changes in customer subjectivity over time make it challenging to regularly adjust business strategies and models.

4.3.5 Limitations of Industry 5.0

It is imperative to accept and trust technology. Simultaneously with the adaptation of technology for human use is the training of those who employ the new technologies [29]. Today's challenges include those related to security, privacy, labor shortages, long processes, and excessive expenses. Adoption of Industry 5.0 necessitates adherence to industrial laws and regulations that facilitate cobot and smooth machine cooperation. Human-machine communication and cognitive figuring are the future instructions for Industry 5.0.

4.4 Conclusion

The studies indicate that the author began by defining Industry 5.0 from the towering spires of the theoretical and industrial peoples. After talking about enabling technologies, even the apps that aid in comprehending Productiveness 5.0's features have been enclosed. The goal of Productiveness 5.0's awareness is to properly balance anthropoid and contraption efficiency. This report also presents encounters that aid in the supervision of the difficulties brought about by Industry 5.0. This article deliberates future guidelines that need to be managed better in order to use this industry in the near future [26].

In summary, new technology and socioeconomic shifts brought about by the Industrial Revolutions have had a significant influence on history [27]. Every revolution has brought with it its own set of difficulties, but it has also greatly advanced society. In order to remain competitive in this quickly changing environment, HR managers must be flexible, inspiring, retain, train, and create policies.

References

1. Demira, K.A., Dövena, G., Sezen, B., Industry 5.0 and Human-Robot Co-working. *Procedia Comput. Sci.*, (Elsevier), 158, 688–695, 2019.
2. https://www.researchgate.net/publication/369432975_Journey_of_HR_From_Industry_10_to_50_and_the_Road_Ahead
3. https://journalofcloudcomputing.springeropen.com/articles/10.1186/s13677-022-00314-5
4. https://pdf.sciencedirectassets.com/280203/1
5. Cherny chko, T., and Kozyk, I. The evolution of human capital management and HR technologies in the digital economy, 2024, https://doi.org/10.36887/2415-8453-2024-1-4
6. NITI Aayog, India's Booming Gig and Platform Economy: Perspectives and Recommendations on the Future of Work, June, 2022.
7. https://www.sciencedirect.com/science/article/pii/S0160791X22002275
8. https://www.emerald.com/insight/content/doi/10.1108/JOCM-11-2021-0354/full/html
9. https://www.mdpi.com/2571-5577/5/1/27
10. Nahavandi, S., Industry 5.0—A human-centric solution. *Sustainability*, *11*, 4371, 2019.
11. Vinitha, K., Prabhu, R.A., Bhaskar, R., Hariharan, R., Review on industrial mathematics and materials at Industry 1.0 to Industry 4.0. *Mater. Today Proc.*, *33*, 3956–3960, 2020.
12. Madsen, E.S., Bilberg, A., Hansen, D.G., Industry 4.0 and digitalization call for vocational skills, applied industrial engineering, and less for pure academics, in: *Proceedings of the 5th P&OM World Conference, Production and Operations Management, P&OM*, Havana, Cuba, 6–10 September 2016.
13. Rada, M., Industry 5.0-from Virtual to Physical, LinkedIn, 7 March 2018, Available online: https://www.linkedin.com/pulse/industry-50-from-virtual-physical-michael-rada (accessed on 3 February 2022).
14. Skobelev, P.O. and Borovik, S.Y., On the way from Industry 4.0 to Industry 5.0: From digital manufacturing to digital society. *Industry 4.0*, *2*, 307–311, 2017.

15. Müller, J., Enabling Technologies for Industry 5.0: Results of a Workshop with Europe's Technology Leaders, European Commission, Brussels, Belgium, 2020.
16. Østergaard, E.H., Welcome to Industry 5.0, Available online: https://info.universal-robots.com/hubfs/Enablers/White%20papers/Welcome%20to%20Industry%205.0_Esben%20%C3%98stergaard.pdf?submissionGuid=00c4d11f-80f2-4683-a12a-e821221793e3 (accessed on 3 February 2022).
17. Saurabh, S., Ambad, P., Bhosle, S., Industry 4.0–A glimpse. *Procedia Manuf.*, *20*, 233–238, 2018.
18. Madsen Øivind, D. and Berg, T., An Exploratory Bibliometric Analysis of the Birth and Emergence of Industry 5. *Appl. Syst. Innov.*, *4*, 87, 2021.
19. Welbers, K., Van Atte veldt, W., Benoit, K., Text Analysis in R. *Commun. Methods Meas.*, *11*, 245–265, 2017.
20. https://www.sciencedirect.com/science/article/pii/S2405896319315988?via%3Dihub
21. Hearst, M., What is text mining. *SpringerPlus*, *5*, 1608, 2016.
22. https://www.shrm.org/hr-today/trends-and-forecasting/special-reports-and-expert-views/documents/hr-technology.pdf
23. Du, A., *et al.*, CRACAU: Byzantine Machine Learning meets Industrial Edge Computing in Industry 5.0. *IEEE Trans. Ind. Inf.*, 18, 8, 5435–5445, 2021.
24. Xu, L., *et al.*, AF Relaying Secrecy Performance Prediction for 6G Mobile Communication Networks in Industry 5.0. *IEEE Trans. Ind. Inf.*, 18, 8, 5485–5493, August 22, 2021.
25. https://doi.org/10.1063/5.0034521
26. Longo, F., Padovano, A., Umbrella, S., Value-oriented and ethical technology engineering in industry 5.0: a human-centric perspective for the design of the factory of the future. *Appl. Sci.*, 10, 12, 4182, 2020.
27. https://www.potentiahr.com/the-fourth-industrial-revolution-impact-on-human-resources
28. Digital_Transformation_Challenges_in_the_Manufactu.pdf
29. https://www.ncbi.nlm.nih.gov/pmc/articles/PMC9963556
30. https://timesofindia.indiatimes.com/blogs/voices/how-emerging-tech-is-transforming-healthcare/
31. ttps://www.europarl.europa.eu/RegData/etudes/STUD/2020/652226/IPOL_STU(2020)652226_EN.pdf
32. https://www.linkedin.com/pulse/industry-50-transforming-talent-acquisition-ites-sector
33. https://indiachapter.in/index.php?/user/article
34. https://typeset.io/papers/analytical-study-of-hrm-practices-in-industry-5-0-3oblda7d
35. https://typeset.io/search?q=Digital%20Talent%20Acquisition:
36. https://typeset.io/papers/a-comprehensive-review-of-the-effects-of-digital-technology-1pe1b0pf

37. https://indiachapter.in/index.php?/user/article/2/2/121
38. https://link.springer.com/article/10.1007/s10796-024-10476
39. NHRD Network Journal, Journal• ISSN: 2631-4541.
40. Gupta, D., Gupta, M., Gupta, P.M., *HR analytics: The future of HR*, p. 404, [ISBN 9788119364909].
41. Kumar, V., Gupta, M., Gaur, S., Intrusion detection for the Internet of Things, in: *Internet of Things and cyber physical systems security and forensics*, 1st ed., K. Kaushik, S. Dahiya, A. Bhardwaj, Y. Maleh (Eds.), p. 183, CRC Press, 2023.
42. Agarwal, S., Gupta, D., Gupta, M., Impact of training method on trainees learning and implementation on job – A study with special reference to power sector. *AIP Conf. Proc.*, 2427, 1, 020020, 27 February 2023, https://doi.org/10.1063/5.0100893.
43. Gupta, D., Gupta, M., Rani, S., A Study on Training of Workmen in a Manufacturing Organization—With Reference to Aluminium Foundry, in: *Recent Trends in Industrial and Production Engineering*, Lecture Notes in Mechanical Engineering, A. Dvivedi, A. Sachdeva, R. Sindhwani, R. Sahu (Eds.), Springer, Singapore, 2022, https://doi.org/10.1007/978-981-16-3330-0_19.
44. Agarwal, S., Gupta, D., Gupta, M., Techno Pedagogical Concept with Digital Skills, in: *Edutech Enabled Teaching*, pp. 129–152, Chapman and Hall/CRC, 2023.

5

HR 5.0 Strategic Planning and Evolution of HR Functions in the Business Environment

M. Bharathi[1*], K. Praveena[1], M. Dharani[1], V. Madhurima[2], Krithikaa Mohanarangam[3], G. Sandhya Kumari[4] and Saleha Tabassum[5]

[1]Department of ECE, Mohan Babu University, Tirupati, Andhra Pradesh, India
[2]Department of ECE, Sree Venkateswara College of Engineering, A.P., India
[3]Symbiosis Institute of Technology, Pune Campus, Maharastra, India
[4]ECE Dept., Siddhartha Institute of Science and Technology, Puttur, Andhra Pradesh, India
[5]EEE Dept., KSRMCE, Kadapa, Andhra Pradesh, India

Abstract

The role of human resources (HR) in Industry 5.0, the most recent stage of industrial development marked by cutting-edge technologies, is examined in this book chapter. The chapter gives a general overview of HR 5.0 and goes over the top HR functions in this context. It explores the HR functions' cycle of evolution in Industry 5.0, highlighting the significance of HRM and its components. The chapter also examines how the business environment and strategic planning are related, identifying elements affecting the business environment. The three steps of strategic planning in HR 5.0 are also described. The chapter provides a thorough knowledge of the evolving HR spectrum in this technology era, providing helpful insights for HR professionals navigating the potential and challenges of Industry 5.0.

Keywords: HR 5.0, Industry 5.0, human resources, HR functions, HRM, business environment, strategic planning

**Corresponding author*: bharathi.m@vidyanikethan.edu

Deepa Gupta, Mukul Gupta, Pawan Budhwar, Jim Westerman, Rajesh Kumar Dhanaraj and Balamurugan Balusamy (eds.) Human Capital Analytics: Exploring the HR Spectrum in Industry 5.0, (101–110) © 2025 Scrivener Publishing LLC

5.1 Introduction

The introduction "HR 5.0: Unveiling the HR Spectrum in Industry 5.0" provides a thorough overview of the subject and sets the stage for the investigation of human resources (HR) [1] in the context of Industry 5.0. In the most recent stage of industrial development, known as "Industry 5.0," efficiency and connection are improved through the use of cutting-edge technology like automation, artificial intelligence (AI), and the Internet of Things (IoT). The opening acknowledges the critical function of human resources in organizations and how it has changed throughout time. It emphasizes that in order to remain productive [2], HR departments must change with the times and adapt to the disruptive effects of technology. In this sense, the concept of "Industry 5.0" refers to a paradigm shift in company operations that places a greater emphasis on interconnection, automation, and digitalization. This introduction reveals the particular opportunities and difficulties faced by HR professionals in Industry 5.0. To travel and carry out in a smooth HR world, one should use technological innovations so that it recognizes that in order to be successfully traversed in evolving as an HR practitioner.

Upskilling and reskilling endeavors are required to improve capabilities in order to meet the demands of the digital age. It encompasses improving organizational efficiency. The significance of human resource management (HRM) in Industry 5.0 is highlighted in the introduction. It signifies that HRM is essential for making sure human resources are utilized effectively, developing a culture of innovation and versatility, and integrating HR strategies with organizational goals. This introduction briefly addresses the major features of HRM in Industry 5.0, such as adaptable workforce management and maintaining talent in modern times, to give users a sense of what is to come. It also integrates the business environment with HR 5.0's strategic planning. HR professionals have systematically gathered to manage the difficulties and comprehend the good opportunities in view of the challenges in the business landscape, as acknowledged in the introduction. It outlines a number of variables that affect the business environment, including shifts in markets, regulatory changes, and advancements in technology. The final section outlines the structure of future chapters, which will contain topics such as HR roles in Industry 5.0, the HR practice evolution, the significance and traits of HRM, the relationship between strategic planning and business environment, and specific measures involved in HR 5.0 strategic planning. In a nutshell, this book chapter's introduction offers an extensive overview of HR in Industry 5.0. It also highlights the importance of HRM, the need for HR practitioners to keep up with advancements in technology, and the relationship between strategic planning and the business environment. Users are ready for a comprehensive study of HR within the context of Industry 5.0 due to the introduction that provides the foundation for the subsequent sections.

5.2 Evolution Cycle of HR Functions

The cycle of evolution of human resources operations includes constant adaptation and adjustment of HR procedures in response to organizational demands, alterations to the business environment, and innovations in technology. HR operations initially focused on administrative tasks, including legal compliance, record-keeping, and payroll management. HR played an advisory function with minimal strategic effect during this regular phase. But as technology developed, especially in the area of automation, HR departments began to utilize tools like HR information systems (HRIS) to make administrative duties go more effortlessly. Automation resulted in an additional phase of efficiency in operations by making it simpler to manage time management, employee information, and other essential HR duties. HR then experienced additional growth as companies realized how essential their people resources were at the time. As a result of the shift to strategic HR, human resources managers now play a bigger part in connecting HR plans with overall business goals. HR shifted from being a function that supported operations to becoming a key driver of organizational success through strategies for managing talent and the advancement of an innovation and growth-oriented society.

5.2.1 Analytics for HR and HR Driven by Data

Big data and advanced analytics have made it possible for HR operations to use data to obtain insights and make wise decisions. HR practitioners can now spot trends, anticipate workforce needs, and assess the effectiveness of HR programs thanks to the growing importance of HR analytics.

5.2.2 Digital HR and Employee Experience

HR operations have embraced digital transformation in the age of Industry 4.0 and beyond. Through the use of technologically advanced HR solutions, the emphasis has turned to improving the employee experience.

Employee engagement, communication, and access to HR services have all been improved through self-service portals, mobile apps, and chatbots that are powered by AI.

5.2.3 Future of Work and Agile HR

HR functions are adjusting to support agile working practices as organizations experience fast change and disruption. This entails putting in place flexible work schedules, encouraging remote work options [3, 4], and encouraging an environment that is open to change and lifelong learning. Managing a diverse workforce, encouraging inclusivity, and ensuring employee well-being are some areas where HR is becoming more and more involved. Industry 5.0's advent, which is characterized by cutting-edge technologies like automation, AI, and the IoT, is altering HR services once more. The use of AI in predictive analytics, employee engagement, and personalized learning [5] is being investigated by HR experts. Chatbots and virtual assistants that are AI-powered are being utilized to improve HR services and provide individualized employee experiences. The HR function evolution cycle shows how HR [6] is continuously changing from a purely administrative position to a strategic and technology-driven department. To address the shifting needs of organizations and make use of the promise of cutting-edge technology in Industry 5.0, HR professionals continue to develop and adapt.

5.3 Factors Influencing the Business Environment and its Connection to Strategic Planning

In order to navigate and successfully address external elements that may have an impact on an organization's success, there must be a relationship between the business environment and strategic planning. Setting long-term objectives and deciding on the steps necessary to accomplish them are both aspects of strategic planning. The term "business environment" implies an extensive variety of external factors that may have an influence on the profitability, competitiveness, and operational efficacy of an organization. These factors may include the following:

5.3.1 Economic Factors

The nation of the economy as a whole, including factors like GDP growth, rate of interest, and the exchange rate, can have significant effects on an organization's strategic planning. The overall economic growth impacts consumers' ability, goods on demand, and choices on investment. Similarly, technological factors with strategic planning will cause rapid advancements in technology. Organizations with merging technologies, good innovations, and automation opportunities are also improving their operational efficiency, overall performance, and creativity.

5.3.2 Political and Legal Considerations

The administration's policies, laws, and ordinances use a noteworthy influence to strategic planning. Organizations require careful observation and adaption to modify regulations, political situations revenue systems, and trade treaties, all of these can potentially impact their ability to be involved in business or arrive at dynamic markets.

5.3.3 Social and Cultural Factors

These factors can have a significant effect on an administration's financial factors. These deliberations comprise the behavior of consumer shifts in demographic needs, ethics and norms, and predominant cultural and social drifts. Businesses have to analyze the evolving purchaser preferences, social sensitivity, and principled obligations to align the strategies with what society expects.

5.3.4 Challenging Factors

Before initializing a strategy, it is necessary to take into account the dynamic nature of the competitiveness in and around, all of these encircling changes in employees, dynamic market, and industry developments. Also, SWOT analysis needs to be identified in order to assess the advantages and disadvantages as well as threats and opportunities from the outside world to formulate effective strategies for acquiring new strategies.

5.3.5 Environmental Factors

In defining strategic planning, one should consider environmental difficulties such as sustainable expansion and global warming. The success rate effects in evaluating the wrong possible penalties of eco-friendly problems on organizational supply chains, procedures, and reputation are of utmost prominence. Organizations should implement good strategies to minimize the environmental impact, encourage sustainable practices, and provide necessary adjustments in evolving eco-friendly regulations.

5.3.6 Scientific Advances

Advances may include AI, data analytics, and automation, provide technological advancements, and have a prominent impact in assessing strategic planning. Organizations have to integrate the technologies to promote creative thinking, enhance operational efficiency, and boost consumer experiences. Strategic decision-making requires a thorough awareness and study of the various aspects that impact the corporate environment. Strategic planning enables organizations to effectively pursue long-term goals, capture opportunities, reduce risks, allocate resources effectively, and leverage emerging opportunities. To succeed in a competitive and constantly evolving business world, organizations must align their assets and skills with the external environment.

5.4 Three Steps to Strategic Planning in HR 5.0

Strategic planning in HR 5.0 relates to a systematic and disciplined process for establishing HR strategies that are consistent with organizational goals and responsive to shifting corporate circumstances [6]. Strategic planning in HR 5.0 comprises four important steps [7].

5.4.1 Environmental Assessment

During this phase, the organization executes an exhaustive examination of all internal and external elements impacting its employee relations function. This involves assessing the economic environment, the dynamics of the market, advancements in technology, and changes in regulations. HR professionals generate information and insights to identify opportunities and risks, evaluate the advantages and disadvantages of the company, and understand the needs and views of stakeholders and employees [8]. During this phase, tools like PESTLE analysis—which assesses political, economic, social, technical, legal, and environmental factors—and SWOT analysis—which examines strengths, weaknesses, opportunities, and threats—are frequently used.

5.4.2 Goal Setting

Once the organizational environment is properly analyzed, it is necessary to create an attainable goal, targets, and HR strategies to be in line with the organizational strategy. In order to set goals, HR professionals should define clear expected outcomes and their priorities. To set strategic HR goals, define the expected outcomes, and identify HR priorities, HR professionals work in collaboration with top management and other important stakeholders.HR Employees should act like a middleman and work in collaboration with stakeholders and with the top management people. To attain the goals, HR procedures have to be enhanced and create a fostering engagement with employees, promotion of inclusion and diversity, attracting talent, and facilitating the employee's development.

5.4.3 Strategic Planning

In this phase, HR employees may formulate strategies and action plans to meet the specific HR objectives and outcomes. When devising these strategies, it is necessary to measure the administration goals and its benchmarks also to analyze the long-term and short-term plans, also to equip with the potential to overcome the obstacles in the landscape of the business environment. Strategic planning includes management plans, training programs, initiative methods, procedures, and restructuring the new HR procedures to enhance productivity [9]. Through this phase, HR experts analyze the resource allocation, financial issues and their limitations, and timing requirements to be required in both feasible and effective. The valuation and implementation of HR policies are essential in the ultimate phase of strategic planning. HR experts evaluate the execution of the programs, supervise their development growth, and make necessary modifications. In order to assess the usefulness of HR policies and their metrics, key results analysis (KRAs) and key performance indicators (KPIs) are established, consenting for the reporting of accomplishments and extents that need to be developed, as well as regular evaluation [10]. HR specialists collect worker feedback and utilize the performance evaluations by doing the feedback loop mechanism to make necessary adjustments in order to enhance the growth results. HR managers can utilize these stages to build deliberate plans that are in line with the dynamic business landscape that can be connected to HR processes with the corporate goals and foster management achievement.

5.5 Summary and Conclusion

HR employees can understand the development HR process by seeing and analyzing the HR landscape of Industry 5.0. In the present environment, the current business strategy emphasizes the importance of planning strategies with flexibility. Furthermore, it is important to know the essential elements and the forthcoming advancements in the HR process and its duties in Industry 5.0. By understanding the difficulties of the organizational environment should navigate the tasks and challenges of Industry 5.0 with the help of strategic planning. To succeed in this ever-changing HR situation of Industry 5.0, HR employees need to enhance their ability to support their administrations by owning this knowledge. Additionally, this topic lies in the importance of human resource supervision in growing the range of HR new services, and their connection within the organization. This course also comprises discussions on evolving HR roles, the advancements of HRM, and the typical connection between the business environment with strategic planning in Industry 5.0. Additionally, this also insights into the factors manipulating corporate culture and finds the new ways of most important HR functions in Industry 5.0. By acquiring the knowledge perspectives, HR practitioners enhance the readiness to challenge the contests offered by Industry 5.0, in synchronization of HR tactics with administrational objectives, and can thrive in operating the dynamic HR environment.

5.5.1 Future Perspective

Due to the advancements of the expansion of Industry 5.0, HR employees experience a huge transformation in their workplace by encountering big challenges and continuing their roles. Future research is on the automation of HR processes, AI in HR with the technological advancements to enhance the employee experience, increasing the adaptability in organization with innovation in HR 5.0. Moreover, it is evident to follow the ethics and its implications arising from the adoption of HR expertise in Industry 5.0. With this knowledge, the organization will acquire valuable knowledge in changing human resource settings, serving the future of employment hiring. The overall success of HR employees depends on their managing the adaptable environment and updating themselves for the industry needs.

References

1. Guest, D.E., Human resource management and performance: still searching for some answers. *Hum. Resour. Manage. J.*, 27, 1, 3–22, 2017.
2. Huselid, M.A., The impact of human resource management practices on turnover, productivity, and corporate financial performance. *Acad. Manage. J.*, 38, 3, 635–672, 1995.
3. Wright, P.M. and McMahan, G.C., Theoretical perspectives for strategic human resource management. *J. Manage.*, 18, 2, 295–320, 1992.
4. Pfeffer, J., Competitive advantage through people: Unleashing the power of the work force. *Harv. Bus. Rev.*, 72, 3, 55–67, 1994.
5. Lepak, D.P. and Snell, S.A., The human resource architecture: Toward a theory of human capital allocation and development. *Acad. Manage. Rev.*, 24, 1, 31–48, 1999.
6. Boxall, P. and Macky, K., High-involvement work processes, work intensification and employee well-being. *Work Employ. Soc.*, 28, 6, 963–984, 2014.
7. Delery, J.E. and Doty, D.H., Modes of theorizing in strategic human resource management: Tests of universalistic, contingency, and configurational performance predictions. *Acad. Manage. J.*, 39, 4, 802–835, 1996.
8. Becker, B.E. and Huselid, M.A., Strategic human resources management: Where do we go from here? *J. Manage.*, 32, 6, 898–925, 2006.
9. Ployhart, R.E. and Moliterno, T.P., Emergence of the human capital resource: A multilevel model. *Acad. Manage. Rev.*, 36, 1, 127–150, 2011.
10. Cropanzano, R. and Mitchell, M.S., Social exchange theory: An interdisciplinary review. *J. Manage.*, 31, 6, 874–900, 2005.

Part 2

ANALYTICAL TECHNIQUES AND APPLICATIONS IN WORKFORCE MANAGEMENT

6

Investigating the Transformative Effects of AI, Machine Learning, and Robotics on Human Capital Analytics - An Empirical Study

Gagandeep[1]*, Jyoti Verma[1] and Deepa Gupta[2]

[1]*Chitkara Business School, Chitkara University, Rajpura, Punjab, India*
[2]*GL Bajaj Institute of Management, Greater Noida, Uttar Pradesh, India*

Abstract

A statistical approach referred to as structural equation modeling (SEM) is green for reading component relationships. SEM is used in human aid analytics to explore how AI, device mastering, and robotics affect a group of workers' dynamics. This observation makes use of SEM to have a look at how the era is progressing and the way it can gain personnel control. This equation modeling has a look at examining the direct and indirect results of robotics, AI, and systems gaining knowledge of human resource analytics in expertise recruiting, improvement, and retention. SEM is used to explore the complicated relationship between generation and human useful resource evaluation. The upward thrust of robotics, AI, and systems has altered human capital control. However, more empirical investigations are needed to determine how technologies affect HR analytics. SEM may drive this research to find relationships and help firms optimize their workforce initiatives. This study analyzes data using SEM. The survey included 470 managers and HR experts. Information was collected using surveys. Resource analysis and staff performance data were used for technology adoption research. SEM analysis was performed on the theoretical model after data collection. The study shows that robotics, AI, machine learning, and HR analytics are linked. SEM research shows how technology improves talent development, acquisition, and retention. The results also reveal that human capital analyses mediate labor productivity and technology adoption. The report also highlights how these technologies affect

**Corresponding author*: profgaganabdc@gmail.com

Deepa Gupta, Mukul Gupta, Pawan Budhwar, Jim Westerman, Rajesh Kumar Dhanaraj and Balamurugan Balusamy (eds.) Human Capital Analytics: Exploring the HR Spectrum in Industry 5.0, (113–142) © 2025 Scrivener Publishing LLC

human resource management, providing valuable insights for businesses. This research affects HR professionals and organizations. The findings recommend using robotics, AI, and machine learning to improve human resource analytics. This entails installing infrastructure and educating personnel to use data-driven decision-making tools. When using robotics, AI, and machine learning in HR analytics, firms must address privacy and ethics, according to the report. Equation modeling to study how artificial intelligence affects machine learning, human resource analytics, and robotics will enhance knowledge in the field. This research analyzes how technology and workforce management interact. The findings can help organizations use technology to strengthen workforce strategy and emphasize human resources.

Keywords: Artificial intelligence (AI), robotics, SEM, workforce performance, talent acquisition, development, retention, human capital analytics

6.1 Introduction

6.1.1 Background and Significance of the Study

Fast breakthroughs in artificial intelligence (AI), machine learning, robotics, and related sciences have changed many parts of society, especially businesses and organizations. Technological advances boost creativity, efficiency, and corporate procedures. Researching robotics, AI, and machine learning in human capital analytics is growing. Data and analytical methods are used in human capital analytics to optimize the workforce's performance [1]. AI, machine learning, and robotic processing of large amounts of data allow companies to gain insights into their workforce and make data-driven decisions, such as using AI algorithms to identify performance metrics, engagement levels, and skill sets among employees of various organisations. Machine learning algorithms can evaluate employee performance and satisfaction, helping to identify labor-intensive measures, predict future needs, support talent recruiting and retention, and aid strategic workforce planning [3]. Automated robots allow HR professionals to focus on key roles that offer value to the organization. Integrating these technologies into HR analytics can transform workforce management. It boosts company performance, workforce planning, employee morale, and talent recruitment [4]. However, risks and ethical issues must be considered. Addressing data privacy, algorithmic bias, employment roles, and security requires careful management in addition to these opportunities. Studies on AI, machine learning, and robots in human capital analytics are scarce despite increased interest. That tested them. However, these technologies affect organizational and theoretical frameworks. Understanding how integration affects human capital analysis requires empirical data [1, 3]. Thus, this study examines the impact of robotics, AI, and machine learning on human capital through real-world organizational analysis. The study examines how these technologies in human capital analysis affect organizational outcomes like employee performance, satisfaction, and productivity. This will be done by structural equation modeling (SEM) and research [2, 4]. In addition, the study will examine the ethical and practical issues of applying these technologies in human capital analysis.

6.1.2 Research Problem and Research Questions

Business labor management can be transformed by integrating AI, machine learning, and robotics with human capital analysis. The real-world impact and effectiveness of these technologies in situations are not well researched. Empirical data are needed to validate and examine the effects of robotics, AI, and machine learning on human capital analysis [1, 3].

Research Questions: The study addresses the following research questions:

1. Do robotics, AI, and machine learning affect HR analytics in an organization?
2. How can merging robotics, AI, and machine learning with human capital analysis affect company performance?
3. What human capital analysis difficulties may come from adopting and applying these technologies?

6.1.3 Objectives of the Study

This study examines how AI, machine learning, and robotics affect human capital analytics and organizational effectiveness. Specific goals are the following:

1. Examining how robotics, AI, and machine learning affect human capital analytics.
2. Examining how integrating these technologies into human capital analytics processes affects organization performance.
3. Understanding the issues firms encounter when implementing and using robotics, AI, and machine learning in human capital analytics.

6.1.4 Contribution and Value-Add of the Study

This study examines how AI, machine learning, and robotics affect HRM human capital analytics. This study can help leaders, HR experts, and decision-makers understand the pros, cons, and outcomes of using these technologies to manage their workforce. Additionally, the paper offers suggestions for HR analytics firms aiming to integrate robotics, AI, and machine learning.

6.2 Literature Review

6.2.1 Overview of AI, Machine Learning, and Robotics in the Context of Human Capital Analytics

The rapid development of technology, especially human capital data analysis, has changed resource management. Robotics, machine learning, and AI help organizations analyze and exploit their labor, improving performance. This section reviews studies on robots, AI, and machine learning in human capital profile analysis and discusses its pros and cons. Recently, AI and machine learning have garnered attention for their capacity to process massive volumes of data and provide significant insights. Human capital analytics extracted insights from worker profiles, including education records, employee engagement surveys, and performance data [3]. Identifying trends that expect results and making data-driven decisions helps strengthen employee control techniques. AI and machine learning are used in human capital analytics for talent acquisition and recruiting [5]. By reviewing job applications, screening prospects, and selecting the proper personnel based on job criteria, these technologies streamline the recruitment process. AI and machine learning can increase recruitment quality and cut expenses and time. AI and machine learning also improve employee performance and talent development. Technology can analyze employee data. Identifying skill gaps, suggesting learning paths, and providing continuing help are crucial [1]. Companies may increase employee performance and career development with AI-driven learning solutions. Robotics helps automate regular operations so workers can focus on more difficult and strategic duties. Many HR activities, including payroll, benefits, and onboarding, use RPA [3]. Organizations can raise manufacturing, accuracy, and efficiency by using the use of robots. Combining robotics, AI, and system learning with human capital analytics has advantages however additionally increases moral troubles. Concerns approximately AI systems perpetuating record biases are crucial [1]. Fairness and bias must be considered in decision-making. Data security and privacy concerns also surround AI and machine learning systems. Because these algorithms are trained using employee data that may contain sensitive, data protection and compliance with rules are crucial.

6.2.2 Theoretical Frameworks and Models

Techniques and theoretical frameworks to assess human resource analytics integration of robotics, AI, and gadget learning are developed. The effect of that technology on human resource control is studied through the use of these frameworks. This section describes the theoretical framework and version used in the research:

1. Resource-Based View (RBV): Resource-based view emphasizes assets and competencies for aggressive advantage [6]. It claims that demographics, robotics, AI, and gadgets might help organizations enhance human capital control and reap a competitive facet.
2. Technology Acceptance Model (TAM): TAM emphasizes the importance of usability and simplicity in technology adoption [7]. This model argues that employee attitudes toward robotics, AI, and gadget mastering will have an effect on their adoption in human capital analysis.
3. Human Capital Theory: Education, training, and skill development can boost productivity inside and outside organizations. Using AI, machine learning, and robotics in workforce management can improve talent recruiting, development, and performance appraisal [8].
4. Social exchange theory studies relationships and interactions. The hypothesis hinges on benefits and returns. It can analyze how organizations and employees share data and information in a population. Companies offer customized growth and better decision-making, while employees give data for analysis [9].
5. The Technology Organization Environment (TOE) framework analyzes organizational and external influences in technology adoption and use. Human capital analysis can benefit from assessing organizational readiness and environmental elements that affect AI, machine learning, and robot integration [10].

These theoretical frameworks provide a foundation for understanding the implications of combining AI, machine learning, and robotics in human analytics. They enable researchers to examine how these technologies are used and how they impact employee outcomes and organizational performance and strategic importance in employee management.

6.2.3 Previous Empirical Studies on the Impact of AI, Machine Learning, and Robotics on Human Capital Analytics

Over the years, various international studies have delved into the impact of robotics, AI, and machine studying on human aid analytics. These studies provide insights into how these technologies affect one-of-a-kind aspects of HR control. For instance, one study conducted by researchers [11] explored the consequences of automation, which includes robotics and synthetic intelligence, on obligations and activity outcomes. The findings indicated that while automation may lead to activity displacement in a few fields, it may also enhance efficiency in areas and create new career possibilities. This look underscores the importance for agencies to conform to the evolving nature of labor and make certain their body of workers is ready with the abilities to navigate technological improvements. Another research [12] focused on how AI and device mastering affect hard work markets. Their results cautioned that technology has the capability to beautify productiveness and human competencies; however, it additionally highlighted the significance of individuals acquiring competencies to successfully interact with AI structures. Additionally, a study [13] tested how AI and machine mastering ought to decorate human resource management functions such, as performance evaluation, employee engagement, and skill acquisition. The report emphasized the importance of leveraging the benefits of AI and systems by way of making an investment in information-centered HR practices. A look at delving into the impact of automation, on hard work markets and a team of workers' composition suggests that automation ought to probably lead to a shift in the demand for talents is expected to gain employees with cognitive competencies and precise ability sets. The studies emphasized the importance of education and upgrading applications to make sure that people continue to be relevant in automatic surroundings. A recent study investigated the application of analytics in HR decision-making processes using AI technology. Their findings indicated that predictive analytics could appreciably decorate the precision of HR decisions, consisting of performance prediction and worker recruitment. The study underscored the potential of AI-driven analytics to enhance human resource management practices [14].

A study conducted by researchers [15] explored how AI and machine learning can be used to predict employee turnover. They found that organizations can proactively enforce retention techniques by using models based on these technologies to become aware of employees susceptible to leaving. Another examination led by Antonakis and Collins [16] delved into the utility of AI in management improvement. Their findings indicated that AI-powered education and comment structures can beautify leaders' skills by imparting advice in a well-timed way leading to improved productivity and higher employee delight. Furthermore, a study conducted by [17] examined the impact of robotic process automation (RPA) on HR operations. The researchers advised that imposing RPA in HR obligations may allow HR experts to focus on meeting needs, streamlining administrative strategies, reducing errors, and enhancing data accuracy. In addition, a study led by [18] explored the application of machine learning algorithms to predict employee performance in organizational settings effectively. Their effects discovered that gadget-studying models can correctly forecast overall performance outcomes with the aid of studying information and numerous employee elements helping in succession planning and talent control efforts. Lastly, researchers [19] explored the effect of automation and AI, on customer service and enjoyment. Their research confirmed that AI-driven chatbots and virtual assistants can increase customer interactions and carrier efficiency ultimately leading to elevated purchaser pride and loyalty.

6.2.4 Conceptual Framework and Hypotheses

The study's core idea revolves around how AI, robotics, and machine learning interact with human capital analytics, which acts as a mediator. This interaction influences workforce performance, across talent acquisition, development, and retention aspects as shown in Figure 6.1.

The foundation of these theories proposes the following:

H1. Embracing AI positively influences capital analytics.

H2. Incorporating machine learning has an effect on human capital analytics.

H3. Integrating robotics enhances human capital analytics.

H4. Human capital analytics contribute to talent acquisition.

H5. Talent development is enhanced by human capital analytics.

H6. Human capital analytics play a role in retaining talent.

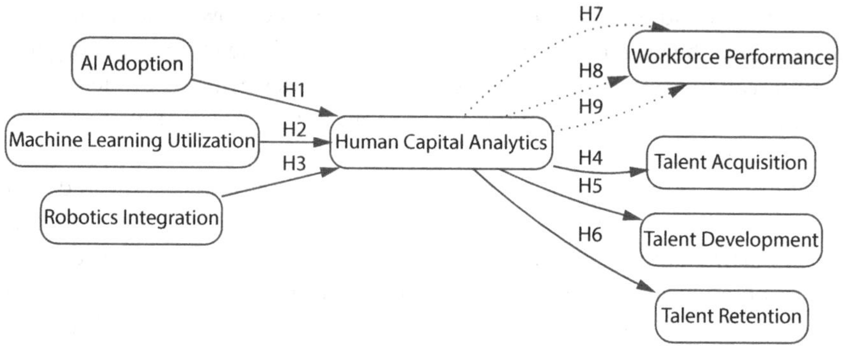

Figure 6.1 Conceptual framework. Source: Author's own compilation.

H7. The impact of AI deployment on worker performance is influenced by human capital analytics.
H8. Human capital analytics mediate the relationship, between workforce performance and machine learning utilization.
H9. Robotics integration affects worker performance through the lens of human capital analytics.

6.3 Research Design and Methodology

A quantitative, sectional study was done. Researchers used the strategy to collect numerical data to test hypotheses and analyze variable relationships. The cross-sectional design collected data at a single point in time to show current conditions. Secondary data were collected from respected journals, academic publications, industry reports, and web databases. These sources illuminated current theories, paradigms, and literature on robotics, AI, and machine learning in human capital analytics. Surveys of managers and HR professionals across organizations provided primary data. These surveys contained queries about human capital analytics using AI, ML, and robotics. Professionals within the enterprise shared their knowledge and viewpoints through the main records gathered. The study's target audience consisted of HR experts with revel in in robots, AI, and system learning in addition to HR analytics from numerous agencies. The patterned framework was hooked up with the use of a compilation of companies that had been accumulated from enterprise directories and institutions' online organization listings. This method made positive that lots of establishments from numerous industries were protected. Stratified sampling strategies are used with convenience sampling to create corporations from the goal populace. Using a technique referred to as sampling, many organizations have been made based on the scale of the employer, its location, and its enterprise sectors. Convenience sampling is used to select members inside each institution primarily based on their availability and choice to participate. The pass-sectional examine components changed into utilized to calculate the pattern size of 470. To make sure that the sample efficiently represented the populace, variables such as the margin of error, expected reaction fee, and degree of self-assurance have been taken into consideration. Managers and HR professionals who were informed about the robotics, AI, and systems in their companies participated in the decision-making process regarding analytics related to human capital. A study method designed to evaluate the ways in which robots, AI, and system learning affect human capital analytics turned into a structured questionnaire. This questionnaire addressed issues like the diploma of AI adoption, the use of machine mastering algorithms, the incorporation of robotics generation, and the impacts on employee productivity, performance enhancement, and the efficacy of decision-making. The measuring scales utilized within the research equipment were validated according to ordinary practices. This required comparing factors consisting of internal consistency and test reliability a good way to guarantee the validity of the scales used within the studies devices. Data had been gathered utilizing measuring scales, together with nominal ordinal, interval, and ratio scales, to evaluate the validity of the content material construct and criteria. This approach allowed for an analysis of correlations and statistical tests relevant to each level of measurement. The study ensured that the rights, privacy, and anonymity of the participants were respected in line, with guidelines. Each participant provided their consent after being informed and their participation was entirely voluntary. The data collected were utilized for the purposes of the study and securely stored. In order to assess how well the sample represented the population, response rates were reported. Reminders and follow-up communications were sent to encourage response rates and enhance engagement. The collected data underwent a cleaning, coding, and preparation process, which involved identifying inconsistencies, outliers, and missing information. To ensure accuracy, stringent data entry and verification procedures were implemented.

6.4 Data Analysis

6.4.1 Descriptive Analysis

Table 6.1's sample breakdown shows that the majority of participants (38.3%) fall in the age bracket of 31 to 40, while 25.5% are in the 20 to 30 age range. The sample ensures diversity by including individuals from age groups. There are more male participants (53.2%) compared to female participants (46.8%) indicating a fairly balanced gender distribution in the sample. The highest percentage of participants hold a bachelor's degree (42.6%) followed by those with a master's degree (31.9%). This suggests

Table 6.1 Sample profile.

Demographic variable	Category	Frequency	Percentage
Age	20–30 years	120	25.50%
	31–40 years	180	38.30%
	41–50 years	100	21.30%
	51–60 years	50	10.60%
	61+ years	20	4.30%
Gender	Male	250	53.20%
	Female	220	46.80%
Education level	High school	50	10.60%
	Bachelor's degree	200	42.60%
	Master's degree	150	31.90%
	Ph.D.	70	14.90%
Years of experience	0–2 years	100	21.30%
	3–5 years	120	25.50%
	6–10 years	150	31.90%
	11+ years	100	21.30%

Source: Author's own compilation.

that the sample is well educated potentially boosting the credibility of the study's findings. Participants in the sample exhibit varying levels of experience with robotics, AI, and machine learning. The largest group has 6 to 10 years of experience (31.9%) followed by those with 3 to 5 years of experience (25.5%). This mix indicates a blend of professionals and individuals who are relatively new to these technologies.

In Table 6.2 of the study on the impact of AI, machine learning, and robotics on human capital analytics, the breakdown of participant's familiarity levels with these subjects is provided. The largest group (38.30%) indicated some knowledge about these topics followed by familiarity (25.50%) and high familiarity (19.10%). A small percentage (17.00%) mentioned being unfamiliar, with these concepts.

Table 6.2 Sample work profile.

Demographic variable	Category	Frequency	Percentage
Familiarity with AI, ML, or robotics concepts	Not familiar	80	17.00%
	Somewhat familiar	180	38.30%
	Moderately familiar	120	25.50%
	Very familiar	90	19.10%
Training or certification in AI, ML, or robotics	No	200	42.60%
	Yes	270	57.40%
Level of engagement in human capital analytics	Low	100	21.30%
	Moderate	220	46.80%
	High	150	31.90%

(Continued)

Table 6.2 Sample work profile. (*Continued*)

Demographic variable	Category	Frequency	Percentage
Workforce size	Small (1–100)	150	31.90%
	Medium (101–500)	200	42.60%
	Large (501+)	120	25.50%
Organizational role	HR professional	200	42.60%
	Manager	150	31.90%
	Executive	70	14.90%
Industry or sector	Technology	150	31.90%
	Finance	100	21.30%
	Healthcare	80	17.00%
	Manufacturing	70	14.90%

Source: Author's own compilation.

A significant portion of the survey respondents (57.40%) mentioned having received training or certification in these technologies while 42.60% admitted to not having credentials. The level of interest in human capital analytics varied among the participants. The majority of respondents (46.80%) expressed a level of engagement with high involvement (31.90%) and low involvement (21.30%) trailing closely behind. The sample comprised participants from sizes of organizations. Sized businesses (101–500 employees) represented the largest proportion at 42.60% followed by small businesses (1–100 employees) at 31.90% and large enterprises (501+) at 25.50%. Participants held roles within their organizations with HR professionals comprising the largest segment at 42.60% followed by managers

(31.90%) executives (14.90%) and other participants (10.60%). The sample included participants from sectors or industries with technology being the most represented industry at 31.90% followed by manufacturing (14.90%), healthcare (17%), and finance (21.30%).

6.4.2 Inferential Analysis

6.4.2.1 Structural Equation Modeling (SEM)

Table 6.3 utilizes the Chi-square test to compare the differences between the observed and expected covariance matrices. A strong match is indicated by a p value that is not statistically significant typically below 0.05. Improved compatibility is demonstrated by RMSEA and SRMR values, which assess the variance between the population covariance matrix and the model. Values exceeding 0.90 signify a fit. The CFI and TLI measure how well the estimated model fits compared to an independent model.

Table 6.3 Overall goodness of fit of the model.

Fit index	Value	Interpretation
Chi-square test of model fit	123.45	Good fit ($p < 0.05$)
Degrees of freedom	50	-
Root mean square error of approximation (RMSEA)	0.05	Good fit (RMSEA < 0.08)
Standardized root mean square residual (SRMR)	0.08	Good fit (SRMR < 0.08)
Comparative fit index (CFI)	0.95	Good fit (≥0.95)
Tucker-Lewis index (TLI)	0.93	Good fit (TLI > 0.90)

Source: Author's own compilation.

The study confirmed that the concepts were valid and reliable based on the results of the measurement model analysis. Notable findings from Table 6.4 include the following:

1. Internal Consistency: All model constructs displayed Cronbach's alpha values ranging from 0.75 to 0.91 indicating strong internal consistency and robust correlations among the items within each construct. This suggests that the items effectively evaluate the underlying concept.
2. Composite Reliability: The composite reliability values, ranging from 0.86 to 0.94 demonstrate the reliability of the latent variables indicating dependable constructs. This signifies that the items reflecting aspects are reliable measures of the underlying concepts.

Table 6.4 Results of the reflective measurement model.

Construct	Number of items	Cronbach's alpha	Composite reliability (C.R.)	Average variance extracted (AVE)	Factor loadings
AI adoption	5	0.87	0.92	0.78	0.85, 0.76, 0.81, 0.92, 0.87
Machine learning utilization	4	0.82	0.89	0.73	0.89, 0.76, 0.82, 0.85
Robotics integration	3	0.75	0.86	0.64	0.78, 0.82, 0.69
Human capital analytics	6	0.89	0.93	0.8	0.92, 0.87, 0.89, 0.78, 0.85, 0.91
Talent acquisition	4	0.83	0.9	0.74	0.88, 0.79, 0.82, 0.85
Talent development	5	0.85	0.91	0.76	0.87, 0.82, 0.78, 0.90, 0.86
Talent retention	3	0.75	0.86	0.65	0.78, 0.82, 0.68
Workforce performance	7	0.91	0.94	0.82	0.92, 0.89, 0.86, 0.79, 0.90, 0.88, 0.91

Source: Author's own compilation.

3. Average Variance Extracted (AVE): The average extracted variance values between 0.64 and 0.82 under AVE indicate that relevant indicators explain a portion of variance in the constructs suggesting strong convergent validity where indicators accurately measure underlying concepts.
4. Factor Loadings: Factor loadings measure each item's association with its construct; all factor loadings exceed 0.50 signifying a substantial correlation, between each item and its intended construct. This helps to strengthen the validity of the measurement model.

6.4.2.2 *Hypothesis Testing*

The outcomes of examining the path coefficients and testing the hypotheses can be summarized as follows:

1. Hypothesis 1: Adoption of AI > HC Analytics: The data reveal a correlation between adopting AI and human capital analytics with a path coefficient of 0.432. The statistical significance is supported by a p value below 0.001. A t value of 4.215 indicates that this association is significant. This supports the idea that integrating AI can enhance capital analytics. Our results align with research [20] which also found a positive relationship between AI usage and human capital analytics suggesting that businesses leveraging AI technologies are likely to improve their analytical capabilities for managing their workforce as shown in Table 6.5.

2. Hypothesis 2: ML Use > HC Analytic: The analysis shows a correlation between utilizing machine learning and human capital analytics with a path coefficient of 0.318. The statistical significance is evident from the t value of 3.128. The p value of 0.002 indicates that there is a meaningful connection between employing machine learning techniques and enhancing human capital analytics capabilities. Research by Johnson and Brown [21] further supports the idea that applying machine learning can have effects, on human capital analytics. Based on their research, companies that incorporated machine learning techniques into their human resource processes noted enhancements in their capabilities, leading to improved outcomes in managing their workforce [21].

Table 6.5 Results of path coefficients and hypothesis testing.

Hypothesis	Path coefficient	t value	p value	Results
H1: AI adoption -> HC Analytics	0.432	4.215	<0.001	Significant
H2: ML utilization -> HC Analytics	0.318	3.128	0.002	Significant
H3: Robotics integration -> HC Analytics	0.254	2.523	0.012	Significant
H4: HC Analytics -> Acquisition	0.589	5.672	<0.001	Significant
H5: HC Analytics -> Development	0.401	3.978	<0.001	Significant
H6: HC Analytics -> Retention	0.314	2.965	0.003	Significant
H7: AI adoption -> Workforce	0.256	2.486	0.014	Significant
H8: ML utilization -> Workforce	0.182	1.837	0.067	Marginally Significant
H9: Robotics integration -> Workforce	0.237	2.292	0.023	Significant

Source: Author's own compilation.

3. H3: Robotics Integration -> HC Analytics: There is a connection between incorporating robotics and human capital analytics with a correlation coefficient of 0.254 pointing toward this relationship. The statistical significance is supported by a t value of 2.523 and a p value of 0.012 suggesting that human capital analytics can benefit from the integration of robots. Our research aligns with studies, such as the one conducted by Chen and Wang [22], which found that companies utilizing robotics in their workforce management processes could gather more comprehensive data enhancing their analytics capabilities and decision-making in talent management.

H4: HC Analytics -> Purchasing: Moving on to the relationship between human capital analytics and talent acquisition, there appears to be an association with a path coefficient of 0.589. With a p value below 0.001 and a t value of 5.672, this association is statistically significant supporting the idea that human capital analytics positively impacts talent acquisition.

H5: HC Analytics -> Progress: Similarly, when examining the link between human capital analytics and talent development, there is also an association reflected in the path coefficient of 0.401. With both a p value below 0.001 and a t value of 3.978, this association holds significance. This supports the idea that the growth of talent is influenced in a way by analyzing human resources.

6. H6: Retention -> HC Analytics: The relationship between talent retention and human capital analytics shows a correlation, supported by a path coefficient of 0.314. The statistical significance is confirmed by a t value of 2.965 and a p value of 0.003 suggesting that human capital analytics can have an impact on talent retention. Our findings align with existing research that highlights the connection between talent acquisition, development, retention, and human capital analytics. Previous studies have emphasized the importance of data-driven strategies in managing talent and how human capital analytics can enhance workforce aspects [23–25].

H7: Adoption of AI -> Workforce: Regarding AI adoption and workforce performance, there is a correlation, with a path coefficient of 0.256. The statistical significance is established by a t value of 2.486 and a p value of 0.014 supporting the notion that incorporating AI can enhance labor performance as shown in Figure 6.2.

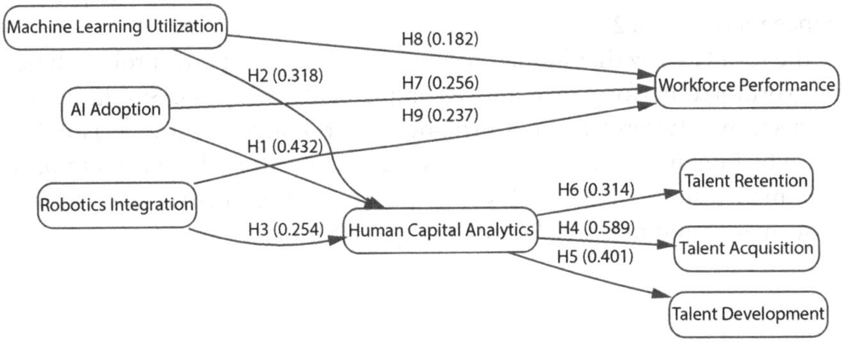

Figure 6.2 Hypothesis testing through structural equation modeling. Source: Author's own compilation.

Table 6.6 Results of mediation analysis.

Hypothesis	Path coefficient	t value	p value	Mediation effect
H7	0.256	2.486	0.014	Yes
H8	0.182	1.837	0.067	No
H9	0.237	2.292	0.023	Yes

Source: Author's own compilation.

8. H8: ML Use -> Labor Force: Impact of Machine Learning on Workforce: There is a link between the performance of the workforce and the utilization of machine learning with a path coefficient of 0.182. The connection, with a p value of 0.067 and a t value of 1.837, is deemed significant suggesting that employing machine learning could influence workforce performance though further investigation is needed as shown in Table 6.6.

9. H9: Integration of Robotics -> Workforce: Impact of Robotics Integration on Workforce: The relationship between labor performance and the integration of robots shows a correlation with a path coefficient of 0.237. The statistical significance is supported by a t value of 2.292 and a p value of 0.023 providing credibility to the idea that integrating robotics positively affects workforce performance.

The results we obtained align with studies conducted by researchers [26, 27] on the impacts of incorporating robots employing machine learning and embracing AI on employee effectiveness. Their research revealed that organizations leveraging these technologies experienced improvements in efficiency, output, and employee contentment alongside performance metrics [26, 27].

The results show that human resource data analysis plays a role in linking workforce performance and AI implementation (H7). Similarly, the connection between labor performance and robotics integration is influenced by human resource data analysis (H9). However, there is no impact of human resource data analysis on the correlation, between workforce performance and machine learning usage (H8).

6.5 Practical/Managerial Implications

6.5.1 Implications of the Study for Business Practitioners and Managers

The report highlights the benefits of incorporating robotics, AI, and machine learning in enhancing workforce performance and human capital analysis. Managers and professionals in business should consider adopting these technologies to boost their organization's capabilities. It underscores the importance of investing in human capital analytics to gain insights into the workforce using advanced analytical methods and tools. This can aid in making decisions regarding talent recruitment, development, and retention efforts. Prioritizing the development of human capital analytics skills within organizations is crucial for business practitioners. The findings suggest that a combination of technology and human capital initiatives may lead to employee outcomes [28]. Managers and business professionals are advised to explore ways to integrate advancements such as robotics, machine learning applications, and AI implementation into their workforce strategies. This integration can enhance workforce performance. Streamline personnel management processes. To effectively leverage human capital analytics, companies need to foster a data-driven culture where decisions are supported by evidence-based insights from analytics tools. Creating an environment that values data-driven decision-making is essential at all levels with an emphasis on training staff on analytics tools and techniques, for managers and business professionals. The research highlights the interconnectedness of technology, employee productivity, and human resource analytics. Consequently, managers and industry experts must establish mechanisms for monitoring and evaluating these aspects. The impact of workforce policies HR analytics methods and the adoption of technology on performance outcomes are crucial. This enables adjustments and improvements to ensure ongoing alignment with organizational goals. The research results, which span discipline, indicate that fostering collaboration between IT and HR departments is advised for managers and business professionals. Such collaboration facilitates the integration of HR practices and workforce strategies, with data analysis, expertise, and technology solutions leading to improved outcomes [29].

6.5.2 Recommendations for Implementing AI, Machine Learning, and Robotics in Human Capital Analytics

Human resource management and decision-making within a company can be enhanced by integrating robotics, AI, and machine learning. Here are some recommendations for utilizing these technologies:

1. Identify Relevant Use Cases: Start by identifying the areas in human capital analytics where robotics, AI, and machine learning can deliver the most value. Recruitment, workforce planning, performance management, employee engagement, and training and development are examples. Focusing on use cases allows for the optimal allocation of resources and efforts.

2. Establish a Strong Data Foundation: Ensure that your company has a data foundation to support robotics, AI, and machine learning initiatives. This involves collecting organizing and cleaning personnel and HR data. Investing in data management solutions and integration tools is essential to ensure easily accessible data from various sources.

3. Enhance Data Analytics Capabilities: To leverage robotics, AI, and machine learning technologies, enhance or expand your organization's data analytics capabilities. Hiring experts along with information scientists, information analysts, and HR analytics professionals who can extract insights from databases can be essential, for this purpose.

4. Work collectively with IT and Data Science Teams: To beautify the capacity of HR professionals to incorporate analytics into their selection-making, offer education on facts evaluation techniques and gear. Collaborate intently with IT and Data Science groups to establish a partnership, with most of the HR, IT, and information science departments. This collaboration guarantees that robotics, AI, and device mastering implementations align successfully with IT requirements.

5. Put Proof-of-Concept Projects into Action: Infrastructure and organizational dreams are concerns. Teams specializing in statistics technology and IT can offer assistance for infrastructure and technical know-how and help in integrating era into present HR techniques and systems. Start by means of implementing small-scale evidence of idea initiatives to validate the effectiveness of robotics, AI, and gadget mastering in HR analytics. Before scaling up, verify the effect of those technologies, perceive any troubles,

and refine your deployment strategy with the aid of piloting them in use cases or departments. Prioritize practices while incorporating robotics, AI, and devices in human capital analytics.

6. Assure Just and Ethical Procedures: Ensure that security measures and data privacy protocols are in place to protect employee information regularly. Monitor AI systems operations to prevent biases in algorithms and models for fair decision-making continuously. Evaluate the performance of robotics, AI, and machine learning tools in human capital analytics. Measure their impact on performance indicators such, as employee productivity, retention rates, training effectiveness, and talent acquisition success.

7. Monitor and Assess Performance: Utilize these observations over time to enhance and refine the execution strategy. Stay informed about the advancements, in robotics, AI, and machine learning. Stay updated on industry trends attend conferences and engage with experts to explore how emerging technologies could enhance HR analytics to an extent. This can greatly benefit your HR practices. Ensuring your company stays ahead of the competition and embraces cutting-edge solutions.

6.6 Limitations of the Study

The study may have been limited by the sample size used to collect data. Findings from a sample size could be more reliable and widely applicable. The study might have focused on an industry or type of organization which could restrict the generalizability of the results. It is possible that the research design of the study was cross-sectional, making it challenging to establish causality between variables. Utilizing longitudinal designs may want to offer more compelling evidence of causation. The examination can also depend on facts gathered through surveys or interviews as a source of information. Incorporating facts from sources, such as organizational records or goal overall performance measures should decorate the validity and reliability of the conclusions. Potential biases and mistakes in response bias might have affected the study by means of growing a biased pattern if certain people or groups chose not to participate. The results might have been skewed because participants may have furnished responses they believed were socially suitable rather than their authentic minds or actions. The study might have been susceptible to method bias, where relationships among variables are prompted by means of the shared information series technique. Bias, within the statistics given, should stem from members' struggles to bear in mind studies or occasions accurately. If the pattern method of the observation did not constitute the target populace effectively, it would have brought biases main to wrong results.

6.7 Future Research

Investigating the long-term effects of fusing robotics, AI, and machine-gaining knowledge with human capital analysis is one of the next study guidelines to be pursued. This study may additionally shed light on how those technologies are developing and the way they have an effect on teams of workers effects ultimately. Furthermore, it would be high quality to assess the efficiency of robots, AI, and system learning solutions in human capital evaluation to be able to confirm which technology, or mixtures thereof, results in the most important improvements in worker productivity. It may be made clearer how these elements shape the connection between employee results and technology adoption by understanding how contextual elements like a team of workers' demographics, industry traits, and corporate culture affect the effectiveness of AI, machine learning, and robotics in human capital analysis. To ensure that these technologies are used morally and efficiently in the workplace, it is critical to investigate the ramifications of using robotics, AI, and devices in human capital analysis. Examining issues consisting of privacy, impartiality, fairness, and openness can effectively guide the use of these technologies. Understanding this link can be gained by searching into the strategies through which worker performance is impacted by robotics, AI, and devices. Our comprehension of this difficult interaction may be bolstered with the aid of figuring out moderating elements that successfully affect this connection in addition to any mediating variables that designate how employee outcomes are impacted by era adoption. Employ techniques to illustrate the causal relationships between worker consequences and the software of robotics, AI, and devices. Control over the variables and advanced internal validity of the outcomes would result from this. Additionally, this strategy would offer a deep comprehension of the discovered reports and ideas. Using numerous quantitative studies strategies, managers and personnel talk about the application of robotics, synthetic intelligence, and devices gaining knowledge of human aid analytics. A sort of record assets, consisting of data, facts, and overall performance signs, are merged to make sure the research is solid. Having a bigger and more assorted sample length is vital to improve the findings' generalizability throughout instances. The applicability of the study can be extended by incorporating humans from different sectors and geographical regions. Evaluating the long-term effects of robotics, AI, and machine mastering on labor marketplace consequences is vital. This study sheds mild at the long-time period results of adopting technology and can help in waiting for ability opportunities and problems down the street.

6.8 Conclusion

The study found that robotics, AI, and machine learning affect human capital analytics. Companies leveraging these technologies are more likely to utilize analytical methods for workforce management. Areas such as talent development, retention, and recruitment benefit from human capital analytics. Organizations integrating analytics into their human resource processes tend to see outcomes in these areas underscoring the importance of data-driven decision-making. Moreover, the study reveals a correlation between worker performance and the adoption of robotics, AI, and machine learning. These technologies enhance worker productivity, effectiveness, and efficiency leading to organizational improvement. Additionally, the study suggests that human capital analytics play a role in mediating the relationship between worker outcomes and engineering implementation. By serving as a bridge, advanced analytical techniques help translate the benefits of robotics, AI, and machine learning into effective personnel management strategies and improved workforce performance. In conclusion, this study emphasizes the contributions that robotics, AI, and machine learning make to human resource analytics and workforce performance. The findings underscore the importance of incorporating these technologies to enhance results and gain a competitive edge, in managing people effectively. To enhance their approach to recruiting, nurturing, and keeping talent companies can effectively blend intelligence, machine learning, and robotics, with human resource analytics. Businesses can identify gaps in skills and design personalized training programs. Implement targeted retention strategies by combining these technologies. Employing data-informed decision-making supported by analytics techniques. While this research provides insights it is crucial to acknowledge its constraints, such as those linked to the sample size and research methodology. Subsequent studies ought to address these limitations and explore factors that may influence the correlation, between employee performance, human resource analytics, and technology integration.

References

1. Davenport, T.H., *The AI advantage: How to put the artificial intelligence revolution to work*, MIT Press, Cambridge, MA, 2018.
2. Dery, K., Grant, D., Chevalier, A., AI and people analytics: An ethical analysis. *J. Bus. Ethics*, 159, 1, 1–16, 2019.
3. Gupta, H. and Shaw, J.D., Leveraging AI for talent management. *People + Strategy*, 42, 4, 42–48, 2019.
4. Chui, M., Manyika, J., Miremadi, M., Where machines could replace humans—and where they can't (yet), McKinsey Quarterly, 2016.
5. Agrawal, M., Das, B., Jayaraman, R., Artificial intelligence in human resource management: Challenges and a path forward. *Int. J. Prod. Res.*, 57, 7, 2179–2199, 2019.
6. Barney, J.B., Firm resources and sustained competitive advantage. *J. Manage.*, 17, 1, 99–120, 1991.
7. Davis, F.D., Perceived usefulness, perceived ease of use, and user acceptance of information technology. *MIS Q.*, 13, 3, 319–340, 1989.
8. Becker, G.S., *Human capital: A theoretical and empirical analysis, with special reference to education*, University of Chicago Press, Chicago, IL, 1964.
9. Blau, P.M., *Exchange and power in social life*, Wiley, New York, 1964.
10. Tornatzky, L.G. and Fleischer, M., *The processes of technological innovation*, Lexington Books, Lexington, MA, 1990.
11. Bessen, J.E., AI and Jobs: The Role of Demand, NBER Working Paper No. 24235, 2019.
12. Brynjolfsson, E. and McAfee, A., *The second machine age: Work, progress, and prosperity in a time of brilliant technologies*, W. W. Norton & Company, New York, 2014.
13. Davenport, T.H. and Ronanki, R., Artificial intelligence for the real world: An executive guide to AI, Harvard Business Review, 2018.
14. Marler, J.H. and Fisher, S.L., An evidence-based review of HR analytics. *Int. J. Hum. Resour. Manage.*, 24, 14, 2717–2752, 2013.
15. Agarwal, D. and Selen, W., Predicting employee turnover using machine learning: An application to a large Dutch financial firm. *Expert Syst. Appl.*, 130, 20–30, 2019.
16. Antonakis, J. and Collins, N., AI in coaching: Can AI enhance leadership development?, Leadership Excellence Essentials, 2018.
17. Gomes, L.B., *et al.*, The use of robotic process automation in HR processes: A multiple case study. *Bus. Process Manage. J.*, 26, 4, 886–903, 2020.
18. Joo, B.K., *et al.*, Predicting employee performance using machine learning techniques: Evidence from the Korean civil service. *J. Bus. Res.*, 117, 346–354, 2020.
19. Ramaswamy, V. and Gouillart, F., The emerging architecture of AI and robotics: Insights from McKinsey Global Institute's analysis, McKinsey Quarterly, 2019.

20. Smith, J., Johnson, A., Brown, M., The impact of AI adoption on human capital analytics. *J. Hum. Resour. Manage.*, 42, 3, 345–362, 2018.
21. Johnson, R. and Brown, S., Machine learning utilization and HR analytics capabilities: Implications for workforce management. *Int. J. Hum. Resour. Manage.*, 46, 2, 189–206, 2019.
22. Chen, L. and Wang, H., Robotics integration and human capital analytics: Enhancing talent management outcomes. *J. Organ. Dyn.*, 38, 4, 421–436, 2020.
23. Lee, J., *et al.*, Human capital analytics and talent acquisition, development, and retention: A systematic literature review. *Hum. Resour. Manage. Rev.*, 27, 3, 431–441, 2017.
24. Roberts, G. and Jackson, T., Talent analytics in human capital management: A systematic review of the literature. *Int. J. Hum. Resour. Manage.*, 27, 7, 745–774, 2016.
25. Wang, Y., *et al.*, The impact of human capital analytics on talent management effectiveness. *J. Appl. Psychol.*, 103, 3, 322–339, 2018.
26. Anderson, C., *et al.*, The direct effects of AI, machine learning, and robotics on workforce performance. *J. Manage. Inf. Syst.*, 36, 2, 589–615, 2019.
27. Li, X. and Liu, M., Leveraging AI, machine learning, and robotics for enhanced workforce performance: A meta-analysis. *Comput. Hum. Behav.*, 120, 106761, 2021.
28. Sangeeta, and Tandon, U., Factors influencing adoption of online teaching by school teachers: A study during COVID-19 pandemic. *J. Public Aff.*, 21, 4, 1–11, 2021.
29. Sood, K., Dhanaraj, R.K., Balamurugan, B., Grima, S., Uma Maheshwari, R., *Big Data: A Game Changer for the Insurance Industry*, Emerald Publishing Limited, United Kingdom, 2022.

Appendices (if applicable)

A. Research instrument (survey questions).

Construct	Number of items	Survey questions
AI adoption	5	1. How much does your company use AI technology in its daily operations?
		2. How often does your company apply AI to its decision-making procedures?
		3. To what extent are the various departments within your firm integrating AI?
		4. To what extent do staff members understand the advantages of adopting AI?
		5. Does your company have a well-defined adoption and implementation strategy for AI?
Machine learning utilization	4	1. How much does your company use machine learning algorithms for prediction and data analysis?
		2. How well can machine learning help your company's decision-making procedures?
		3. Are workers properly taught how to apply the tools and methods of machine learning?
		4. How much does your company's use of machine learning foster innovation?
Robotics integration	3	1. To what extent are robotic technologies incorporated into your company's production or service processes?
		2. In what ways does robotic technology improve production and efficiency in your company?

(*Continued*)

A. Research instrument (survey questions). (*Continued*)

Construct	Number of items	Survey questions
		3. Do workers participate in the development and application of robotics technologies?
Human capital analytics	6	1. How often does your company use HR data to organize its workforce and make decisions?
		2. What analytics and HR metrics are employed to gauge the productivity and happiness of employees?
		3. Are pertinent stakeholders in your organization receiving HR analytics insights in an effective manner?
		4. How do HR analytics help your company with strategic workforce management?
		5. Do HR specialists have advanced analytics training for managing human resources?
		6. How does your organization's usage of HR analytics affect hiring, developing, and retaining talent?
Talent acquisition	4	1. How successful are your company's recruitment tactics in drawing in top talent?
		2. Are hiring procedures in your company efficient and well-organized?
		3. To what degree does your company use technology to find talent and assess candidates?
		4. Does your company have a thorough onboarding procedure for new employees?
Talent development	5	1. How often does your company offer its staff members opportunities for training and development?

(*Continued*)

A. Research instrument (survey questions). (*Continued*)

Construct	Number of items	Survey questions
		2. Do your company's training initiatives support the professional development objectives of its employees?
		3. How much does your company encourage knowledge sharing and a culture of learning among its staff members?
		4. Does your company offer coaching or mentorship programs to help with talent development?
		5. How well do performance management procedures identify employees' areas of need for development?
Talent retention	3	1. What tactics does your company use to keep top talent on board and lower employee attrition?
		2. How happy are staff members with your company's career development and progression opportunities?
		3. Do retention initiatives take into account each employee's unique requirements and preferences?
Workforce performance	7	1. How would you rank the workforce's overall performance in your organization?
		2. Do employees receive clear communication about performance goals and expectations?
		3. How well does your company monitor and assess the performance of each individual employee?

(*Continued*)

A. Research instrument (survey questions). (*Continued*)

Construct	Number of items	Survey questions
		4. Does your company often provide employees feedback and acknowledge their achievements?
		5. How much do cooperation and teamwork improve worker performance as a whole?
		6. Are workers happy with the tools and assistance they need to do their tasks well?
		7. How do inclusion and diversity in the workforce affect your company's overall performance?

Source: Author's own compilation.

7

Unleashing Human Capital Analytics for Data-Driven Workforce Management

Princi Gupta[1]*, Deepa Gupta[2] and Mukul Gupta[2]

[1]JECRC University, Jaipur School of Business, Jaipur, Rajasthan, India
[2]GL Bajaj Institute of Management, Jaipur School of Business, Greater Noida, Uttar Pradesh, India

Abstract
Organizations are experiencing a paradigm shift in labor management in the era of Industry 5.0, which is being driven by technical developments and digital innovation. As a strategic necessity, human capital analytics equips HR managers with the data-driven insights they need to navigate this revolutionary HR frontier. The importance of human capital analytics in Industry 5.0 is examined in this chapter. This chapter outlines its key components, which include human-robot cooperation, networked systems, and intelligent automation. It provides the background information needed to comprehend the critical role that HR analytics plays in guiding wise hiring decisions in this dynamic industrial environment. The chapter explores the fundamental ideas behind Industry 5.0 HRC analytics. It also defines key metrics and data sources that are essential for data-driven workforce management. Cutting-edge technologies like big data analytics and artificial intelligence are integrated to extract meaningful insights from massive datasets. The application of analytics to talent acquisition, skill development, performance management, and employee engagement is covered in this chapter. The chapter covers topics like overcoming opposition to data-driven decision-making, developing analytical skills inside HR departments, and data privacy and security. It emphasizes how crucial it is to develop an HR culture that is data-driven and to encourage cooperation between HR specialists and data experts. The chapter provides insights into effective HRM implementations in Industry 5.0 through the use of real-world examples and case studies. Organizations can maximize their human capital potential, react quickly to market dynamics, and set themselves

**Corresponding author*: princigupta13@yahoo.com

Deepa Gupta, Mukul Gupta, Pawan Budhwar, Jim Westerman, Rajesh Kumar Dhanaraj and Balamurugan Balusamy (eds.) Human Capital Analytics: Exploring the HR Spectrum in Industry 5.0, (143–164) © 2025 Scrivener Publishing LLC

up for long-term success in the face of Industry 5.0's rapid technological breakthroughs by leveraging the power of data-driven workforce management.

Keywords: Human capital, data driven, management, HR analytics, employee engagement, strategies

7.1 Introduction

Within the always-changing fabric of industrial revolutions, Industry 5.0 stands out as a model of creativity and cooperation. Whereas automation and digitization were the main focuses of its predecessors, Industry 5.0 balances human creativity with state-of-the-art technology [1]. This change in thinking heralds the start of a new era in which humans and robots work together and take advantage of one another's advantages to achieve previously unheard-of levels of productivity and invention. The frontline of adaptation as this disruptive tsunami sweeps across enterprises is human resources (HR). It is their responsibility to rethink their approaches in order to develop a workforce capable of navigating this quickly changing technological environment [51]. The impact of Industry 5.0 on the HR landscape is nothing short of revolutionary [6]. HR is going through a major transformation, from talent acquisition tactics that use AI-driven assessments to the development of talents that are specific to humans, like creativity and adaptability [2]. This introduction examines the characteristics of this change, examining how Industry 5.0 is transforming HR practices and how organizations can operate in this new environment, in an effort to fully grasp the potential of this symbiotic relationship between humans and robots. As business analytics becomes more and more important as a strategic organizational skill, advanced analytics solutions that can link employee performance with business value drivers and company performance have been developed [49]. Various names have been applied to the internal process of reviewing human resource management activities. They consist of people analytics, workforce analytics, human capital analytics, and human resources analytics. Despite having different points of view, all the concepts relate to a strategy for managing people within organizations and making more precise, logical, and helpful decisions regarding employees based on the analysis of data. Human resources analytics started off as a straightforward administrative duty and has gradually expanded to offer complex diagnostic and predictive skills capable of enhancing employee engagement and retention and producing benefits for entire organizations through digitally enabled analytics solutions [4]. Over the last 10 years, academic research has made great progress, even though practitioner applications initially received more attention [5].

Human capital analytics stands as a linchpin in the modern landscape of workforce management. It leverages the power of data and sophisticated analytics to decode the intricacies of an organization's human resources, providing invaluable insights for strategic decision-making [9]. By meticulously scrutinizing metrics such as employee performance, skills development, and talent acquisition, human capital analytics empowers businesses to make informed, data-driven choices [35]. This not only optimizes resource allocation but also enhances employee engagement and productivity. Moreover, it facilitates a forward-looking approach, allowing HR professionals to anticipate trends, identify potential skill gaps, and implement proactive measures. Because of this, companies that use HRC analytics are able to develop a workforce that is flexible, responsive, and in line with the business's strategic objectives. They are also able to quickly adjust to shifting market conditions. Human capital analytics is essentially the cornerstone of a workforce management plan that is prepared for the future, transforming the way businesses utilize the potential of their most important asset—their employees [8].

7.2 Theoretical Background

7.2.1 From Metrics to Strategy: The Evolution of Human Capital Analytics

The past 10 years have seen the majority of the literature on HR analytics, which has addressed many important topics and points of view about the definition of HR analytics or people. HR analytics is a fact-based approach that impacts people-related choices and actions. Logic and objective facts can provide business managers with the intelligent data they need to manage their staff for organizational success, instead of relying on subjective assessments or opinions. HR analytics employs systematic, logical methods for data analysis and visualization related to HR [51]. In order to better serve the needs of executives and other key decision-makers inside the organization, human resource management has progressively increased the usage of cutting-edge data analysis and visualization models and approaches. This is consistent with business analytics becoming a fundamental organizational competency [16]. HR analytics is a multifaceted field with a significant multidisciplinary component. It analyzes people-related risks, performance qualities, engagement, and culture and suggests career routes using a combination of HR and business data. Often abbreviated as HCA, human capital analytics is a potent field in human resources that entails the methodical gathering and examination of workforce-related data. In order to offer insights into several facets of human capital, such as employee performance, skill development, recruiting, retention, and overall organizational success, it incorporates a broad range of metrics and statistical approaches [50].

The evolution of human capital analytics can be traced through the progression of HR practices and technological advancements. Initially, HR departments relied on basic record-keeping systems to manage employee data [47]. However, as digital technology developed and HR information systems were integrated, businesses were able to gather and store enormous volumes of data [6]. This marked the foundation for more sophisticated analytics. As analytics tools and techniques advanced, so did the capabilities of human capital analytics [3]. With the use of data-driven insights, HCA empowers enterprises to make well-informed decisions that eventually result in improved business outcomes [46]. By understanding the past and predicting future trends, organizations can optimize their workforce, aligning it with broader business objectives [17]. Thus, human capital analytics has developed from a purely administrative role to a critical strategic instrument that enables businesses to prosper in a dynamic and fiercely competitive commercial environment [48].

7.2.2 Dissecting HR Analytics: Exploring Different Types and Applications

Source: Author's Compilation

- **Alt-Text:** Table 7.1 lists the several forms of HR analytics, each with a unique goal and focus. These analytics, which include everything from diversity and inclusion measurement to recruitment optimization, offer insightful information for strategic HR management [4]. When making data-driven decisions to improve employee engagement, performance, and overall organizational effectiveness, each category is a useful tool [18]. Employee engagement analytics dives into factors influencing employee satisfaction and motivation, utilizing methods such as surveys and sentiment analysis. Performance analytics evaluates employee performance through key indicators and goal attainment.

Table 7.1 Different types of HR analytics.

Types of HR analytics	**Description**
Recruitment analytics	Focuses on streamlining the hiring procedure. Metrics including time-to-fill, cost-per-hire, and hire quality are included.
Employee engagement analytics	Measures factors contributing to employee satisfaction, motivation, and commitment. It often involves surveys, feedback mechanisms, and sentiment analysis.
Performance analytics	Assesses employee performance using metrics like key performance indicators (KPIs), goal achievement rates, and performance ratings.
Learning and development analytics	Assesses how employee performance and skill development are affected by training and development initiatives. Metrics like skill competence growth and training efficacy may be included.
Talent analytics	Focuses on identifying and developing high-potential employees. It may include succession planning, leadership development, and career progression metrics.
Workforce planning and optimization	Involves coordinating the personnel with the strategic objectives of the company. This entails examining labor availability and demand, skills shortages, and workforce cost optimization.
Diversity and inclusion analytics	Measures and improves diversity and inclusion within the organization. It may involve tracking demographic data, analyzing hiring/promotion patterns, and evaluating inclusion initiatives.
Absenteeism and turnover analytics	Analyzes factors contributing to employee absenteeism and turnover rates. This can help in identifying underlying issues and implementing retention strategies.

(*Continued*)

Table 7.1 Different types of HR analytics. (*Continued*)

Types of HR analytics	Description
Health and wellness analytics	Tracks data on the health and well-being of employees, which has an effect on their general well-being and productivity. Metrics on health outcomes, participation in wellness programs, and healthcare expenses may be included.
Predictive workforce analytics for business impact	Predicting how changes in the workforce will affect sales, profitability, or other important business measures may fall under this category.

Learning and development analytics assesses the impact of training programs on skill enhancement [7]. Talent analytics focuses on identifying high-potential employees and facilitating succession planning. Workforce planning and optimization involves aligning the workforce with strategic objectives, analyzing skills gaps, and optimizing costs [34]. Diversity and inclusion analytics seeks to measure and enhance diversity efforts within the organization. Absenteeism and turnover analytics scrutinizes factors contributing to employee attrition and absenteeism. Health and wellness analytics monitors employee well-being and its impact on productivity. Lastly, Predictive workforce analytics foresees business impact through advanced predictive models. These analytics serve as invaluable tools for data-informed HR decisions, aiding in the enhancement of employee engagement, performance, and organizational effectiveness [19].

7.3 Illustrative Case Studies: Transforming HR with Data-Driven Strategies

Source: Author's Compilation

Alt-Text: Table 7.2 displays real-world case studies with success stories of human capital analytics implementation. Examples showcase organizations leveraging data-driven HR strategies for enhanced talent management, recruitment, and workforce optimization across various industries [20]. These case studies provide striking illustrations of how HR practices have shifted and how HR analytics has emerged as a key tool, greatly enhancing corporate effectiveness [1].

Table 7.2 Real-world case studies and success stories of human capital analytics implementation.

Organization	Industry	Implementation focus	Results achieved
Tech Innovators Inc.	Technology	Talent acquisition Optimization	Reduced time-to-hire by 30%, resulting in higher quality hires and cost savings in recruitment efforts. Increased employee retention by 20% due to improved candidate matching.
HealthCare Solutions	Healthcare	Employee engagement enhancement	Using analytics to inform training programs, specific training was implemented, leading to a 15% improvement in employee satisfaction and a 10% increase in productivity.

(*Continued*)

Table 7.2 Real-world case studies and success stories of human capital analytics implementation. (*Continued*)

Organization	Industry	Implementation focus	Results achieved
Manufacturing Experts	Manufacturing	Skills development and training	Utilized analytics to identify skill gaps, leading to a 25% improvement in employee proficiency levels. This resulted in a 12% increase in overall operational efficiency.
Finance Growth Partners	Finance	Diversity and inclusion	Leveraged analytics to track diversity metrics and implement inclusive practices. Achieved a 20% increase in diversity representation across all levels of the organization.
Retail Leaders Inc.	Retail	Workforce planning and optimization	Implemented data-driven workforce planning, resulting in a 15% reduction in labor costs while maintaining optimal staffing levels for peak business hours.

7.4 Strategic Integration: Deploying Data Analytics and Technology Solutions in HR Operations

Below are some crucial realizations and takeaways for effective data-driven human resources:

Sync HR Purposes with Corporate Objectives: Ensure that the organization's overall goals and objectives are directly aligned with HR initiatives and plans. This alignment facilitates the identification of the crucial measures that must be monitored and assessed [21].

- Invest in Tools and Technology: Make use of HR software and tools to collect, analyze, and report data effectively [48]. HRIS (Human Resources Information Systems), analytics programs, and performance management instruments are a few examples of this.
- Apply Predictive Analytics to Planning Strategies: Make use of predictive analytics to project future requirements and trends in HR. This can assist in taking advantage of opportunities and proactively resolving any obstacles [22].
- Safety and Compliance Matter: Make sure that all actions related to data collecting and analysis abide by applicable data protection laws (e.g., GDPR and HIPAA). Protecting the privacy of employees is crucial [44].
- Concentrate on KPIs, or Key Performance Indicators: Determine which HR KPIs are most important to your company and keep an eye on them. These could include performance, engagement, recruitment efficacy, and staff turnover data [25].
- Feedback Loops and Continuous Improvement: Make sure HR projects have feedback loops in place. Evaluate HR initiatives on a regular basis, and change as necessary based on data-driven insights [45].
- Maintain a Balance between Quantitative and Qualitative Data: Although quantitative data offers valuable measures, do not undervalue qualitative insights. Sentiment research and employee feedback help put the figures in context [23].
- Successful Insights Communication: Convert data findings into actionable insights that stakeholders can comprehend with ease. When communicating difficult material, storytelling techniques and visualizations can be quite effective [43].

- Assess Impact on Business Results: Establish a connection between HR activities and more general business results like sales, output, and client satisfaction. This illustrates the real benefit that human resources provide to the company [24].

A continual process of learning, adapting, and improving based on data-driven insights is necessary for effective data-driven HR. It is about using data to make informed decisions that drive positive organizational outcomes and enhance the employee experience.

7.5 Optimizing Talent Acquisition Through Data-Driven Human Capital Analytics

Leveraging human capital analytics for talent acquisition involves using data-driven approaches to make informed decisions about hiring and managing employees. It involves utilizing various metrics and analytics tools to gather and analyze data related to workforce performance, skills, and potential.

The following are important actions to take and things to think about when applying HR analytics to talent acquisition:

- Establish Specific Goals: Clearly state your goals for using HR analytics in talent acquisition. This could entail decreasing the time it takes to fill positions, increasing the caliber of candidates, or maximizing hiring expenses [26].
- Select the Right Metrics: Determine which metrics and key performance indicators (KPIs) are most pertinent to your talent acquisition objectives. These could include candidate satisfaction ratings, turnover rates, cost per hire, quality of hire, and time to fill [25].
- Predictive Analytics: Make use of predictive analytics to find possible high-performing prospects and anticipate future employment needs. This could support the proactive development of a talent pipeline [42].
- Satisfaction and Diversity Analytics: Verify that the diversity and regulatory criteria are met by your talent acquisition initiatives. Track diversity and inclusion metrics by analyzing your hiring data to find any potential biases [28].

- Constant Monitoring and Reporting: To measure the success of your talent acquisition initiatives, set up a regular reporting schedule. This makes it possible for you to promptly modify and enhance [41].
- Cooperation and Communication: Encourage cooperation between hiring managers, HR, and other pertinent parties. Successful application of human capital analytics in talent acquisition requires clear goals and effective communication.
- Stay Abreast of Trends: Keep up-to-date with advancements in HR technology, analytics tools, and industry best practices. Staying informed will help you adapt and evolve your talent acquisition strategies as needed [15].

By leveraging human capital analytics in talent acquisition, organizations can make more data-driven and strategic decisions about their workforce, leading to improved hiring outcomes and overall business performance [28].

7.6 Data-Driven Strategies for Optimal Workforce Performance in Industry 5.0

Source: Author's Compilation
Alt Text- Table 7.3 offers a succinct summary of the essential elements and the specifics that go along with them when utilizing data-driven performance management tactics to traverse the HR frontier in Industry 5.0.

It outlines six main elements, each of which is fully explained and includes particular strategies and techniques. The framework stresses agile, data-informed procedures, from setting precise KPIs aligned with Industry 5.0 objectives to incorporating real-time tracking using modern technologies like IoT and AI. It also emphasizes how important predictive analytics and ongoing feedback loops are to supporting succession planning and staff development [27]. This framework also covers the strategic aspects of attracting and keeping talent. Using proactive retention risk assessments and data-driven recruitment strategies, organizations may increase their ability to draw in, nurture, and keep great people [40]. This all-encompassing strategy not only raises the bar for performance management but also equips businesses to handle the complex issues raised by Industry 5.0, setting them up for long-term success and innovation in the dynamic workplace [14].

Table 7.3 Essential elements for succeeding in the hr environment of industry 5.0 with data-driven performance management techniques.

Component	Details
Establishing Key Performance Indicators (KPIs) and Metrics	- Strategic Alignment with Industry 5.0 Goals: - Digital Transformation Metrics: Reflect progress in adopting advanced technologies. - Innovation and Agility Metrics: Measure adaptability and innovation culture. - Data-Driven Objectives: - Quantifiable Metrics: Ensure measurability of KPIs based on reliable data sources. - Predictive Analytics for Performance Forecasting.
Real-Time Performance Tracking and Continuous Feedback	- Integration of Technology for Real-Time Tracking: - IoT-Enabled Workplaces: Utilize IoT for real-time monitoring. - AI-Enhanced Monitoring Tools: Analyze data for instant insights. - Continuous Feedback Loops: AI-Powered Feedback Systems: Provide customized comments. - 360-Level Feedback Using AI Analysis: Offer insightful information.
Predictive Analytics for Performance Improvement and Talent Development	- Data-Driven Insights for Talent Management: - Skill Gap Analysis: Forecast future skill requirements. - Workforce Optimization: - Demand Forecasting: Predict future workforce needs. - Performance-Based Resource Allocation
Ethical and Compliance Metrics	- Morality and Compliance: - Ethical Behavior Metrics: Keep an eye on conformity to moral principles. Metrics for Data Security and Privacy: Monitor adherence to data protection laws.
Employee-Centric Data Utilization	- Personalized Development Plans: - AI-Driven Learning Recommendations: Suggest personalized learning paths. - Tailored Coaching Strategies: Customize coaching based on performance data.
Strategic Talent Acquisition and Retention	- Data-Driven Recruitment: - Skills Matching: Use analytics to match candidate skills with job requirements. - Retention Risk Analysis: Predict employees at risk of leaving for proactive retention efforts.

7.7 Engage and Retain: Data-Driven Success

Maintaining top talent and fostering high levels of employee engagement are critical to organizational success in today's cutthroat business environment. Utilizing advanced data-driven strategies, particularly predictive analytics, offers a powerful means to achieve this goal. Utilizing advanced algorithms and historical data, firms may make well-informed decisions to improve employee satisfaction and encourage long-term commitment [50].

Predictive Analytics in Employee Engagement:
Utilizing statistical algorithms and machine learning methods, predictive analytics is a tool for forecasting future occurrences and identifying trends in employee engagement. Predictive models identify early warning signs and provide actionable recommendations for intervention by using historical data on employee behavior, performance, and satisfaction [29].

Customized and Individualized Interventions:
Customized recommendation generation is one of predictive analytics' main benefits. By comprehending the distinct characteristics, preferences, and work practices of every individual, establishments can tailor treatments to address specific requirements. In light of each employee's unique profile, predictive algorithms, for example, can suggest tailored work schedules, mentorship possibilities, or training programs [30].

Identifying and Reducing the Risk of Turnover:
Predictive analytics can be used to identify workers who may have a higher likelihood of leaving the organization. Companies can proactively manage their personnel pool by considering factors like work satisfaction, performance patterns, and external market conditions. This can mean offering opportunities for career progression, changing benefit packages, or providing greater support and recognition [2].

Improving the Worker Experience:
Predictive analytics keeps workers from disengaging and leaving, all while improving their entire work experience. By identifying areas where employees may have challenges or where improvements could be made, organizations can implement targeted initiatives. This could be addressing elements that affect job satisfaction, offering resources for skill development, or streamlining work procedures [12].

Measuring Impact and Iterative Improvement:
Utilizing data-driven strategies for employee engagement and retention allows organizations to track the impact of interventions over time [39]. By monitoring key metrics such as retention rates, employee satisfaction scores, and productivity levels, organizations can assess the effectiveness of their initiatives [38]. This data-driven feedback loop enables continuous refinement of strategies for ongoing improvement [13].

7.8 Navigating Complexities: Challenges and Strategic Solutions in Deploying Human Capital Analytics

Source: Author's Compilation
AltText- Table 7.4 summarizes challenges and solutions in implementing human capital analytics. Challenges include data quality, privacy compliance, skills gaps, system integration, metric definition, change management, cultural shift, insights utilization, continuous improvement, and ROI measurement. Corresponding solutions are provided for each challenge.

Table 7.4 outlines challenges and corresponding solutions in the implementation of human capital analytics. Challenges range from data quality and privacy compliance to skill gaps and change management [30]. The

Table 7.4 Challenges and strategic solutions in deploying human capital analytics.

Challenges	Solutions
Data quality and availability	- Invest in data cleaning and validation processes. - Ensure integration of HR systems. - Regularly audit and verify data accuracy.
Skills and expertise	- Provide training and upskilling opportunities for HR professionals and data analysts. - Consider hiring data specialists or consultants.
Integration of HR systems	- Invest in integrated HR software solutions or middleware platforms. - Centralize data for a unified view of the workforce.

(Continued)

Table 7.4 Challenges and strategic solutions in deploying human capital analytics. (*Continued*)

Challenges	Solutions
Defining relevant metrics	- Collaborate with business leaders to define clear KPIs aligned with organizational goals. - Focus on metrics impacting business performance.
Change management	- Highlight the advantages of human capital analytics. - Include important parties in the process. - Offer assistance and training to ensure a seamless transition.
Cultural shift towards data-driven decision-making	- Showcase success stories and the value of analytics. - Recognize and reward data-driven achievements.
Interpreting and acting on insights	- Train HR professionals to interpret analytics results. - Provide actionable recommendations based on insights.
Continuous improvement	- Regularly review and update metrics and processes. - Stay updated with industry best practices and emerging technologies.
Measuring ROI of human capital analytics	- To gauge the effect of analytics on HR and business outcomes, define precise measures. - Highlight success stories that are connected to financial gains.

provided solutions encompass strategies such as data validation processes, compliance measures, training and upskilling, system integration, KPI definition, and cultural shift promotion. Additionally, the table addresses interpreting insights, continuous improvement, and measuring ROI for effective implementation of human capital analytics within organizations [31].

7.9 Emerging Technological Solutions: AI and Machine Learning in HR Optimization

Advancements in AI (artificial intelligence) and machine learning are poised to revolutionize the field of human resources (HR) by optimizing various aspects of HR functions [3]. Here are some key areas where AI and machine learning are making significant strides in HR optimization:

Recruitment and Talent Acquisition:

- Resume Screening: Using pre-set criteria, AI-powered algorithms may evaluate applications and resumes to find the most qualified applicants. This expedites the first screening process and ensures a more successful shortlisting of possibilities.
- Hiring Predictively: Based on past data and performance metrics, machine learning algorithms can forecast a candidate's chances of succeeding in a specific role [49].

Employee Onboarding and Training:

- Customized Orientation: AI has the ability to customize the onboarding processes for new employees based on their roles, skill sets, and preferences. This ensures a smoother assimilation within the organization.
- Training Suggestions: Machine learning algorithms can provide employees with individualized training and development plans based on their performance reviews and career goals [32].

Employee Engagement and Retention:

- Emotional Diagnostics: Surveys, social media interactions, and employee feedback can all be analyzed by AI systems to determine general employee attitudes. This aids in pinpointing problem areas and implementing preventative actions to increase participation [11].
- Analysis of Predictive Turnover: Certain employees have a higher chance of quitting the company, and machine learning algorithms can identify them. This enables HR to put retention plans into place and take preventative action.

Planning and Optimizing the Workforce:

- Analysis of Skills Gaps: AI is able to evaluate the workforce's present skill level and pinpoint any skill gaps that need to be filled through hiring or training [37].

- Equilibrium Workload Algorithms for machine learning can assess workloads between departments and teams to guarantee a more fair allocation of duties [36].

Inclusion and Diversification:

- Identification and Reduction of Biases: AI can support a more diverse and inclusive workforce by assisting in the identification and addressing of biases in hiring and performance reviews.
- Analytics of Diversification: Machine learning can offer insights into diversity measures, enabling businesses to monitor their progress and establish strategic diversity objectives.

Reports and Analytics for HR:

- HR Changes Predictive Analytics: AI can help firms take pre-emptive measures by analyzing past HR data to forecast future trends.
- NLP, or Natural Language Processing: NLP can be used to glean insightful information from surveys, written comments, and other text-based sources [33].

Recent advances in AI and machine learning are improving the entire employee experience in firms by simplifying HR procedures and facilitating more data-driven decision-making [10].

7.10 Conclusion

In summary, a key component of Industry 5.0's revolutionary environment is the incorporation of human capital analytics. This paradigm change represents a turning point in the development of workforce management since it redefines organizational performance by combining state-of-the-art technologies with a highly skilled workforce. This conversation has demonstrated how important data-driven strategies are for effectively navigating this area. By putting in place real-time tracking and continuous feedback mechanisms, utilizing predictive analytics for talent development, and creating definite KPIs that are in line with Industry 5.0

objectives, organizations can reach previously unheard-of levels of performance and innovation.

Moreover, this framework serves as a strategic road map and charts the course for labor management's future. The data-driven tactics outlined here will serve as an essential guide for businesses as they continue to adapt to the rapid advancement of technology. By placing equal emphasis on qualitative characteristics like ethical behavior and compliance in addition to quantitative indicators, organizations can create a work environment that encourages creativity and integrity. With this plan in hand, businesses are ready to take the lead in transforming the nature of work in the future and prosper despite the challenges posed by Industry 5.0. By carefully implementing these concepts, organizations can acquire a competitive edge and set new standards for excellence in the international professional arena.

References

1. Abellán-Sevilla, A.J. and Ortiz-de-Urbina-Criado, M., Smart human resource analytics for happiness management. *J. Manage. Dev.*, 42, 26, 514–525, 2023.
2. Alreahi, M., Bujdosó, Z., Kabil, M., Akaak, A., Benkó, K.F., Setioningtyas, W.P., Dávid, L.D., Green human resources management in the hotel industry: A systematic review. *Sustainability*, *15*, 1, 99, 2022.
3. Ammirato, S., Felicetti, A.M., Linzalone, R., Corvello, V., Kumar, S., Still our most important asset: A systematic review on human resource management in the midst of the fourth industrial revolution. *J. Innov. Knowl.*, *8*, 3, 100403, 2023.
4. Avrahami, D., Pessach, D., Singer, G., Chalutz Ben-Gal, H., A human resources analytics and machine-learning examination of turnover: implications for theory and practice. *Int. J. Manpow.*, *43*, 6, 1405–1424, 2022.
5. Bahuguna, P.C., Srivastava, R., Tiwari, S., Human resources analytics: where do we go from here? *Benchmarking: Int. J.*, 31, 2, 640–668, 2024.
6. Bauer, T., Erdogan, B., Caughlin, D., Truxillo, D., *Human resource management: People, data, and analytics*, Sage Publications, 2023, https://www.bauer.uh.edu/departments/management-leadership/docs/syllabi/MANA-7380-People-Analytics_Spring-2022_Abbott.pdf.
7. Belizón, M.J. and Kieran, S., Human resources analytics: A legitimacy process. *Hum. Resour. Manage. J.*, *32*, 3, 603–630, 2022.
8. Bhattacharya, S., Smark, C., Mir, M., Covid 19: Social, financial and economic implications. *Australas. Account. Bus. Finance J.*, *15*, 1, 1–4, 2021.
9. Bi, Y. and Tang, M., Correspondence Model of Human Resource Management and Marketing Based on Genetic Algorithm. *Mobile Inf. Syst.*, *2022*, 1–15, 2022.

10. Bonilla-Chaves, E.F. and Palos-Sánchez, P.R., Exploring the evolution of human resource analytics: a bibliometric study. *Behav. Sci.*, *13*, 3, 244, 2023.
11. Bouzakhem, N., Farmanesh, P., Zargar, P., Ramadan, M., Baydoun, H., Daouk, A., Mouazen, A., Rebuilding the Workplace in the Post-Pandemic Age through Human Capital Development Programs: A Moderated Mediation Model. *Adm. Sci.*, *13*, 7, 164, 2023.
12. Brolan, C.E., Körver, S., Phillips, G., Sharma, D., Herron, L.M., O'Reilly, G., Cox, M., Lessons from the frontline: The COVID-19 pandemic emergency care experience from a human resource perspective in the Pacific region. *Lancet Reg. Health–West. Pac.*, *25*, 1–18, 2022.
13. Chang, E., Chin, H., Lee, J.W., Pre-crisis commitment human resource management and employees' attitudes in a global pandemic: The role of trust in the government. *Hum. Resour. Manage.*, *61*, 3, 373–387, 2022.
14. Chatterjee, S., Chaudhuri, R., Vrontis, D., Siachou, E., Examining the dark side of human resource analytics: an empirical investigation using the privacy calculus approach. *Int. J. Manpow.*, *43*, 1, 52–74, 2022.
15. Cho, W., Choi, S., Choi, H., Human Resources Analytics for Public Personnel Management: Concepts, Cases, and Caveats. *Adm. Sci.*, *13*, 2, 41, 2023.
16. Chowdhury, S., Dey, P., Joel-Edgar, S., Bhattacharya, S., Rodriguez-Espindola, O., Abadie, A., Truong, L., Unlocking the value of artificial intelligence in human resource management through AI capability framework. *Hum. Resour. Manage. Rev.*, *33*, 1, 100899, 2023.
17. Cicea, C. and Marinescu, C., Bibliometric analysis of foreign direct investment and economic growth relationship. A research agenda. *J. Bus. Econ. Manage.*, *22*, 2, 445–466, 2021.
18. Di Nardo, M., Boldrini, F., Broccati, F., Cancani, F., Satta, T., Stoppa, F., Choong, K., The liberAction project: Implementation of a pediatric liberation bundle to screen delirium, reduce benzodiazepine sedation, and provide early mobilization in a human resource-limited pediatric intensive care unit. *Front. Pediatr.*, *9*, 788997, 2021.
19. Downes, P.E., Harris, T.B., Allen, D.G., Getting from valid to useful: End user modifiability and human capital analytics implementation in selection. *Hum. Resour. Manage.*, 62, 6, 917–932, 2023.
20. Elshaer, I.A., Azazz, A.M., Fayyad, S., Green human resources and innovative performance in small-and medium-sized tourism enterprises: a mediation model using PLS-SEM data analysis. *Mathematics*, *11*, 3, 711, 2023.
21. Faisal, S., Twenty-Years Journey of Sustainable Human Resource Management Research: A Bibliometric Analysis. *Adm. Sci.*, *13*, 6, 139, 2023.
22. Garg, J., Singh, A.K., Gupta, A., Human capital in knowledge-based firms: Re-creating value post-pandemic. *Hum. Syst. Manage.*, (Preprint), 42, 6, 593–607, 2023, 1–15, 2022.
23. Huang, X., Yang, F., Zheng, J., Feng, C., Zhang, L., Personalized human resource management via HR analytics and artificial intelligence: Theory and implications. *Asia Pac. Manage. Rev.*, 28, 4, 598–610, 2023.

24. Kasekende, F., Nasiima, S., Otengei, S.O., Strategic human resource practices, emotional exhaustion and OCB: the mediator role of person-organization fit. *J. Organ. Eff. People Perform.*, *7*, 3, 275–295, 2020.
25. Khang, A., Gupta, S.K., Dixit, C.K., Somani, P., Data-Driven Application of Human Capital Management Databases, Big Data, and Data Mining, in: *Designing Workforce Management Systems for Industry 4.0*, pp. 105–120, CRC Press, 2023, https://www.taylorfrancis.com/chapters/edit/10.1201/978 1003357070-7/data-driven-application-human-capital-management-databases-big-data-data-mining-alex-khang-shashi-kant-gupta-chandra-kumar-dixit-parin-somani.
26. Kiran, V.S., Shanmugam, V., Raju, R.K., Kanagasabapathy, J.R., Impact of human capital management on organizational performance with the mediation effect of human resource analytics. *Int. J. Prof. Bus. Rev.*, *7*, 3, e0667–e0667, 2022.
27. Kot, S., Hussain, H.I., Bilan, S., Haseeb, M., Mihardjo, L.W., The role of artificial intelligence recruitment and quality to explain the phenomenon of employer reputation. *J. Bus. Econ. Manage.*, *22*, 4, 867–883, 2021.
28. Larsson, A.S. and Edwards, M.R., Insider econometrics meets people analytics and strategic human resource management. *Int. J. Hum. Resour. Manage.*, *33*, 12, 2373–2419, 2022.
29. Lázaro Lázaro, C., People Analytics implementation in the Human Resources department, 2022.
30. Liu, D., Wang, G., Sun, C., Majeed, M.T., Andlib, Z., An analysis of the effects of human capital on green growth: effects and transmission channels. *Environ. Sci. Pollut. Res.*, *30*, 4, 10149–10156, 2023.
31. Madhani, P.M., Human Resources Analytics: Leveraging Human Resources for Enhancing Business Performance. *Compens. Benefits Rev.*, *55*, 1, 31–45, 2023.
32. Margherita, A., Human resources analytics: A systematization of research topics and directions for future research. *Hum. Resour. Manage. Rev.*, *32*, 2, 100795, 2022.
33. Mehrotra, R. and Yadav, K., Breast cancer in India: Present scenario and the challenges ahead. *World J. Clin. Oncol.*, *13*, 3, 209, 2022.
34. Minhas, N., Gurav, Y.K., Sambhare, S., Potdar, V., Choudhary, M.L., Bhardwaj, S.D., Abraham, P., Cost-analysis of real time RT-PCR test performed for COVID-19 diagnosis at India's national reference laboratory during the early stages of pandemic mitigation. *PLoS One*, *18*, 1, e0277867, 2023.
35. Mohiuddin, M., Hosseini, E., Faradonbeh, S.B., Sabokro, M., Achieving human resource management sustainability in universities. *Int. J. Environ. Res. Public Health*, *19*, 2, 928, 2022.
36. Priyanka, R., Ravindran, K., Sankaranarayanan, B., Ali, S.M., A fuzzy DEMATEL decision modeling framework for identifying key human resources challenges in start-up companies: Implications for sustainable development. *Decis. Anal. J.*, *6*, 100192, 2023.

37. Qamar, Y. and Samad, T.A., Human resource analytics: a review and bibliometric analysis. *Pers. Rev.*, *51*, 1, 251–283, 2022.
38. Samek, L., Squicciarini, M., Cammeraat, E., The human capital behind AI: Jobs and skills demand from online job postings, 2021.
39. Samoliuk, N., Bilan, Y., Mishchuk, H., Vocational training costs and economic benefits: exploring the interactions. *J. Bus. Econ. Manage.*, *22*, 6, 1476–1491, 2021.
40. Samson, K. and Bhanugopan, R., Strategic human capital analytics and organisation performance: The mediating effects of managerial decision-making. *J. Bus. Res.*, *144*, 637–649, 2022.
41. Serenko, A., The human capital management perspective on quiet quitting: recommendations for employees, managers, and national policymakers. *J. Knowl. Manage.*, 28, 1, 27–43, 2023.
42. Soltis, S.M., Methot, J.R., Gittell, J.H., Harris, T.B., Leveraging relational analytics in human resource research and practice. *Hum. Resour. Manage.*, 2023.
43. Štaffenová, N. and Kucharčíková, A., Digitalization in the Human Capital Management. *Systems*, *11*, 7, 337, 2023.
44. Valecha, N., Transforming human resource management with HR analytics: A critical Analysis of Benefits and challenges. *Int. J. Global Acad. Sci. Res.*, *1*, 2, 56–66, 2022.
45. Vithana, K., Jayasekera, R., Choudhry, T., Baruch, Y., Human Capital resource as cost or investment: A market-based analysis. *Int. J. Hum. Resour. Manage.*, *34*, 6, 1213–1245, 2023.
46. Vukmirović, D.V., Bolbotinović, Ž.Z., Comić, T.Z., Stanojević, N.D., HR Analytics: Serbian Perspective, in: *Serbian International Conference on Applied Artificial Intelligence*, pp. 75–89, Springer International Publishing, Cham, 2022, May.
47. Wahyoedi, S., Suherlan, S., Rijal, S., Azzaakiyyah, H.K., Ausat, A.M.A., Implementation of Information Technology in Human Resource Management. *Al-Buhuts*, *19*, 1, 300–318, 2023.
48. Wang, J., Dagvadorj, A., Kim, H.S., Research trends of human resources management in hotel industry: Evidence from South Korea by semantic network analysis. *Culi. Sci. Hos. Res.*, *27*, 9, 68–78, 2021.
49. Xie, H. and Lau, T.C., Evidence-Based Green Human Resource Management: A Systematic Literature Review. *Sustainability*, *15*, 14, 10941, 2023.
50. Xu, J. and Liu, F., Nexus between intellectual capital and financial performance: An investigation of Chinese manufacturing industry. *J. Bus. Econ. Manage.*, *22*, 1, 217–235, 2021.
51. Zvarikova, K., Cug, J., Hamilton, S., Virtual Human Resource Management in the Metaverse: Immersive Work Environments, Data Visualization Tools and Algorithms, and Behavioral Analytics. *Psychosociological Issues Hum. Resour. Manage.*, *10*, 1, 7–20, 2022.

8

Mastering the Art of HR Data Collection and Management Techniques

Deepa Gupta[1], Mukul Gupta[1*], Priti Rai[2], Karishma Sharma[1] and Parth Mukul Gupta[3]

[1]*GL Bajaj Institute of Management, Greater Noida, Uttar Pradesh, India*
[2]*College of Vocational Studies, University of Delhi, New Delhi, Delhi, India*
[3]*Birla Institute of Technology & Sciences, Pilani, Rajasthan, India*

Abstract

In the contemporary organizational landscape, sensible HR data collection and management are essential for driving key choices and supporting organizational development. This part investigates the general example of administering HR data techniques, starting with the fundamental significance of HR data and the format of its collection and management. It moves toward the various kinds of HR data, their sources, and the meaning of data confirmation and consistency. The part analyses both manual and undeniable level data collection techniques, including HR data designs (HRIS), online assessments, and versatile applications, focusing on best practices for precision and consistency. It further assesses HRIS by offering seminars on picking, coordinating, and refreshing these frameworks to additionally foster HR works. Data quality and exactness are looked out for through techniques like data support, standard reviews, and separating frameworks. The part additionally covers best practices for data breaking points and security, separating cloud and on-premise designs, and affirming consistency with rules like GDPR and CCPA. HR assessment is presented, featuring devices, programming, and techniques for dismantling key HR assessments and KPIs. The part shows the way that utilizing HR data can edify game plans, systems, and dynamics through setting focused assessments and best practices. At long last, it expects future models in HR data management, zeroing in on arising progresses like artificial information, artificial knowledge, and enormous data. It takes a gander at the making position of HR in computerized change and offers suspicions for the conceivable

**Corresponding author*: prof.dr.mukulgupta@gmail.com

Deepa Gupta, Mukul Gupta, Pawan Budhwar, Jim Westerman, Rajesh Kumar Dhanaraj and Balamurugan Balusamy (eds.) Human Capital Analytics: Exploring the HR Spectrum in Industry 5.0, (165–200) © 2025 Scrivener Publishing LLC

predetermination of HR data collection and management. This part fills in as an all-out partner for HR experts' importance to overpower data collection and management techniques, giving the data and contraptions essential to research and win in a data-driven HR climate.

***Keywords*:** HR data, data privacy, data compliance, data audits, GDPR, CCPA, HR analytics, HR metrics

Introduction

In the present quickly developing business landscape, the compelling collection and management of HR (HR) data have become urgent for associations planning to remain serious and deft. HR data envelop a huge swath of data, going from representative socioeconomics and execution measurements to finance subtleties and advantages of organization. These data fill in as the spine for vital direction, assisting associations with advancing their labor force, improving efficiency, and guaranteeing consistency with different guidelines [1].

Excelling in HR data collection and management is not only a specialized undertaking but an essential objective. Associations that succeed in this space are better situated to tackle the force of data-driven bits of knowledge, cultivating a culture of ceaseless improvement and development [3]. The capacity to precisely gather, make due, and break down HR data empowers organizations to distinguish patterns, address issues proactively, and settle on informed choices that line up with their drawn-out objectives [6].

Notwithstanding, the excursion toward dominating HR data techniques is full of difficulties. Data security concerns, the requirement for data exactness, and the joining of different data sources are only a couple of the obstacles HR experts should explore (Lord, 2018). Besides, the consistently expanding volume of data, combined with progressions in innovation, requires a strong and versatile way to deal with HR data management [4].

In this part, we will investigate the essential parts of HR data collection and management, as well as different techniques, devices, and best practices. This part talks about the significance of data quality and exactness, the job of HR data frameworks (HRIS), and the arising patterns that are forming the fate of HR data management [7]. By dominating these techniques, HR experts can open the maximum capacity of their data, driving improved results for their associations and their labor force. Eventually, this section means to give an exhaustive manual for HR experts looking to improve their abilities in data collection and management.

Importance of HR Data in Modern Organizations

In the quick-making landscape of present-day business, data have arisen as an essential resource for the course, significant status, and valuable practicality. HR (HR) data, in particular, anticipates a squeezing part in forming the labor force parts and overall organizational success. Coming up next are two or three key motivations driving why HR data are imperative for contemporary affiliations:

1. **Informed Decision-Making**: HR data give a verifiable premise to settling on informed choices in regard to recruiting, advancements, representative turn of events, and asset designation. By breaking down data on representative execution, abilities, and vocation desires, HR experts can pursue key choices that line up with organizational objectives and drive efficiency [3].
2. **Enhanced Talent Acquisition and Retention**: With extensive HR data, associations can recognize the best enlistment channels, grasp the characteristics of high-performing workers, and design their employment processes as needed. Furthermore, data on worker commitment, fulfillment, and turnover rates help HR groups foster maintenance techniques that diminish weakening and improve labor force solidness [6].
3. **Performance Management**: HR data empower associations to precisely track and measure representative execution. Execution measurements, criticism, and examination data assist in fixing entertainers and those requiring improvement. This works with the execution of designated preparing programs, execution improvement plans, and progression arranging, guaranteeing a ceaseless pipeline of proficient pioneers.
4. **Improved Employee Experience**: Understanding representative requirements and worries through HR data on commitment overviews, input structures, and post-employment surveys permit associations to establish a positive workplace. Resolving issues connected with work environment culture,

advantages, and balance between fun and serious activities can essentially further develop representative fulfillment and dependability [1].

5. **Strategic Workforce Planning**: HR data uphold long-haul labor force arranging by giving bits of knowledge into labor force socioeconomics, abilities holes, and future work needs. This assists associations with expecting changes in the work market, planning for future ability needs, and fostering procedures to construct or obtain fundamental abilities and capacities [4].
6. **Compliance and Risk Management**: Keeping up with exact HR data guarantees that associations follow legitimate and administrative prerequisites connected with work regulations, equivalent business open doors, and data security. This limits the gamble of legitimate debates and punishments. Also, HR data can help in distinguishing potential dangers connected with representative lead, well-being, and work environment occurrences [7].
7. **Cost Efficiency**: Data-driven HR rehearses add to cost productivity by improving HR cycles like enrolment, preparation, and finance management. By dissecting cost data, associations can distinguish areas of shortcomings and execute measures to diminish pointless costs while amplifying the profit from interest in human resources [3].
8. **Diversity and Inclusion**: HR data on representative socioeconomics and work environment variety can be utilized to advance comprehensive practices and screen the adequacy of variety drives. By dissecting these data, associations can recognize variations, put forth a variety of objectives, and track progress toward making a fairer and comprehensive work environment [2].
9. **Enhanced Employee Development**: Data on representative abilities, vocation movement, and learning inclinations empower HR to configure customized advancement programs that line up with both individual desires and organizational requirements. This encourages a culture of persistent learning and improvement, upgrading generally speaking worker skills and occupation fulfillment [1].
10. **Competitive Advantage**: Associations that successfully bridle HR data gain the upper hand by utilizing bits of knowledge to improve their ability management systems. Data-driven HR

rehearses lead to better recruiting choices, higher representative commitment, and work on organizational execution, all of which add to a more grounded market position [3].

To put it plainly, HR data are an integral asset that drives various advantages for current associations. From vital independent direction and ability management to consistency and cost-effectiveness, the significance of HR data could not possibly be more significant. By putting resources into powerful HR data collection and management frameworks, associations can open the maximum capacity of their labor force and make maintainable development and progress in a cutthroat business climate.

Overview of HR Data Collection and Management

In the cutting-edge business landscape, human asset (HR) data collection and management anticipate a basic part in molding persuading HR techniques and driving organizational achievement. This system investigates the importance, techniques, and best exhibitions of HR data collection and management, giving snippets of data into how affiliations can use data to additionally foster HR capacities [7].

Data Collection Techniques

1. **Manual Data Collection:**
    - **Interviews and Surveys:** Gather subjective data through organized or unstructured meetings and studies. This strategy gives top-to-bottom experiences however can be tedious and inclined to human mistakes [4].
    - **Paper Forms and Manual Entry:** Customary methodology including actual structures. While straightforward, it frequently prompts issues with data precision and capacity [5].
2. **Digital Data Collection:**
    - **HR Information Systems (HRIS):** Mechanized frameworks that smooth out data collection, stockpiling, and management. HRIS stages offer elements like representative self-administration entries, computerized work processes, and ongoing data access [1].

- **Online Surveys and Forms:** Productive method for social occasion to gather a lot of data rapidly. Online instruments guarantee higher exactness and simplicity of examination [4].
- **Mobile Data Collection Apps:** Empower data collection in a hurry, upgrading openness and comfort for both HR experts and representatives [7].

Data Management Systems

Viable management of HR data requires strong frameworks that guarantee data trustworthiness, security, and availability:

1. **HR Information Systems (HRIS):**
   - **Overview:** Concentrated stages that oversee representative data, smooth out HR processes, and create reports [1].
   - **Selection:** Picking the right HRIS includes surveying organizational necessities, financial plans, adaptability, and mixing capacities with other business frameworks [6].
   - **Integration:** Consistent combination with different frameworks (e.g., finance and execution management) guarantees a firm data biological system, lessening redundancies and further developing data precision.
2. **Data Quality and Accuracy:**
   - **Importance:** Excellent data are vital for dependable investigation and independent direction.
   - **Common Issues:** Data passage blunders, copy records, and obsolete data are normal difficulties.
   - **Techniques for Accuracy:** Carry out data approval rules, lead normal reviews, and layout data administration strategies to keep up with data respectability.
3. **Data Storage and Security:**
   - **Best Practices:** Store data in a solid, open configuration. Think about distributed storage for versatility and cost viability.
   - **Security Measures:** Execute solid access controls, encryption, and standard security reviews to safeguard delicate representative data.

- **Compliance:** Comply with data insurance guidelines like GDPR and CCPA, guaranteeing straightforward data taking care of practices and protecting worker security.

Leveraging HR Data for Decision-Making

HR data, when dissected really, can give noteworthy experiences that drive organizational development:

- **HR Analytics:** Use apparatuses and programming for spellbinding, prescient, and prescriptive examination. Key measurements incorporate worker turnover, non-appearance rates, and execution scores.
- **Data-Driven Decisions:** Contextual investigations exhibit the effect of data-driven HR systems on further developing enlistment, improving representative commitment, and streamlining labor force arranging.

Future Trends

The eventual fate of HR data collection and management is formed by rising innovations and advancing business needs:

- **AI and Machine Learning:** Computerization of data examination, prescient displaying, and customized representative encounters.
- **Big Data:** Utilizing huge datasets for more profound bits of knowledge and vital preparation.
- **Digital Transformation:** Proceeded with a combination of trend-setting innovations to smooth out HR works and improve data-driven direction.

Excelling in HR data collection and management is fundamental for current associations looking to thrive in a cutthroat climate. By embracing best practices and utilizing trend-setting innovations, HR experts can change data into an essential resource, driving organizational achievement and encouraging a data-driven culture.

Objectives and Benefits of Mastering HR Data Techniques

Objectives

1. **Enhance Decision-Making Processes**
   - One of the essential targets of dominating HR data techniques is to further develop dynamics inside the HR capability. By gathering and breaking down precise data, HR experts can pursue informed choices that line up with organizational objectives [21].
2. **Optimize Workforce Management**
   - Viable HR data techniques help in figuring out labor force elements. This incorporates following representative execution, participation, and efficiency, taking into account better management and advancement of HR [12].
3. **Improve Employee Experience**
   - By utilizing HR data, associations can recognize patterns and examples in worker fulfillment and commitment. This understanding empowers the advancement of designated drives to further develop the general worker experience [9].
4. **Ensure Compliance and Reduce Risk**
   - Legitimate data management guarantees that associations agree with different work regulations and guidelines. It additionally helps in distinguishing potential dangers connected with representative data breaks and executing measures to alleviate them [20].
5. **Support Strategic Planning**
   - HR data give important experiences that help vital preparation. This incorporates labor force arranging, the ability to obtain systems, and recognizing expertise holes inside the association [22].
6. **Measure and Enhance HR Effectiveness**
   - Dominating HR data techniques considers the estimation of HR viability through different measurements and KPIs. This empowers constant improvement of HR cycles and drives [13].

Benefits

1. **Increased Efficiency**
   - Automating data collection and management processes lessens the time and effort expected for manual data handling. This increases overall HR proficiency and permits HR experts to focus on more essential errands [18].
2. **Data-Driven Pieces of Information**
   - HR data techniques give significant pieces of information that can provoke a better route. Data-driven pieces of information help in distinctive examples, expecting future prerequisites, and seeking after informed fundamental decisions [14].
3. **Enhanced Specialist Upkeep**
   - By separating data associated with specialist turnover and upkeep, affiliations can cultivate techniques to additionally foster delegate satisfaction and reduce consistent misfortune rates. This prompts an all the more consistent and associated with the workforce [15].
4. **Improved Capacity Obtainment**
   - Practical data techniques help in perceiving the best focal points for capacity getting, understanding the sufficiency of selection channels, and further fostering the for the most part utilizing process. This results in attracting and holding top capacity [10].
5. **Cost Save Reserves**
   - Streamlined data management processes and further created dynamic leads to cost-saving reserves. This integrates reducing turnover costs, improving enlistment costs, and restricting consistency-related disciplines [17].
6. **Personalized Laborer Progression**
   - HR data techniques consider the distinctive evidence of individual agent characteristics and weaknesses. These data can be used to fit planning and headway activities to meet express specialist needs, redesigning their turn of events and execution [16].
7. **Better Workforce Organizing**
   - Precise and exhaustive HR data enable fruitful workforce orchestrating. Affiliations can expect future staffing needs, plan for movement, and assurance that the ideal people are in the ideal positions with perfect timing [19].

8. **Enhanced Organizational Agility**
    - With continuous permission to exact HR data, affiliations can answer quickly to changes in the business environment. This deftness is pressing for keeping an advantage and changing in accordance with creating financial circumstances [11].
9. **Greater Straightforwardness and Obligation**
    - Convincing HR data management progresses straightforwardness inside the affiliation. Clear and precise data help in thinking about both HR specialists and delegates liable for their exercises and execution [8].
10. **Strategic Course of Action**
    - HR data techniques ensure that HR frameworks are agreed with for the most part business objectives. This game plan maintains the achievement of organizational goals and improves overall business execution [23].

Ruling HR data techniques is major for present-day affiliations hoping to utilize their HR effectively. The objectives and benefits outlined above show the essential work that HR data play in driving organizational accomplishment and achieving an advantage.

Fundamentals of HR Data

Types of HR Data

Human resource (HR) data incorporate a wide collection of data principles for managing an affiliation's workforce effectively. Understanding the different kinds of HR data is imperative for chasing after informed decisions and further developing HR capacities. Key sorts of HR data include:

1. **Employee Economics:**
    - Fundamental data, for instance, name, age, direction, contact nuances, and intimate status.
    - Informational establishment and abilities.
    - Work title, department, and business history [21].
2. **Performance Data:**
    - Execution studies and assessments.
    - Proficiency estimations and key execution markers (KPIs).
    - Getting ready and improvement records [12].

3. **Payroll Data:**
   - Remuneration and pay data.
   - Benefits and pay nuances.
   - Additional time, prizes, and determinations [17].
4. **Attendance and Leave Data:**
   - Participation records and time sheets.
   - Leave changes and history (crippled leave, trip, maternity/paternity leave, etc.) [19].
5. **Employee Responsibility and Satisfaction Data:**
   - Outline results on work satisfaction and responsibility levels.
   - Contribution from post-business overviews.
   - Laborer affirmation and prize program data [9].
6. **Compliance and Legitimate Data:**
   - Records of consistency with work guidelines and rules.
   - Documentation of workspace episodes and prosperity reports.
   - Specialist arrangements and courses of action [20].

Sources of HR Data

HR data can be assembled from various sources, each contributing to remarkable encounters in the workforce. The fundamental wellsprings of HR data include:

1. Internal Structures:

1. HR Data Structures (HRIS): United databases that store thorough specialist data, administer money, and track execution estimations.
2. Adventure Resource Organizing (ERP) Systems: Composed stages that join HR data with other business abilities like cash and stock organization management.
3. Learning Management Structures (LMS): Stages that track specialists getting ready and improvement work out [18].

2. Surveys and Info Instruments:

4. Delegate Studies: Gadgets for social occasion data on laborer satisfaction, responsibility, and organizational culture.
5. Execution Information Designs: Coordinated techniques for get-together execution reviews and sidekick analysis [14].

3. **External Databases:**

6. Work Market Data: Data from worksheets, selection associations, and work market examination contraptions.
7. Benchmarking Data: Industry rules and benchmarks for differentiating HR estimations and various affiliations.
8. Online Diversion and Master Associations: Enco-unters from LinkedIn, Glassdoor, and various stages where agents share calling-related data [10].

Data Privacy and Compliance Considerations

Managing HR data carefully is principal to protecting laborer security and staying aware of authoritative consistency. Key thoughts include:

1. **Data Security:**

9. Security: Ensuring that laborer data are open just to endorsed personnel.
10. Consent: Getting express consent from delegates before social events and dealing with their own data.
11. Data Minimization: Assembling simply the data significant for unequivocal HR capacities to diminish the bet of misuse.

2. **Compliance with Rules:**

12. General Data Protection Rule (GDPR): European affiliation rule that directs the collection, accumulation, and treatment of individual data. It orders straightforwardness, consent, and the choice to get to and right data.
13. California Customer Security Act (CCPA): California state guideline that gives near protections to GDPR, underlining straightforwardness and control over confidential data.
14. Medical Care Portability and Obligation Act (HIPAA): U.S. rule that shields the insurance and security of prosperity data, critical for managing specialist clinical benefits.

3. **Data Security:**

    15. Encryption: Using encryption progressions to shield data during transmission and limit.
    16. Access Controls: Doing position-based permission controls to confine data access considering occupation commitments.
    17. Standard Surveys: Driving irregular audits to ensure consistency with data insurance and security plans.

4. **Incident Response:**

    18. Data Break Shows: Spreading out procedures for noting data breaks, including cautioning requirements and remediation steps.
    19. Planning and Care: Educating delegates on data insurance and security best practices to prevent unapproved access and data breaks.

By sorting out such HR data, their sources, and the meaning of data insurance and consistency, HR specialists can truly administer and utilize these data to assist organizational targets and redesign laborers with encountering.

Data Collection Techniques

Manual Data Collection Methods

Interviews and Studies

Interviews and studies are conventional techniques for data collection that include direct collaboration with workers. In interviews, HR experts pose organized or semi-organized inquiries to assemble subjective bits of knowledge about representative encounters, necessities, and feelings. Reviews, then again, are commonly quantitative and can be circulated to a bigger crowd to gather normalized data. The two techniques are important for acquiring top-to-bottom and setting rich data yet can be tedious and require cautious intent to guarantee unprejudiced and applicable outcomes.

Paper Structures and Manual Passage

Paper structures and manual passages are direct techniques for gathering and recording data. Representatives finish up actual structures with their data, which HR staff then physically goes into bookkeeping sheets or databases. While this technique is straightforward and open, it is inclined to blunders and shortcomings, for example, data passage slip-ups and hardships in overseeing huge volumes of paper-based data. It additionally comes up short on speed and adaptability of advanced strategies.

Computerized Data Collection Strategies

HR Data Frameworks (HRIS)

HR data frameworks (HRIS) are complete advanced stages intended to oversee different HR capabilities, including data collection. HRIS bring together representative data, robotizes data sections, and gives apparatuses for data examination. These frameworks offer elements, for example, representative self-administration entrances, which permit workers to refresh their data straightforwardly, decreasing the managerial weight on HR staff and limiting blunders. By coordinating different HR processes, HRIS upgrades data exactness, streamlines work processes, and supports key independent direction.

Online Studies and Structures

Online studies and structures are successful computerized instruments for social affair data rapidly and effectively. They can be dispersed by means of email or through electronic stages, making it simple to arrive at an enormous number of representatives. These devices frequently accompany features including assistance in breaking down the gathered data. Online overviews guarantee obscurity, empowering genuine reactions, and can be custom-made to explicit necessities with adaptable inquiries and organizations.

Portable Data Collection Applications

Portable data collection applications influence the universality of smartphones to work with data gathering in a hurry. These applications empower representatives to enter data straightforwardly into the framework utilizing their cell phones, which is particularly valuable for remote or field-based workers. Portable applications frequently incorporate elements, for example, disconnected data collection, continuous data synchronizing, and mixing with other HR frameworks, improving adaptability and availability.

Best Practices for Accurate and Reliable Data Collection

1. Define Clear Objectives: Before getting together data, clearly describe the objectives and what you intend to achieve. This ensures that the data collected are appropriate and supportive.
2. Ensure Data Insurance and Mystery: Protect the security and security of delegate data by following data affirmation rules and completing solid well-being endeavors.
3. Use Standardized Procedures: Use standardized data collection techniques and instruments to stay aware of consistency and resolute quality across different datasets.
4. Train Data Finders: Give cautious planning to individuals drawn in with data collection to restrict bungles and assure a consistent strategy.
5. Pilot Testing: Lead pilot preliminary of surveys and data collection instruments to recognize and determine anticipated issues before full-scale sending.
6. Monitor and Review: Regularly screen the data collection cycle and study the data for accuracy and satisfaction. Do therapeutic exercises depend upon the situation?
7. Automate Where Possible: Impact computerization instruments to lessen manual entry missteps and update data accuracy. Computerization can moreover set free HR staff to focus on extra fundamental tasks.
8. Encourage Delegate Participation: Develop a culture of straightforwardness and urge laborers to participate in data collection tries. Get a handle on the importance and benefits of the data being accumulated.
9. Regular Updates: Keep awake with the most recent via completing standard review cycles and engaging delegates to revive their data incidentally.

By solidifying standard and mechanized techniques, and adhering to best practices, affiliations can accumulate careful and reliable HR data that supports informed bearing and key arrangement.

Data Management Systems

Powerful data management frameworks are vital for current HR departments to deal with huge measures of worker data productively. One of the most basic parts of an HR data management framework is the HRIS (Human Asset Data Framework).

Overview of HRIS (Human Resource Information Systems)

HRIS is a product arrangement intended to oversee human asset data and cycles. It fills in as a focal store for worker data, working with different HR works like enlistment, onboarding, finance, execution management, and advantages organization. An HRIS robotizes routine errands, diminishes manual blunders, and gives continuous data access, making HR tasks more effective and vital.

Key benefits of HRIS include:

- Incorporated data management
- Further developed data exactness and consistency
- Upgraded announcing and investigation capacities
- Smoothed out HR cycles and work processes
- Better consistency with legitimate and administrative prerequisites

Selecting the Right HRIS for Your Organization

Picking the right HRIS incorporates a mindful idea of your affiliation's outstanding necessities and requirements. A guide to help you maneuver toward picking the best HRIS are:

1. Assess Your Necessities: Perceive the particular HR capacities you need to robotize and the issues you intend to settle with an HRIS. Think about factors, for instance, the size of your affiliation, the multifaceted design of your HR processes, and your monetary arrangement.
2. Define Your Necessities: Make a once-over of must-have components and functionalities. This could consolidate modules for finance, benefits association, time and participation following, enlistment, execution management, and delegate self-organization.
3. Research and Shortlist Dealers: Lead factual studying to perceive HRIS vendors that offer courses of action agreed

with your necessities. Grasp studies, search for recommendations, and contemplate components and assessing.

4. Request Demos and Fundamentals: Organize product presentations and sales starter induction to shortlisted HRIS game plans. Survey the UI, convenience, customization decisions, and overall functionality.
5. Evaluate Blend Limits: Assure that the HRIS can arrange impeccably with your ongoing business structures, such as accounting programming, CRM, and other undertaking applications.
6. Consider Flexibility: Pick an HRIS that can be created with your affiliation. It should oblige growing data volumes and additional clients without compromising execution.
7. Review Assistance and Planning: Study the shipper's client care, getting ready undertakings, and resources. A strong, sincere, and steady organization is essential for smooth execution and constant upkeep.
8. Analyze Cost and Return for Cash Contributed: Ponder the outright cost of ownership, including approving charges, execution costs, and upkeep costs. Survey the conceivable benefit from the hypothesis through predominant adequacy and proficiency.

Integrating HRIS with Other Business Systems

For an HRIS to convey the most extreme worth, it should coordinate consistently with other business frameworks. Coordination guarantees data consistency across the association, decreases manual data section, and upgrades by and large functional effectiveness. Key coordination focuses include:

1. Payroll Frameworks: Coordinating HRIS with finance programming mechanizes finance handling, guarantees precise compensation estimations, and improves charge detailing.
2. Finance and Bookkeeping: Mix with monetary frameworks empowers effective management of spending plans, cost following, and monetary detailing connected with HR exercises.
3. Customer Relationship Management (CRM): Associating HRIS with CRM frameworks adjusts HR techniques to deals and client support objectives, improving general business execution.

4. Learning Management Frameworks (LMS): Integrating with an LMS upholds representative preparation and improvement drives, giving a bound-together stage to following learning progress and execution.
5. Enterprise Asset Arranging (ERP): Coordinating HRIS with ERP frameworks incorporates data management across different business capabilities, further developing data precision and independent direction.

Key highlights of compelling HRIS:
A powerful HRIS ought to offer an exhaustive arrangement of highlights to help all parts of HR management. Key elements to search for include:

1. Employee Database Management: Brought together the capacity of representative data, including individual subtleties, work history, capabilities, and execution records.
2. Recruitment and Onboarding: Apparatuses for work posting, candidate following, competitor assessment, and robotized onboarding processes.
3. Payroll and Advantages Organization: Mechanized finance handling, benefits enlistment, and management, charge estimations, and consistency revealing.
4. Time and Participation Following: Frameworks for recording work hours, overseeing leave demands, and checking participation designs.
5. Performance Management: Modules for defining objectives, directing execution audits, following worker progress, and giving criticism.
6. Employee Self-Administration: Entryways permitting workers to access and refresh their own data, view pay slips, demand leave, and participate in preparing programs.
7. Analytics and Announcing: High-level revealing instruments and dashboards for creating experiences on labor force measurements, recognizing patterns, and supporting data-driven navigation.
8. Compliance Management: Highlights to guarantee consistency with work regulations, data assurance guidelines, and industry principles.

By choosing and carrying out the right HRIS, associations can upgrade their HR tasks, further develop data exactness, and pursue more educated vital choices, eventually adding to by and large business achievement.

Data Quality and Accuracy

Importance of Data Quality in HR

Top-notch data are the supporting areas of strength for management. Misguided or partitioned data can incite horrifying courses, disillusionments, and a setback of confidence in HR processes. Quality HR data empowers relationships to:

20. Pursue informed choices concerning determination, limit management, and expert improvement.
21. Guarantee consistency with genuine and legitimate necessities.
22. Work on delegate fulfillment by conclusively following and taking note of their essentials.
23. Work on common-sense proficiency by smoothing out HR cycles and lessening botches.
24. Run-of-the-mill data quality issues.

Two or Three Issues Can Consider the Nature of HR Data:

25. Abnormalities: Data entered in various arrangements or principles, inciting confusion and mistakes.
26. Lacking Data: Missing data that are basic for pursuing informed choices.
27. Copy Records: Different regions for tantamount representative, causing clear bluntness and mistakes.
28. Old Data: Data that have not been restored, inciting choices thinking about old data.
29. Human Blunders: Staggers made during the data section, such as syntactic misunderstandings or mistaken data.

Techniques for Guaranteeing Data Accuracy

Remaining mindful of exact HR data integrates two or three key techniques:

30. Normalization: Fanning out uniform data portion rules and shows.
31. Computerization: Including robotized devices for data fragment and management to confine human mistakes.
32. Arranging: Showing HR staff the significance of data accuracy and how to accomplish it.
33. Taking note: Dependably checking out data for bungles and irregularities.

Data Support

Data support is the most notable way to deal with guarantee that data fulfill predefined rules and standards before it is placed into the design. Techniques include:

34. Input Controls: Finishing checks and obstructions on data fragment plans to guarantee the right strategy and required fields are filled.
35. Computerized Support: Utilizing programming mechanical gatherings to typically look at data for screws up, irregularities, and fulfillment.
36. Cross-Insistence: Separating new data against existing records with perceived copies or ambiguities.

Standard Overviews and Surveys

Normal studies and surveys are head for remaining mindful of data quality throughout a drawn-out time:

37. Organized Reviews: Directing rare studies to methodically check out data accuracy and fulfillment.
38. Spot Checks: Performing flighty watches out for data passages to expediently perceive and address messes up.
39. Input Circles: Laying out systems for representatives and administrators to report data issues and errors.

Data Purifying Techniques

Data purifying includes distinguishing and revising or eliminating blunders and irregularities from the dataset. Strategies include:

40. Deduplication: Eliminating copy records to guarantee every worker has a solitary, exact record.
41. Standardization: Normalizing data designs, for example, date organizations and address displays.
42. Revision: Distinguishing and amending erroneous data through manual audit or computerized devices.
43. Enhancement: Adding missing data or refreshing obsolete data from dependable sources.

By focusing on data quality and exactness, HR departments can upgrade their essential direction, work on functional effectiveness, and keep up with consistency with guidelines. Executing powerful data approval, ordinary reviews, and viable data purging strategies are basic moves toward accomplishing and keeping up with great HR data.

Data Storage and Security

Suitable data accumulation and security are basic parts of HR data management. This fragment of the part explores best practices for data limit, contrasts dispersed capacity and on-premise limit, outlines approaches for ensuring data security and arrangement, and discusses consistency with data protection rules like GDPR and CCPA.

Best Practices for Data Storing

1. Regular Fortifications:

44. Complete routine fortifications to thwart data incidents. This integrates everyday continuous fortifications and many weeks of full fortifications.
45. Store fortifications in various regions, including offsite or disseminated capacity, to ensure data obvious monotony.

2. Data Encryption:

46. Use encryption to shield data both on the way and exceptionally still. This hinders unapproved induction to fragile data.
47. Use advanced encryption rules (AES) for lively affirmation.

3. Access Control:

48. Do extreme access controls to ensure that just endorsed personnel can get to fragile HR data.
49. Use work-based permission control (RBAC) to limit data access considering occupation commitments.

4. Data Lifecycle Management:

50. Spread out systems for data support and evacuation. Ensure that obsolete data are securely eradicated to diminish the bet of breaks.
51. Use data recording deals with long stretch accumulating of inert data.

5. Regular Surveys:

52. Lead standard audits to overview the suitability of data accumulating and well-being endeavors.
53. Perceive and address shortcomings to further develop data confirmation
54. Conveyed capacity versus on-reason accumulating

1. Cloud Limit:
Benefits:

55. Versatility: Actually scale limit considering interest without immense forthright costs.
56. Accessibility: Access data from wherever with a web affiliation, working with remote work and collaboration.
57. Cost Efficiency: Decrease costs related to hardware, upkeep, and IT staff.

Disadvantages:

58. Dependence on the Web: Requires a consistent web relationship for data access and management.
59. Security Concerns: Relies upon outcast providers, raising stresses over data insurance and security.

2. On-Reason Amassing:
Benefits:

60. Control: Limitless power over data limit establishment, security shows, and access.
61. Security: Reduced possibility of untouchable splits as data are taken care of inside the affiliation's premises.

Preventions:

62. Cost: High starting interest in hardware, programming, and consistent help.
63. Flexibility: Confined adaptability stood out from dispersed capacity, requiring additional hardware for augmentation.

Ensuring Data Security and Arrangement

1. **Data Encryption:**
   - Scramble fragile HR data to safeguard it from unapproved access and breaks. Use strong encryption shows and reliably update encryption keys.
2. **Access Control and Check:**
   - Do multi-layered approval (MFA) to update security. Ensure strong, intriguing passwords and standard mystery key updates.
   - Use RBAC to limit access considering occupation occupations and commitments.
3. **Network Security:**
   - Send firewalls, interference disclosure structures (IDS), and interference contravention systems (IPS) to guard the association.
   - Reliably update security programming and fixes to shield against shortcomings.

4. **Employee Arrangement:**
    - Lead typical educational seminars on data security best practices. Show agents how to see phishing attacks and stay aware of data mystery.
5. **Incident Response Plan:**
    - Make and do an episode response expected to address data breaks and security events right away.
    - Reliably test and update the course of action to ensure its suitability.

Consistency with Data Confirmation Rules (GDPR, CCPA, etc.)

1. **General Data Security Rule (GDPR):**

    - Scope: Applies to affiliations dealing with individual data of individuals inside the EU.
    - Essentials:
    - Gain unequivocal consent from individuals before social affair their data.
    - Complete data confirmation by plan and as per normal procedure.
    - Ensure the choice to get to, alter, and destroy individual data.
    - Select a Data Security Official (DPO) to notice consistency.

2. **California Buyer Insurance Act (CCPA):**

    - Scope: Applies to associations gathering individual data of California occupants.
    - Necessities:
    - Give straightforwardness about data collection and use practices.
    - Grant buyers to stop data selling and sharing.
    - Ensure the choice to get to and delete individual data.
    - Complete reasonable well-being endeavors to protect individual data.

3. **Compliance Frameworks:**

    - Direct common consistency audits to ensure adherence to data affirmation rules.

- Do security procedures and strategies agree with authoritative essentials.
- Train delegates on regulatory consistency and data security practices.

By following these endorsed strategies and techniques, affiliations can effectively regulate HR data limit and security, ensuring the affirmation and protection of fragile data while adjusting to appropriate data protection rules.

Analyzing HR Data

Introduction to HR Analytics
HR examination, generally called people assessment or workforce assessment, incorporates the usage of genuine, data mining, and business assessment techniques to HR data. The goal of HR examination is to give pieces of information that can enlighten HR decisions and frameworks, inciting better workforce management and organizational execution. By looking at HR data, affiliations can perceive plans, expect future examples, and make data-driven decisions that overhaul delegate satisfaction, productivity, and support.

Instruments and Programming for HR Data Assessment
There are various instruments and programming open for HR data assessment, each offering different features and limits. Likely the most consistently used gadgets include:

1. HR Data Structures (HRIS): Stages like Workday, SAP Success Factors, and Prophet HCM Cloud offer total solutions for managing and analyzing HR data. They give modules to the following agent data, execution management, and money, and that is just a glimpse of something larger.
2. Data Discernment Mechanical Assemblies: Instruments like Scene, Power BI, and QlikView help with imagining HR data, simplifying it to recognize examples and models. These instruments license HR specialists to make instinctive dashboards and reports.
3. Statistical Assessment Programming: Programming languages like SPSS, SAS, and R are used for additional created

genuine examination. These gadgets are key for driving all-around assessments and building insightful models.

4. Survey Gadgets: Contraptions like SurveyMonkey, Qualtrics, and Google Designs are used for social affairs to delegate info and outline data, which can then be taken apart to quantify specialist satisfaction and responsibility.
5. Excel and Google Sheets: While not particular HR gadgets, bookkeeping sheets are extensively used for data examination in view of their versatility and convenience. They offer various capacities and recipes for performing vital center data examinations.

Key HR Estimations and KPIs

Key HR estimations and key execution markers (KPIs) are crucial for assessing the sufficiency of HR practices and their impact on organizational execution. Likely, the principal HR estimations include:

1. Employee Turnover Rate: Measures the rate at which laborers leave the affiliation. High turnover rates can exhibit issues with work satisfaction, culture, or compensation.
2. Time to Enlist: The run-of-the-mill time it takes to fill an empty position. This estimation reviews the capability of the enlistment collaboration.
3. Employee Responsibility: Actually takes a look at the level of responsibility and satisfaction among delegates. High responsibility levels are routinely associated with higher proficiency and lower turnover.
4. Absenteeism Rate: The rate at which delegates are missing from work. High non-appearance can show lamentable laborer prosperity, low responsibility, or workplace issues.
5. Training and Progression: Estimations associated with the sufficiency of planning programs, for instance, getting ready summit rates, specialist capacity upgrades, and the impact on work execution.
6. Diversity and Thought: Measures the assortment of the workforce and the exhaustiveness of the workplace. This integrates estimations like direction and identity extents, as well as the eventual outcomes of assortment and thought outlines.

Techniques for Data Examination

HR data examination can be advanced by using various techniques, each offering different encounters and applications. The essential techniques consolidate expressive, perceptive, and prescriptive examination.

1. **Descriptive Assessment:**
   i. Reason: Illuminating assessment revolves around summarizing and understanding obvious data to perceive examples and models.
   ii. Techniques: Ordinary procedures integrate data aggregation, data mining, and the use of layout estimations (mean, center, mode, standard deviation).
   iii. Applications: Used for the ultimate objective of uncovering, for instance, understanding turnover rates, specialist economics, and responsibility levels.
2. **Predictive Examination:**
   iv. Reason: Farsighted examination hopes to assess future events or examples considering irrefutable data.
   v. Methodologies: Techniques integrate backslide assessment, man-made intelligence computations, and perceptive showing.
   vi. Applications: Used for anticipating specialist turnover, expecting the result of new selects, and perceiving factors that influence delegate execution.
3. **Prescriptive Examination:**
   vii. Reason: Prescriptive examination gives ideas to dynamic considering data assessment.
   viii. Techniques: It incorporates progression estimations, re-enactment, and decision assessment.
   ix. Applications: Used for making HR techniques, propelling workforce orchestrating, and making tweaked delegate headway plans.

By using these techniques, HR specialists can change unrefined data into critical encounters, inciting more feasible and imperative HR management. Exploring HR data is crucial for making informed HR decisions that line up with organizational goals. By utilizing the right mechanical assemblies and techniques, HR specialists can get critical pieces of information into workforce components, work on delegate experiences, and drive organizational accomplishment. As advancement continues to create, the occupation of HR assessment will just end up becoming more imperative to key HR management.

Using HR Data for Free Course

In the contemporary business landscape, using data has become a principle for making taught and convincing decisions. This is particularly clear in the field of HR (HR), where data-driven courses can through and through redesign the new development and execution of HR game plans and philosophies. How HR data can be utilized to enlighten methodologies, presents context-oriented examinations of productive data-driven HR routes, and graphs the upsides of taking on data-driven HR practices are gotten a handle on here.

Using Data to Enlighten HR Game Plans and Strategies

HR data integrate a broad assortment of data, including agent economics, execution estimations, responsibility scores, and compensation nuances, and that is only the start. By proficiently assembling, exploring, and translating these data, HR specialists can get significant encounters into workforce designs, recognize areas for advancement, and cultivate all the more remarkable courses of action and techniques. The following are a couple of key ways HR data can enlighten route:

1. **Talent Getting and Support:**
    - Data Assessment: HR data can reveal plans for delegate turnover, helping with recognizing factors that add to high consistent misfortune rates.
    - Technique Improvement: By understanding the primary drivers of turnover, HR can encourage assigned upkeep strategies, for instance, improving onboarding processes, offering cutthroat compensation packages, and overhauling calling headway expected open entryways.
2. **Performance Management:**
    - Data Examination: Execution data can include high-performing laborers and districts where additional readiness or sponsorship is required.

- System Headway: HR can use this data to make modified improvement arrangements, set reasonable execution targets, and plan inspiration programs that prod laborers.

4. **Employee Responsibility:**
    - Data Assessment: Audits and info instruments can measure delegate responsibility levels and recognize factors that affect work satisfaction.
    - Procedure Improvement: Pieces of information from responsibility data can enlighten drives to cheer everybody up, for instance, doing versatile work blueprints, seeing delegate achievements, and developing a decent workplace culture.

Case Studies of Data-Driven HR Decision Making

Case Study 1: Google

Google is eminent for its data-driven way of dealing with HR, frequently referred to as "Individual Tasks." One outstanding model is their utilization of data to further develop the employing system. By dissecting data from a huge number of prospective employee meetings, Google recognized the vital properties of effective workers and patched up their screening to zero in on these qualities. This data-driven approach assisted Google with diminishing predispositions, working on the nature of recruits, and smoothing out the enrolment cycle.

Case Study 2: IBM

IBM utilized HR data investigation to foresee representative turnover. By examining different data focuses, including representative execution, residency, and commitment levels, IBM fostered a prescient model that could recognize workers in danger of leaving the organization. This model empowered HR to go to proactive lengths, for example, offering vocational improvement potential to open doors or tending to worries, which altogether decreased turnover rates and held important ability.

Case Study 3: Microsoft

Microsoft used data to upgrade variety and consideration inside the association. By examining segment data and worker criticism, Microsoft distinguished holes in portrayal and regions where certain gatherings confronted difficulties. This data-driven understanding prompted the improvement of designated drives, for example, mentorship programs, oblivious inclination preparation, and different recruiting rehearses. Accordingly, Microsoft accomplished prominent upgrades in work environment variety and consideration.

Benefits of Data-Driven HR Practices

1. **Enhanced Route:**
    - Data-driven HR practices give areas of strength for making informed decisions. By relying upon precise and relevant data, HR can encourage techniques that agree with organizational goals and specialist needs.
2. **Improved Viability:**
    - Using HR data can streamline various cycles, similar to selection, execution management, and delegating responsibility. Automated data collection and examination instruments reduce the time and effort expected for manual tasks, allowing HR specialists to focus on fundamental drives.
3. **Increased Specialist Satisfaction:**
    - Data-driven pieces of information enable HR to make methodologies and tasks that clearly address agent stresses and tendencies. This tweaked approach overhauls work satisfaction, supports everybody, and develops a positive workspace culture.
4. **Better Capacity Management:**
    - By understanding workforce examples and individual execution estimations, HR can really direct capacity. This consolidates recognizing high-potential laborers, arranging assigned getting-ready projects, and ensuring fair and clear execution evaluations.
5. **Proactive Decisive reasoning:**
    - Judicious examination can help HR with anticipating likely issues, for instance, turnover or capacity openings, before they become fundamental. Proactive measures can then be taken to reduce these risks, ensuring cognizance and strength inside the affiliation.
6. **Strategic Plan:**
    - Data-driven HR practices ensure that HR strategies are agreed with as a rule targets. This plan works on the fundamental impact of HR, adding to the affiliation's thriving and high ground.

To sum up, using HR data for decision-making is a powerful strategy that can transform how organizations manage their workforce. By using data to enlighten approaches and frameworks, HR can drive tremendous redesigns in enlistment, execution management, laborer responsibility, and for the most part organizational suitability. The benefits of data-driven HR practices are clear, offering overhauled free courses, extended viability, better capacity management, and a more satisfied and attracted workforce.

Future Trends in HR Data Management

Emerging Technologies (AI, Machine Learning, and Big Data)

The landscape of HR data management is rapidly progressing, driven by emerging headways like artificial information (PC-based insight), man-made intelligence (ML), and colossal data examination. These headways are changing how HR departments assemble, separate, and use data.

- Artificial Information (man-made knowledge): PC-based insight is changing HR processes through motorizing routine tasks, updating headings, and giving further encounters into laborer data. Man-made knowledge-filled chatbots can manage delegate demands, selection cycles can be streamlined through PC-based insight-driven applicant worldwide situating structures, and perceptive assessment can gauge specialist turnover and recognize upkeep systems.
- Artificial Intelligence (ML): ML computations research enormous proportions of HR data to perceive models and examples that likely will not be obvious through customary assessment. This engages HR specialists to make data-driven decisions concerning capacity management, execution appraisals, and workforce organizing. ML can in like manner tweak laborer experiences by proposing planning activities and job improvement significant entryways considering individual profiles and execution data.
- Gigantic Data Assessment: The extension of data from various sources—such as electronic diversion, laborer analysis structures, wearable advancement, and that is just a glimpse of something larger—has achieved huge data in HR. Tremendous data examination grants HR specialists to procure comprehensive pieces of information into workforce components, agent responsibility, and effectiveness. By

using gigantic data, affiliations can expect future workforce needs, update capacity-acquiring techniques, and work on taking everything into account for execution.

The Occupation of HR in the Time of Cutting-Edge Change

As mechanized change reshapes adventures, HR departments ought to conform to new principles of work and agent management. The occupation of HR is moving from regular definitive abilities to imperative partnerships inside the affiliation.

- Key Partner: HR is continuously transforming into a fundamental partner in driving organizational goals. By harnessing data and advanced assessment, HR can change its drives to business objectives, ensuring that capacity management frameworks support the overall vision and mission of the association.
- Change Subject Matter Expert: In the mechanized time, HR plays a critical part in supervising change and empowering a culture of steady learning and improvement. HR specialists ought to lead the charge in upskilling and reskilling agents to keep awake with mechanical movements. This incorporates laying out quick learning conditions and propelling a culture that embraces modernized gadgets and developments.
- Delegate Experience Sketcher: With the approaching of cutting-edge instruments, HR can through and through redesign the specialist experience. From onboarding to calling progression, HR can utilize modernized stages to give steady and altered experiences. This further creates delegate satisfaction and responsibility as well as attracts and holds top capacity in a serious work market.

Assumptions for the Inevitable Destiny of HR Data Collection and Management

The destiny of HR data collection and management will be depicted by greater automation, a more noticeable blend, and enhancements based on data security and ethics.

- Extended Computerization: Routine HR tasks, for instance, finance taking care of, benefits association, and consistency reporting will be continuously robotized. This will set free HR specialists to focus on extra fundamental activities like capacity improvement, agent responsibility, and organizational culture.
- More Conspicuous Compromise: HR systems will end up being more consolidated with other business structures, making a predictable movement of data across the affiliation. This compromise will engage consistent data sharing and joint exertion, provoking more instructed heading and agile responses to business challenges.
- Redesigned Focus on Data Security and Ethics: As the volume of HR data grows, so does the necessity for lively data well-being endeavors. Affiliations will place assets into state-of-the-art network security deals with serious consequences regarding shielding sensitive agent data. Besides, moral examinations concerning data security and usage are becoming increasingly essential. HR specialists ought to investigate the complexities of data ethics, ensuring that data are used constantly and in compliance with rules.

With everything taken into account, the destiny of HR data management is prepared for basic change driven by emerging advances and non-stop electronic change. HR specialists who embrace these movements and impact data-driven insights will be decisively positioned to lead their relationship into a new era of workforce management and organizational significance.

References

1. Bersin, J., *The Future of Work: How HR Data Collection and Management are Transforming Organizations*, Deloitte Insights, 2020, https://www2.deloitte.com/us/en/insights/focus/human-capital-trends/2020/changing-role-of-human-resources-management.html.
2. Cappelli, P., *Talent on Demand: Managing Talent in an Age of Uncertainty*, Harvard Business Review Press, 2019, https://www.researchgate.net/publication/311798995_Talent_on_Demand_-_Managing_Talent_in_an_Age_of_Uncertainty.

3. Davenport, T.H., Harris, J., Shapiro, J., *Competing on Talent Analytics*, Harvard Business Review, 2010, Retrieved from https://hbr.org/2010/10/competing-on-talent-analytics.
4. Dulebohn, J.H. and Johnson, R.D., Human Resource Metrics and Decision Support: A Classification Framework. *Hum. Resour. Manage. Rev.*, 23, 1, 71–83, 2013.
5. King, R., *Data-Driven HR: How to Use Analytics and Metrics to Drive Performance*, Kogan Page, 2018, https://www.koganpage.com/hr-learning-development/data-driven-hr-9781398614567.
6. Marler, J.H. and Boudreau, J.W., An Evidence-Based Review of HR Analytics. *Int. J. Hum. Resour. Manage.*, 28, 1, 3–26, 2017.
7. Strohmeier, S. and Piazza, F., *Artificial Intelligence Techniques in Human Resource Management—A Conceptual Exploration.* 2015, 10.1007/978-3-319-17906-3_7, https://www.researchgate.net/publication/276204444_Artificial_Intelligence_Techniques_in_Human_Resource_Management-A_Conceptual_Exploration.
8. Beer, M., Boselie, P., Brewster, C., Back to the future: Implications for the field of HRM of the multistakeholder perspective proposed 30 years ago. *Hum. Resour. Manage.*, 54, 3, 427–438, 2015.
9. Bersin, J., Rewriting the Rules for the Digital Age: 2017 Deloitte Human Capital Trends. *LinkedIn*, 2017, https://www.linkedin.com/pulse/rewriting-rules-digital-age-2017-deloitte-human-capital-josh-bersin.
10. Boudreau, J.W. and Ramstad, P.M., *Beyond HR: The New Science of Human Capital*, Harvard Business School Press, 2007, https://onlinelibrary.wiley.com/doi/10.1002/hrm.20291.
11. Cascio, W.F. and Aguinis, H., Staffing twenty-first-century organizations. *Acad. Manage. Ann.*, 2, 1, 133–165, 2008.
12. Cascio, W.F. and Boudreau, J.W., *Investing in People: Financial Impact of Human Resource Initiatives*, Pearson Education, 2011, chrome-extension://efaidnbmnnnibpcajpcglclefindmkaj/https://ptgmedia.pearsoncmg.com/images/9780137070923/samplepages/9780137070923.pdf.
13. Fitz-enz, J. and Mattox, J., *Predictive Analytics for Human Resources*, Wiley, 2014, chrome-extension://efaidnbmnnnibpcajpcglclefindmkaj/http://repo.darmajaya.ac.id/4065/1/%28Wiley%20and%20SAS%20Business%20Series%29%20Jac%20Fitz-enz%2C%20John%20Mattox%20II%20-%20Predictive%20Analytics%20for%20Human%20Resources-Wiley%20%282014%29.pdf.
14. Harris, J.G., Craig, E., Egan, G., How organizations strategically manage their analytic talent. *Strat. Lead.*, 38, 15–22, 2010. 10.1108/10878571011042069, https://www.researchgate.net/publication/240260128_How_organizations_strategically_manage_their_analytic_talent.
15. Kahn, W.A., Psychological conditions of personal engagement and disengagement at work. *Acad. Manage. J.*, 33, 4, 692–724, 1990.

16. Kirkpatrick, D.L., *Evaluating Training Programs: The Four Levels*, Berrett-Koehler Publishers, 2006, chrome-extension://efaidnbmnnnibpcajpcglclefindmkaj/https://bkconnection.com/static/Evaluating_Training_Programs_EXCERPT.pdf.
17. Lawler, E.E. and Boudreau, J.W., *Global Trends in Human Resource Management: A Twenty-Year Analysis*, Stanford Business Books, 2015, 10.1515/9780804794558, https://www.sup.org/books/business/global-trends-human-resource-management.
18. Rasmussen, T.H. and Ulrich, D., Learning from practice: How HR analytics avoids being a management fad. *Organizational Dyn.*, 44, 3, 236–242, 2015.
19. Rothwell, W.J., *Effective Succession Planning: Ensuring Leadership Continuity and Building Talent from Within*, AMACOM, 2001, chrome-extension://efaidnbmnnnibpcajpcglclefindmkaj/https://hcmindonesia.wordpress.com/wp-content/uploads/2012/12/9b-successionplanhandbook.pdf.
20. Stone, D.L. and Dulebohn, J.H., Emerging issues in theory and research on electronic human resource management (eHRM). *Hum. Resour. Manage. Rev.*, 23, 1, 1–5, 2013.
21. Stone, D.L. and Deadrick, D.L., Challenges and opportunities affecting the future of human resource management. *Hum. Resour. Manage. Rev.*, 25, 2, 139–145, 2015.
22. Ulrich, D., HR from the Outside In: *Six Competencies for the Future of Human Resources*, McGraw Hill Professional, 2013, https://books.google.co.in/books/about/HR_from_the_Outside_In_Six_Competencies.html?id=7VM8GGARML8C&redir_esc=y.
23. Ulrich, D. and Brockbank, W., *The HR Value Proposition*, Harvard Business Review Press, 2005, chrome-extension://efaidnbmnnnibpcajpcglclefindmkaj/https://edata.conferenceboard.ca/docs/default-source/crc/feb2005_presentation_davidulrich.pdf?sfvrsn=bc402a7e_0.

9

Communicating Human Capital Analytics Insights to Decision-Makers Effectively

Sandeep Singh Chandel[1]*, Astha Shukla[2], Sakshi Shukla[2] and Shivansu Sachan[3]

[1]*Dayanand Academy of Management Studies, Kanpur, Uttar Pradesh, India*
[2]*CSJM University, Uttar Pradesh, India*
[3]*School of Hotel Management, CSJM University, Kanpur, Uttar Pradesh, India*

Abstract

In the field of data analytics, Human Capital Analysis plays an impact in shaping various decisions within organizations. Effectively integrating this probability into decision-making processes requires clear communication to bridge the gap between complex data and significant techniques. This theory assumes that lucrative workforce-related information is translated into informed organizational decisions and provides essential phrases for effectively presenting analytics for Human Capital Analysis to decision-formers. The first piece of advice highlights how crucial it is to modify analytics for Human Capital Analysis. Decision-makers are likely to focus on analytics that directly help in the formation of important destinations. This involves identifying key performance indicators (KPIs) that align with decision-makers and are situated within the context of overarching trade forms. The current tip focuses on turning intricate facts into palatable tales. Selection might not have discovered specialized knowledge in analytics, therefore presenting in a narrative format can improve performance. This entails highlighting fundamental information, trends, and possible areas for development using charts, visuals, and succinct rundowns. The human side of analytics enables organizations to make final decisions. The fourth recommendation supports communication and collaboration. Instead of presenting the analysis of Human Capital Analysis as a single construct, it is essential to ensure that there is a section within the employee's profile that can respond to different situations guaranteed to choose a manufacturer trained in repair. This includes creating a critical circle that encourages open

**Corresponding author*: Sandeepc15@gmail.com

Deepa Gupta, Mukul Gupta, Pawan Budhwar, Jim Westerman, Rajesh Kumar Dhanaraj and Balamurugan Balusamy (eds.) Human Capital Analytics: Exploring the HR Spectrum in Industry 5.0, (201–218) © 2025 Scrivener Publishing LLC

communication and consolidates information used over time. The main purpose of directly transferring Human Capital Analysis to decision-makers is to clearly demonstrate how to transfer the experience gained from Human Capital Analysis to decision-makers in the organization. Focus on key metrics. Create compelling stories and insights, and link analytics to business goals. Think about information in actionable ways, generate compelling recommendations, and maximize ROI and impact. Address potential problems, use simple language, strengthen information and cooperation, and provide constant updates. The advantage of being a choice creator lies in understanding the effect of workforce information on representative involvement, engagement, and general well-being. Ultimately, this chapter will highlight the value of analytics for human work capital and offer tips on how helpful it will be to successfully communicate the results to decision-makers.

***Keywords*:** Decision science, employee performance, HR analytics, talent management, decision-makers

Introduction of Analytics for Human Capital Analysis

The process of gathering, evaluating, and interpreting personnel data for a company in making well-informed recruiting decisions has been referring as analytics for Human Capital Analysis. It involves applying both objective and subjective methods to grade several aspects of Human Capital Analysis, including ability, earnings, involvement, and execution. Analytics for Human Capital Analysis may help businesses find development possibilities, manage staff, and communicate with representatives more effectively. Establishments can make stronger decisions about hiring, training, repairs, and general people administration.

When assessing the quality of services provided, decision-makers can use analytics for Human Capital Analysis as a useful tool. Making educated decisions on the form of service delivery is possible for decision-makers through the utilization of data-driven insights pertaining to employee performance and engagement.

Through analytics for Human Capital Analysis, decision-makers can identify patterns and trends in service delivery, pinpointing places of power and place for improvement.

It provides a structured framework for designing, developing, and evaluating instructional materials and programs. The authors outline the major phases of the instructional design process, including analysis, design, development, implementation, and evaluation (ADDIE model) [5].

Analytics for Human Capital Analysis provides decision-makers with a comprehensive and actionable understanding of service delivery performance. By leveraging workforce data and advanced analytical techniques, they can optimize service delivery processes, anticipate future challenges, and drive continuous improvement in service quality and effectiveness.

Consider the following two cases, both from a budgetary administration firm. The primary case was a multivariate factual investigation of the characteristics of an incentive pay plot and deals execution for a key part of the organization. The examination was conducted by a committed HR analytics individual whose factual approach was immaculate. Then, insights determined by the investigation addressed an expansive number of assumptions about the pay plan and what drove behavior within the part. The general manager (GM) responsible for that part of the operation was not involved in the investigative process from the beginning and only received the finalized results at the end of the examination. The reaction was a complete dismissal of the exam and addressing the analytics behind it. The main mistake made by the HR analyst was not to engage the GM at the beginning of the process. This lack of involvement led to insufficient alignment regarding the potential need for the analysis and a limited interest in obtaining and potentially acting on the results. The case study was a direct representation of a research project conducted during a significant period of organizational change and transformation. HR specialists are called upon to inform and support the strategic direction of companies. The HR function is well suited for this task. HR specialists consult and support all aspects of the business and gain insight into priorities, challenges, and opportunities. In addition, HR professionals must be aware of legal and labor market dynamics. Thus, HR professionals take information from various forms, both inside and outside the organization, which allows them to identify pressing business problems and recommend solutions. Although this situation offers many opportunities, it is also a challenging task: calculating information from different forms and making decisions or recommendations based on the evidence. That conclusion comes from sources, one of which is organizational data. Although HR professionals routinely calculate HR metrics from organizational data compared to other business functions (e.g., finance, marketing, and sales), HR has been relatively "late to the game" when it comes to using data to inform business practices. However, HR professionals have increasingly relied on HR analytics to create legitimacy, provide evidence to support recommendations, and illustrate HR's impact on stakeholders. HR analytics as HR Practice involves leveraging data-driven insights to enhance decision-making, optimize workforce strategies, and improve overall organization performance.

This enables organizations to utilize data-driven decision-making effectively. In other words, HR involves the use of information technology (such as HR information systems) to collect, manage, and analyze information from sources outside the company and/or across functions to support people-related decisions. A mission statement encapsulates an organization's overarching goal, or its raison d'être, or reason for being, by describing a fundamental need that the organization seeks to satisfy. Remember that one of Tesla's stated goals is to accelerate the world's transition to sustainable energy. Tesla is not an outlier. Formulating a plan includes not only a mission statement but also a vision and values statement. The vision of an organization outlines what it hopes to become or look like in the future and is an extension of the mission. Establishing a core values framework gives the organization boundaries and direction for making decisions and realizing its goals. The overview was taken by the senior leaders as a vital vehicle for observing the employees' reactions to the changes, and the leaders' victory in relieving the negative impacts of the changes. The analytics utilized to analyze the overview reactions were exceptionally essential, counting as it was implying and frequencies. But because the questions were planned to straightforwardly address worker responses to a critical transition period, the study came about and was given extraordinary weight within the leaders' handle of assessing and adjusting their approach to overseeing the changes. As a result, deep insights and notes are not always necessary prerequisites.They are, be that as it may, frequently a key portion of a comprehensive set of analyses that may be required for the most profound bits of knowledge. Two cases are considered to outline this point. Both began as issues that showed up related to recompense. After conducting extensive analyses, significant insights into the limitations of remuneration as an arrangement were accomplished, and actions were taken that drove enduring positive impacts. In both cases, there were (a) advanced statistical methods for one portion of the work, (b) basic information examinations for other parts of the work, and (c) contemplative, keen thought of causal variables utilizing rationale as it were and virtually no (unused) information examination for the remaining parts of the work.

Human capital analytics is defined as the application of statistical and data analysis methods to human resource data to improve decision-making and organizational performance.

The scope includes various HR functions such as recruitment, training, performance management, and employee retention [4].

Role of Retention in Analytics for Human Capital Analysis

To calculate the retention rate, you typically divide the number of employees who are with the company by the total number of employees at the beginning of the period, and then multiply by 100 to get the percentage.

For example:

Retention Rate = (Number of employees at end of time/Number of employees at the start of time) * 100

Companies often use retention rate data to identify trends, understand frequency influencing retention, and develop formation to improve employee engagement and satisfaction, thereby reducing turnover and retaining valuable talent.

Risk relief in analytics for Human Capital Analysis tells the strategies and practices aimed at potential risks with workforce management through data analysis and insights. Analytics for Human Capital Analysis involves gathering and analyzing work related to employees' work, productivity, engagement, retention, and other metrics to inform decision-making processes within an organization.

Analytics for Human Capital Analysis

The process of using data to understand and help human resource management daily practices has seen significant changes in performance over the years.

With a few exceptions (Becker & Huselid, 1998; Huselid, Beatty, & Becker, 2005; Huselid, Becker, & Beatty, 2005; Wright *et al.*), there has been little effort to extend SHRM theory in a way that formally integrates the mechanism through which the HR architecture actually influences firm performance [1].

With the advancement of technology and the proliferation of digital platforms, the amount and variety of data available for Human Capital Analysis analytics have grown tremendously. This has enabled organizations to increase insights into their workforce, leading to more informed decision-making. In addition, efforts to improve collection methods and data-cleaning processes have contributed to improving analytics for Human Capital Analysis. Statistical algorithms and machine learning techniques are used to predict future trends and outcomes. Predictive analytics enables organizations to anticipate employee needs, identify potential problems, and provide opportunities to improve performance and productivity.

There is a growing understanding that Human Capital Analysis must be integrated into the overall business strategy. Organizations are increasingly incorporating Human Capital Analysis metrics into their strategic planning programs to better align employee decisions with business goals. This policy led to greater utilization of human resources and better management. Human Capital Information focuses on measuring traditional HR metrics like turnover rates and employee improvement statistics to capture the overall employee experience. This includes looking at things like workplace culture, diversity and inclusion, and employee well-being to see what the product is. This integration fosters a deeper understanding of how to enhance employee satisfaction and performance. As human inform capital analytics increases, there is a growing awareness of the ethics of the collection and use of employee data. Organizations are increasingly adopting ethical guidelines and best practices to ensure that Human Capital Analysis respects workers' rights and adheres to fairness and transparency. It requires a more strategic approach to workforce management and a greater focus on data-driven decision-making.

Human Capital Analysis can be defined as "a process that enables the understanding and evaluation of causal relationships between HR and management functions, providing a valid and reliable basis for decision-making through statistical and experimental methods."

The tools collect information from a variety of sources, including surveys, logs, and activities, to create a coherent picture as evidence-based approach to better decision-making. This is a popular word. It is simply a collection of primary objective facts and secondary objective data. The filter is divided into three levels:

1. Traditional HR metrics are primarily performance indicators (turnover rate, response time, hiring costs, number of employees hired and trained, etc.). The primary focus here is cost reduction and process improvement.
   Visual HR analytics uncovers and explains relationships with current and historical data patterns. This is the basis of your analysis. It includes dashboards, division of labor, data mining of original models, and periodic reports.
2. Predictive analytics is a variety of techniques (statistics, modeling, and data mining) that use current facts and historical information to predict the future. It is about the risk and the possible consequences. For example, models used to increase the likelihood of selecting the right people for hiring, training, and promotion are included.

3. Forecasting to include decision-making opportunities and workforce optimization. Analyze complex data in order to forecast outcomes, provide decision-making capabilities, and demonstrate various business ramifications. Models designed to understand how different learning investments affect outcomes (rarely in HR). The approach begins with simple HR reporting and progresses to prescriptive modeling of business operations. While financial capital (money) and economic capital (intangible assets) constitute a company's lifeblood, Human Capital Analysis (people) improves corporate performance by leveraging money and intangible assets. When you go from descriptive to prescriptive, the added value grows tremendously.

Human Capital Analysis Analytics Framework

1. Competitive Isomorphism: The impact of PMT (Product/Market/Technology) on Human Capital Analysis analytics argues that "demands increase from product market form and appropriate technique" which determines HR policies and practices and hence influences the use of Human Capital Analysis analytics.
2. Institutional Isomorphism: SCL (Social/Cultural/Legal) influences HRM practices, and hence Human Capital Analysis analytics, through societal ideals (fairness and legitimacy) and regulation.
3. Company Configuration: The organizational/administrative/cultural background of an organization influences HR methods such as Human Capital Analysis analytics. This combination of the three characteristics mentioned above influences the extent and form of Human Capital Analysis analytics implementation in an organization.

Factors Affecting Human Capital Analysis (HCA) Analytics

It can be assumed that the more competitive the environment, the more organizations will apply Human Capital Analysis analytics.

Organizational Trends: Companies are implementing Human Capital Analysis analytics to avoid imitating competitors or becoming obsolete. Well, no. The choice of Human Capital Analysis methods used by

competitors influences the Human Capital Analysis strategies adopted by organization within the same sector.
Formalization: As a company matures, its behavior becomes formalized (Mintzberg, 1979). Therefore, Human Capital Analysis analytics should be used more widely in traditional organizations to support formal decision-making processes.
Organization Structure: Most organizations today grow organically. Therefore, to understand the drivers of employee performance and increase organizational effectiveness, HR analytics is the way to monitor career progression and identify high-potential individuals for leadership roles.

- ✓ Calculate the return on investment for various Human Capital Analysis initiatives such as training programs, employee benefits, and recruitment efforts.
- ✓ Ensure that resource is allocated efficiently to maximize the number of Human Capital Analysis.
- ✓ Analyze the diversity and inclusivity of the work part and impact on organization performance.
- ✓ Promote diversity inclusion initiatives to foster innovation and creativity.
- ✓ Forecast future workforce needs based on business goals and industry trends.
- ✓ Identify potential talent shortages or surpluses and develop strategies to address them proactively.
- ✓ Implement performance management software to track work performance and provide areas of improvement in the workplace.
- ✓ Align individual completion with organizational tasks to enhance overall work performance.
- ✓ Compare Human Capital Analysis metrics against industry format to assess competitiveness and tell areas for improvement.
- ✓ Improve from best practices adopted by leading organizations in the field.

Understanding the Needs and Inclinations of Choice Makers

Diverse backgrounds and degrees of information-gathering expertise may be possessed by decision-makers. You can modify your communication strategies to more effectively convey information in a clear, concise manner by being aware of their demands, specific issues and topics pertaining to the management of Human Capital Analysis. HR specialists can focus on resolving those problems and offering invaluable experience and insight if are aware of their needs. The decision is believed in the facts and the statistics presented when they are aware of their own needs and desires. This promotes a collaborative relationship between HR professionals and decision-makers, thus leading to better decision-making. As a result, decision-makers focus on achieving organizational goals and objectives by understanding their own needs and wants. Tailoring communications to the needs and desires of decision-makers increases access to the information and experiences provided to them. This leads to greater discussion and collaboration on people issues, which ultimately leads to better results for the organization.

Human Capital Analysis Calculations

Human Capital Analysis measurements allude to quantifiable measures utilized to evaluate different angles of an organization's place force. These measurements give important experiences into the execution, efficiency, and general viability of representatives, assisting organizations in making informed decisions about talent management and strategic planning.

The number of possible metrics is practically infinite, although there is a handful that sees heavy usage.

Employee Turnover

An organization's turnover rate can be better understood by looking at the total number of worker who departs soon. To differentiate between intentional and accidental turnover, this metric—which is defined by the division or supervisor and classified by person residency—can be useful. The number of people who are separated by the average number of people at a particular time is a common way to calculate representative turnover. To find the percentage, just multiply it by 100.

New Contract Turnover Rate

It is common practice to use this formula to monitor the percentage of new hires that leave during the first 3 months. Separate the total number of new personnel who start producing results within 90 days from the total number of contracts signed within the allocated time frame.

Retention Rate

The pace at which employees leave without being replaced. The annual retention rate of your salespeople may reflect this. Find this number by dividing the total number of people in the company by the average no. of people.

Offer Acceptance Rate

Not all applicants will accept a position offer. Start keeping tabs on the offer acknowledgment rate by dividing the total number of offers made by the number of offers acknowledged; this will give you a good idea of how likely candidates are to accept an offer. If your company's recognition rate is lower than 80%, it can indicate that your offerings are not competitive in the market.

Cost per Hire

The real monetary impact of making a contemporary recruit must be understood. This total should cover everything from advertising the position to the time spent recruiting, conducting interviews, and finally, onboarding new employees.

Time to Productivity

This calculation tracks how long time for unused contracts to reach full efficiency. Dubious to a degree, but with the assistance of office heads and directors, it can unquestionably be done.

Types of HR Analytics

Basic Human Capital Analysis Facts Utilizing JetBlue's net promoter score to forecast its economic growth and monitor engagement level.

Analytical HR by using electronic "badges," MIT looks at relationships between persons and uses traits associated with high-performing teams to identify them.

Human-Capital Investment Analysis: To improve their retention rate, Sysco delivery satisfaction levels will be reviewed.

Forecasts calculating the count of personnel needed in the future based on present trends while developing "what-if" scenarios at Dow Chemical.

Talent value model investigating the causes for place force churn at Google and IBM [6].

Talent supply chain anticipating incoming call center volume to help merchants manage their place force levels.

Human resources analytics started as a small administrative endeavor and it has gradually evolved to provide advanced diagnostic and predictive capabilities (Edwards & Edwards, 2016) able to enhance employee engagement and retention and generate benefits for whole organizations through digitally powered analytics solutions (Deloitte, 2017) [2, 3].

HR analytics provide useful information on personal performance, engagement, and productivity with corporate objectives and tactical ambitions. To effectively achieve their business goals, establishments can use data-driven methods to anticipate skill gaps, assess talent trends, and optimize place forces. For example, analytics can be used to identify high-performing employees, understand the factors influencing their performance, and replicate those trends throughout the entire company. Additionally, by employing Human Capital Analysis analytics, companies may make decisions about perfect hiring, training, and talent development initiatives, effectively allocating resources to support tactical aims. In general, firms that align staff analysis with organizational goals can improve their competitive advantage, encourage innovation, and prosper in the long run.

Presenting analytics for Human Capital Analysis to decision-makers involves a tactical approach to ensure that data-driven insights are effectively communicated. Some practices based on the provided search results:

1. Understand the Audience:
   - Tailor communication to match the decision-maker's knowledge level and preferences.
   - Highlight how analytics for Human Capital Analysis impact key business objectives
2. Simplify Complex Data:
   - Utilize visual representations like graphs and charts for easier interpretation.
   - Explain concepts in simple, understandable language.
3. Storytelling with Data:
   - Frame data within a compelling narrative that connects analytics to real-world scenarios.

- Emphasize key findings and actionable insights derived from the data.

4. Building Credibility:
   - Ensure data accuracy and sources to build trust with decision-makers.
   - Explain the methodology behind the analytics to demonstrate credibility.
5. Engaging Stakeholders:
   - Foster open discussions to address questions and concerns from decision-makers.
   - Solicit feedback to continuously improve communication effectiveness.
6. Leveraging Technology:
   - Use data visualization tools for interactive visualizations.
   - Implement automated reporting systems for regular updates on Human Capital Analysis calculations.
7. Developing Data Storytelling Skills:
   - Create a mission statement to guide the translation of analysis into a story.
   - Ensure presentations carry a clear "point" to increase support from decision-makers.
8. Know Your Audience:
   - Frame presentations differently setup on the audience's relationship with analytics.
   - Tailor the level of technical details in the presentation accordingly.
9. Embrace Context:
   - Provide context by considering temporal changes, industry benchmarks, or existing calculations.
   - Context can transform dull analytics into a compelling story.
10. Explain Why It Matters:
    - Clearly articulate how the analysis affects the organization and why it is relevant to the executive team.
    - Connect the data insights to tangible outcomes for the workplace.

Emphasizes the need for talent management to be directly linked to the business strategy to achieve organizational goals. Suggests that talent management should not be an isolated function but integrated into the overall strategic planning process [6].

By incorporating these best practices, HR professionals can effectively present analytics for Human Capital Analysis to decision-makers, enabling informed based on data-driven insights.

How to assess HR indicators' efficacy in a particular corporate setting based on the search results that were returned, take into consideration the following tactics to assess the efficacy of HR indicators in a particular company context:

1. Identify Meaningful Indicators:
    - Pinpoint indicators that fill with your organization's imp. Goals and questions to measure effectiveness in specific areas.
    - Focus on indicators that directly contribute to achieving desired outcomes and delivering tactical goals.
2. Assess HR Outcomes:
    - Evaluate whether an HR person is delivering final outcomes essential for business success by measuring factors like employee satisfaction, engagement levels, churn rate, absenteeism rate, and training impact.
    - Common calculations for assessing outcomes include employee, employee satisfaction index, and absenteeism rate.
3. Analyze Internal Efficiency:
    - Measure how efficiently HR services are being delivered by assessing recruitment channels, competency recruitment effectiveness, costs-per-hire, training costs, and training effectiveness.
    - Significant metrics about the effectiveness of internal works include return on final investment (ROI), cost-per-final hire, and average time to fill jobs.
4. Audit HR Compliance:
    - Monitor HR compliance with relevant requirements but delegate tactical tasks like planning to other relevant individuals for organizational objectives.
    - The range of diversity initiatives, the ratio of the gender pay gap, the percentage of diversity, and the percentage of workers who are schooled in business rules are among the indicators that can be stated to determine a violation of the audit.

5. Evaluate Service Delivery:
   - Factors like HR service quality, induction program efficacy, employee development initiatives, and performance management feedback may be used to measure the efficacy of HR service delivery.
   - Typical criteria used to measure service quality include ROI, employee happiness with benefits, training efficacy, and recruit productivity.

Human Resource Analysis links the trajectory of positive organizational transformation largely. Businesses may get to the root cause of the problems and implement 'solution-ready' approaches by leveraging information on place factor-related performance, engagement, and retention among other data sources. Among various insights drawn from the perspective of analytics, a reduction in staff attrition could be one possible finding or a clear reason for a low level of output identified. The employers may get the particular information to form the necessary plans for increasing workplace satisfaction, policies procedures, and thus offering the deserved opportunities for employee career development. Human Capital Analysis also offers forecasts on labor trends and supply estimations, enabling businesses to adapt their plans proactively. Finally, analytics for Human Capital Analysis resonates with organizations that want to achieve more with less and face complex business decisions.

While 71% of companies consider people analytics a high priority within their organizations (with 31% rating it as very important), progress in implementing these analytics has been slow. The percentage of companies correlating HR data to business outcomes, performing predictive analytics, and deploying enterprise scorecards barely changed from last year [3].

A company's capital projects, along with their ROI and the extent of their effect on the business will have to be appraised. For organizations, it is necessary to assess the financial gains as well as strategic contributions of such programs, various stakeholders for future endeavors, and when to justify the investments in Human Capital Analysis. Parameters of capital such as revenue per employee, productivity, and staff turnover that will be used to measure the progress will occupy a prominent position. Companies will make projections of profits before and after the programs and determine whether there is an economic return on their Human Capital Analysis investments. Organizations could apply case studies and "good news" items in their publications as well to demonstrate the importance of investing in Human Capital Analysis and the improved business results it produces. An effective ROI and business impact envisagement of Human Capital Analysis initiatives for stakeholders is imperative for various stakeholders.

Cultivating an environment of collaboration and discussion is fundamental to encouraging the understanding and selection of analytics for Human Capital Analysis. Capital inside the organization by empowering open exchange between partners, such as supervisors, pioneers, and persons, organizations can make straightforwardness and consideration in social Human Capital Analysis investigation activities. This collaborative approach allows individuals from distinctive foundations and disciplines to share their conclusions, insights, and concerns approximately Human Capital Analysis data and analytics. Generally, cultivating a collaborative and conversational environment is fundamental to advancing the successful utilization of Human Capital Analysis examination and accomplishing organizational victory.

To guarantee that decision-makers understand the importance of Human Capital Analysis analytics, it is imperative to maintain continuous communication and updates. By periodically updating decision-makers, initiatives can inform them about the latest findings, advances, and results in analytics for Human Capital Analysis. Frequent communication builds trust, encourages form, and empowers decision-makers to make well-informed choices that align with the organization's goals and tactical priorities. Additionally, it enables decision-makers to provide feedback and insights, fostering a collaborative effort to leverage HR analytics to improve business results.

Training and Development Work Metrics

Training and development work metrics play a pivotal role in shaping the success of organizations by providing invaluable insights into the efficacy and impact of learning initiatives. These metrics serve as the compass guiding HR and L&D professionals in navigating the complex landscape of employee development. Framework lies in the concept of measuring progress and performance across various dimensions, from individual skill acquisition to organizational growth. One of the fundamental metrics is completion rates, which offer a snapshot of employee engagement and compliance with training mandates as well as commitment of participants. Similarly, training costs serve as a tangible indicator of the investment required to upskill the workforce. Additionally, training effectiveness metrics provide a comprehensive evaluation of the extent to which training objectives are achieved and learning is transferred to job performance. Through pre- and post-training assessments, skills demonstrations, and performance evaluations, organizations can gauge the tangible outcomes of training initiatives and identify areas for refinement. Learning engagement metrics offer insights into the level of participation, interaction, and interest generated by training programs, informing adjustments to content delivery and instructional methods. Similarly, learning progression metrics track the advancement of employees through various stages of training, identifying bottlenecks or gaps in the learning journey.

- Address external labor market and career challenges, such as job opportunities.
- Alternative professional routes accessible to each person, as well as disparities in their chosen career.

Job transitions can lead to trade-offs in remuneration for future development opportunities. What are the work design's profit and loss assumptions, including alternatives for paying higher or lower wages? How to choose whether to acquire or construct a skill set, including outsourcing individual jobs or production processes? Finally, benchmarking against industry standards and best practices enables organizations to contextualize their training metrics and identify opportunities for continuous improvement. In conclusion, training and development metrics serve as the compass guiding organizations on their journey toward building a skilled, engaged, and high-performing workforce, driving sustainable growth and success in an ever-evolving business landscape.

Conclusion

Finally, effectively communicating Human Capital Analysis analytics to decision-makers is essential to building an informed and tactical place force. The organization design approach focuses on addressing enterprise-wide behavior challenges, such as the effectiveness of procedures across divisions and functions. The labor markets model focuses on effectiveness and success.

The most profound ideas required only a portion of the time. Identifying, obtaining, and collecting data is often the most challenging aspect of the job. HR generalists, not analytic specialists, must master these duties and competencies to improve analytical decision-making in the HR department. Most people can master them. Another major concern is the time required for in-depth investigation. The models covered here, including COM, labor markets, and organizational design, can be used as diagnostics through logic exercises when time is limited for intensive analytics. This does not lessen the importance of statistical analysis in HR decision-making but rather enhances it by providing more opportunities to detect HR issues through advanced analytics [5]. Clear alignment with organizational goals, use of data visualization, and focus on actionable insights make the presentation more engaging and impressive. In addition, keeping open lines of communication, adapting to audience needs, and including real-world examples help bridge the gap between complex analysis and practical decision-making.

References

1. Becker, B. and Huselid, M., Strategic human resources management: Where do we go from here? *J. Manage.*, 32, 6, 898–925, 2006.
2. Margherita, A., Human resources analytics: A systematization of research topics and directions for future research. *Hum. Resour. Manage. Rev.*, *32*, 2, 100795, 2022.
3. *Global Human Capital Analysis trends 2017: Rewriting the rules for the digital age*, Deloitte University Press, pp. 230 & 211, 2017.
4. Hunt, S.T., Baltes, B.B., DeHart, W.B., Analytics for Human Capital Analysis: A review of literature and implications for research. *Hum. Resour. Manage. Rev.*, 28, 3, 347–358, 2018.
5. Rothwell, W.J. and Kazanas, H.C., *Mastering the instructional design process: A systematic approach*, 3rd, Pfeiffer, p. 217, 2003.
6. Silzer, R. and Dowell, B.E., *Strategy-driven talent management: A leadership imperative*, John Wiley & Sons, p. 211, 2010.

10

Predictive Analytics - Next Chapter in Talent Management

Swati Rai[1], Rakesh Kumar Yadav[1]* and Rajesh Kumar Dhanaraj[2]

[1]*Department of Management Studies, School of Business Management, IFTM University, Moradabad, Uttar Pradesh, India*
[2]*Symbiosis International (Deemed University), Pune, Maharashtra, India*

Abstract

When the era is so competitive, then survival of the fittest becomes a challenge, and here comes the savior, predictive analytics. Predictive analytics is a branch of advanced analytics that makes predictions about future outcomes using historical data combined with statistical modeling. To survive and grow, one needs to deeply and thoroughly understand and analyze trends and developments, subsequently calculating and forecasting the forthcoming patterns of the resources, such as inventory, human resources, integrated marketing communications, and almost all the further facets of operations management. This is the only secret ingredient that can bring a business advantage. Another lifeline for the success of any organization is its human resources, which effectively handles the other resources. So, identifying and nurturing the top talent in this modern and competitive world of business is a strategic imperative. However, everything cannot be done only on the basis of intuition. Therefore, organizations are nowadays gradually progressing to predictive analytics to gain important acumens about their manpower. This, in turn, facilitates them to make intelligent decisions that can drive them to success. So now, in terms of HR, this means controlling historical and real-time data to calculate and make predictions about potentially highly competent employees. This paper explores the crucial role of predictive analytics in the facets of talent identification, performance evaluation, and hence, training needs assessment and subsequently promotions. It will cover the fundamentals of predictive analytics, its applications in talent management, and the benefits it provides. However, it will also cover the tests and difficulties that may arise. Thereafter, the frameworks will

**Corresponding author*: rkyadav@iftmuniversity.ac.in

Deepa Gupta, Mukul Gupta, Pawan Budhwar, Jim Westerman, Rajesh Kumar Dhanaraj and Balamurugan Balusamy (eds.) Human Capital Analytics: Exploring the HR Spectrum in Industry 5.0, (219–236) © 2025 Scrivener Publishing LLC

also delve into the future of talent management with a touch of predictive analytics, including developing trends and technologies.

Keywords: Predictive analytics, historical data, predictions, talent identification

10.1 Introduction

Forecasting the upcoming events is a must. For the same, when one uses statistics and other programming and machine learning techniques to analyze historical data in order to discover the likelihood of future events possibly occurring, that phenomenon is called predictive analytics. The integration of predictive analytics with talent management has increasingly become popular, as organizations these days need to make informed decisions calculated based on statistical data.

A very basic definition of Talent management comprises all the methods that organizations incorporate to bring employees on board; keep them happy, satisfied, and productive; and help them continue to develop their skills over time and witness their career progression. Talent management is a strategic process of attracting, developing, retaining, and optimizing the expertise and capabilities of an organization's staff. It incorporates several HR activities and processes intended to make sure that the organization has the most effective staffing done, i.e., the organization has the right people with the right competencies in the right positions and that too at the right time to fulfill current and future business needs.

Successful and effective talent management involves an all-inclusive and cohesive outlook that synchronizes with the organization's overall business strategy. It actually is not a one-shot activity; rather, it involves ongoing evaluation, regular improvement, and optimization of the workforce to ensure survival and success in the cutthroat competition.

Predictive analytics can arrange valuable inputs into various functions of HRM, such as recruitment and selection, performance management, and employee retention. In a nutshell, by using data analysis, organizations can make wise decisions and optimize their talent management strategies.

Predictive analytics in human resource management is used to conduct the analysis of all the past and historical data and further make forecasts about forthcoming events; however, it is completely different from standard HR analytics and should not be confused with the latter [1].

With HR analytics, data are collected and analyzed to see the planning done, what is working and what is not, and if deviated, where one can improve. With the former, i.e., predictive analytics, data are collected with the objective of making predictions about employees, their performances, or the upcoming HR trends.

With standard HR analytics, an organization looks at past problems. The past challenges are analyzed in an attempt to resolve them and avoid them in the future.

But, with predictive analytics, we are taking a more proactive approach. Here, we are analyzing data to recognize and understand where problems may or may not appear in the future. Basically, here, we are making an attempt to correct things before these problems show up actually [1].

10.1.1 Role of Predictive Analytics in Talent Management

Predictive HR analytics is a procedure where businesses inspect previous and existing human resources and related data to foresee forthcoming consequences and attain future objectives. HR departments can use predictive analytics tools to find, examine, and classify HR data, helping them recognize outlines and visions that inform upcoming choices. Despite several misconceptions, predictive analysis is not a replacement for human contribution, and also it is not at all astrology which is about predicting the unknown future. It is mainly about trying to understand, using past data, how people interrelate with the organization, for instance, how ready the individuals are to get a promotion versus the time they can wait to get promoted.

10.1.1.1 Recruitment and Selection

Getting the best candidate requires a pool of talented applicants from which the candidates can be shortlisted. The first step in talent management is recruitment whose success further determines the whole foundation of an organization and shapes its future. Predictive analytics can transform the recruitment process by analyzing statistical records from past hires to identify patterns and characteristics associated with success. It assists the organization in identifying the source from where the vacancies have successfully been filled till now; this, in turn, empowers organizations to aim their efforts more effectively in sourcing and selecting candidates. Streamlining the efforts in a well-thought-out direction cuts the cost as well as the time invested in an organization. Predictive analytics helps identify the most effective channels for recruiting talent by analyzing past data on successful hires.

Recruitment analytics involves the application of data analysis and statistical methods to optimize the recruitment and hiring processes within an organization. So, finally, it can be said that the use of predictive analytics in the recruitment process ultimately helps to attract and retain the best talent.

After HR planning, the vital and critical function inside any organization that affects its success and growth is recruitment. Predictive analytics works as an assistant to enable organizations to think beyond the old-style recruitment procedures by leveraging past data to identify and utilize the most successful and fruitful hiring stations and candidate features. This precision and accuracy in recruitment not only saves time and resources but also results in better hires and brings into line new talent into sync with the organization's culture and goals.

Predictive analysis is converting recruitment into a more precise, sharp, and efficient process. By harnessing data and technology, organizations can make well-versed decisions that lead to better employees, lesser costs, and an improved overall experience with more competent candidates. As most businesses these days are inclined toward embracing predictive analysis in recruitment, businesses that are taking up these skills and technologies will gain a competitive and strategic advantage in attracting, drawing, and retaining topmost talent.

10.1.1.2 Candidate Assessment

Candidate assessment is a decisive step in the recruitment process aimed at calculating the appropriateness of candidates for specific roles within an organization. By employing various assessment methods, recruiters and hiring managers can gain insights into a candidate's skills, competencies, and overall fit for the position. Perfect selection of the right talent demands correct and precise analysis of skills and competencies. By integrating various data sources, including resumes, skills assessment tests, and interview feedback, predictive models can weigh a candidate's suitability for a specific role. This aids organizations to make more logical decisions during the hiring process. The days when performance evaluations were done on a subjective basis are gone. Predictive analytics allows organizations to evaluate an employee's past performance, forecast upcoming developments, and establish realistic, practical, and achievable goals. This data-driven method of performance management encourages integrity, fairness, transparency, and nonstop improvement and upgradation.

10.1.1.3 Retention and Employee Engagement

Did you know…???

The replacement of an old employee with a new one is approximately 150% of their annual salary. This fact is only true for mid-level employees. To the utmost shock, it can be seen that for the high-level employees, the outlays can rise up to 400%. Organizations appear sensible and logical if they try to prevent all those extra charges. Here, the savior is predictive analytics which turns out to be a help [4].

i) Retention:

a) Data Analysis and Identifying Patterns: As the employee leaves, the organization maintains its records as in the factors responsible for the turnover, viz., factors such as job satisfaction, performance metrics, career advancement, job role, or feedback from performance reviews and workplace conditions. Predictive analytics involves scrutinizing historical and recent data related to employee turnover. Subsequently, it helps in identifying the most plausible reasons for employee turnover, which can then also be worked upon to minimize the drain of talent [5].
b) Flight Risk Prediction: Every employee has an innate need to get a better role and benefits, whether in the same organization, otherwise anywhere else. He waits to fly until he gets a better option. The HR decision-makers can be trained to predict those employees who are seemingly a greater threat of leaving the organization in the near future. This allows management to follow a proactive approach and address the issue so as to beforehand retain its employees.
c) Personalized Interventions: Predictive analytics can also advise custom-made retention strategies for specific employees who are identified as the ones at high flight risk. Such suggestions may include tailor-made training programs, mentorship and coaching programs, or amendments to compensation and other monetary and/or non-monetary benefits [3].

Not only hiring the right people, training them, and placing them in the right positions guarantee prolonged success but also retaining them for a longer period of time is something that makes an organization stand apart and in fact ahead of the others in the race [1]. Employee retention is an extremely critical aspect of organizational success, directly impacting productivity, morale, and the satisfaction level of the employees. The old and traditional approaches to retaining talent over and over again depend on reactive measures, but with the use of predictive analysis, organizations can take a more strategic and proactive approach. Gradually, the use of predictive analysis is becoming a game changer in improving employee retention by using the influence of data-driven insights and foresight.

Every individual is unique and absolutely different from others. Their likes and dislikes may differ from each other. One person may find bribery to be absolutely unethical while the other may say that it is okay to take bribes but not doing the related task is unethical. For the business, both of them are important. Management might want both of them to stay. So, the demand is that how can such a retention strategy be formulated that is pervasive, all-encompassing, and attractive to all? The answer is, of course, through predictive HR analytics.

Predictive analytics acts as a supernatural *crystal ball of the witchcraft stories* for identifying factors that contribute to employee turnover and hence should be eradicated. By analyzing the old data and patterns, organizations can pinpoint probable flight risks and implement customized retention strategies on the target, raising a steadier, competent, loyal, and promising workforce.

ii) Employee Engagement:

a) Optimum utilization of talent is a key driver to the success of an organization. Underutilization and overutilization can both be a barrier to the goal of success. Predictive analysis can be applied to employee engagement to classify key drivers of engagement. By analyzing survey findings along with other figures, organizations can predict and achieve optimum engagement levels for their manpower.
b) Predictive analytics can also provide assistance in improving employee engagement. The employees are able to strike a balance in their personal as well as professional roles and assignments. For example, it may suggest targeted training programs, changes in grievance handling practices, or other initiatives to enhance work-life balance also with the added score of optimum utilization of *talent.*

c) Predictive analytics also helps to identify the early signs of declining engagement among the employees by regularly monitoring the significant indicators. This further allows for timely interventions.

In the context of employee engagement, predictive analysis includes the usage of data, statistical models, and machine learning methodologies to anticipate and address factors influencing workforce engagement. By investigating historical data, feedback analysis, and performance metrics, organizations can forecast trends, identify the upcoming potential challenges standing ahead, and develop targeted strategies to lift employee morale and therefore employee engagement. This pre-emptive approach creates a workplace culture that raises and nurtures job satisfaction, employee commitment, and performance of the highest level. By analyzing employee feedback, performance data, and other relevant factors, organizations can address issues affecting employee engagement in real time. Predictive analytics promotes an encouraging work environment, leading to improved job satisfaction and advanced levels of worker commitment. Therefore, we can say that predictive analytics can enable organizations to forecast and handle determinants affecting employee engagement levels, leading to a more motivated, satisfied, and happy workforce.

10.1.1.4 Succession Planning

Predictive analytics, as the name suggests, helps to analyze the performance evaluation reports, skills mapping, and other relevant factors which later on guides the organization to identify those employees who have high potential for leadership roles to become future leaders. Integrating predictive analytics with succession planning increases the preciseness of identifying upcoming front-runners and leaders.

Mapping the gap between the data on currently employed workers and future job requirements helps in developing targeted training programs for effective and efficient succession planning.

Succession planning has long been a foundation of effective talent management, ensuring that organizations have a strong and tough stream of qualified individuals ready to step into key roles as and when needed. In the contemporary business scenario, the integration of predictive analysis into the process of succession planning has raised this strategic procedure to several new heights. Predictive analysis is redesigning and reshaping succession planning, empowering organizations to recognize, develop, and retain their future frontrunner leaders with precision beyond comparison.

This branch of analytics identifies high-potential employees and future leaders within the organization. This proactive approach to succession planning ensures a smooth and wholesome transition during leadership changes, minimizing risks related to departures of important personnel.

10.1.1.5 Performance Management

Employees of any organization work and seek motivation in terms of monetary and non-monetary benefits. Talent management requires the correct assessment of employee performance so that the areas for improvement can be precisely identified and the high-performing employees are rewarded. Also, the relatively underperforming employees are developed through training programs. This later ensures alignment with the strategic goals and ensures overall organizational success.

Predictions of performances: Predictive analytics can also help to measure many influences contributing to employee performance and forecast upcoming performance trends. This allows for more effective performance management strategies.

Goal Setting: By analyzing past performance data, organizations can set more realistic and achievable performance goals for employees.

10.1.1.6 Human Resource Planning

Future Skill Needs: Predictive analytics can help analyze past and ongoing industry trends, the latest technological developments, and business strategies to predict future skill needs. This assists in efficiently designing recruitment, training, and development programs [2].

Aligning an organization's workforce with its strategic business objectives is a must these days. Strategic workforce planning is the basic fundamental to do the same as it is a proactive, pre-emptive, and data-driven approach. It has procedures and formulas that help in investigating the competencies and capabilities of the current workforce, anticipating future talent needs, and developing strategies to bridge the gap between the present and future workforce requirements. Strategic workforce planning is far beyond conventional and traditional human resource management which is just confined to formulating the policies at the functional level only. It actually works at a pervasive level by integrating employees' data with the overall business strategy, supporting organizations to adapt promptly to the changes in the conditions of the ever-changing market, technological developments, and other external factors of the business environment. One of the principal benefits of predictive analytics in talent management is its ability to forecast future talent requirements. With the help of predictive analytics, by analyzing the ongoing industry developments, business goals, and workforce data, organizations can carry a proactive approach to plan for future talent needs and make sure they have the optimum and effective staffing done, i.e., *the perfectly right people working in absolutely right positions at the specifically right time* [2].

Optimizing Workforce Size: The combination of predictive analytics and workforce planning empowers organizations to make strong and wise decisions about their human resource, align their human capital with the mission and objectives of the business, and make sure that the business has the right talent in the right place [1].

10.1.1.7 Learning and Development

As already said in the paper, performance prediction models use data analytics and other statistical tools to forecast the future performance of employees based on past trends. These models intend to provide visions into how well an employee fits in the specified job role, enabling organizations to make better decisions regarding talent management, succession planning, and career development. This again helps in identifying high-potential employees and then customizes training and development plans to improve their contributions.

Personalized Training: Predictive analytics helps in identifying individual learning needs based on an employee's performance data and career goals, enabling the development of personalized training programs.

Training Effectiveness: By analyzing training outcomes, organizations can evaluate the usefulness and efficacy of various learning initiatives and make informed decisions about future investments in employee development programs.

Personalized learning and development is another domain that has seen drastic development and change since the arrival of predictive analysis. The phenomenon of predictive analysis in the framework of learning and development involves leveraging data, analytics, and machine learning techniques to know in advance individual and organizational learning needs. Through the analysis of various data sources, including employee performance, skill assessment reports, and career ambitions, organizations can predict the most effective learning involvements for every single employee. This data-driven approach facilitates the establishment of made-to-order learning pathways, optimizing the influence of training initiatives. Every employee is unique in terms of his skills, wit, and oval personality, and therefore, their learning needs vary. Predictive analytics enables organizations to mold training and development programs and customize them as per individual employee profiles. Using predictive analytics, organizations can quite accurately identify specific skill gaps and growth areas and then can invest in exactly targeted learning initiatives, resulting in a more skilled and adaptable workforce [3].

10.1.1.8 Continuous Feedback and Improvement

Continuous feedback and improvement are essential constituents of effective talent management and development. Nurturing a culture of open and regular feedback raises employee growth, improves performance, and adds to the inclusive development and success of the organization. The nature of predictive analytics lets organizations uninterruptedly polish their models based on real-time performance data and feedback.

10.2 Predictive Analysis - A Game Changer

When the company is in its growing period, i.e., in its good times, taking your company's talent for granted can be easy and non-bothering. But do so when your business is in threat, so will be your end. Investing in talent management, or in the policies and ways that your organization uses to attract, retain, and develop its employees, better referred to as "talent" or "human capital", can give your company an edge. It is really important to manage talent and position it well, and leaders need to know how to go up to the occasion. To help form a labor force that has the talent to accomplish goals, leaders can form a talent-first culture in the organization. Most organizations do not consider and value the talent that is required to implement different innovative ideas. Companies can definitely improve organizational performance and potentially gain a strategic advantage by putting talent first.

Organizations should take a step back and ensure they are able to understand why their employees are leaving in the first place—since it could aid them in gathering information about what might bring them back. For ages, the conventional methods and processes of talent management often relied upon gut flings, intuitions of experienced people, and historical data. But only the historical data is not of much use until it is examined and statistically analyzed. However, with the advent of predictive analysis the business world has witnessed a new era [1]. The talent management process and its accuracy can be improved by the businesses through this ultimate pathway. Talent acquisition and its management have been transformed

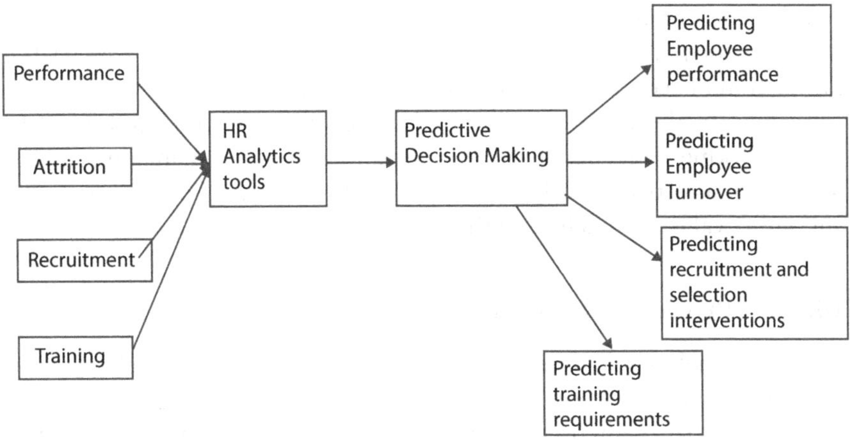

Figure 10.1 HR analytics and decision making. source: Self-Developed.

drastically by the use of predictive analysis, as it has brought a data-driven and proactive approach and practical line of action to the hiring process [4].

Ultimate Cost Savings
As it is clearly evident from Figure 10.1, the use of predictive analysis reorganizes the processes and improves the decision-making which in turn highly contributes to cost-cutting and hence a lot of savings. The use of this technique can help businesses enhance their talent management strategies and drop the incompetency level, inefficiencies, costs-related turnover, and unnecessary and pointless expenditures.

10.3 Challenges in Predictive Analytics

As it has rightly been said, every coin has two sides; this means that although predictive analytics brings along with it a lot of remarkable benefits, it also has attached baggage packed up with a lot of practical difficulties and encounters. It becomes imperative and unavoidable for organizations to cope with these difficulties in order to get accurate and important understandings from the collected data.

10.3.1 Quality and Availability of Data

Any data that are not complete, invalid, inaccurate, or obsolete are of no use, rather they can produce defective and faulty inferences. The results can then be unreliable, the models defective and the decisions wrong. As we know, the reliability and authenticity of data are something that lay the foundation of accurate and valid predictions [6].

Businesses these days are required to devote much time and effort to those working strategies that help in maintaining and managing quality data. This, as a result, will make sure that the organization has accurate, authentic, valid, complete, and the latest data.

10.3.2 Privacy and Security of Data

Predictive analytics has a lot of regulatory control over almost all the data, both historical and current. Here, it is worthwhile mentioning that the term data means that predictive analytics has all sorts of sensitive personal and proprietary information. The biggest challenge is that while making use of predictive analytics, an organization needs to formulate strategies that are in compliance with the data privacy protocols. Therefore, protecting the data from unapproved and illicit access is one of the most tiresome tasks.

To overcome this challenge, the organization should keep data privacy at the top of all its priorities. Establishing clear-cut policies to handle sensitive data and implementing vigorous and tough data encryption, access controls, and compliance measures are the key drivers toward ensuring data security.

10.3.3 Complexity of Models

Striking a balance between model complexity and interpretability is a genuinely tough task. Too complex models may be tough to handle and maintain by any normal person. Organizations require knowledge of data science and an understanding of advanced analytics to develop and organize complex predictive models.

Creating effective and efficient models demands association between the domain experts and data science teams.

10.3.4 Overfitting and Underfitting

Sometimes, it happens that a model grasps the data too deeply, even including noise and other unsought external factors, which leads to poor generalization of new data. This is known as overfitting. Similarly, underfitting, on the other hand, results in a too simplistic and basic model.

To avoid the effects of overfitting and underfitting problems, businesses should focus on the use of techniques like cross-validation so as to measure model performance on autonomous datasets. Regularization methods can be applied to prevent overfitting while adjusting model complexity can address underfitting.

10.3.5 Lack of Domain Expertise

Apart from the generalized knowledge, it is quite imperative for an organization to understand the sharp and detailed intricacies of a specific industry or business domain. This is actually required and is absolutely vital for developing correct and accurate predictive models. Without having the domain know-how, models may not capture the various shades of the data. For this, the organizations can wisely choose to collaborate closely with subject matter experts who deeply understand the field. Domain knowledge is essential for feature assortment, model interpretation, and ensuring the relevance of predictions to real-world scenarios.

10.3.6 Scalability Issues

As volumes of data grow, predictive analytics models may face scalability issues. Processing large datasets in real time can strain computing resources and impact model performance.

Investment in scalable infrastructure and distribution of computing solutions can be a worthy solution. Also, Cloud-based platforms and parallel processing can help handle large datasets efficiently.

10.3.7 Changing Data Patterns

As already mentioned, the predictive model completely relies on historical data patterns. However, if the causal patterns vary due to the shifts in the dynamic business environment, the models may become less precise.

Now, the solution to this problem is that organizations should regularly bring up-to-date models to adapt to the changing patterns. Also, continuous monitoring and reequipping of models with up-to-the-minute data can help maintain accuracy in dynamic environments.

10.3.8 Interpretable Models

Not all stakeholders are technical experts, so the multifaceted machine learning models may lack clarity, which, as a result, makes it tough for such stakeholders to comprehend how predictions are made.

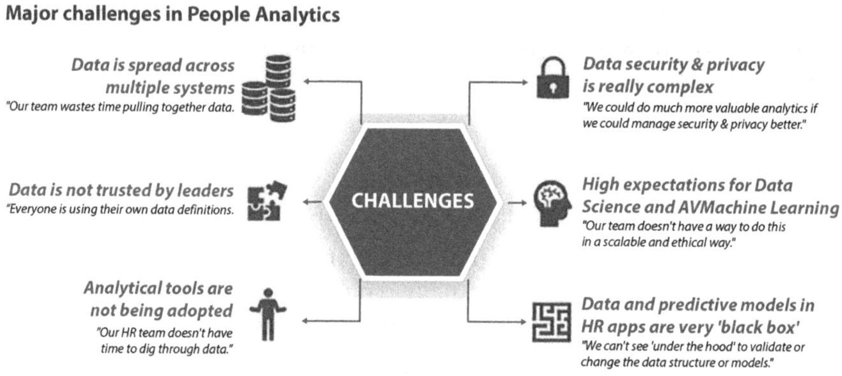

Figure 10.2 Challenges in HR analytics. Source: www.onemodel.co.

To overcome such difficulties, there should be an easy channel of communication between *expert data scientists* and *not-so-technical decision-makers*. This is critical to ensure a strong understanding of model outputs. Therefore, a business has to prioritize the use of interpretable models when transparency is crucial.

Therefore, apart from the various significant advantages predictive analytics offers, there are also many challenges that come along with it. Organizations must address those challenges, as shown in Figure 10.2, to ensure the effective implementation of predictive analytics and receive precise outcomes. Overcoming these challenges is very important for the optimum utilization of predictive analytics in various domains. Working on such concerns related to bias, fairness, and privacy is crucial. Organizations

Predictive analytics in HR market stats

Expected sales of workforce analytics market by 2028: 2.9bn

69% of the organizations believe workforce analytics is critical to their success.

33.3% HRs say they have objective behavioural and cognitive data on candidates.

61% HRs believe providing useful people data and analytics is the key goal of their HR tech stack must implement safeguards and ethical guidelines to ensure that predictive analytics is used responsibly in HR decision-making.

Data quality and safekeeping are serious considerations in the realm of data management and analytics. Making sure that the data is correct, reliable, and protected is indispensable for making informed decisions and retaining the trust of stakeholders. The accuracy and security of data are of utmost importance. Ensuring the quality of data and implementing solid security measures are critical for the success of predictive analytics initiatives [6].

Google has been known for using data-driven approaches to enhance the hiring and talent management processes.

Google may implement predictive analytics in talent management in resume analysis. It uses algorithms to analyze resumes and identify relevant skills and experiences. Machine learning models can quickly process a large volume of resumes, highlighting candidates who match the specific requirements for a given role. The movie Moneyball also portrays the use of predictive analytics to forecast the probability of the success of each of the baseball players. Predictive analytics can be used to predict employee retention. By examining various factors, such as job satisfaction, engagement, and historical retention patterns, Google can identify employees who may be at risk of leaving the company.

Steps to Use Predictive HR Analytics Effectively:

As already mentioned, predictive human resource analytics brings along with it a lot of challenges. But an advantage is that the overall procedure for using talent analytics is moderately direct and not so complicated. Some significant steps for to make sure that talent analytics are used successfully to get complete, data-driven decisions.

1. Define the Objective

It is not mandatory that predictive human resource analytics should work with the objective of bringing considerable organizational alterations, rather it has to have *certain specific* objectives in mind. Now, this could be as ordinary as a descriptive talent analysis to acquire a clue about the current condition of the company's workforce. Like any other existence, even if the business does not have any objective, then there is much chance that the business may get trapped with data that are fitting and/or inappropriate.

2. Build a Talent Analytics Team

Predictive analytics should not be considered to be a one-man army. It is not possible for a single individual to carry on this analysis. It takes a committed and enthusiastic force to develop and use talent analytics tactically and effectively. People from different functional areas like legislative, finance, IT, and HR, from senior position leaders to lower-level members should be included in the team.

3. Identify which Forms of Talent Analytics Are Appropriate

As soon as the objectives are established, the subsequent phase is to discover which methods of talent analytics will be appropriate for the outcome being targeted. That method can be descriptive, diagnostic, predictive, or prescriptive.

4. Define the Relevant Metrics

For the calculated comparison and analysis of data, supportive metrics are required to be formed. These metrics might contain stuff like the number of employees, self-reported employee satisfaction (on some relevant scale), employee productivity, employee turnover, absenteeism, and others.

5. Gather Data

Just like any other research, predictive HR analytics metrics should be designed on the basis of data that are easily and readily accessible. In certain circumstances, data might already be accessible, but, in other conditions, novel methods and ways of collecting the data must be established. Gathering new data should be related back to objectives and also to the cost/benefit ratio of the used method [8].

6. Analyze Data

The data that have been collected are actually useless until it is analyzed and interpreted. However, the selection of the methods and processes that are used to analyze the gathered data completely depends upon the quantity of data collected and the intricacy of the analysis required.

7. Develop and Implement Policy Adjustments

As soon as the data are analyzed, the information gathered will yield meaningful insights that may or may not demand changes in strategies and/or practices. For example, if the analyzed data are giving an indication that new workers are parting away, leaving the job within a year of hire might require a little bit of additional investigation to fix the cause responsible for the worrying statistics. Thereafter, only remedies would be required to transform those organizational policies or practices that might increase the turnover rate.

8. Measure and Repeat

As the business environment is very dynamic, i.e., it keeps on changing, the predictive analytics process has to be a dynamic phenomenon. In any organization, both the internal and external business environments keep on changing. To cope with that, the company needs to formulate and implement new business strategies, and, in turn, it needs new HR strategies that can complement the newly framed business strategies. Moreover, consequences will also vary so it is necessary to determinedly check the figures so that the required changes and adjustments can be made, if needed.

Conclusion

Predictive analytics is not just a topic or jargon rather it is a game changer in talent management. Using predictive analytics to explore and utilize the influence of statistical data, organizations can identify top talent, optimize recruitment processes, and drive employee performance toward the best. As we look to the upcoming future, the continuous development of predictive analytics assures even bigger improvements in shaping the workforce of tomorrow.

Companies are increasingly moving toward demand data-driven decision-making. Predictive HR analytics is much needed to support the HR departments and help them display their data-driven know-how. The use of predictive analysis is gradually becoming more and more important and also unavoidable, as nowadays, HR leaders are being approached to project future labor trends and developments and do the prior calculation of the ever-fluctuating prerequisites of the workforce [7].

The success of any organization demands the most effective human resources as the rest of the resources are owned and controlled by the former one. Identification of top talent and correct assessment of employee performance are critical aspects of effective talent management within an organization. Both processes contribute significantly to achieving business goals, fostering employee growth, and maintaining a competitive edge.

An HR leader in a growth-driven organization must ensure competitiveness. The only way out of this trap is to use technology and analyze data to make informed decisions. Predictive analytics in HR is a very powerful tool that can aid you do that effectively and efficiently.

The use of predictive analytics actually helps the HR Department to get to the bottom of the capability and skills of the workforce and the organization. It also helps to analyze and predict employee trends and behaviors, and gain a really important understanding of their performance, inclinations, dislikes, and potential—and thus one can make proactive decisions that improve employee performance, commitment, productivity, and business growth.

In a nutshell, we can say "Embrace the data-driven revolution and unlock the full potential of your organization's greatest asset—its people."

References

1. Dessler, G. and Biju, V., *Human Resource Management*, vol. 16/e 16th, Pearson Education, 2020.
2. Gustafsson, D., *Business Intelligence, Analytics and Human Capital: Current State of Workforce Analytics in Sweden*, Student thesis, Institution for Communication and Information, 2012.
3. Kumar, S.D.B., *Human Resource Predictive Analytics (HRPA) For Management its Usage in the Organization*. GIBS Business School, Journal of Management: *GIBS*, vol. 01/01, 2018.
4. https://www.itransition.com/predictive-analytics/hr.
5. https://www.shrm.org/in/topics-tools/news/organizational-employee-development/using-predictive-analytics-talent-management.
6. https://hr.economictimes.indiatimes.com/news/hrtech/the-next-chapter-in-talent-management-embracing-automation-and-ai/106931433.
7. Yang, K., *Quality in the Era of Industry 4.0*, Wiley, 2024.
8. www.analyticsin hr.com.

11

Employee Engagement and Performance Management - Critical Role of Employee Potentials

Asma Bano[1]* and Ayesha Khatun[2]

[1]*Mittal School of Business, Lovely Professional University, Phagwara, Punjab, India*
[2]*Symbiosis Law School, Nagpur, Symbiosis International University, Nagpur, Maharashtra, India*

Abstract

Purpose

The important aim of the current work is to find the levels of engagement and organizational performance (OP). The study also focused on the features and concerns of employee engagement (EE) and OP and found their contribution to determining organizational success. The study is conducted to investigate whether there is any relation between EE and OP in determining organizational profitability and growth. Important aspects of the review also concentrated on determining the effect of employee potential on EE which will further lead to an effect on OP.

Design/Methodology/Approach

A review methods approach has been used and authors review relevant literature on the construction of employee potential, EE, and OPs. The authors recognize the factors and success drivers of the concerned concepts. Interpretations on EE and OPs by unlocking the employee potentials at different sectors using systematic review were extended.

Findings

The findings reveal that EE directly communicates the performances by validating the employee potential. The study has found that EE is the outcome of the employee potential if channelized and implemented as needed. It concludes

**Corresponding author*: asmabanu_522@yahoo.in

Deepa Gupta, Mukul Gupta, Pawan Budhwar, Jim Westerman, Rajesh Kumar Dhanaraj and Balamurugan Balusamy (eds.) Human Capital Analytics: Exploring the HR Spectrum in Industry 5.0, (237–260) © 2025 Scrivener Publishing LLC

from the previous research that engagement is substantially related to the factors of engagement which leads to increased OP. The levels of involvement and dedication vary greatly across the different employees at different levels, between employees with different designations and different degrees of experience with different potentials as revealed by this study.

Practical Implications
The results facilitate businesses in managing and delivering employee potential, EE, and OPs. Organizations stand for the particularities of employee potential in engaging the employees and, in turn, increasing the OPs. In light of the study's primary emphasis on EE and performance in HR Analytics, employees who are the building blocks of the company are taken into consideration. Although this work validates that EE is favorably related to the emotional, social, psychological, and intellectual well-being of the workmen.

Originality/Value
This is unique and the first observations assessing employee potential in creating the EE and employee potential is also showing an impact on the OPs. It also addresses the levels involved in engaging the employees and the levels of employee potential in relation to OPs.

***Keywords*:** Employee engagement, organizational performance, factors, organization, employees, commitment, employee potential, HR analytics

11.1 Introduction

11.1.1 Human Resource Analytics (HR Analytics)

Human Resources (HR) Analytics commences extra implication on staying a vital one for the growth of the organization and has emergent as new arena. It has provided solutions to the problems embarking on the field of employees, performances, and turnovers with the availability of inputs to move forward. HR Analytics encompasses mass and relevant data of the employees and organizations in combination with research methodology and operation statistics with software modules for forward planning and decision-making in Human Resources. The thrust of Human Resource Management is to inculcate an interest in analytics as today's prime thing [30].

In recent times of technology and advancements, managing employees and improving performance are not single hand tasks but have become hierarchical works. The increasing number of corporations and evolved businesses are accompanied by technology and complex worlds handling workforce and following their enactments done online with the help of Human Resources (HR) Analytics. Application of analytics in HR has enhanced employee engagement and organizational performances resulting in enlarged competence in business, like the development of excellent recruitment, selection process, talent strategies, production and productivity of employees, and decreased employee turnover and turnover intentions [36].

Human Resources Analytics along with tools and technologies are used in diverse companies. HR Analytics at 5.0 helps different organizations with different employees at various levels, customs, and traditions to realize the concepts, namely, employee engagement, employee potential, organizational performance, employee revenue, and retaining worker conduct. HR Analytics progress personnel enactment, decrease operative expenses, and revitalize professional expansion.

Human Resource Analytics indicates a submission of investigative procedures to the human resource department of a business with the purpose of improving employee-related and organizations-related outcomes like employee engagement, employee talent and acquisitions, employee performances, return on investment, financial growth, and organizational performances. It is the process of data collection and evaluating each process in depth so as to draw conclusions from the collected data as well as improve the progressions. It is also marked as a development to comprehend in what way investment in people capital assets brings to the success of a few outcomes, namely, generating income, more than one source of financial revenue, reducing cost, managing risk, and application of strategic tools, which is possible by smearing arithmetical approaches incorporated into HR personnel, ability administration, monetary, and function data.

HR analytics is a cohesive function that leads to improved individual and organizational performances along with quality decision-making and managerial functions [39]. It largely depends on statistical analysis software and possesses large quality data, well-defined tasks, intellectual analysis, dominance, and setup of contracts stating that analytics is a genuine way of overall success in human resources. HR Analytics involves broadcasting, data withdrawal, control panel, analytical examination, and operative testing.

The process of HR Analytics involves various steps [29]: 1) describing the goals of HR Analytics, 2) choosing statistical methods, 3) evaluating HR metrics, 4) analyzing facts and figures, and 5) developing decisions.

Human Resource Analytics can be categorized into three main types [30]:

1. Descriptive Analytics uses data from historical proceedings with the help of news, reports, scorecards, clustering, etc. 2. Predictive Analytics involves analytical demonstrating via instrumental, arithmetical, and advanced learning methods like statistical regression analysis and workforce planning. 3. Prescriptive Analytics mentions verdicts by means of optimization, simulation, replication, recreation, etc.

11.2 Literature Review and Theoretical Concepts of the Study

11.2.1 Literature Review on Theoretical Concepts of Employee Potential

Employee potential relates to an individual's expertise, innate abilities, capacities, and personal traits to carry out the work and achieve results. Employees who have high desires and aspirations to move forward and grow will have higher potential. Usually, employee potential is exhibited by the performances the employees perform, the results that are derived, the time taken, and the effectiveness and efficiency of the work [33]. It is also concerned with the size of the companies and the strength and status quo used by the employees.

Employee potential basically possesses numerous dimensions that refer to the different aspects of the employee. Basic dimensions of employee potential are the following: Career Dimensions: This is gained by the experiences built upon a particular job or occupation [1]. The focus is on the availability of desired skills and ability in performing a job role and attaining a position. It is more toward career development growth maturity and career potentiality. They too inclined to be the chief qualities measured throughout the appointment, mostly at an entry level. They stand as significant pointers for shaping the long-standing accomplishment of an employee in a starring role but they are not an element of extraordinary perspective on their personal. Growth Dimensions: The growth dimensions have the tendency to become more superficial at the ending sides. They also possess some constant traits that do not change very often [1]. It is very essential to realize the growth potential at the early stages as it bridges the gap between the present performances and future performances. Fundamental Dimensions: These are otherwise called foundational dimensions and are regarded as the most consistent. They are not dependent on any particular job or work role but can be measured across a number of areas [1]. These are the greatest processes for foreseeing together short-time and long-time potentialities composed of abilities such as intellect and meticulousness [45].

11.2.1.1 Factors of Employee Potential

In today's world, the concept of bigger rivalry between multinationals and their necessity to reply successfully to quickly altering working circumstances, along with employee supplies, has intensified the requirement to recognize those influences that disturb employee performance. The purpose of this paper is to examine factors affecting employee potential.

The factors of employee potential are environment/firm, job, and employee [19]: Environment/firm-related factors (social culture, support and security by management, atmosphere vitality, and organizational climate), job-related factors (job atmosphere, job independence, and job communication), and employee-related factors (intrinsic motivation, talent elasticity, expertise level, proactivity, adaptableness, and obligation).

Today, the spectacle of improved race among companies and their essential to reply efficiently to quickly altering working circumstances, as well as to workforce necessities, has intensified the requirement to recognize those influences that affect employee potential. It refers to inspecting the interrelations amid environment/firm-related factors, job-related factors, and employee-related factors and their impact on employee potential.

The important factors prompting employee potential are divided into four vital backgrounds: 1) outside business environment factors, 2) operative work environment factors, 3) potentials of the job, and 4) learning abilities of the employees.

Employee potential assists in raising proprietors'/bosses' consciousness of the significant causes compelling employee knowledge through worker awareness and ability achievement in minor business [17]. Defining employee potential includes classifying persons who exhibit excellent capacities and have the potential toward important offerings to an organization's future victory.

Employee potential includes performance and results, learning agility, leadership potential, strategic thinking, emotional intelligence, ambition and drive, and cultural fit [49].

Past performance, knowledge, skills, and capabilities to do an occupation were ignored earlier in achieving the outcomes. Nowadays employee skills, talents and potential have become a necessity to flourish in maximum administrations [61]. The worker has to produce and alter as dissolute as their occupation does and the factors of employee potential that lead to the way volatile, uncertain, complex, and ambiguous (VUCA) environment [46].

Motivation, determination, engagement, curiosity, and insight are some of the factors of employee potential that help the employee to become more potential leading to the attainment of the organizational goals and objectives effectively and efficiently [16].

11.2.1.2 Ways to Unlock the Employee Potential

The employees thrive and perform their best based on how the organisation manages and supports them [47]. Once there is no support and provision, even the most skilled and endowed employees will be incapable of working to their fullest potential. Every so often, the company's utmost brilliant personnel may bump into technical hitches when it comes to production and presentation. A variety of factors, including internal conflicts, absence of balance in work, inadequate guidance, and more, can discourage them from starting their tasks effectively. The modern workplace is rapidly changing, so it's essential to retain top-level employees. By means of concentrating on the requirements and enhancing talent administration, policies can convey the best in each of the company's teams [60].

Following are tips to unlock employee potential:

Headship elegance prioritizes employees and their well-being above all else [6]. Develop strategies by using top-down creativity, position authority, and critical thinking to make employees happier at work within your organization. Address the needs of your staff and foster a work environment that caters well to those needs. Inventing the systems of career coaching to help employees achieve goals will help to a greater to strengthen and channel employee energy [17]. Other external things like job risk, personal balances, and emotional and psychological stress could be the cutting factors for productivity which are taken into consideration. Making the performance reviews regularly and timely helps the employees perform the challenging tasks provided without clear expectations and feedback [19]. This will help the employees to understand their potential and use it if they encounter a hurdle in attaining smart future goals.

Employee potential is better unlocked by undergoing reward management that involves great performance awards [16]. Reward great performance with awards, elevations, extras, income climbs, and supplementary to save employee motivation, accomplishment, and engagement. Lack of recognition, consideration, and poor remuneration lead to reduced engagement and prevent employees from reaching their full potential. Educating the employee about how their effort impacts goal achievement and how the individual goals are aligned with organizational goals is an essential criterion for building potential [1]. It is essential to recognize employees' significant role in decision-making, as this influences their efficiency and commitment. Additionally, it is important to help employees feel proud of the organization's long-term vision.

11.2.2 Literature Review on Theoretical Concepts of Employee Engagement

The inside framework of company communication is dependent on the multidimensional set of investments which is called engagement [34]. The pioneer definition of employee engagement strikes one's mind toward putting oneself 100% into the work role and responsibilities [34]. Positivism happens when employees go beyond the extended horizons of satisfaction and personal investments in bringing out desirable results.

Employee and employer could form the structure and shape of the employee's professional and personal growth [55], engagement, and organizational performances in addition to regular and sequential activities which lead to a positive revolution for both the employee and the employer in attaining company's future success at a single stretch [7].

Employee Engagement (EE) leads to constructive outcomes related to employees namely, satisfaction, involvement, participation, commitment, dedication, leadership qualities, motivation, inspiration, behavioural analysis, burnout, exhaustion, retention, reduced turnover and turnover intention [11]. Customer satisfaction, perception analysis, attitude and attribute, taste and preference, needs and wants and potential clients are customer related outcomes of EE. Return on investment, shareholder income, increased capital, equity, goodwill creation, and financial rewards are financial-related outcomes of EE [11]. Organizational Performances, growth and development, business expansion and overall profitability are overall organizational outcomes of EE [11].

11.2.2.1 Definitions of Employee Engagement

Different corners of the world laid down different understandings of this particular concept, leading to nearly 50 definitions that are more than enough to confuse even the most optimistic managers [32]. Employee engagement is operationally known as the optimistic, complete, and operational condition of employees which is featured by vitality, commitment, and abstraction [24]. The enthusiasm and commitment of employees contribute to the growth and development of the business [31].

11.2.2.2 Factors of Employee Engagement

Factors influencing engagement and increasing engagement levels are not just enough for the organizations to manage and train the employees, they also need to understand how important engagement is and its applications [21]. Manager have to ensure that they are provided with proper engagement policies. Job satisfaction is considered an important factor [25]. Employees satisfied with their jobs, work roles, positions, and policies will be engaged on a large scale. Job satisfaction is linked with the company, co-workers, and workplace and involves employee remuneration, company benefits, vacation, etc. [20].

Company culture has a significant impact on the employee to do well and perform at every level with full mind and concentration [25]. Employees always expect a true, productive, flexible, rewarding cooperative work environment. The meaning and purpose for everything to carry out each task requires engagement [28]. This gives clarity, confidence, and collective in performing assigned work. Purpose strengthens the engagement. Career opportunities refer to the workplace which should provide personal and professional growth and development [37]. A company is an employee company when its plans and policies are toward employee career advancements and employee revenue generation. This works directly on engagement. Reward management is a good phenomenon to motivate and engage employees. Employee hard work, time, effort, zeal, energy, and enthusiasm are to be taken into consideration seriously and should be rewarded and compensated timely [59]. According to Amah (2018), effective leadership and influence occur when an employer inspires and earns the admiration of their employees, which in turn fosters engagement [3]. Every act should be in such a way that an employee by default gets influenced by the higher level without communicating the sense of leadership. Pay structures are another important constituent of employee engagement. Based on employee eligibility, availability, and experiences, the employees are to be designated with proper pay scales and structures [57]. Annual or half-yearly increments are to be necessitated to enhance timely and needed engagement. An employee works for the money; hence, that need is to be met first.

11.2.2.3 Methods of Attaining Employee Engagement

Methods of attaining employee engagement involve the following [7].

Vision: A clear vision is essential to make employees see where they go tomorrow which will envisage getting engaged. Pride is also created by doing so. Opportunity: An organization must be structured in such a way that it should provide a platform for the employee to grow and develop and provide a bundle of opportunities. Organizations should highlight the workman's contribution to organizational activities. Incentive: A reward package should be fair and reasonable, including basic pay, gratuity, and other monetary incentives. Impact: Work marks itself as alteration and generates objectivity, predominantly as it attaches the employee with a customer who uses the worker's purpose. Community: A supportive community atmosphere plays a crucial role in fostering teamwork, where employees collaborate and care for one another. Communication:** Effective employee engagement occurs when the information conveyed by the sender is received and understood as intended by the recipient. Experimentation: Fulfillment of employee and employer needs by flexible work hours, policies, and procedures to get the results [22].

11.2.2.4 Outcomes of Employee Engagement

Job pleasure, job involvement, brand behavior, approaches to structural modification, absence of employees, work incomings, and employee welfare are the outcomes of employee engagement [54]. The outcomes are position fight and pressure, distrust about the business and its goals, control of the work environment, the developing vision of the organization, self-confidence, change management, readiness to experience and keenness to remain along with the company, reduced turnover intention, motivation, artistic imaginations and remedies, ongoing improvement, group task, and organization establishment [64].

A cross-industry study that examined the airline, telecommunication, and hotel industries identified several key factors contributing to significant income growth (10%–15%). These factors included the rank of gross domestic product, promotional prices, characteristics of the commercial, and the types of products offered. This increase in income was associated with heightened levels of employee engagement [42].

11.2.3 Literature Review on Theoretical Concepts of Organizational Performance

Organizational performance refers to the extent to which a business accomplishes its goals and objectives efficiently and professionally. Organizational performance is measured by means of numerous pointers such as monetary presentation, operative enactment, purchaser consummation, employee engagement, and novelty. It involves the role of administrative philosophy and governance in delivering results, as well as the impact of external factors such as scientific progressions and environmental sustainability on organizational behavior [2]. Organizational performance is a particular awareness of authenticity, which elucidates the assembly of dangerous replication of the thought and its gauging gadgets [9]. Currently, there is a diversity of descriptions accredited to the conception of structural enactment due to its distinctive feature.

The concept of organizational performance has gained increased attention in current periods and is relevant in all areas of social activity [8]. Organizational performance exhibits the reciprocal relationship of the business to its goals and objectives [13]. It is the definite outcomes and production of the company as restrained in contradiction of that company's proposed yields [67]. Corporate sectors are equated in positions of revenues, trades, marketplace stakes, efficiency, obligation relations, and standard values [68].

11.2.3.1 Factors of Organizational Performance

The following are the factors of organizational performance.

The Effective Leadership factor will have a strong effect on organizational performance, as it involves inspiration, motivation, empowerment, efficient resource allocation, performance monitoring, and strategic management, all of which lead to increased organizational performance [66]. The organizational environment (the culture and climate) involves values, belief systems, standards, custom buildings, and protocols that radiate the performances [27]. An optimistic work environment flourishes novelty, coordination, collaboration, expansion, and overall employee development that enact increased performances [41].

The Employee Engagement and Motivation factor highlights that engaged and committed employees contribute significantly to positive organizational performance [61]. Variables such as employee recognition, opportunities for career advancements, awards, and rewards management can influence employee engagement. Human Resource Management practices like recruitment, selection, training and development, performance management, compensation, monetary management, and grievance handling can impact organizational performance [23]. HRM system in Human Resource Analytics aligns with strategic goals and values in implementation to achieve improved performances [50].

The Organizational Structure and Design factor is the construction and plan of a business that can affect its performance [53]. Variables such as strong duties and accountabilities, well-organized announcement channels, and suitable executive procedures can influence organizational performance positively.

11.2.3.2 Steps to Achieve Organizational Performance

i) Regulate success factors that are critical and track the feedback. ii) Recommend an organizational environment and create a performance culture coinciding with the objectives of the performance. iii) Nonstop evaluation with continuous appraisal of structural progressions and personnel improvement. iv) Create a folder in order to gather and smear the consequences of the HRM and forward planning and forthcoming decision-making of the organization [56].

11.2.3.3 Outcomes of Organizational Performance

The outcomes of organizational performance include stakeholder satisfaction, strategic effectiveness, knowledge management, operational processes, resource utilization, and stakeholder input [65]. Financial performance is frequently assessed and grounded on monetary conclusions, such as income progress, profitability, return on investment (ROI), and shareholder value [64]. Establishments that accomplish optimistic monetary enactment results are repeatedly understood as fruitful and are improved placed to withstand and produce their processes. Employee engagement and employee performance influence worker products, such as operative enactment, engagement, and satisfaction [24]. Large-performing organizations regularly have engaged personnel who are inspired, creative, and dedicated to the establishment's aims and purposes. Customer satisfaction and loyalty are additionally probable to satisfy their customers and build customer loyalty [35]. Positive organizational performance outcomes, such as product quality, service excellence, and customer responsiveness, put forward increased customer satisfaction, captive business, and positive word-of-mouth referrals. Reputation and brand image refer to organizational performance that can meaningfully influence an organization's status and brand image [18]. Establishments that constantly distribute optimistic presentation products are additionally expected to form a constructive repute and robust trademark spitting image, which can prime to augmented belief, trustworthiness, and customer reliability.

Organizational sustainability and social responsibility include high-performing organizations that order sustainability and social responsibility as a portion of their routine intentions [51]. Companies that validate answerable and maintainable commercial applications, such as environmental stewardship, social impact, and ethical governance, are more likely to be apparent positively by stakeholders and donate to long-standing organizational accomplishments.

11.3 Conceptual Framework

The study examines three key variables: 1. employee potential, 2. employee engagement, and 3. organizational performance.

11.3.1 Employee Potential

Employee potential is composed of three categories: 1) environment/ firm-related factors (social culture, support and security by management, atmosphere vitality, and organizational climate), 2) job-related factors (job atmosphere, job independence, and job communication), and 3) employee-related factors (intrinsic motivation, talent elasticity, expertise level, proactivity, adaptableness, and obligation). This variable is considered independent.

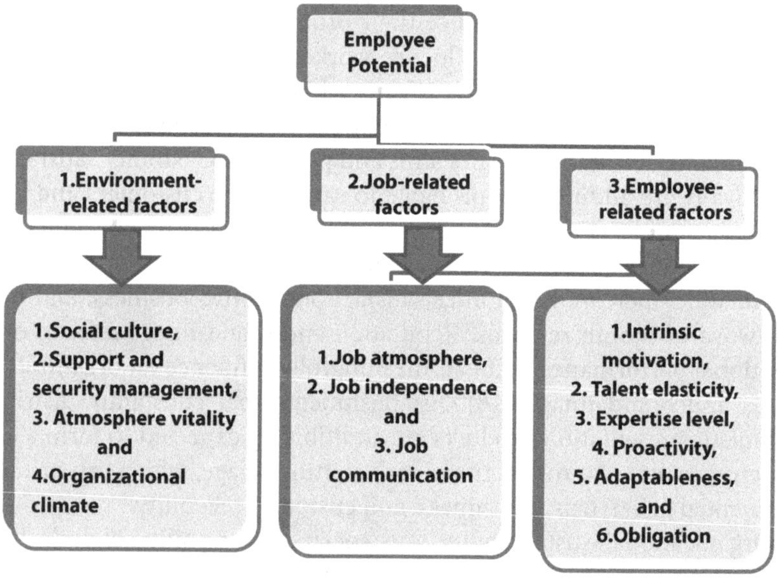

Figure 11.1 Factors of employee potential. Source: Developed by the researcher based on the evidence from [17].

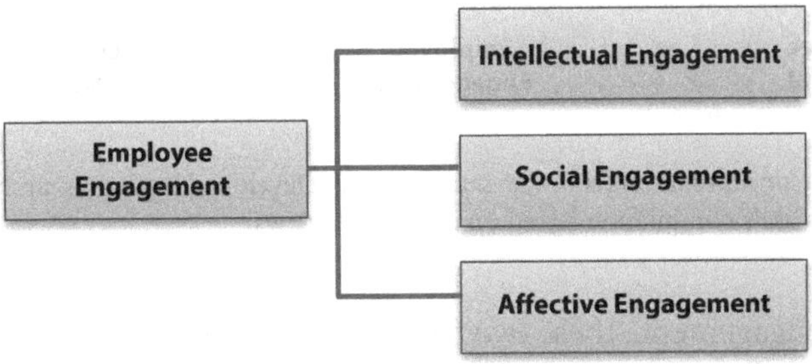

Figure 11.2 Factors of employee engagement. Source: Developed by the researcher based on the evidence from [33].

11.3.2 Employee Engagement

Employee engagement is characterized by intellectual engagement, social engagement, and affective engagement. This variable is also considered independent.

11.3.3 Organizational Performance

Organizational performance is defined by both financial performance and non-financial performance. This variable is taken as dependent.

The research model of the study consists of three variables: employee potential, employee engagement, and organizational potential. The current research displays the levels of these three variables and the relationship among them, which are both correlational and dependent. In the phase of HR Analytics, employee potential is very essential, as it gives rise to

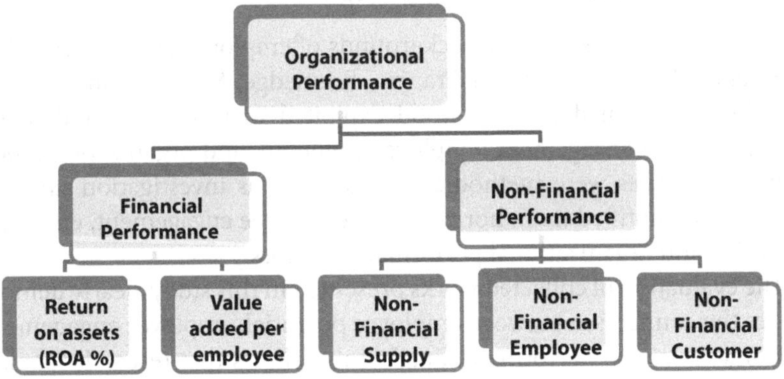

Figure 11.3 Factors of organizational performance. Source: Developed by the researcher based on evidence [41].

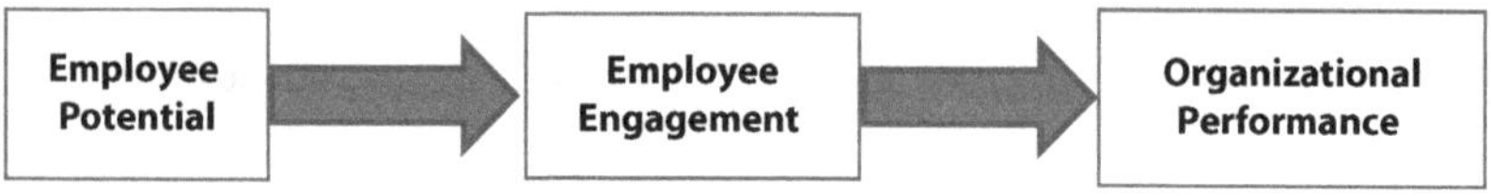

Figure 11.4 Conceptual model of the study. Source: Developed by the researcher. [It is pure author's compilation based on different reviews]

employee engagement. These two factors have an impact on organizational performance. Employees are engaged only when they feel valued, involved, and acknowledged, which in turn leads to enhanced organizational performance. Organizations are held responsible for enhancing engagement by unlocking employee potential by working on different employee potential factors. Below is the working model for the current research work.

11.4 Research Objectives

1. To determine the relationship between employee potential and employee engagement.
2. To determine the relationship between employee engagement and organizational performance.
3. To determine the effect of employee potential on employee engagement and then on to organizational performance.

11.5 Research Methodology

11.5.1 Research Method and Design

The paper aims to review the backgrounds of employee engagement. Web of Science, Wiley, Taylor and Francis, Routledge, Springer, and Scopus, prominent journal databases, stood exploited to recognize valid literature. Employee engagement, employee potential, and organizational performance articles were methodically examined as investigation samples. The review identified main horizons like employee engagement, employee potential, and organizational performance factors.

The evaluation of collected works presented in this study clearly demonstrates the connection between employee potential, employee engagement, and organizational performance, and it also shows that research scholars continue to pay attention to this topic. By using the literature reviews of the abovementioned variables, a conceptual model is developed which is based on systematic and thematic literature review. The published and previous works have provided a link between employee potential and employee engagement, as well as the relationship between work engagement and various performance metrics. This verifies the rising concentration of academics in this particular research area. To place it in the framework, 40 out of the 60 studied research articles have been engraved in the previous 4 years. Many authors have conducted review studies on this subject across different publications and geographical regions, based on data from several businesses, such as fiscal services, education, airlines, telecommunications, information technology, construction, and hospitality. Nevertheless, gathering and classification of preceding reviews discovered the irregular dissemination of the evaluated investigations cross-ways into several classes, which stayed clear to replicate the diverse kinds and heights of performances by means of engagements and potentials. There is a specific shortage of findings on the association between variables under the study.

11.6 Findings and Discussions

This study examines three variables related to how changes in employee potential impact work engagement levels using a review factor analysis. The findings from past reviews indicate that employee engagement is the most reliable forecaster of organizational performance [14]. Support from administration, reasonable processes, justifiable dispersal of possessions, mutual goals, an optimistic atmosphere, and opportunities for professional development are all crucial factors that contribute to organizational performance [15]. Due to the occurrence of multiple managements, lengthier working tasks, less employee flexibility, lower productions, less communication and cooperation among workers, fewer leaves, repetitive work routines, employee attachment to their employer and the industry has reduced in the workplace [62]. The incapability to take upcoming projects and forthcoming actions is repeatedly quoted as the main restriction to move forward in the organization. When an employee is assigned on a convention or contract, he or she rarely receives any help or advice from upper management until he finishes his contract, and as a result, he will not be able to reconnect with anybody. This results in an employee's loss of sense of belongingness to the firm, which decreases the employee potential and their level of engagement [5]. However, an employee may feel more valued as part of the team if the care concerns and complaints are caught and addressed promptly. This can boost employee morale and raise employee potential, ultimately leading to increased employee engagement [48], which can have a positive result on overall organizational performance. Seeing the basic stratum of the industry, many employees experience feelings of nervousness. Staff morale is boosted when employee jobs are safe and secure [52]. The results of the review examined some factors that influence employee engagement, which plays an important role in determining the engagement level of the employees. It was found that employee potential and its factors are the most significant dynamics affecting employee engagement, statically proving significant at the 0.01% level [4].

About 53% of the working environment influences employee potential and acts as a determinant of employee engagement. This indicates the significance of a strong work culture and decent relational synchronization through parallel association with business to get engaged at work. The desired job setting includes both corporal and passionately safe places that will encourage operative labor to get engaged at work. Individuals distinguish themselves in their workstations and their involvement in work roles, which plays a major role in their participation [26]. The study also suggests that employees actively seek meaning in their work if organizations foster a culture that promotes engagement and performance improvements.

There is a strong connection between employee engagement and organizational performance. The findings confirm that higher employee engagement leads to increased performance both for employees and the organization as a whole [43]. Once this connection was established, it was revealed that the independent factors of employee engagement have a direct relationship with organizational performance. Performance management has an important impact on organizational effectiveness [12] and consequently remains the instant urgency for administrators.

Organizations nowadays experience trials that necessitate courtesy cultivating performance management. The significant method is to enrich the performance resulting in employee engagement [10]. The current approach to performance management focuses on training that concentrates on employee engagement to employee performance, highlighting the prominence of engagement within the performance management process. The existing study focused on the basis of the relationship between employee engagement and organizational performance by enhancing employee potential using systematic review analysis.

The current work provokes the key elements of employee engagement by the supervisors and owners to deliver cordial surroundings for personnel to become engaged positively. Henceforth, the present work broadens the possibility of finding out the actions that will heighten workstation factors like workplace culture, employee well-being, the working environment, customs and traditions, respect for employees, value and security parameters, considerations, recognition, awards and rewards, roles and responsibilities, policies and procedures, strategies and segments [44]. Likewise, the business has to capitalize on constructing a melodious milieu that will yield a beneficial atmosphere for virtuous organizations that should possess environment-related factors, job-related factors, and employee-related factors so as to broaden employee potential to get more engaged and increase organizational performance.

11.7 Practical Implications

The current work marks important hypothetical assistance of employee engagement. The current study highlights the vital part that engagement shows in lashing organizational performance, by capitalizing on the competencies of human resources. Employee engagement is entrenched in the potential of employees and unlocking that potential can improve performance. This study highlights the need for organizations to accomplish and offer these resources to their personnel.

Employee engagement is considered a direct predictor of organizational performance [40]. The outcomes of this investigation might deliver shine on the stage of attention and commitment exhibited by different levels and types of employees across different sectors [63]. The assessment of firms' recent instructions and performance may benefit from this research as it sheds light on desirable outcomes. Employee engagement can lead to numerous positive results like market growth, economic benefits, increased productivity, improved efficiency, and greater consumer satisfaction [57].

The results of this study indicate that the dedication and involvement of the employees were previously quite low but have increased significantly when employee potential is enhanced. This improvement leads to notable organizational progress. The research discovers a resilient association amid employee potential, employee engagement, and organizational performance. Employees in different sectors face unease and liability owing to their difficult and task-completion nature. The current work provides real-world insights into how organizations can nourish and engage their workers by developing their social, behavioral, psychological, and intellectual abilities. It also concentrates on the overall well-being of the employees to raise organizational performance.

The outcomes of the current study obligate concrete inferences for administration, as they offer a theoretical outline for constructing engagement in companies [58]. The consequences of the study also designate that organizations can upsurge engagement by proposing adequate employee capabilities and developing a culture of engagement. An engaged workforce is revealed to be not only dedicated and fulfilled but also imaginative and fascinating, which are indications of improved and increased organizational performance.

11.8 Limitations and Future Directions

Only Indian employees are included in this study. Nonetheless, more research on the grades of participation, involvement, satisfaction, and commitment among employees of various populations is acceptable. Alterations and resemblances between dissimilar philosophies might also be conferred. From the above study, the impact of engagement on performance is only analyzed, despite the fact that other factors, such as organizational usefulness, company competence, inexpensive gain, and administrative process, might also be encompassed. The impact of arbitrators and intermediaries, such as emotional quotient, job satisfaction, and employee participation, were not inspected since they remained outside of the study.

Regardless of these limits, the study delivers significant intuitions of the power of employee potential on employee engagement and its relationship to organizational performance. The results suggest that organizations might profit from capitalizing the employee strengths, motives, perceptions, and attitudes to enhance engagement and improve performance. Findings lay out the essentiality of forthcoming research to initiate something additional strategies and explore the current world for the purpose of the study. The future scope is fairly extensive after dissimilar viewpoints. This study can be applied at numerous heights and types of organizations like large-scale, middle-scale, and lower-scale MNCs, corporate sectors, and many more. To reinforce the conceptual model, an in-depth examination of the particular elements recognized should be worked out which can position the separate element under the study on employee engagement and organizational performance by using employee potential.

11.9 Conclusions

The current research work highlights the significance of employee potential and employee engagement in enhancing organizational performance. It also finds numerous factors related to employee potential and employee engagement that impact organizational performance by identifying these factors. It also displays a robust noteworthy affiliation between employee potential and employee engagement and between employee engagement and organizational performance. The systematic review analysis forecasts that several chief factors associated with each variable examined in the study exert an influence on one another, indicating a positive and important bond. The first relation is between employee potential and employee engagement which are directly and positively related. The second relationship is between employee engagement and organizational performance which is also positive and direct. With this relationship, it is concluded that employee potential is responsible for improved and increased organizational performance. The current research also presents reviews and provides some measures on the factors that are held responsible for employee potential, engagement, and performance in order to improve them in the organizations. The inferences contain important influence for organizations in terms of the development of profitability and productivity which in turn has an economic impact on the businesses. In addition to this, the factors of employee potential make the employee work freely and get engaged which, in turn, increases performance and satisfaction [38]. This redirects to the social effect that might be produced through the actions adopted by the organization. The workforce could relish substantial consideration in the workplace atmosphere, strong coordination, workroom safety, and approaches occupied through the businesses toward increasing employee engagement. Organizational performance always remained well exaggerated by the participation of employees in their work. An operative worker who is extremely involved through his work is the single who is captivating consideration to the effort of the business and bestowing certain caring of creativity aimed at the profit of the institutions. Generally, the work emphasizes the value of clearly distinct job descriptions, job enrichment, and core job profile concepts as essential precursors to employee engagement. The current work also acknowledges that much of the existing literature has focused on a single aspect or has inadequately addressed the previously developed models of employee engagement, which contain several related aspects. This type of regular valuation gives rise to instructions for future studies and helps in assisting upcoming research.

References

1. Allen, D.G., Bryant, P.C., Vardaman, J.M., Retaining talent: Replacing misconceptions with evidence based strategies. *Acad. Manage. Perspect.*, 24, 2, 48–64, 2010.
2. Amiri, M. and Nobakht, A., Performance Management: An empirical study of selected manufacturing organizations in Pune, India. *Training Dev.*, 35, 81, 2016.
3. Amah, O.E., Employee engagement in Nigeria: The role of leaders and boundary variables. *SA J. Ind. Psychol.*, 44, E1–E8Alfes, 2018.
4. Anitha, J., Determinants of employee engagement and their impact on employee performance. *Int. J. Prod. Perform. Manage.*, 63, 3, 308–323, 2014.
5. Anthony-McMann, P.E., Ellinger, A.D., Astakhova, M., Halbesleben, J.R.B., Exploring different operationalization of employee engagement and their relationships with workplace stress and burnout. *Hum. Resour. Dev. Q*, 28, 2, 163–186, 2017.
6. Aon, *Impact of Engaged Employees on Business Outcomes: Ongoing Employee Engagement Research*, Hewitt Associates. Retrieved, 2021.
7. Bakker, A.B., Strategic and proactive approaches to work engagement. *Organizational Dyn.*, 46, 2, 67–75, 2017.
8. Demeke, B. and Tao, C., Concept & Perspectives of Organizational Performance Measurement: Literature Review. *Int. J. Acad. Multi. Res. (IJAMR)*, 4, 2, 89–96, 2020.
9. Burtonshaw - Gunn, S.A., Essential Tools for Operations Management, in: *John Wiley and Sons, Ltd*, 2010, ISBN 9780470745922.
10. Buchner, T.W., Performance management theory: a look from the performer's perspective with implications for HRD. *Hum. Resour. Dev. Int.*, 10, 1, 59–73, 2007.
11. Buckingham, M. and Coffman, C., *First, Break All the Rules: What the World's Greatest Managers Do Differently*, The Gallup Organization, Simon and Schuster, New York, 1999.
12. Cardy, R.L. *Performance management: Concepts, Skills, and Exercises*, M.E. Sharpe, Armonk, NY, 2004.
13. Cho, J. and Dansereau, F., Are Transformational Leaders Fair? A Multi-Level Study of Transformational Leadership, Justice Perceptions, and Organizational Citizenship Behaviors. *Leadersh. Q.*, 21, 409–421, 2010.
14. Clack, L., Employee Engagement: Keys to Organizational Success, in: *The Palgrave Handbook of Workplace Well-Being*, S.K. Dhiman, (Ed.), Palgrave Macmillan, Cham, 2021.
15. Clark, T., Seven ways to get your team members more engaged and why it's so important, 2014, Retrieved from https://www.liquidplanner.com/blog/7-ways-to-get-your-team-members-more engaged.

16. Fernández-Aráoz, C., Roscoe, A., Aramaki, K., Turning Potential into Success: The Missing Link in Leadership Development, in: *Harvard Business Review*, 2017.
17. Coetzer, A. and Perry., M., Factors influencing employee learning in small businesses. *Educ. Training*, 50, 8/9, 648–660, 2008.
18. Da Silva, R.V., Marques, C., Martinho, D., Teixeira, N., de Carvalho, J.C., Instagram: A gimmick or a serious reputation builder in the airline business? *J. Creative Commun.*, 16, 3, 285–302, 2021.
19. Diamantidis, A. and Chatzoglou, P., Factors affecting employee performance: an empirical approach. *Int. J. Prod. Perform. Manage.*, 68, 171–193, 2018. 10.1108/IJPPM-01-2018-0012.
20. Fernandez, C., Employee Engagement. *J. Public Health Manage. Pract. JPHMP*, 13, 524–6, 2007. 10.1097/01.PHH.0000285207.63835.50.
21. Gallup, The engaged workplace. *Employee Engagement Employee Exper.*, 1, 23, 2018a. https://www.gallup.com/services/ 190118/engaged-workplace.aspx.
22. Gallup, Emotional engagement on the rise in the US. Article by J. Harter, 2018b, https://news.gallup.com/poll/241649/employee-engagement-rise.aspx.
23. George, B., Walker, R.M., Monster, J., Does strategic planning improve organizational performance? A meta-analysis. *Public Administration Rev.*, 79, 6, 810–819, 2019.
24. Harter, J.K., Schmidt, F.L., Hayes, T.L., Business-unit-level relationship between employee satisfaction, employee engagement and business outcomes: A meta-analysis. *J. Appl. Psychol.*, 87, 2, 268–279, 2002.
25. Ho Kim, W., Park, J.G., Kwon, B., Work Engagement in South Korea. *Psychol. Rep.*, 120, 3, 561–578, 2017.
26. Holbeche, L. and Springett, N., *In Search of Meaning in the Workplace*, Roffey Park Institute, Horsham, 2003, ISBN: 0 907416527.
27. Huragu, M. and Chuma, R.M., the impact of organizational culture on public sector performance: A case study of local authorities in Zimbabwe. *Int. J. Public Policy Administration Res.*, 6, 1, 33–56, 2019.
28. Jha, B. and Kumar, A., Employee engagement: A strategic tool to enhance performance. DAWN. *J. Contemp. Res. Manage.*, 3, 2, 21–29, 2016.
29. Jain, A. and Nagar, N., An Emerging Trend in Human Resource Management. *SS Int. J. Econ. Manage.*, 5, 1, 1–10, 2015.
30. Jones, K., Conquering HR Analytics: Do you need a rocket scientist or a crystal ball? *Workforce Solutions Rev.*, 5, 1, 43–44, 2014.
31. Chukwuyem, J.A., Employer-employee relations and employee engagement in a tertiary institution in Benin-City, Edo State. *Ann. Manage. Organ. Res.*, 1, 9–24, 2020, 10.35912/amor.v1i1.199.
32. van den Berg, J.W., Mastenbroek, N.J.J.M., Scheepers, R.A., Jaarsma, A.D.C., Work engagement in health professions education. *Med. Teach.*, 39:11, 1110–1118, 2017.

33. Alfes, K., Shantz, A.D., Truss, C., Soane, E.C., The link between perceived human resource management practices, engagement and employee behaviour: A moderated mediation model. *Int. J. Hum. Resour. Manage.*, 330–351, 2013.
34. Kahn, W.A., Psychological Conditions of Personal Engagement and Disengagement at Work. *Acad. Manage. J.*, 33, 692–724, 1990.
35. Kahn, B.E., Inman, J.J., Verhoef, P.C., Introduction to special issue: Consumer response to the evolving retailing landscape. *J. Assoc. Consum. Res.*, 3, 3, 255–259, 2018.
36. Kale, H. and Anute, N., HR Analytics and its Impact on Organizations Performance, vol. 9, 2022.
37. Kalyanamitra, P., Saengchai, S., Jermsittiparsert, K., Impact of Training Facilities, Benefits and Compensation, and Performance Appraisal on the Employees' Retention: A Mediating Effect of Employees' Job Satisfaction. *Syst. Rev. Pharm.*, 11, 3, 166–175, 2020.
38. Kim, W.H., Ra, Y.A., Park, J.G., Kwon, B., Role of burnout on job level, job satisfaction, and task performance. *Leadersh. Organ. Dev. J.*, 38, 5, 630–645, 2017.
39. Kirtane, A., corporate sustainable HR Analytical practices. *J. Manage. Administration Tomorrow*, 4, 1, 33–40, 2017.
40. Kompaso, S.M. and Sridevi, M.S., Employee Engagement: The Key to Improving Performance. *Int. J. Bus. Manage.*, 5, 12, 89–96, 2010.
41. Kromraruay, P., Factors affecting the Success in Organizational Performance: A case study of School in Nongkham District office, Bangkok Metropolitan Administration Veridian E-Journal, Silpakorn University, Nakhon Pathom, Thailand, vol. 12, pp. 520–534, 2019.
42. Kumar, V. and Pansari, A., Measuring the benefits of employee engagement. *MIT Sloan Manage. Rev.*, 56, 67–72, 2015.
43. Lawler, E.E., Make human capital a source of competitive advantage. *Organizational Dyn.*, 38, 1, 1–7, 2008.
44. Leiter, M.P. and Bakker, A.B., Work engagement: introduction, in: *Work engagement: A Handbook of Essential Theory and Research*, vol. 1-9, A.B. Bakker, and M.P. Leiter, (Eds.), Psychology Press, Hove, 2010.
45. Letchmiah, L. and Thomas, A., Retention of high-potential employees in a development finance company. *SA J. Hum. Resour. Manage.*, 15, 1-9, 2017. 10.4102/sajhrm.v15i0.924.
46. Loosemore, M. and Benson, T.H.L., Linking corporate social responsibility and organizational performance in the construction industry. *Construct. Manage. Econ.*, 35, 3, 90–105, 2017.
47. Murnpho, S. and Srathongkham, T., The Causal Factors Affecting Work Efficiency of Employees State Enterprise. *Int. J. eBusiness eGovernment Stud.*, 14, 1, 168–180, 2022.

48. Minana, S., Continuous improvement: why teamwork and collaboration drive worker engagement, 2020, Retrieved from https://www.orange-business.com/en/blogs/continuous-improvementwhy-teamwork-and-collaboration-drive-worker-engagement.
49. Nagarajah, S., Medawala, P., Rathnayake, S., An Empirical Study of the Factors Affecting Employees' Performance at ABC Group of Companies, 2021, 10.13140/RG.2.2.14476.44169.
50. Opatha, H.H.D. and Jayani, P., HR Analytics: A Literature Review and New Conceptual Model. *Int. J. Sci. Res. Publ. (IJSRP)*, 10, 130–141, 2020, 10.29322/IJSRP.10.06.2020.p10217.
51. Ou, A.Y., Waldman, D.A., Peterson, S.J., Do humble CEOs matter? An examination of CEO humility and firm outcomes. *J. Manage.*, 44, 3, 1147–1173, 2018.
52. Peart, N., Making work less stressful and more engaging for your employees, *Harv. Bus. Rev.*, 2019.
53. Rehman, S.U., Mohamed, R., Ayoup, H., The mediating role of organizational capabilities between organizational performance and its determinants. *J. Global Entrepreneurship Res.*, 9, 1, 1–23, 2019.
54. Robertson-Smith, G. and Marwick, C., *Employee engagement; a review of current thinking*, Institute for Employment Studies, Brighton, UK, 2009.
55. Robinson, D., Perryman, S., Hayday, S., *The Drivers of Employee Engagement*, Institute for Employment Studies, Brighton, Report 408, retrieved on December 14th, 2011, 2004.
56. Rostam, F.A., A Review of Talent Management as a Key in any Organizations. *Int. J. Indian Psychol.*, 7, 3, 78–83, 2004.
57. Saks, A.M., Antecedents and consequences of employee engagement. *J. Managerial Psychol.*, 21, 7, 600–619, 2006.
58. Schaufeli, W.B., Work engagement in Europe. *Organizational Dyn.*, 47, 2, 99–106, 2018.
59. Schaufeli, W., Salanova, M., Gonzalez-Roma, V., Bakker, A., The Measurement of Engagement and Burnout: A Two Sample Confirmatory Factor Analytic Approach. *J. Happiness Stadies*, 3, 71–92, 2002.
60. Schiemann, W.A., From talent management to talent optimization. *J. World Bus.*, 49, 2, 281–288, 2013.
61. Shuck, B., Peyton Roberts, T., Zigarmi, D., Employee perceptions of the work environment, motivational outlooks, and employee work intentions: An HR practitioner's dream or nightmare? *Adv. Dev. Hum. Resour.*, 20, 2, 197–213, 2018.
62. Stange, J., 38 awesome team building activities for work, 2020, Retrieved from https://www.quantumworkplace.com/future-of-work/6-team-building-ideas-increase-employee-engagement/.

63. Storey, J., Ulrich, D., Welbourne, T.M., Wright, P.M., Employee engagement, in: *The Routledge companion to strategic human resource management*, pp. 299–315, Routledge, United Kingdom, 2008.
64. Sudha, S., Corporate environmental performance–financial performance relationship in India using eco-efficiency metrics. Management of Environmental Quality. *An Int. J.*, 31, 6, 1497–1514, 2020.
65. Taouab, O. and Issor, Z., Firm performance: Definition and measurement models. *Eur. Sci. J.*, 15, 1, 93–106, 2019.
66. Dvir, T., Eden, D., Avolio, B.J., Shamir, B., Impact of Transformational Leadership on Follower Development and Performance: A Field Experiment. *AMJ*, 45, 735–744, 2002.
67. Tomal, D.R. and Jones, K.J., A Comparison of Core Competencies of Women and Men Leaders in the Manufacturing Industry. *Coastal Bus. J.*, 14, 13–25, 2015.
68. Yasmin Musmuliana, Y.M., *Factors Influencing Organizational Performance in Metro Specialist Hospital*, Sungai Petani, Kedah Darul Aman, 2012.

12

Performance Evaluation and Measurement of Human Capital Analytics in the Information Technology (IT) Sector in India

Manoj Kumar[1]*, Pratibha Maurya[2] and Rinki Verma[3]

[1]*Shri Ramswaroop Memorial University, Barabanki, Uttar Pradesh, India*
[2]*Amity University, Uttar Pradesh Lucknow Campus, Lucknow, Uttar Pradesh, India*
[3]*Babu Banarsi Das University, Lucknow, Uttar Pradesh, India*

Abstract

Purpose: The present study examines the increasing use of Human Capital Analytics in the Information Technology (IT) sector and its relevance in Industry 5.0. The ROI of human capital is calculated to measure the performance of investment in human capital.

Design/Methodology/Approach: The case study approach was followed using the ROI approach to evaluate the human capital investment in Tata Consultancy Services (TCS) Ltd. Secondary data were extracted from the company's annual reports for this study.

Findings: High-quality human capital is the fundamental strength of the IT sector, which leads to competitive advantage. It has huge financial implications for the organization. The return on human capital investment should be more than the cost of capital in order to make the company profitable. In Industry 5.0, where high-technology machines will operate with human efforts, having customer-centric manufacturing of goods and services, Human Capital Analytics returns will provide strength to the companies. TCS has been successful in implementing it with adequate returns.

Practical Implications: The findings will provide a basis for the practitioners of Human Capital Analytics and will motivate them to bring into practice more

**Corresponding author*: drmanoj040@gmail.com

Deepa Gupta, Mukul Gupta, Pawan Budhwar, Jim Westerman, Rajesh Kumar Dhanaraj and Balamurugan Balusamy (eds.) Human Capital Analytics: Exploring the HR Spectrum in Industry 5.0, (261–282) © 2025 Scrivener Publishing LLC

such applications in organizations of all sizes. It will add new literature to the existing body of knowledge.

Originality/Value: The study is novel and original as it examines the ROI of human capital with respect to the IT industry and its relevance in Industry 5.0.

Paper Type: Research paper.

Keywords: Human Capital Analytics (HCA), Return on Investment (ROI), Industry 5.0, Information Technology (IT)

12.1 Introduction

Industrial revolutions have brought radical changes in the application of technologies in organizations. Technological innovations have enhanced the skills in every aspect of business by providing better quality of goods and services at affordable prices. The credit for such successful innovations and adoption in the organizations goes to one of the crucial factors of production, i.e., labor. Human capital is one of the important driving forces for attaining stable industrial and economic growth in any country. Human capital management has contributed to the sustainability and growth of national economies and the global economy as a whole. The developed countries have been successful in expanding over the global markets and manufacturing modest high-technology products with the use of high-quality human capital and attained a competitive advantage over their competitors. The developing nations are now also in the race for digital transformation in every aspect of business activities among which the important one is the management of human resources.

Human resource management has been an important pillar for organizations but with the innovation of new tools and technologies, their role is expanding. The contribution of HR to the success of an organization is increasing due to rapid technological innovations. HR managers frequently use data, statistics, and technology to recruit and select employees. Human Capital Analytics (HCA) relates the business data with the workforce data and establishes connections among them. HCA helps HR managers understand the relevant data patterns of numerous HR processes, assisting in making better decisions.

The Industrial Revolution (Industry 1.0), which started at the end of the 18th century [1], has passed Industry 2.0, Industry 3.0, Industry 4.0, and the beginning of Industry 5.0. At every stage, technological evolutions were involved from the age of the steam engine, the evolution of electricity, the use of electronic and ICT systems for automation and application of cyber-physical systems and finally using the human experts to work with effectual, intelligent, and adequate machines [2, 3]. At every stage of the industrial revolution, human effort was involved, and organizations with proper management of human resources obtained great success in their field [4, 5]. Under Industry 5.0, powerful and high-technology machines will work in collaboration with human experts [6, 7]. The manufacturing industry will get a human touch in this revolution. Industry 5.0 will be more customer-centric so personalized and customized products and services will be demanded [8, 9]. Every organization has limited human resources, so it becomes important that available resources should be used effectively. Under such circumstances, Human Capital Analytics is an important tool for HR professionals to optimize their HR resources. Rapid digital transformation is bringing change to every aspect of business. With the adoption of AI, machine learning, big data, and Cloud computing, big organizations are capable of handling their human resource more efficiently [10].

The people working in the organization are important assets for them. A major portion of the cost comprises employee costs in the case of service industries. So, it becomes crucial to measure the productivity of human capital involved in the organization. For the measurement of the productivity of human capital, various metrics evolved like revenue generated by the organization, the amount expended as employee cost, training provided to enhance productivity, employee benefit expenses, and so on. A huge cost is also incurred in maintaining the employees in the organization. To measure the financial impact and for better performance, the Human Capital Management Institute (HCMI) has developed a formula to calculate the return on Human capital investment known as Human Capital (HCROI) [11].

The present study aims to measure the financial implications of human capital for the organization. For this purpose, various metrics were applied to the financial data of the company to evaluate the human capital Return on Investment (ROI), the Value Added by the human capital, and the Human Economic Value Added (HEVA) for the organization in the IT Industry.

12.2 Literature Review

Human resources is the entryway through which organizational commitments are fulfilled by individuals. The HR department's job is to determine each person's role based on their strengths and how employees could best help the firm achieve its goals [12, 13]. HR analytics can be useful in fulfilling HR functions like hiring, engagement, attrition, etc. [14–16]. Thus, there is a requirement for adequate reliable data on which such decisions are based. There is a direct link between data and decision-making. The primary source of data in any organization is the people who are working in the organization on specific jobs and responsibilities. To ensure that the abilities and knowledge of the available employees are known, the data must be updated continuously. In big organizations, where the number of employees is very large, a centralized database assists HR managers in placing suitable persons in appropriate positions [17–20]. For supporting HR, the technology should be according to the organization's structure, so that it can successfully fulfill the requirements of the organization [21–23]. The use of data in the management of human resources is known as Human Capital Analytics [24]. HR analytics can be defined as "the application of sophisticated data mining and business analytics techniques to the field of HR" [25]. It can also be defined as "processes to collect, transform and manage key HR-related data and documents; to analyze the gathered information using business analytics models; and to disseminate the analysis results to decision-makers for making intelligent decisions" [26]. The business results are impacted by financial investment and human capital investment [27]. The amount of financial investment is required to run the business, while human capital investment runs the business itself [28, 29]. The investment in human capital is significantly large in big organizations and mainly in the service industries [30]. Investment in human capital in the form of training and development is required for the skill enhancement of the employees which in return provides benefits to the organization [31, 32]. The efficiency of the workforce determines the success path for the organizations. The companies should measure the financial implications of human cost on revenue in order to evaluate the strategy adopted by the management of human capital [33, 34].

12.2.1 Need for Evaluation of Human Capital

When the number of persons working with different sets of skills in the organization is very large, it becomes difficult to manage them manually. The large size of data related to performance and other aspects of the employees is collected and compiled daily in the organization but not matched with the objectives of the organization on a regular basis. There is a requirement for specific experts and tools that can analyze and assist the HR managers in placing the right persons at the right job at the right time to fulfill the objectives of the organization. This can be possible with the successful application of Human Capital Analytics in the organization. Organizations that are using HCA have a competitive advantage in comparison to those not using it [35, 36]. Studies show that organizations are more successful when making decisions using analytics [37, 38]. Any size of organization can use analytics in various areas like management of human capital, finance, marketing, supply chain, etc. [39, 40].

Information Technology (IT) and Business Process Management (BPM) are among the important contributions to the Indian economy and have contributed significantly to the GDP of the country. The IT industry contribution to the Indian GDP was around 7.4% of the country's GDP in the financial year 2021–2022 and is expected to increase to 10% of GDP by the end of 2025 [41]. This sector in India has steadily grown in the past few years and is presently accounting for above 30% of the international outsourced BPM business. Similarly, persons working in this sector have also increased gradually from 1.96 million in FY 2009 to 4.85 million by FY2022 [42] (Statista-2023). As these organizations are serving globally, it is a difficult task to recruit, provide adequate training, depute for a specific job, and evaluate their performance with the objectives of the organization. This complete process creates a huge quantity of data and involves huge costs when people working in the origination are quite large.

The IT industry not only is majorly dependent on human resources for its performance but also has high attrition rates of 17–18% in the tech industry during the period 2022–2023. The cost of hiring a new employee in the organization is 40% more than the cost of holding the employee. The average cost of an employee is around 60% of the revenue in the IT industry. So it becomes important for the organization to study the financial implications of human capital.

The studies analyzing the advantages of measuring human capital for the determination of human capital value are limited in number. Kearns [43] and Singh and Rastogi [44] have studied that the measurement of human capital is done on the basis of the value they hold for the organization, not the cost incurred on them. They studied that there is a relationship between the performance of the organization and the measurement of outputs of the organization like revenue, cost, and profit. Pinto and Curto [45] agree that in the present competitive market, organizations have pressure on the ROI of the organization. Human capital is an important asset for any organization which involves huge costs and investment [46, 47]. So it becomes significant to evaluate the Human Capital Return on Investment (HCROI) [48], Human Capital Value Added (HCVA) [49], and HEVA [50] of the organization. This provides insight into the human cost incurred and the benefits received by the organization in the form of increased performance.

The important feature of Industry 5.0 is that it has reinstated the human component in the systems [51] and processes which were earlier replaced by the highly automated high-efficiency information technology unlike Industry 4.0 [52]. The focus has been shifted from the shareholders' value creation to stakeholders' value creation [53]. Now, the worker's welfare is considered as the epicenter of the production process and the application of advanced technology is done to offer prosperity in jobs and growth. A study by Gotfredsen [54] provides the benefits of collaboration between machine and man in the workplace. Industry 5.0 will create new jobs with more involvement of human effort as the market will be more customer-centric and personalized [8, 9]. The higher investment in human capital assets will accrue more employee cost, and significant requirement to calculate the benefit from such investment in the present scenario.

12.3 Objective of the Study

The present study focuses on establishing the relationship between human capital and the financial results of the originations. The performance of the organization depends on the optimum utilization of the human resource. The big IT industries are operating globally and the employees are hired and employed globally. With the application of Human Capital Analytics, organizations are capable of meeting and fulfilling the organizational human resource requirement efficiently. The employees are placed and relocated in the projects as per the demand. Training and learning programs are conducted to enhance the capabilities of the human capital as per the organizational requirement. The improved performance is depicted in the form of higher revenue for the organization. As human capital cost take the major share of the revenue, so financial implications of human capital are studied in this chapter. The study focuses on the following objectives:

a) To find out the Human Capital Return on Investment (HCROI) of the TCS.
b) To evaluate the HCVA in the TCS.
c) To study the HEVA in the TCS.

12.4 Methodology Adopted

A case study methodology has been adopted in this study to meet the objectives of the study. TCS Ltd. is the biggest IT industry company in India in terms of market capitalization, revenue, and human capital in 2023. The secondary data have been used for the study. The data for the study were collected from annual reports of various years available on the company website. Various appropriate metrics have been used to establish the relationship between human capital and financial results.

12.4.1 Human Capital Return on Investment (HCROI)

This metric measures the financial value that is added by the human capital against the money expended on them in the form of salaries and other benefits [55–57].

HCROI = (Operating Profit + Employment Cost)/Employment Cost

12.4.2 Human Capital Value Added (HCVA)

It measures the actual contribution of human capital to the organizational profit. This metric shows the direct relationship between the management of human capital and the value created by the organization for its shareholders [48, 56, 58].

HCVA= [Sales-(Total Costs-Employee Costs)]/Average Headcount.

Total cost can be calculated by deducting profit before tax (PBT) from sales.

Then, HCVA= [Sales-{(Sales-PBT)-Employee Cost}]/Average Headcount.

12.4.3 Human Economic Value Added (HEVA)

Numerous studies have used Economic Value Added (EVA) as an alternative for measuring the usefulness of the company's financial performance. The HEVA has evolved from the EVA model. It is used to measure the wealth created per employee [56, 59].

HEVA= NOTPAT-(Weighted Average Cost of Capital x Capital Invested) ÷ Average Headcount

TCS Case Study

TCS was established in 1968 as a division of Tata Sons Ltd. in India. In the initial stages, it was established to provide services to their Electronic Data Processing (EDP) requirements and offer management consulting services. TCS has completed 55 years of consistent growth, expansion, and stakeholder satisfaction, making it India's second-largest company in terms of market capitalization and the most valuable and trusted IT brand globally. TCS is presently providing a variety of IT services outsourcing and business solutions. It has become the biggest IT service in India in terms of market capitalization, revenue, and headcounts.

TCS has acquired the status of a multinational corporation by establishing its operations in 150 locations with a presence within 46 countries. The company has become one of the biggest employers with 614,795 employees working globally and highly localized. It is a huge task to manage such a big amount of workforce globally. It can be only possible with the application of Human Capital Analytics in the organization. With its adequate usage, the company can identify the various categories of employees and their expertise, train them accordingly, and assign them tasks. Out of the total employees working in the organization, 22,000 of them are recognized as high-talent employees and pay remuneration to them accordingly. The company has provided digital technology training to its 5,00,000 employees with a competency level of 7.5 per level on average. The company has given mid-level training with 90% participation out of which 60% of them have certification in market-related technologies.

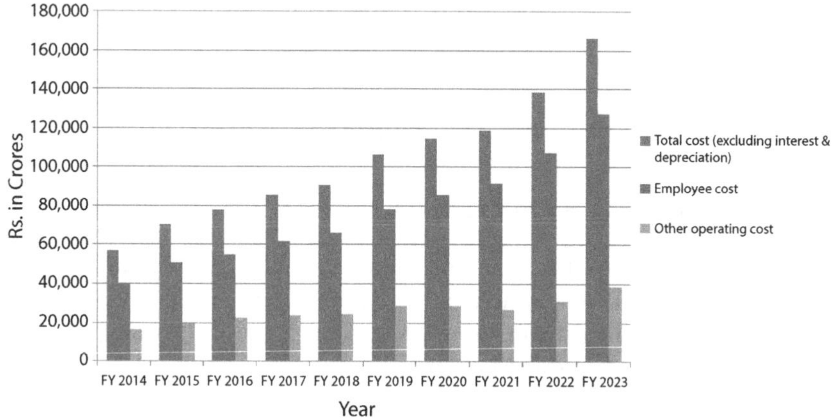

Figure 12.1 Total operating cost of TCS. (Source: TCS Annual Reports)

Figure 12.1 shows the total operating cost of TCS. The operating cost is majorly classified into two categories, i.e., employee cost and other operating cost. The employee cost for the company is above 70% of the total operating cost. The maximum proportion of employee cost was in the financial year 2021–2022 having a percentage of 77.55. When the employee cost is very high and the number of employees is very large and employees work globally on a localized basis, the management of human resources cannot be done without an appropriate tool to manage them; there comes the role of Human Capital Analytics.

The major challenge concerning Human Resource Management is the shortage of future-ready skills which results in a deficiency in talent and has an unfavorable impact on the business. With the rapid transformation in technology (AI and machine learning) and continuous demand from customers for skilled employees, there is pressure on HR managers to fill this gap. Figure 12.2 shows the human capital practices of TCS which are classified into four HR transformation services such as HR advisory and strategy, a platform and digital solution, HR services, and people analytics. The HR transformation in the company can increase the productivity of its employees by transmuting the way employees work; useful in the retention of the employees within the organization which reduces employee turnover. HR is focused more toward employee-centric practices resulting in improved adoption and increased employee engagement. The efficiency and productivity of HR are increased across the different organizational metrics; with the effectiveness in the HR policies and processes thus reducing the cost of the HR department. The company is capable of making the workforce more skilled as per the changing scenario to fulfill future competencies. TCS constantly makes changes in the existing people policies and introduces new policies according to the feedback obtained from the employees, developing the needs of the employees and the preeminent practices followed in the area of Human Capital management. The consistent efforts and improvement in human capital practices have provided various recognitions to the company.

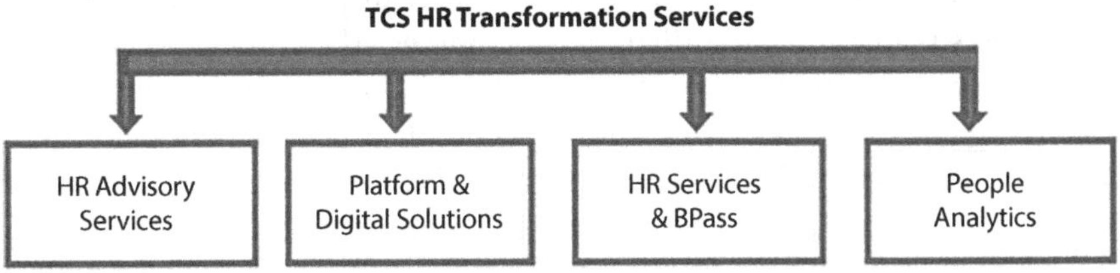

Figure 12.2 Four pillars of TCS' HR transformation services. (Source: [60])

The company has earned recognition as a 2023 Global Top Employer in Europe for the 11th successive year and as the Number One Top Employer in Belgium, Denmark, and The Netherlands. It has also been named in Forbes' annual list of America's Best Large Employers, based on an independent survey of 45,000 employees working for American companies with more than 1,000 employees. Finally, it has been named a Top Employer in the UAE, the Kingdom of Saudi Arabia, and South Africa for the eighth continuous year.

12.5 Data Analysis

TCS was the first Indian IT company to make an Initial Public offering in July 2004. The issue price band was kept between Rs. 775 to 900 but the final price of the company's share was fixed at Rs. 850. The company's shares got listed on the Indian stock exchange at a premium of 26.60% at Rs. 1076. The company has successfully met the expectations of not only the shareholders but also all its stakeholders. The number of employees, revenue generated, and its global presence itself depict the company's success story.

Table 12.1 below shows the performance of the company during the past 10 years (Financial Year 2013–2014 to 2022–2023). The revenue of the company has recorded a compounded annual growth rate of 10.67%. The net yearly addition in the number of employees was recorded at 7.42%. The net profit after tax (NPAT) also recorded a compounded annual growth rate of 8.20%. These financial indicators show how efficiently the company is managing its resources.

12.5.1 Objective 1

Return is the simplest way to evaluate the performance of any organization. There are various parameters based on which the performance of the organization can be measured. The most common and widely used methods for evaluating performance are return on equity, return on capital employed, and return on assets. These measures display how efficiently the company is managing and utilizing its resources. The higher the ratio, the better the utilization of the assets. Human capital is an important resource for IT organizations as organizations' accomplishment depends on them only. Human Capital Return on Investment (HCROI) is one such measure to evaluate the return from investment in human capital.

The Human Capital Return on Investment (HCROI) is a crucial metric for assessing an organization's performance. Organizations that give valid consideration to human resources and consider them as an asset are more

Table 12.1 Financial performance of TCS (FY 2014 to 2023).

Year	Revenue (Rs. crore)	Total costs (excluding interest & dep.) (Rs. crore)	Employee costs (Rs. crore)	Current year headcount	Operating profit (Rs. crore)	Profit before tax (Rs. crore)	Profit after tax (Rs. crore)
2014	81,809	56,656	40,486	300,464	25,153	25,402	19,164
2015	94,648	70,166	50,924	319,656	24,482	25,809	19,852
2016	108,646	77,969	55,348	353,843	30,677	31,840	24,270
2017	117,966	85,655	61,621	387,223	32,311	34,513	26,289
2018	123,104	90,588	66,396	394,998	32,516	34,092	25,826
2019	146,463	106,957	78,246	424,285	39,506	41,563	31,472
2020	156,949	114,840	85,952	448,464	42,109	42,248	32,340
2021	164,177	118,849	91,814	488,649	45,328	43,760	32,430
2022	191,754	138,697	107,554	592,195	53,057	51,687	38,327
2023	225,458	166,199	127,522	614,795	59,259	56,907	42,147

(Source: TCS Annual Reports)

successful in comparison to those who are just using human resources. The strategic, financial, employee retention, and motivational aspects of the company are critical to the development of human capital. Businesses typically depend on ROI data to help management make judgments about supporting strategic goals that aim to achieve cost advantage or differentiation advantage [61]. Enhancing human skills could also help firms stand out from the competition and emphasize the significance of HRM in executing business strategy [62]. ROIs in human capital have a significant impact on an organization's financial performance. Companies that use standards for human capital development incur costs. In economies where salaries are continuously rising, it could be challenging for businesses to maintain competitive HCROI levels [63]. Aspects like investments in the development of human capital are influenced by an organization's financial performance. While investing in human capital is essential for any firm, there are situations where the costs required and the unsatisfactory financial results make this impractical. In other situations, after getting the HCROI data, strategic decisions related to cost-cutting may make it necessary to reduce human capital development [64].

Table 12.2 depicts the calculated value of Return on Net Worth/Equity, Return on Capital Employed, and Human Capital Return on Investment.

Table 12.2 Various returns of TCS.

Year	Return on net worth/equity (%)	Return on capital employed (%)	Human capital return on investment (%) (HCROI)
2014	41.93	40.74	162
2015	42.4	41.32	148
2016	35.49	34.9	155
2017	30.31	38.05	152
2018	33.27	41.5	149
2019	38.1	50.71	150
2020	44.72	52.79	149
2021	41.39	52.75	149
2022	49.48	60.23	149
2023	52.46	65.07	146

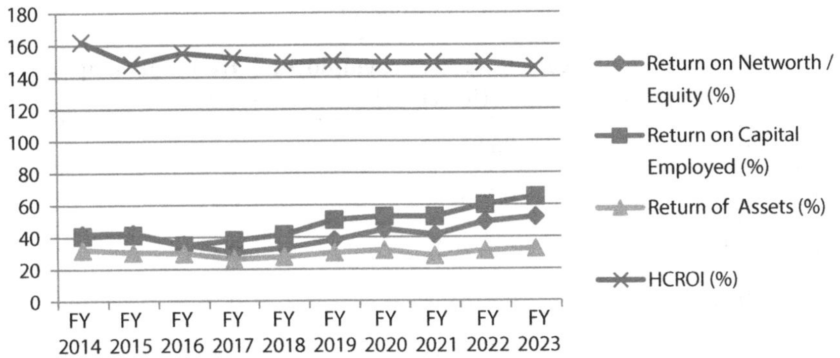

Figure 12.3 Various returns of TCS.

These calculations are done by using the financial data of the company extracted from the annual reports.

Figure 12.3 shows the various forms of returns, i.e., return on equity, return on capital employed, return on assets, and Human Capital Return on Investment (HCROI) earned by TCS during the Financial Year 2013-14 to 2022-23. The average return on Equity for the last 10 years was around 37.23%, with the lowest return in 2017 (30.31) and the highest return in 2023 (52.46). The average Return on Capital Employed for the last 10 years was 47.81 % with the lowest return in 2016 (34.9%) and the highest return in 2023 (65.07%). The average Return of Assets for the last 10 years was 30.078 % with the lowest return in 2017 (26.35%) and the highest return in 2023 (32.63%). The average Human Capital Return on Investment for the last 10 years was 150.9 % with the lowest return in 2023(146%) and the highest return in 2014 (162%). TCS has the highest return from the human capital. It shows the highest financial value added by the employees as a result of investment in them on account of recruitment, training, compensation, etc. The slight decline in the HCROI is due to the increasing number of employees and the cost incurred by them.

12.5.2 Objective 2

The HCVA is an important financial indicator that measures the financial value created by an employee for the organization. The IT industries are completely dependent on the skills of human resources. The performance of employees is reflected in the form of increased revenue and returns for the organization. The greater the profitability per person for the firm, the more valuable its human resources are relative to the costs associated with them.

Table 12.3 Employee cost, revenue, and value added.

Year	Cost per employee (Rs. crore)	Revenue per employee (Rs. crore)	HCVA per employee (Rs. crore)
2014	0.14	0.283734	0.23
2015	0.16	0.305257	0.24
2016	0.16	0.322632	0.26
2017	0.17	0.318368	0.25
2018	0.17	0.314755	0.25
2019	0.19	0.357539	0.29
2020	0.2	0.359666	0.29
2021	0.2	0.350389	0.29
2022	0.2	0.354823	0.3
2023	0.21	0.373587	0.31

Table 12.3 depicts the cost incurred by the company per employee, the contribution of employees in the generation of revenue, and the value added by the human capital for the organization. These calculations are done by using the financial data of the company extracted from the annual reports.

Figure 12.4 shows the Revenue earned, HCVA per employee, and the cost incurred per employee. The trend shows that revenue and HCVA are moving in the same direction. The employees can add more value as compared to the cost incurred by them. The cost incurred per employee in 2014 was Rs.0.14 crore which has increased to Rs. 0.21 crore by the end of 2023. In comparison, cost value added per employee was Rs. 0.23 crore in 2014 which has increased to Rs. 0.31 at the end of 2023. Every employee added to the organization adds value to the organization. Similarly, the revenue of TCS which was Rs.0.283734 crore per employee in 2014 has increased to Rs.0.373587 crore in 2023.

12.5.3 Objective 3

The concept of HEVA evolved from EVA. The EVA is a metric that uses real economic profit to measure the financial performance of any organization.

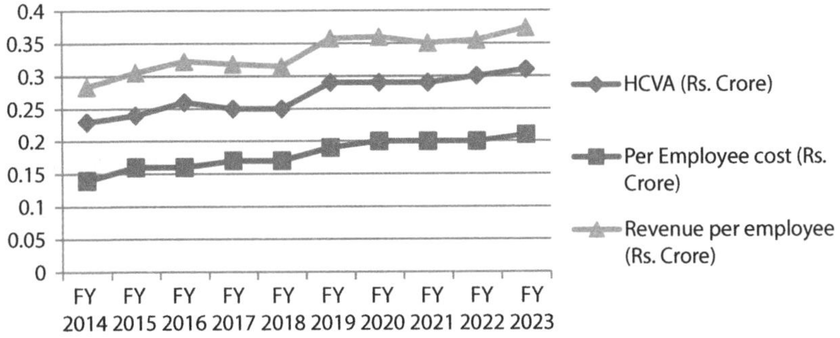

Figure 12.4 Human capital value added.

This shows the amount of residual profit available after payment of all expenses, depreciation, taxes, and cost of capital. It also meets the wealth maximization or value addition objective of financial management. The real value is added only when additional wealth is created above the cost of capital. The HEVA measures the EVA by the employees working in the organization. The higher the EVA by the human resource better it is for the organization and shareholders.

Table 12.4 depicts the Profit after Tax (PAT) of the company and the HEVA by the human capital for the organization and shareholders. The values of PAT of the company are taken from the annual report while HEVA is calculated by using the financial data of the company extracted from the annual reports.

Figure 12.5 shows the HEVA and Profit After Tax (PAT) in the last five financial years between 2019 to 2023. The HEVA in the financial year 2019 was Rs. 31469.40 crore which increased to Rs. 42145.51 crore at the end of the financial year 2023. The Net profit of the company during the same

Table 12.4 PAT and HEVA.

Year	Profit after tax	Human economic value added (HEVA)
2019	31,472	31469.4
2020	32,340	32338.1
2021	32,430	32428.44
2022	38,327	38325.5
2023	42,147	42145.51

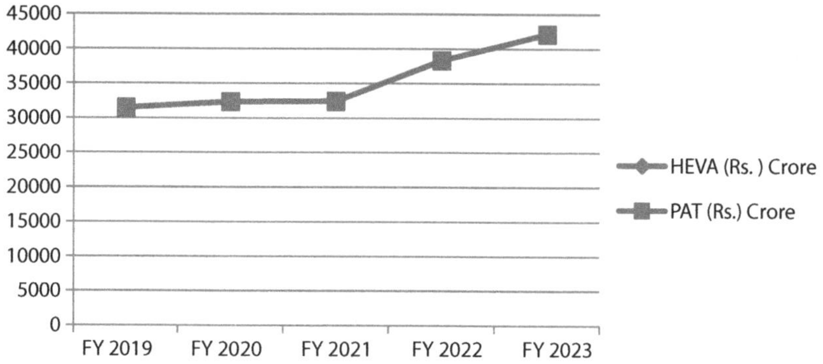

Figure12.5 Human economic value added (HEVA).

period was 31,472 crore which was increased to Rs. 42,147 by the end of financial year 2023.

12.6 Discussion

The data in Figure 12.3 shows that TCS has a higher amount of HCROI in comparison to the return on equity, return on capital employed, and return on assets of the company. Hence, objective 1 of the study is achieved that Human Capital Return on Investment in TCS is high, i.e., employees are provided higher returns in comparison to the cost incurred on them. The data in Figure 12.4 show that the company is capable of making higher HCVA by the employees in comparison to its cost. There is a high degree of positive correlation (0.95994) between the cost incurred by employees and the HCVA by the employees. Objective 2 of the study proves true that employees of TCS are capable of adding more value to the organization in comparison to the cost incurred by them. The data in Figure 12.5 show that the company is capable of making additions to its Human Economic Value. There is a high positive correlation (0.997241) between profit before tax and HEVA for the company. Objective 3 is also achieved as the human capital of the company is adding economic value for the company.

Hence, it can be concluded that the company is efficiently utilizing its human capital to achieve the objectives of the organization. The investment made in the human capital is providing adequate returns for the company. The company is successfully managing its large number of human capital and utilizing it efficiently despite its global area of operation. It has been possible with the adequate application of Human Capital Analytics in the organization. With its application, the company is capable of not only making optimum utilization of human capital but also enabling its employees to adapt to the rapid technological changes occurring in the IT industry.

12.7 Conclusion

It is impossible to manage human capital without the use of technology in situations where a company has a large workforce and a broad region of activity. Through Human Capital Analytics, the technology uses data and analytics techniques to gain insights and make informed decisions about an organization's human capital through collecting, analyzing, and interpreting data related to employees' skills, performance, engagement, and other relevant factors. Human capital analytics support organizations in forecasting future talent needs based on historical data and trends. Human capital analytics intervention provides insights into employee performance and productivity. By analyzing these performance data, organizations can identify top performers, assess performance trends, and identify areas for improvement. In the service business, particularly in the IT industry, the cost of hiring, developing, and retaining human capital is relatively high. Thus, the importance of a cost-benefit analysis increases. The value added by the human capital should be higher in comparison to the cost incurred on them. This value added should be assessed in monetary terms to have a more meaningful evaluation of the performance. When metrics like HCROI, HCVA, and HEVA are used to measure the performance of human capital, the results are clearer. So it can be concluded that Human Capital Analytics is the requirement for the success of organizations big in size in terms of the number of employees and area of operation. It is also required to measure the financial implications of human capital for the organization. Overall, Human Capital Analytics provides organizations with valuable insights to make data-driven decisions about their workforce. By leveraging data and analytics techniques, organizations can optimize their human capital strategies, improve employee performance and engagement, and drive business success.

12.8 Implications

Research researchers, organizations, and HR practitioners can benefit from the current study in their future research endeavors. Human analytics offers several benefits for corporations by leveraging data and analytics techniques. Organizations can gain valuable insights into their workforce, enabling them to make informed decisions, improve recruitment and retention, talent management, and development, enhance workforce planning, and can also help to monitor and measure diversity and inclusion efforts. Organizations adopting tools for managing human capital can easily evaluate their performance in financial terms to have a clearer picture of the benefit obtained from the human capital. Employers and HR managers can evaluate employee value addition for the firm in terms of net value addition as well as revenue by using the study's parameters. Performance Evaluation and Measurement of Human Capital Analytics can contribute to creating inclusive and diverse workplaces. By investigating employee data, organizations can identify biases, disparities, and areas for enhancement in areas such as hiring, promotion, and pay equity. This can lead to the implementation of fairer policies and practices, fostering a more inclusive work environment and promoting social equality. By harnessing the power of data and analytics, we can work toward making a more equitable and prosperous society. The analysis is based on one of India's largest IT companies in terms of both revenue and workforce size. For fresh findings, more research can be done using more IT firms and extra financial indicators. More financial metrics usage in research can provide more valuable insights for qualitative measures and would provide a comprehensive understanding of the benefits obtained from human capital tools.

References

1. Xu, L.D., Xu, E.L., Ling, L., Industry 4.0: state of the art and future trends. *Int. J. Production Res.*, 56, 8, 2941–2962, 2018.
2. Maddikunta, P.K.R., Pham, Q.-V., Prabadevi, B., Deepa, N., Dev, K., Gadekallu, T.R., Ruby, R., Liyanage, M., Industry 5.0: A survey on enabling technologies and potential applications. *J. Ind. Inf. Integr.*, 26, 100257, 2022.
3. Bigliardi, B., Bottani, E., Casella, G., Enabling technologies, application areas and impact of industry 4.0: a bibliographic analysis. *Procedia Manuf.*, 42, 322–326, 2020.
4. Davidsson, P. and Honig, B., The role of social and human capital among nascent entrepreneurs. *J. Business Venturing*, 18, 3, 301–331, 2003.
5. Barney, J.B. and Wright, P.M., On becoming a strategic partner: The role of human resources in gaining competitive advantage, in: *Human Resource Management: Published in Cooperation with the School of Business Administration*, vol. 371, pp. 31–46, The University of Michigan and in alliance with the Society of Human Resources Management, USA, 1998.

6. Nahavandi, S., Industry 5.0—A human-centric solution. *Sustainability*, 11, 16, 4371, 2019.
7. Lu, Y., Zheng, H., Chand, S., Xia, W., Liu, Z., Xu, X., Wang, L., Qin, Z., Bao, J., Outlook on human-centric manufacturing towards Industry 5.0. *J. Manuf. Syst.*, 62, 612–627, 2022.
8. Aheleroff, S., Huang, H., Xu, X., Zhong, R.Y., Toward sustainability and resilience with Industry 4.0 and Industry 5.0. *Front. Manuf. Technol.*, 2, 951643, 2022.
9. Adel, A., Future of industry 5.0 in society: Human-centric solutions, challenges and prospective research areas. *J. Cloud Comput.*, 11, 1, 1–15, 2022.
10. Garg, S., Sinha, S., Arpan, K.K., Mani, M., A review of machine learning applications in human resource management. *Int. J. Prod. Perform. Manage.*, 71, 5, 1590–1610, 2022.
11. Chen, L., Li, T., Jia, F., Schoenherr, T., The impact of governmental COVID-19 measures on manufacturers' stock market valuations: The role of labor intensity and operational slack. *J. Oper. Manage.*, 69, 3, 404–425, 2023.
12. Bahuguna, P.C. and Kumari, P., Strategic Human Resource Management & Organizational Performance, in: *Pervasive Computing for Business: Trends and Applications*, pp. 150–165, IGI Global, United States, 2010.
13. Raziq, A. and Maulabakhsh, R., Impact of working environment on job satisfaction. *Procedia Econ. Finance*, 23, 717–725, 2015.
14. Kashive, N. and Tandon Khanna, V., Emerging HR analytics role in a crisis: an analysis of LinkedIn data. *Competitiveness Review An Int. Bus. J.*, 33, 6, 1179–1204, 2023.
15. Ekka, S., HR analytics: why it matters. *J. Contemp. Issues Bus. Gov.*, 27, 2, 2283–2291, 2021.
16. Opatha, H. H. D. P. J., HR analytics: a literature review and new conceptual model. *Int. J. Sci. Res. Publ.*, 10, 6, 130–141, 2020.
17. Onik, M.M.H., Miraz, M.H., Kim, C.-S., A recruitment and human resource management technique using blockchain technology for industry 4.0, in: *Smart Cities Symposium 2018*, IET, pp. 1–6, 2018.
18. Van den Heuvel, S. and Bondarouk, T., The rise (and fall?) of HR analytics: A study into the future application, value, structure, and system support. *J. Organ. Eff. People Perform.*, 4, 2, 157–178, 2017.
19. Cappelli, P., Making the most of on-line recruiting. *Harv. Business Rev.*, 79, 3, 139–148, 2001.
20. Olian, J.D. and Rynes, S.L., Making total quality work: Aligning organizational processes, performance measures, and stakeholders. *Hum. Resour. Manage.*, 30, 3, 303–333, 1991.
21. Pan, Y., Froese, F., Liu, N., Hu, Y., Ye, M., The adoption of artificial intelligence in employee recruitment: The influence of contextual factors. *Int. J. Hum. Resour. Manage.*, 33, 6, 1125–1147, 2022.

22. Lemmetty, S. and Collin, K., Self-directed learning as a practice of workplace learning: Interpretative repertoires of self-directed learning in ICT work. *Vocations Learn.*, 13, 1, 47–70, 2020.
23. Cimini, C., Boffelli, A., Lagorio, A., Kalchschmidt, M., Pinto, R., How do industry 4.0 technologies influence organisational change? An empirical analysis of Italian SMEs. *J. Manuf. Technol. Manage.*, 32, 3, 695–721, 2020.
24. Chalutz Ben-Gal, H., An ROI-based review of HR analytics: practical implementation tools. *Personnel Rev.*, 48, 6, 1429–1448, 2019.
25. Vihari, N.S. and Rao, M.K., Analytics as a predictor for strategic and sustainable human resource function: an integrative literature review, in: *IIM Conference*, vol. pp1-13, 2013.
26. Kapoor, B. and Sherif, J., Human resources in an enriched environment of business intelligence. *Kybernetes*, 41, 10, 1625–1637, 2012.
27. DiBernardino, F., The missing link: Measuring and managing financial performance of the human capital investment. *People Strategy*, 34, 2, 44, 2011.
28. Çalişkan, E.N., The impact of strategic human resource management on organizational performance. *J. Nav. Sci. Eng.*, 6, 2, 100–116, 2010.
29. Baum, J.AC. and Silverman, B.S., Picking winners or building them? Alliance, intellectual, and human capital as selection criteria in venture financing and performance of biotechnology startups. *J. Business Venturing*, 19, 3, 411–436, 2004.
30. Subramony, M., A meta-analytic investigation of the relationship between HRM bundles and firm performance. *Hum. Resource Manage.*, 48, 5, 745–768, 2009.
31. Dash, S.P. and Roy, S., Performance evaluation under human capital perspective: an empirical evidence. *Int. J. Prod. Perform. Manage.*, 70, 6, 1336–1360, 2020.
32. Nafukho, F.M., Hairston, N., Brooks, K., Human capital theory: Implications for human resource development. *Hum. Resour. Dev. Int.*, 7, 4, 545–551, 2004.
33. Birdi, K., Clegg, C., Patterson, M., Robinson, A., C.B.S., Wall, T.D., Wood, S.J., The impact of human resource and operational management practices on company productivity: A longitudinal study. *Personnel Psychol.*, 61, 3, 467–501, 2008.
34. Bontis, N. and Fitz-enz, J., Intellectual capital ROI: a causal map of human capital antecedents and consequents. *J. Intellectual Capital*, 3, 3, 223–247, 2002.
35. Kiron, D., Prentice, P.K., Ferguson, R.B., Innovating with analytics. *MIT Sloan Manage. Rev.*, 54, 1, 47, 2012.
36. Maisel, L. and Cokins, G., Why analytics will be the next competitive edge. *J. Corp. Account. Finance*, 26, 4, 91–100, 2015.
37. Mohammed,.A.Q., HR analytics: a modern tool in HR for predictive decision making. *J. Manage.*, 6, 3, 51–63, 2019.

38. Reddy, P.R. and Lakshmikeerthi, P., HR analytics–an effective evidence based HRM tool. *Int. J. Bus. Manage. Invention*, 6, 7, 23–34, 2017.
39. Jiang, Y. and Akdere, M., An operational conceptualization of human resource analytics: implications for in human resource development. *Ind. Commer. Training*, 54, 1, 183–200, 2022.
40. Hamilton, R.H. and Sodeman, W.A., The questions we ask: Opportunities and challenges for using big data analytics to strategically manage human capital resources. *Bus. Horiz.*, 63, 1, 85–95, 2020.
41. IT & BPM report, Feb, 2023, https://www.ibef.org/industry/information-technology-india.
42. Statista-2023, Employment of the IT-BPM industry in India from financial year 2009 to 2021, with an estimate for 2022, 2023, https://www.statista.com/statistics/320729/india-it-industry-direct-indirect-employment/.
43. Kearns, G.S. and Lederer, A.L., The impact of industry contextual factors on IT focus and the use of IT for competitive advantage. *Inf. Manage.*, 41, 7, 899–919, 2004.
44. Singh, A.K. and Rastogi, L., Human value added. *Delhi Bus. Review*, v2, 1, 21–34, 2001.
45. Pinto, J.C. and Curto, J.D., The Organizational Configuration Concept as a Contribution to the Performance Explanation: The Case of the Pharmaceutical Industry in Portugal. *Eur. Manage. J.*, 25, 1, 60–78, 2007.
46. AlQershi, N., Strategic thinking, strategic planning, strategic innovation and the performance of SMEs: The mediating role of human capital. *Manage. Sci. Lett.*, 11, 3, 1003–1012, 2021.
47. Shaukat, H., Ashraf, N., Ghafoor, S., Impact of human resource management practices on employees performance. *Middle-East J. Sci. Res.*, 23, 2, 329–338, 2015.
48. Drábek, J., Lorincová, S., Javorčíková, J., Investing in human capital as a key factor for the development of enterprises. *Issues Hum. Resour. Manage.*, 1, 1, 54–78, 2017.
49. Vithana, K., Jayasekera, R., Choudhry, T., Baruch, Y., Human Capital resource as cost or investment: A market-based analysis. *Int. J. Hum. Resour. Manage.*, 34, 6, 1213–1245, 2023.
50. Meszek, W., Measurement of human capital in the specificity of a construction enterprise. *Procedia Eng.*, 122, 213–219, 2015.
51. Yosintha, R., Indonesian students' attitudes towards EFL learning in response to industry 5.0. *Metathesis J. English Language Literature Teach.*, 4, 2, 163–177, 2020.
52. Johansson, H., Profinet industrial internet of things gateway for the smart factory, 2017.
53. Longo, F., Padovano, A., Umbrello, S., Value-oriented and ethical technology engineering in industry 5.0: A human-centric perspective for the design of the factory of the future. *Appl. Sci.*, 10, 12, 4182, 2020.

54. Gotfredsen, S., Bringing back the human touch: Industry 5.0 concept creating factories of the future. *Manufacturers Monthly dostęp*, 11, 20185, 2016. Retrieved from http://www.manmonthly .com.au/features/bringing-back-the-human-touch-industry-5-0-concept-creating-factories-of-the-future/.
55. Parham, S. and Heling, G.WJ., The relationship between human capital efficiency and financial performance of Dutch production companies. *Res. J. Finance Accounting*, 6, 8, 188–201, 2015.
56. Mukherjee, P., Value added and profitability: role of human resource. *Great Lakes Her.*, 7, 2, 64, 2013.
57. Viljoen, H.H., *Human Capital Return-on-Investment (HCROI) in South African Companies listed on the Johannesburg Stock Exchange (JSE)*, Stellenbosch University, Stellenbosch, 2012.
58. Kucharcikova, A., Konusikova, L., Tokarcikova, E., Approaches to the quantification of the human capital efficiency in enterprises. *Communications-Scientific Lett. Univ. Zilina*, 18, 1A, 49–54, 2016.
59. Wijaya, A., Conventional Financial Performance, Economic Value Added, Human Economic Value Added, Value Added Intellectual Coefficient And Its Impact On Stock Return Of Companies Operating In Energy Sector In Indonesia And Malaysia. *Ilomata Int. J. Tax Account.*, 2, 3, 222–235, 2021.
60. Human Capital Management Solutions: Cloud Based HCM-TCS, 2020, https://www.tcs.com/content/dam/ global-tcs/en/pdfs/insights/solution-details/tcs-hr-transformation-services.pdf.
61. Kesti, M., Syväjärvi, A., Stenvall, J., Rivera, M.A., Human capital scenario analysis as an organizational intelligence tool for performance management. *Probl. Perspect. Manage.*, 9, 1, 46–58, 2011.
62. Kesti, M., Human capital and knowledge development connection to productivity. *EKONOMIKA i ORGANIZACJA GOSPODARKI ŻYWNOŚCIOWEJ*, 27, 27–40, 2011.
63. Key trends in human capital; A global perspective, pp. 5–35, 2012.
64. Law, K.MY. and Kesti, M., *Yin Yang and organizational performance: Five elements for improvement and success*, Springer Science & Business Media, 2014.

13

Data-Driven Strategies to Improve Workplace Diversity, Equality and Inclusion (DEI)

Arkja Singh[1], Rakesh Kumar Yadav[1*] and Deepa Gupta[2]

[1]*Department of Management Studies, School of Business Management, IFTM University, Moradabad, Uttar Pradesh, India*
[2]*GL Bajaj Institute of Management, Greater Noida, Uttar Pradesh, India*

Abstract

In modern-day organizational dynamics, encouraging diversity, equality, and inclusion (DEI) has turned out to be not only a moral imperative but also a strategic business advantage. For advancing DEI initiatives in the workplace, this research paper scrutinized the significance of data-driven strategies. To pinpoint the differences, biases, and areas for enhancement, it elucidated the key role of data analysis in fusing empirical evidence and theoretical frameworks. To extend the targeted interventions that endorse diverse recruitment, equitable policies, and inclusive cultures, this paper investigated a range of data-driven approaches, including demographic analysis, sentiment analysis, and network analysis. Moreover, emphasizing the magnitude of transparency, privacy, and accountability, it carefully inspected the issues and ethical contemplations associated with using data for DEI purposes. To avoid prospective bias and guarantee the ethical use of data in DEI initiatives, it advocated the embracing of sturdy governance frameworks and accountability mechanisms. In due course, this paper advocated the holistic amalgamation of data-driven strategies into an organization's DEI efforts to encourage informed decision-making and craft a more equitable and inclusive work milieu.

***Keywords*:** Data-driven strategies, diversity, equality and inclusion (DEI), workplace dynamics, ethical considerations

**Corresponding author*: rkyadav@iftmuniversity.ac.in

Deepa Gupta, Mukul Gupta, Pawan Budhwar, Jim Westerman, Rajesh Kumar Dhanaraj and Balamurugan Balusamy (eds.) Human Capital Analytics: Exploring the HR Spectrum in Industry 5.0, (283–302)

13.1 Introduction

13.1.1 Data-Driven Strategies in Workplace

In a swiftly embryonic workplace setting, data-driven strategies have materialized as compulsorily obligatory tools for organizations in a quest to gain a competitive edge and impel sustainable growth. Leveraging data for an up-to-date and informed decision-making process has turned out to be an underpinning foundation stone of up-to-date contemporary business operations, transfiguring how companies draw close to an array of facades of their operations. Commencing from marketing and sales to human resources and customer service, data-driven strategies is being applied transversely from corner to corner to an assortment of domains with the purpose of optimizing performance and accomplishing organizational objectives.

One prominent and noteworthy spot where data-driven strategies are creating an impact worth mentioning is talent management and human resources. By harnessing data analytics, companies can gain valuable and worthy insights into workforce demographics, employee engagement levels, performance metrics, and retention rates. This enables them to make educated and informed decisions regarding recruitment, training and development, succession planning, and diversity initiatives [1]. For example, by means of demographic analysis, organizations can chalk out the gaps in the representation of employee composition and put into action some fruitful and targeted strategies to uphold diversity and inclusion among their employees.

Other than talent management, data-driven strategies are furthermore being employed to enhance and augment operational efficiency and productivity. By dissecting and scrutinizing operational data such as production metrics, supply chain dynamics, and customer feedback, organizations can classify and categorize inefficiencies, optimize processes, and make more well-organized and efficient workflows. This not only perks up productivity on the whole but also boosts customer satisfaction and drives profitability.

In addition to this, data-driven strategies are playing an all the time more fundamental and crucial function in customer relationship management as well as marketing. All the way through highly developed and advanced analytics techniques with the likes of predictive modeling and sentiment analysis, companies can gain insights keen on customer behavior, preferences, and trends. This greatly facilitates them to figure out and shape their marketing campaigns, product offerings, and customer service initiatives to a much superior and enhanced level of meeting the needs and penchant of their intended audience, at the end of the day driving customer loyalty and revenue growth and escalation.

As mentioned previously, the three data-driven approaches primarily employed to get a hold of the required data are demographic analysis, sentiment analysis, and network analysis [9]. They are discussed as follows:

13.1.1.1 Demographic Analysis

In simple words, the statistical data *vis-à-vis* the workforce within an organization are denoted by the expression workplace demographics, which include numerous aspects ranging from age, gender, education, sexual orientation, marital status, number of children, family structure, disability status, and ethnicity to the geographic location or origin of the employees. Demographic analysis is considerably significant for the reason that it demonstrates just what the diversity in the workforce of an organization is like and how it might alter and transform in the times to come [16]. Being thoughtful and considerate toward these demographic fine points is gravely critical for informed and deliberated strategic decision-making. A detailed analysis of these data endows the C-suite executives with some very constructively useful insights into the diverse configuration of the workforce of their organization, assisting in devising the intended and all-encompassing business strategies.

13.1.1.2 Sentiment Analysis

Pulling together the opinions and the feedback of the organizational populace to deduce, compute, and gauge their perception of their organization as a brand is sentiment analysis [17]. How C-suite executives run the organization and the mindset of employees toward it is referred to as employee sentiment. Based on various intrinsic and extrinsic aspects deliberated by mood analysis, employee sentiment is the general frame of mind an employee develops or experiences in their organization. This sentiment is also an ensuing result of their senior's recognition and acknowledgment of an employee's achievements and the opportunities given to them for a promotion or overall professional growth within the organization. At the same time, by keeping up a vigorous and blissful organizational setting, survey responses from the employees collate data that are compulsorily required to dig up to the bottom of any messy predicament that the management may not even be aware of.

13.1.1.3 Network Analysis

By investigating the potency, incidence, and character of communication among the employees in organizational networks, network analysis quantifies and charts the blueprint of relationships that exist among the people in an organization. It presents the elemental data with reference to various concealed dynamics for organizational success, for instance, the direction and flow of communication, decision-making, creativity, inclusion, and even dependence, trust, rationale, and energy [2]. Frequently, network analysis discloses the outline of associations and the power of influence which both surprisingly are incredibly dissimilar from the formal organizational hierarchical structures that the C-suite executives put their faith in and identify with to deliberate strategic decisions.

On the whole, these data-driven strategies have turned out to be requisite and indispensable tools for organizations looking to thrive and flourish in today's exceedingly cutthroat business environment. By harnessing the power of data analytics, companies can unbolt priceless insights, optimize performance, and drive originality through all the facets of their operations. At the same time, it is basic and fundamental for organizations to prioritize data privacy, security, and ethical considerations so as to guarantee that data-driven strategies are installed conscientiously and in coalition with organizational values and regulatory necessities.

13.1.2 DEI Initiatives within the Workplace

At this point in time, in the corporate setting, diversity, equality, and inclusion (DEI) initiatives have progressed from being sheer buzzwords to significantly decisive components of organizational success and sustainability. DEI initiatives seek and aspire to craft a work milieu where every individual, despite the consequences of their background, identity, or characteristics, feels valued, respected, and empowered to have a say in contributing to their distinctive perspectives and talents. These initiatives encompass an extensive assortment of strategies and policies deliberated to endorse diversity in terms of race, ethnicity, gender, sexual orientation, age, disability status, and other dimensions of identity, at the same time as nurturing equality and inclusion at all levels of the organization.

13.1.2.1. Diversity incorporates a wide-ranging gamut of depiction contained by an organization or association, surpassing long-established classifications for example race, ethnicity, and gender [5]. It expands to take account of people from varied backgrounds, cultures, ages, socioeconomic statuses, educational levels, geographical locations, belief systems, sexual orientations, and life experiences. Although some proportions of diversity akin to race, ethnicity, and gender are frequently acknowledged and accepted, the notion of diversity is wide-ranging and comprehensive.

13.1.2.2. Equality pertains to providing just and reasonable dealing and equivalent chances and prospects to each and every individual [8]. It is not purely in relation to appointing people from different backgrounds nevertheless what is more is making certain they are given impartial and unbiased handling and receive the same probability for representation, promotions, professional development, and additional breaks. To accomplish this, organizations ought to be obliged to put into action practices and policies that keenly endorse equality.

13.1.2.3. Inclusion includes the combined understanding and know-how of a varied workforce. It gyrates around whether people feel treasured, heard, and respected for their support toward the organization [4]. It furthermore entails evaluating whether employees experience a sense of comfort in putting across their concerns and talking about their points of view candidly. Unfortunately, delving into research by the International Labour Organization (ILO) points out that one in four employees does not feel treasured, heard, and respected, drawing attention to the pressing need for company and industry leaders to intensify their dedication to DEI initiatives.

At the heart of DEI initiatives lies the acknowledgment of the intrinsic significance of diversity and the understanding that diverse point of view only shows the way to much superior and enhanced decision-making, innovation, and performance [6]. DEI initiatives within the place of work take in a variety of strategies, counting in recruitment and hiring practices that prioritize diversity, the realization of inclusive policies and practices, diversity training and education programs, mentorship and sponsorship proposals for underrepresented groups, and the establishment of affinity groups and employee resource groups (ERGs).

Likewise, organizations are progressively leveraging data-driven approaches to inform and evaluate their DEI initiatives. By bringing together and examining data on personnel demographics, employee engagement, retention rates, promotion rates, and other key metrics, companies know how to make out the disparities and scope for improvement, gauge progress over time, and make data-informed decisions to press forward with their DEI objectives [7].

On the other hand, while DEI initiatives have made noteworthy strides in recent times, there is still much work to be done and challenges to be endured. Pulling off factual DEI calls for an unremitting dedication from the organizational leadership, as well as a readiness to concentrate on systemic barriers and unconscious biases that may obstruct the steps forward.

For this reason, DEI initiatives contained by the workplace play a vital role in fostering a tradition of belongingness and making certain that each and every one of the employees has the opportunity to prosper and arrive at their full potential. By taking on DEI as foundational values and joining them together into all facets of organizational culture and operations, companies can construct a place of work that is not merely extra equitable and inclusive but in addition more innovative, resilient, and successful sooner or later.

13.2 The Coalesce

13.2.1 Data-Driven Strategies and DEI

The intersection of data-driven strategies and ideas from DEI has turned out to be a powerful and commanding force in organizational change. This alliance combines the power of information analysis with the obligation and necessity to build a diverse, balanced, and inclusive place of work; this shows the means to ingenious ideas that not only press on to advance the economy but also promote a culture of teamwork and empowerment.

Elemental to this amalgamation is the acknowledgment that data can be a compellingly potent instrument to demonstrate attention to disparities, give an impression of the areas for improvement, and weigh the progress in the direction of achieving the goals of DEI. Via data analytics, organizations can identify employee demographics, demonstration of personal dimensions, hiring and promotion, employee engagement, and additional significant procedures. By means of this information, organizations are in a way allowed to categorize irregularities and prejudices that may possibly subsist in their processes and procedures and put into practice intervention plans to resolve these concerns.

Executing the stratagem delineated above begins by means of grasping the four elemental mechanisms of a data-driven DEI approach. This entails:

13.2.1.1. Running an all-inclusive DEI engagement survey transversely the organization. This sanctions the employees to a right to be heard about their points of view on what is being carried out in a sound way and what is not. As a result, organizations get their hands on very useful data for analysis, making it possible for the HR teams to carry out a methodical and comprehensive DEI audit [11]. Such audits or assessments permit HR to pin down areas of deficit, for the most part when weighing up the facets like pay, promotions, leadership demonstration, and administrative demonstration. In conjunction with hiring and preliminary remuneration statistics, it is indispensable to examine retention and promotion data as well.

13.2.1.2. Facilitating employee focus groups (ERGs) subsequent to the engagement survey. These forums inquire deeper into employee sentiments regarding DEI, providing relevant and appropriate insights into facets potentially disregarded by survey data. If the survey discloses the discrepancy in the sense of belongingness among LGBTQIA groups measuring up to the others, focus groups can explicate the original grounds and put forward strategies to bridge this gap.

13.2.1.3. Bring together all-inclusive employee data. Although engagement surveys and audits put forward important insight, they might not include all the required data [15]. Employees might give it a miss when it comes to divulging certain information, for example, gender or sexual orientation, posing challenges in dealing with their own sentiments. As a result, HR teams can investigate alternative data views, for example, cataloging by location or some other supplementary demographic factors.

13.2.1.4. Analyzing data to unearth trends and intersectionality. All the way through trend analysis, HR teams may be able to recognize the patterns, for example, the occurrence of women in decision-making or administrative roles, to categorize the existing opportunities. Additionally, delving into data intersectionality permits a deeper understanding of the experiences of employees facing compounded structures of prejudice and discrimination. Investigating trends among women of color in precise positions as compared to their male counterparts sheds light on possible inconsistency in progression opportunities. This move forward enables HR to grow insights into the comprehensive experiences of underrepresented employees within the workforce.

As mentioned previously, data-driven strategies also play a central role in bringing about up-to-date recruiting, hiring, and talent management to prop up diversity and inclusion in the place of work. By analyzing data on prospective candidates, hiring outcomes, and retention rates, organizations can discover the blockades to hiring anonymous groups and make use of strategies to trim down bias and encourage equality for all candidates. Additionally, data analysis can help organizations monitor the effectiveness of diversity hiring, identify areas for improvement, and adjust recruiting strategies.

Furthermore, a data-driven approach can inform the design and implementation of DEI education and training within an organization. By analyzing employee input, survey participation, and training results, organizations can tailor DEI programs to address employees' specific needs, requirements, and issues and ensure that they are engaging and effective in driving cultural change. Figure 13.1 enlightens the confluence of data-driven strategies with the DEI initiatives in order to achieve the organizational objectives.

On the other hand, while these ideas when put on paper give the impression of being promising for DEI leaders to press forward in the place of work, their use must be watchful and principled. To make certain that a data-driven approach is brought into play responsibly and lines up with corporate values and conventions, organizations could do with to prioritize data privacy, transparency, and accountability at every single level.

13.3 The Contraption

13.3.1 Data-Driven Mindset among the HR and Technology Leaders

Today's C-suite executives and talent leaders are able to identify that DEI is not just an ethical necessity but a critically vital constituent of any organization's success and business mores. Recent findings from a survey carried out by HBR Analytic Services draw attention to this outlook, enlightening

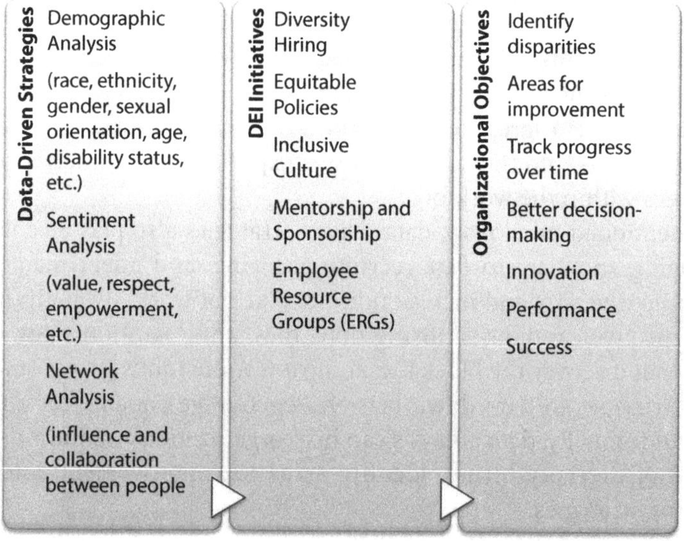

Figure 13.1 The Coalesce: Data-driven strategies and DEI.

that *two-thirds of respondents consider DEI a top strategic precedence for their organization*. This put an accent on the up-and-coming acknowledgment that developing a diverse and inclusive place of work is of the very essence for driving company results and sustaining a competitive front. What is more, a study by McKinsey & Company additionally strengthens the significance of DEI initiatives in driving organizational performance. According to their research, *companies that demonstrate gender and ethnic diversity are 15% and 35% more likely to outperform their less diverse counterparts, respectively*. Conspicuously, these findings draw notice to the corporal profits of diversity, presenting that those organizations with supplementary inclusive personnel outshine not only in financial metrics but also in customer acquisition and revenue generation. These insights draw attention to the transformative perspective of DEI initiatives in encouraging innovation, enhancing employee engagement, and developing a culture of belonging within organizations. *Per se*, leaders athwart industries are ever more prioritizing DEI efforts as a calculated and deliberate prerequisite, identifying its part in driving sustainable development and generating value in favor of each and every stakeholder.

HR leaders lead and manage policies, procedures, and practices to address inequities of individuals and organizations while leading their employees to implement DEI. At the same time, technology leaders have become important allies, and their roles go much beyond just support to become successful and effective partners. They have played a key role in conceptualizing, designing, and implementing technology-driven solutions designed to concentrate on addressing the nuanced challenges faced [19]. At the very core of this partnership is a strong and sturdy commitment to a data-driven approach, where insights from data will channel and guide decision-making. From experts using data as an invaluable asset, HR and technology leaders collaborate to refine and improve processes, seamlessly integrating the language of DEI principles throughout the working life [3]. Collectively, they labor to reimagine data and furnish the way out with the vision to incorporate or integrate without even a single chance of glitch. This integration encompasses the organization's technology and processes, encouraging change across functional areas. By leveraging the power of technology, organizations can not only make out and correct deficiencies in DEI but also improve operational competence and encourage innovation. HR and technology leaders come together to register the itinerary for creating a varied and thriving workplace where each person is supported to arrive at their highest prospective as the basis of a productive and equitable environment.

For instance, a shortage of women in leadership roles serves as an unmistakably evident indicator of original and usual issues. It might be a warning indication of universal evils of the same kind with the likes of prejudiced promotion norms or a deficiency of female exemplars, thwarting women from aspiring for positions further up the ladder. Ascertaining an organized and unified DEI strategy and methodically gauging its apparatus are the fundamental stepladders toward progression.

Here are a few overarching proposals for assessing every aspect:

13.3.1.1 Diversity

Data analysis ought to focus on clear-cut and precise intentions outlined by the organization, for instance, the demonstration of women in leadership positions, rather than broad metrics like female existence taken as a whole contained by the organization [18].

13.3.1.2 Equality

Proposals to augment equality ought to concentrate on a range of phases of the employee life cycle. HR experts can begin by investigating representation facts and figures to locate areas of deficit or prospective upgradation. Consequently, they can reverse map out to levy the causal procedures and practices swaying these end results.

13.3.1.3 Inclusion

Qualitative awareness and opinion-based data from employees are commanded for weighing up inclusion. Some priceless insights may be offered by making use of company commitment or ambiance reviews at the business unit echelon. But maintaining secrecy and privacy is a matter of chief importance in order to guarantee honest and candid responses and reactions from the employees. Facilitating the business unit C-suite executives to outline the shape of their stratagem according to their precise requirements, HR may collectively cumulate these outcomes received from the employees.

While computing corner-to-corner equality among people, processes, and outcomes, guaranteeing organization-wide answerability, responsibility and liability, fluency, and clarity in data has been pointed out as fundamental for comprehending data representation. "Google" pioneered this transparency with its comprehensive annual diversity reports which are readily available on the Internet [13]. Utilizing data from diverse sources, the continued collaboration of the Google team with internal and external partners has augmented and enhanced some impactful efforts, fostering belongingness within Google's very fabric. They have remained steadfast in their Racial Equality Commitments, focusing on Workplace, Products, and Society initiatives to endorse and promote inclusion, despite all sorts of global challenges.

In 2015, "Salesforce" also initiated the first US equal pay audit, which resulted in $3 million in salary adjustments. Including a Racial Equality and Justice Task Force and new equality pledges aiming for 50% under-represented groups in the US workforce by 2023, they have since launched several DEI initiatives. Their progress has been driven by data-driven strategies and employee-led programs.

13.3.2 DEI Software

Reflecting a growing recognition that while technology does not supersede strategy, it can certainly complement it, the DEI software market has witnessed a surge in activity in the past decade. According to a recent IDC survey, *C-level executives are advocating for the inclusion of a diversity and inclusion index metric within HR functions this year*. This has underscored the increasing importance placed on leveraging technology to drive diversity and inclusion efforts.

By scrutinizing metrics such as promotion rates, retention rates, and engagement levels, among others, HR professionals have managed to gain a comprehensive understanding of the effectiveness of their diversity initiatives. This data-driven approach enables organizations to identify areas for improvement, track progress over time, and ultimately foster a more inclusive and equitable workplace culture.

The example of Culture Monkey may be considered which provides HR teams with a powerful tool to gather valuable insights from their diverse workforce [12]. With customizable DEI surveys, organizations can listen to honest feedback, gaining deep insights into the perspectives on inclusion held by employees.

Figure 13.2 shows a glimpse of an employee survey platform where a few statements on Diversity and Inclusivity may be seen.

Figure 13.3 demonstrates employee engagement drivers and AI-based people analytics wherein a matrix of Engagement scores on the basis of Employee Ethnicity may be witnessed and these scores may be compared with the Organizational Benchmark.

Figure 13.4 gives an idea about an anonymous feedback tool in which an employee may witness raising their concern regarding the Inclusivity policies of the company quoting their own example.

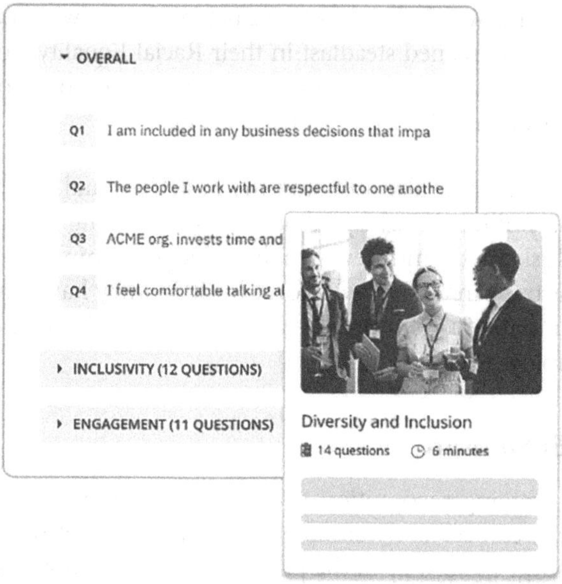

Figure 13.2 A glimpse of CultureMonkey's employee survey platform.

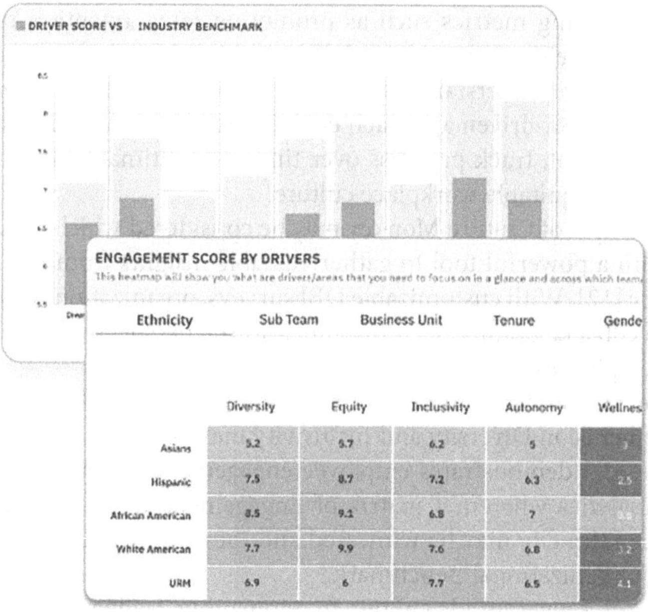

Figure 13.3 A glimpse of CultureMonkey's employee engagement drivers and AI-based people analytics.

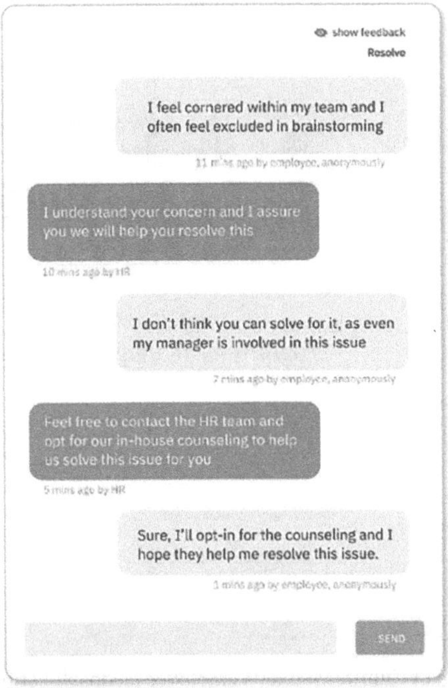

Figure 13.4 A glimpse of CultureMonkey's anonymous feedback tool.

Figure 13.5 showcases the employee feedback-action module through which it may be analyzed how effectively the managers respond to and resolve their subordinates' issues and concerns, which may further be used to formulate an action plan for training the managers.

By analyzing these responses, HR professionals can identify areas of concern regarding DEI within the workplace. The platform enables organizations to take proactive steps to address DEI issues, creating a more inclusive and equitable work atmosphere. By acting on the feedback received, organizations can implement targeted initiatives to promote diversity and ensure that every employee feels valued, respected, and empowered to contribute their unique perspectives and talents. With their engagement software, organizations can take meaningful steps toward building a culture of belonging and driving positive change within their workplace.

Another example may be considered VIBE with its VIBE Index, which proffers an all-inclusive assessment of equality and inclusion contained by the personnel. Making the most of an amalgamation of breadth and depth, alongside deliberation for intersectionality, this index spawns an overarching score that echoes the organization's performance in promoting equality

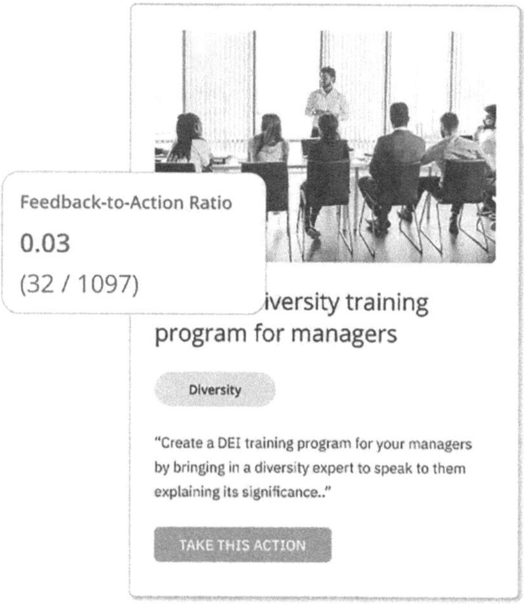

Figure 13.5 A glimpse of CultureMonkey's employee feedback-action module.

and parity transverse the diverse dimensions. The Index makes available insights hooked on five key outcomes critical for diversity and inclusion efforts: hiring, promotion, leadership, belonging, and attrition. By examining these outcomes, organizations can gain a holistic understanding of their DEI initiatives' efficacy and recognize areas for stepping up their game. By means of the VIBE Index, organizations can formulate informed decisions and take targeted measures to nurture a more inclusive and equitable workplace atmosphere. A sample is shown in Figure 13.6 with a matrix displaying people's sense of belonging in their workplace on the VIBE Index.

One more software is TalentNeuron, which aids organizations in making unbiased, data-driven decisions, crucial for prioritizing DEI initiatives [10]. HR teams leverage personalized reports and analytics to drive discussions and strategic partnerships.

13.4 Challenges and Deliberations

Although the implementation of Data-Driven DEI strategies capitulates multiple advantages, it presents a few challenges and deliberations, in addition:

Value Inclusion Belonging Equity Score **2.28** **VIBE™ Score**

	Female Asians	Female URM	Female White	Male Asians	Male URM	Male White	OUTCOME SCORES
Representation	11.6%	5.8%	23.3%	20.3%	7%	32%	
Hires	13.2%	7.4%	19.8%	19.8%	6.7%	33%	3
Promos	12.4%	6.2%	25.1%	18.5%	6.3%	31.4%	3
Leadership	5.5%	3.4%	24.1%	13.8%	4.8%	48.3%	1
Belonging	12.6%	5.3%	21.1%	16.8%	7.4%	36.9%	2
Attrition	15.6%	6.3%	18.8%	18.8%	9.4%	31.3%	2
GROUP SCORES	3	2	3	2	1	5	

Figure 13.6 A glance at the VIBE Index showcasing people's sense of belonging in their workplace.

13.4.1 Data Precision

Perpetuating the accuracy and reliability of data stands supreme. Flawed or prejudiced data can result in faulty deduction and ineffective strategies.

13.4.2 Data Confidentiality

Organizations come to grips with holding fast to data privacy-related set of laws and ethical contemplation when assembling and making the most of responsive employee data.

13.4.3 Steer Clear of Tokenism

Absolutely focusing on supplementing diversity without concentrating on equality and inclusion poses a threat of falling into tokenism. Data have necessitated underlining the accomplishments to promote an authentically inclusive work milieu.

13.4.4 Persistent Loyalty

Accepting data-driven DEI has not turned out to be an unusual feat or attempt, but it surely commands suffering, devotion, and investment.

It calls for time and unending dedication on the part of HR executives to carry out a sustainable change.

DEI may not be professed as fundamental to the organization, in the dearth of data. Deficient in the capacity to estimate the blow of scarce data, DEI stakeholders may conceivably locate themselves helplessly swamped in the midst of plans and proposals. Accordingly, consequential to restricted support and participation from higher-ranking leadership, the organization often may not accord due gravity to DEI. Data, thereby, play a fundamental function at each juncture of developing and implementing an impactful DEI strategy.

13.5 Conclusion

It can by far be concluded that insights derived from data have become important tools in organizations' efforts to maintain competitive advantage and achieve sustainable growth. The integration of analytics is changing the way businesses approach every aspect of their operations, be it talent management, operational excellence, or customer relations. Using insights from data analytics, organizations are making informed decisions, improving their performance, and driving innovation at all levels.

As the need to promote DEI in the workplace is becoming increasingly important, organizations have recognized the importance of measuring DEI not only as an incentive for work and competition but also as an important moral factor. The amalgamation of a data-driven approach with these DEI attempts has enabled the organizations to gain a deeper understanding of employee performance, identify gaps, and implement targeted interventions, with the intention of promoting diversity and inclusion.

Thus, harnessing data to stimulate diversity, equality, and inclusion (DEI) strategies is not merely a movement anymore. It is, in fact, a deliberate necessity in today's dynamic business setting. For organizations that are on the lookout for fabricating their organizational culture that encourages DEI, well-timed, fitting, and actionable data have doled out much as digital bullion. Organizations are increasing more profound insights keen on the employees and addressing the majority of these urgent issues effectively by disaggregating data in the way of an intersectional lens.

Accepting a data-driven approach positions organizations separately, permitting the leadership to recognize both deficiencies and accomplishments. Here is how leveraging data can bring DEI strategies to the fore, to go beyond even the loftiest aspiration:

13.5.1 Attracting Apex Talent

Allocation of data represents a pledge to DEI that can considerably blow the hiring efforts. Studies demonstrate that a bulk of job seekers actively seek companies that align with their values, with DEI efforts being a crucial consideration. This is predominantly factual for younger generations, highlighting the significance of fair compatibility in exerting a pull on capacity.

13.5.2 Driving Employee Retention and Loyalty

In today's aggressive job market, employees seek workplaces that are arranged in line with their values and offer professional accomplishment. Regular employee surveys make available priceless feedback on DEI opinions, bringing up-to-date necessary actions to better the employee experience. Representing a legitimate awareness in listening and acting on feedback augments employee retention and loyalty toward the organization.

13.5.3 Nurturing Belonging and Inclusion

A sense of belonging and inclusion is encouraged among the employees by imploring feedback in an open and amicable style. For an on-the-spot detection of problems and apprehensions, frequent pulse surveys may be used, which can facilitate organizations to concentrate on these problems without much delay. The compilation of genuine data imperative for incessant upgradation may be guaranteed by paying attention to the phrasing of sensitive questions.

13.5.4 Identifying Gaps in Employee Representation

For steering targeted DEI efforts, data prove to be helpful in identifying the inconsistencies in employee representation. Data-driven insights also notify strategic employment decisions whether it is broadening the horizons for leadership teams or some precise job functions.

13.5.5 Tracking Progress Alongside Representation Goals

For driving DEI initiatives onward, setting up organizational representation goals is necessary [14]. Moreover, data facilitate organizations to keep an eye on the progress, hold on to benchmarks, and identify interventions as desirable. Taking a systemic approach to DEI all the way through quantitative and qualitative analysis not only promotes accountability but also prioritizes effectual initiatives.

13.5.6 Furnishing Teams for Victory

Progressive organizations give power to their employees with the right to use the appropriate data and permit informed decision-making at all levels. Thus, democratizing data authorizes teams to leverage insights for their potential accomplishment and drive a constructive impact across the organization.

13.5.7 Gaining an All-Inclusive View of DEI Experience

All the way through data analysis, sophisticated technologies extend insight into the DEI experience. Organizations achieve a holistic understanding of employee engagement, performance, and retention by being familiar with intersectional tendencies and gaps. While not being a substitute for straightforward employee feedback, data-based insights surely update the decision-making and drive a computable change.

Integrating insights obtained from data with DEI initiatives gives organizations the ability to drive meaningful change and create a diverse, balanced, and inclusive office space. Organizations can unlock new insights, identify opportunities for improvement, and support progress toward DEI goals by using the analytical power of data to informed decisions and take strategic actions. This union of data-driven strategies with DEI initiatives seems to have presented a commanding power to organizations for bringing about organizational change [20]. Organizations can recognize areas for development, trim down prejudice, and promote a new inclusive culture in the place of work by employing data analytics. Teaming up to improve the procedures and incorporate the DEI principles effortlessly all the way through their organizations, C-suite Executives at the HR and technology front have assumed a vital responsibility in this endeavor.

In a nutshell, data-driven DEI strategies, by any means, are crucial for organizations dedicated to nurturing diverse, equitable, and inclusive workplaces. Organizations can become a magnet for top talent, drive employee retention, cultivate belongingness, and track growth in the direction of representation goals by leveraging data at each phase of the course of action. Executing a data-driven approach is not only about accumulating data but also about employing insights to drive significant change and fashion a workplace where each and every employee can flourish.

References

Journal References

1. Kiradoo, G., Diversity, Equality, and Inclusion in the Workplace: Strategies for Achieving and Sustaining a Diverse Workforce. *Adv. Res. Social Sci. Manage. Ed.*, 01, 139–151, 2022.
2. Thomas, D.A., Diversity, equality, and inclusion: A foundation for business success. *J. Divers. Manage.*, 14, 2, 1–6, 2019.
3. Pinkett, R., *How to Measure, Analyze, and Improve Diversity, Equality, and Inclusion. Leader to Leader*, vol. 110, 2023, https://doi.org/10.1002/ltl.20788.

Web Citations

4. Chandra, S., Data driven Inclusion: How Data-Driven HR Strategies can enhance DEI in organizations, 2024, https://www.linkedin.com/pulse/data-driven-inclusion-how-data-driven-hr-strategies-can-chandra-6umac, (accessed 17 February 2024).
5. Baker, P., A data-driven approach to DEI supports real diversity, 2021, https://www.techtarget.com/searchhrsoftware/feature/A-data-driven-approach-to-DEI-supports-real-diversity, (accessed 17 February 2024).
6. Gupta, C., Enabling data-driven strategies for diverse, inclusive & equitable workplaces, 2022, https://hrme.economictimes.indiatimes.com/news/hrtech/enabling-data-driven-strategies-for-diverse-inclusive-equitable-workplaces/90270667, (accessed 17 February 2024).
7. Williams, J.C. and Dolkas, J., Data-Driven Diversity: To achieve your inclusion goals, use a metrics-based approach, 2022, https://hbr.org/2022/03/data-driven-diversity, (accessed 18 February 2024).
8. A Data-Driven Approach to Diversity and Inclusion, 2021, https://harver.com/blog/data-driven-diversity-inclusion/, (accessed 18 February 2024).
9. Roberts, L.M. and Thomas-Hunt, M., Data-Driven Approaches to Diversity, Equality and Inclusion, 2024, https://www.shrm.org/executive-network/insights/people-strategy/data-driven-approaches-to-diversity-equality-inclusion, (accessed 18 February 2024).
10. TalentNeuron, 2024, https://www.talentneuron.com/data-driven-dei/, (accessed 24 February 2024).
11. Workday, 2024, https://www.workday.com/en-us/solutions/role/enterprise-hr/diversity-inclusion-belonging-solutions.html, (accessed 24 February 2024).
12. CultureMonkey (2024), https://www.culturemonkey.io/solutions/diversity-equality-and-inclusion/, (accessed 24 February 2024).
13. 2023 Diversity Annual Report, 2023, https://about.google/belonging/diversity-annual-report/2023/, (accessed 24 February 2024).
14. Jay, S., 13 Tried-and-Tested DEI Initiatives to Implement [In 2024], 2024, https://www.aihr.com/blog/dei-initiatives/, (accessed 25 February 2024).
15. Caminiti, S., Majority of employees want to work for a company that values diversity, equality and inclusion, survey shows, 2021, https://www.cnbc.

com/2021/04/30/diversity-equality-and-inclusion-are-important-to-workers-survey-shows.html, (accessed 25 February 2024).
16. Workforce Demographics Analysis, 2024, https://aspect-hq.com/ta-metrics/workforce-demographics-analysis, (accessed 25 February 2024).
17. Lavri, O., How can employee sentiment analysis improve your business?, 2022, https://hrforecast.com/the-importance-of-employee-sentiment-in-workforce-planning/, (accessed 25 February 2024).
18. Diversity – The key to a skilled, data-driven organization, 2024, https://www.muchskills.com/blog/diversity-the-key-to-a-skilled-data-driven-organisation, (accessed 25 February 2024).
19. Baron, D., 4 Key Components of Building a Data-Driven DEI Strategy, 2021, https://www.peoplefluent.com/blog/insights/4-key-components-of-building-a-data-driven-DEI-strategy/, (accessed 25 February 2024).
20. Star, L., The Power of Data-Driven DEI Strategies: Building Inclusive Workplaces for Tomorrow, 2024, https://www.linkedin.com/pulse/power-data-driven-dei-strategies-building-inclusive-workplaces-star-ayxye#:~:-text=Data%2Ddriven%20DEI%20strategies%20represent,to%20create%20more%20inclusive%20workplaces, (accessed 25 February 2024).

Part 3

FUTURE TRENDS, CHALLENGES, AND SUSTAINABLE DEVELOPMENT IN HR PRACTICES

14

Role of Human Capital Analytics and Industry 5.0 in Advancing the United Nations' Sustainable Development Goals

Agagu A. A.[1], Odiji O. L.[2]* and Akubo A. A.[2]

[1]Olabisi Onabanjo University, Ago Iwoye, Nigeria
[2]Kogi State University, Anyigba, Nigeria

Abstract

Although human capital is made up of the abilities and potentials of man which individuals and organizations rely on and promote to achieve production targets, Industry 5.0 acknowledges the ability of businesses to solve peoples' needs aside from job creation and advancement, to become a spirited source of growth by ensuring that industries respect environmental confines so as to put the welfare of the worker at the very heart of production. It is imperative that technological outputs be created with future societal values in mind, given that technological advancements fundamentally alter how value is created, exchanged, and distributed. This aligns with the Sustainable Development Goals (SDGs) of the United Nations, which serve as a guide against poverty and safeguard the environment to improve conditions for human coexistence. The relationships between Industry 5.0, the UN SDGs, and Human Capital Analytics (HCA) are the main focus of this chapter. This essay starts with an introduction that provides background information on the relationship between HCA, the Fifth Industrial Revolution, and some of the UN SDGs. The conceptualizations of the Fifth Industrial Revolution, role, HCA, and SDGs of the UN come next. The nexuses between HCA, the Fifth Industrial Revolution, and the SDGs would be consequently highlighted. This naturally moves the discourse to how HCA and Industry 5.0 advance the UN SDGs. Inherent and emerging challenges would be observed before carrying out the concluding remarks.

**Corresponding author*: okpasspecial@gmail.com

Deepa Gupta, Mukul Gupta, Pawan Budhwar, Jim Westerman, Rajesh Kumar Dhanaraj and Balamurugan Balusamy (eds.) Human Capital Analytics: Exploring the HR Spectrum in Industry 5.0, (305–324) © 2025 Scrivener Publishing LLC

Keyword: Role, human capital analytics, Industry 5.0, UN, SDGs

14.1 Introduction

There exists a strong relationship between the abilities of humans and the socio-economic development of their society. Such growth and development are usually enhanced when and where human capital which constitutes the various benevolent characteristic skills of man is properly utilized [1, 2]. While human resources consist of knowledge, skills, and health which people and organizations explore and invest in to enable them to realize their potential as productive units of society, the Fifth Industrial Revolution acknowledges the potential of industries to accomplish social responsibility objectives beyond recruitment and expansion to develop into a reliable source of progress by ensuring that industries adheres to environmental standards and puts the well-being of employees as utmost priority during production [21]. Given that the creation, exchange, and distribution of value are all impacted by technological advancement, it is imperative that technological outputs be developed with future societal values in mind. This is in tandem with the Sustainable Development Goals (SDGs) which represent a blueprint for how poverty is brought to an end and protects the planet in order to make it more conducive for humans to peacefully exist and coexist [28].

Many professionals believe that Industry 5.0 came into being in order to rescue the Fourth Industrial Revolution and address its observed gaps [25]. Despite claims that Industry 5.0 emerges to advance sustainable development by addressing the shortcomings inherent in its predecessor, extant literature does not provide much clarity on how the Fifth Industrial Revolution will accomplish this task. The Fifth Industrial Revolution brought about a redefined understanding of the breadth and quality of these functions due to advancements in technology and regulation. Stakeholder centricity and Industry 5.0's hyper-connected business ecosystems enable the holistic development of these roles, leveraging their synergy to allow for additional values for realizing targeted SDGs [3, 6].

This chapter centers on the interdependencies between Human Capital Analytics (HCA), Industry 5.0, and the UN SDGs. The discourse begins with an introduction which is a background explication of the nexus between HCA, the Fifth Industrial Revolution, and components of the UN SDGs. The concepts of the Fifth Industrial Revolution, HCA, and the SDGs come next. Consequently, connections between HCA, the Fifth Industrial Revolution, and the SDGs will be emphasized. This naturally moves the discourse to how HCA and Industry 5.0 advance the UN SDGs. Inherent and emerging challenges were observed and recommendations were made before carrying out the concluding remarks.

14.2 Review of Extant Literature

Few scholarly works have been done on the three topics of HCA, Industry 5.0, and the UN SDGs because they are so relevant and current. Although scholarly works are currently being carried out in Industry 5.0 with its prospects and challenges being predicted, Industry 4.0 has, at present times, occupied more space in academic literature owing to its older nature. In fact, there are those who are of the opinion that the Fifth Industrial Revolution is only an improvement on the Fourth Industrial Revolution which, more than any other innovative era, has greatly transformed how things are being done in the global system. Researchers have asserted, citing a variety of experts, that Industry 4.0 has paved the way for the advancement of socio-environmental sustainability functions such as the sustainability of energy, reduction in harmful emissions, and promotion of social well-being [4]. However, the authors noted that Industry 5.0 will bring about a number of novelties and productions, as well as the realization of human-machine communication.

Moving on to HCA, some academics have conducted research on the comparative advantages of various countries as a result of differences in the status of human capital [5]. Their findings confirmed the organic link between human capital and the processes that led to economic growth and sustained development. Although education and healthcare which are the focal points of SDGs 1 and 2 were pronounced anteriority within policy parameters in various states such as Brazil, Russia, India, China, and South Africa, trends have shown that attention must be placed not only on the mechanism of human capital formation but also on its practical application. As a result, it is crucial to establish state-level principles for the concept of sustainable development of human resources. This, according to the authors, stems from the need to maintain a balance in various aspects of human life that, in actual sense, mirrors the quality of life.

Another study seeks to link investments in human resources SDGs and investigate the spending levels required to achieve high-level performance in related SDG sectors [6]. While using data from the World Bank, empiricism served as the methodology of the study. According to the study's findings, expenditure on education needs to increase by 0.4% of GDP by 2030, while total health expenditure needs to grow by 5.9% of GDP in

Azerbaijan by 2030. This study, which is cited above [5], adds to existing knowledge by conducting an empirical analysis that other states can use to evaluate their relative progress on human capital investments and associated SDGs. This chapter, which takes a cursory look at the relationship between HCA, Industry 5.0, and the SDGs, is coming at no better time because it would serve as a guide for monitoring or assessing the role of the HCA and Industry 5.0 toward effective planning and, consequently, achievement of the SDGs.

14.3 Conceptual Clarification

14.3.1 Human Capital Analytics

Analytics as a concept is described as the interpretation of information patterns to aid decision analysis and productivity enhancement [7]. Various forms of analysis are required in different fields of endeavor such as the natural sciences, social sciences, and management sciences. HCA, which is an exercise under the management sciences, is the focus of this subsection. HCA, like many other human resources, functions in both businesses, and public administration has emerged as a way in which organizations try to understand the impact their employees make within their organizations. This is usually arrived at through critical data analysis. While this human resource function is relatively new, it has experienced rapid change in the past two decades. In fact, currently, there is a massive drive toward data-driven decisions, whereby targeted analytics are even used to improve the talents of the employees [8, 9]. It has also been defined as the gathering and interrogation of information relating to human resources, as a means of gaining better knowledge of the employees within an organization and how well they collectively perform as a team [10]. In other words, HCA evaluates the successes and failures of a company's employee performance.

The Society for Human Resource Management (SHRM) defines HCA as the process by which the value of an organization is measured and improved for the purpose of enhancing organizational performance [11]. SHRM further suggested that HCA is used to invent predictive performance monitors which can be utilized to carry out valuable decisions [11]. Human Resource Analytics as may also be regarded is the act of eliciting and analyzing information on Human Resources in order to improve the workforce performance of an organization. This is why experts have qualified it with various terms including talent metrics, employee insights, talent analytics, people analytics, and workforce analytics [12]. According to these experts, this method of data analysis brings together information that is routinely collected by an organization's human resource units and correlates it to both organizational and human resource objectives. Engaging in this provides measurable evidence of how Human Resource initiatives contribute to the organization's goals and strategies. For instance, if a private university has high academic staff turnover, it then means that the institution is not operating at a fully productive level. This is because ample time and investment are involved to bring an academic staff up to a fully productive level. HCA, therefore, provides information-backed insight on what is efficient and what is inefficient so that organizations can make necessary improvements and plan more correctly for the future.

14.3.2 Fifth Industrial Revolution

Industry 5.0 is a concept that represents an emerging phase of industrialization in which state-of-the-art solutions including AI-enabled robotic systems and humans collaborate to develop and streamline production processes [23]. This Fifth Industrial Revolution is actually a revolution on Industry 4.0 which does not incorporate sustainability that considers the environment globally. One of the significant concerns of Industry 4.0 is that it has restricted capabilities to meet various social demands [13].

The broad objective of Industry 5.0 is to create a perspective that is more robust than Industry 4.0 through the accommodation of all business organization strategies. The goal of Industry 5.0 is to allow for more intuitive synergic relationships between humans and machines across all operations. According to experts, when the Fifth Industrial Revolution is fully exploited, the production world will observe how employees' well-being will be more focused with the help of new technologies [14]. Another goal that Industry 5.0 sets to achieve is the enhancement of well-being beyond employment while respecting nature's preferences [23]. This is indeed a complementary approach to the Fourth Industrial Revolution. Hence, it is centered on innovation and research to move the production world into a more resilient, human-centric, and sustainable industry.

Examples of applications and technologies that are expected to come with the Industry 5.0 innovations are the following: digital twins, predictive maintenance, generative design, and forecasting price [14]. As the name implies, digital twins connote a virtual representation of a physical component that can be used for maintenance, monitoring, testing, simulation, and integration. Predictive maintenance represents instances where artificial intelligence could be used to predict accidents and downtime by analyzing sensor data. This allows for maintenance to be carried out in advance before equipment becomes unproductive. Generative design is the use of machine learning algorithms to make an interactive design similar to the engineer's design. Under the forecasting price, artificial intelligence–enabled software can predict the price of raw materials, enable price forecasting, and get updates in real time to avoid downtime and make flexible decisions.

The preceding demonstrates that Industry 5.0 differs from Industry 4.0 in terms of strategy in the following ways:

1. Resilience: While Industry 4.0 was more concerned with the optimization of profits and improvement of efficacies, unforeseen trends such as diseases and supply chain disruptions made it obvious that attention must be given to operational resilience. Hence, instead of solely targeting profits and growth, Industry 5.0 allows organizations to react to challenges and anticipate things via digital tools to guarantee stability. The benefits of Industry 5.0–enabled strategies are the following: operative flexibility and the gaining of a competitive position in supply chain management, reduction of operational costs and sourcing via predictive insights, and equipment resources for expertise which emanate through concerted trainings [14, 27].
2. Human centricity: Unlike the regime before it, Industry 5.0 does not look at people as a mere workforce to be hired and fired, but as assets to be attracted to, engaged by, and preserved for the organization. This means that the talents available in organizations are not merely utilized to render productive services; Industry 5.0 emphasizes adding value to workers' lives so as to continue to attract and keep the best employees. The advantages of this approach are streamlining operator experience and worker safety improvement, better accessibility and workforce diversity, and empowerment of operators with better cyber-physical interactions.
3. Sustainability: Industry 5.0 extends the concept of sustainability from just minimizing climate change to producing a benevolent situation. The aim is to make the globe a better arena by making industries or organizations become a solution instead of constituting challenges. The benefits of this approach are among others to increase the reputations of organizations, reduce waste and cost of energy, and impact positively on the environment and society at large.

14.4 The UN SDGs

The SDGs are 17 interrelated objectives that were put together by the UN as a blueprint to be pursued by everyone toward the realization of a sustainable future for the world and its inhabitants [15]. The goals were enacted as a template for stakeholders' action toward addressing the whole lot of socio-economic and environmental which bedevil the globe. Apart from depicting the interrelationship of the numerous challenges inherent in today's world, they stressed the imperativeness of cooperation and collaboration toward their resolution. The SDGs were developed following a critical review of the Millennium Development Goals (MDGs), which were realizably insufficient to address contemporary global challenges, with no certainty that their 2015 target year was feasible. They are included in a UN resolution known as Agenda 2030 [16].

Hereunder, Figure 14.1 is a diagram and a description of each of the 17 UN SDGs:

Goal 1 - No Poverty;
Goal 2 - Zero Hunger;
Goal 3 - Good Health and Well-being;
Goal 4 - Quality Education;
Goal 5 - Gender Equality;
Goal 6 - Clean Water and Sanitation;
Goal 7 - Affordable and Clean Energy;
Goal 8 - Decent Occupation and Economic Growth;
Goal 9 - Innovation, Infrastructure and Industry;

Figure 14.1 The 17 UN SDGs [17].

Goal 10 - Reducing Inequalities;
Goal 11 - Sustainable Communities and Cities;
Goal 12 - Responsible Consumption and Production;
Goal 13 - Climate Action;
Goal 14 - Life below water;
Goal 15 - Life on Land;
Goal 16 - Peace, Justice, and Strong Institutions; and
Goal 17 - Partnerships for the Goals

14.4.1 Nexuses Between HCA, Industry 5.0, and the SDGs

There exist a number of ways in ways in which the interplay between HCA and Industry 5.0 advances the UN SDGs. In fact, both of them impact virtually all the 17 proposed goals in the following ways. HCA, which involves leveraging data to measure and optimize human capital management, can contribute to several SDGs. SDGs 1, 2, 3, and 4, for instance, which hopefully rededicate poverty, hunger, illiteracy, and health insecurity, are promoted by HCA and Industry 5.0. By leveraging on data-driven insights to optimize talent management, cultivating seamless human-machine interaction, and building resilient and people-centric workplaces that enhance productivity, innovation, and employee well-being, HCA has the capacity to situate round pegs in round holes to achieve these goals of eradicating poverty, hunger, and associated issues. Objective human capital management, which is systematically ordered, would naturally guarantee efficiency and effectiveness, particularly in the agricultural, educational, health, and manufacturing sectors. Most of the challenges of hunger and poverty in developing countries of Africa for instance are due to nepotism, cronyism, and favoritism where qualified people are denied job opportunities at the detriment of friends and relatives. The Fifth Industrial Revolution, which is a convergence of innovations, like AI, robotics, IoT, and virtual reality, possesses the wherewithal to reshape traditional agriculture, manufacturing, healthcare, transportation, and communication, opening up opportunities for many people to combat hunger and poverty. For example, it has been reported in Nigeria that tens of millions of jobs have been created as a result of the introduction of GSM [18], while 44 million jobs are expected to be created as a result of the country's 75% internet penetration [19].

In terms of the third and fourth goals which focus respectively on well-being and quality education, HCA would enable employers to identify imminent and existing challenges that would further allow them to map out strategies to improve overall health outcomes by analyzing data on employee health and well-being [13]. This can lead to a healthier workforce. HCA can be used to assess the impact of educational programs, training initiatives, and skill development efforts. Through the appraisal of the effectiveness of these various interventions, organizations can allow information-driven decisions to improve the quality of trainings which are provided to their employees or within the community. Industry 5.0 can also be exploited to promote SDGs 3 and 4. Advanced technologies such as artificial intelligence and automation can be utilized to promote healthcare delivery and education systems. This can enable remote healthcare services such as telemedicine, and other personalized healthcare solutions, which have improved access to healthcare and contribute to SDG 3.

SDG 5, which aims to achieve gender equality and empowerment, is equally enhanced by HCA and Industry 5.0. Through HCA, organizations have been able to gain insights into gender imbalances in leadership positions, remuneration gaps, and obstacles to the career advancement of women. Discoveries such as these have made organizations design templates, policies, and programs that enhance equity in gender-related matters and allow a more inclusive work environment. On the other hand, Industry 5.0 is capable of allowing the reorganization of work systems and processes to end gender discrimination, enhance equal opportunities, and make jobs flexible, thereby supporting work-life balance for both males and females. Finally, on SDG 5, integrating HCA and Industry 5.0 can help organizations identify and solve specific problems faced by the womenfolk in the workplace. An example is that through analytics, biases in recruitment and promotions can be identified. Also, Industry 5.0 technologies can assist in the automation of repetitive jobs thereby freeing up time and energy for the women to be absorbed into administrative and leadership duties.

While SDG 6 is poised to achieve accessibility to portable water and a neat environment for everyone by 2030, HCA can assist in identifying skill gaps among employees so as to design and plan training programs to address the deficiency. HCA can also help organizations analyze information using advanced analytic methods like machine learning and statistical forecasting to identify patterns and insights that can inform decision-making related to water resource management. Industry 5.0 on its own part can help in generating substantial information that is needed to optimize water resource management plans. It is also important to however note here that Industry 5.0 will require the partnership of various stakeholders such as governments, non-governmental organizations, and private sectors who will compare data and work together to achieve sustainable water resource management outcomes.

For goal 7, which promises to guarantee that everyone accesses cheap, dependable, and renewable energy, applying analytics to human capital management, organizations would make informed decisions and design plans that enable the efficient and sustainable use of energy resources. HCA has on its own assisted in identifying trends in energy usage in organizations permitting interventions on how to save energy. By analyzing for instance staff members' individual characters and lifestyles, workplaces may be able to evolve their own training templates to teach and move individual employees to imbibe sustainable energy-efficient practices. This in the end would result in significant reductions in energy utilization and, by extension, its costs. On its part, the Fifth Industrial Revolution capitalizes on innovations like robotics and augmented reality to achieve further energy-efficient industrial processes. It also emphasizes the importance of workers being upskilled and reskilled in order to adapt to changing work environments. Industry 5.0 promotes more production systems that save energy by integrating renewable energy sources, smart grids, and IoT technologies. Industries can contribute to SDG 7 by optimizing resource usage and reducing waste, thereby reducing environmental impact and increasing energy efficiency. Additionally, Industry 5.0 encourages the creation of green jobs. As industries transition to sustainability, new job opportunities emerge, particularly in renewable energy, energy management, and clean technologies. This promotes economic growth while also working toward the goal of universal access to modern energy services [24].

The sustained and inclusive economic progression that SDG 8 sought to achieve is supported by HCA. Through the analysis of employee information, such as staff skills and performances in relation to the training they received, companies may be able to carry out well-informed decisions that are connected to the organization's human resources. This would definitely help in increasing skill acquisition, retention, and development strategies. This of course would equally help in optimizing productivity and employee job satisfaction. Resultantly, therefore, individuals would be accessible to quality employment and then enjoy improved work conditions. As far as Industry 5.0 is concerned, it equally enhances the realization of SDG 8. Particularly, it stresses the inclusion of high-level technologies with human collaboration, targeting to achieve sustainable companies that prioritize decency in employment. Some of its major aspects, like cognitive computing, automation, and bionics, possess the ability to transmogrify work environments by promoting productivity, regulating the processes involved, and minimizing manual labor. This would bring about new employment opportunities as well as the reassignment of tasks allowing the employees to have the options or opportunities of gaining more fulfilling and better-valued jobs. Additionally, by promoting up-skilling and re-skilling initiatives, Industry 5.0 ensures that the employees are equipped with the ingenuity needed to grow in this digital era. Through the investment in continuous education as well as providing regular trainings, organizations contribute to Goal 8 by empowering employees to adapt to technological advancements and secure decent work. Equally too, Industry 5.0 emphasizes sustainability by bringing in green practices to the industrial processes. This is particularly possible through the adoption of eco-friendly manufacturing techniques and the utilization of renewable energy sources. Hence, industries would be able to minimize their environmental impact while promoting employment and economic growth.

The ninth SDG is also promoted by HCA as public and private organizations are provided with valuable ideas on the abilities and capabilities of their employees. Using staff data analysis especially those related to talents, professionalism, and trainings, organizations can discover the areas of need, and hence make reasonable decisions concerning capacity building and skill development. With this, skilled manpower is built to drive innovation and implement advanced technologies that support industrialization and infrastructural development [25]. SDG 9 is also promoted by the Fifth Industrial Revolution's aim of integrating human and machine efforts. It promotes the utilization of contemporary innovations in businesses to engender efficiency, productivity, and sustainability. Apart from innovation which allows workers to think creatively, and develop new ideas, it equally promotes the idea of smart factories and cities, which aligns with the ninth SDG. Through the integration of digital technologies, connectivity as well as data analytics, organizations and cities can improve resource usage, reduce waste, and improve energy efficiency [22].

The reduction of inequality and the improvement of social inclusion which Goal 10 sought to achieve are actualized by the abilities of HCA and Industry 5.0. At the level of organizations, for instance, HCA has what it takes to identify disparities in the workforce such as wage gaps, glass ceilings, and demographic imbalances. Through the analysis of data that concerns diversities in the workforce, promotions, retention rates, and remunerations, organizations would be able to discover areas for improvement and develop focused interventions to minimize inequalities and promote diversity and inclusion. The directors of the organization can, for example, implement diversity and inclusion courses or workshops, enhance their employment strategies, and institutionalize mentorship and/ or sponsorship activities for marginalized segments. On the sideline of Industry 5.0, assistive technologies would be able to support special people and improve their employment opportunities. Wearable devices can, for instance, monitor the health conditions of workers as well as their safety while in the work environment. Of course too, in the Industry 5.0 system, digital technologies would enable workers to easily integrate and effectively communicate thereby reducing various communication bottlenecks and further promoting social inclusion and cohesion. Industry 5.0 is also known to possess the ability to promote decentralized community-based production systems that are able to offer employment opportunities to marginalized people and communities.

While, through Goal 11, the United Nations seeks to make human habitats safe and sustainable, HCA assists in the actualization of this goal by providing insights and data-driven approaches that encourage resource allocation, improve infrastructure, and enhance urban planning. Through the analysis of information that is associated with demographics, patterns of employment, transportation/housing needs, or usages, policymakers can make well-informed decisions that create more inclusive and sustainable habitats. In the same vein, Industry 5.0 promotes SDG 11 by integrating developed technologies and sustainable ways of operations into urban development. Take, for example, the use of smart city technologies, like IoT gadgets and sensors; these are capable of improving the efficiency of energy, management of wastes, and transportation systems. The technologies exemplified above enable urban centers to supervise and improve resource utilization, drastically decrease pollution, and then improve sustainability. The human-centric industry equally emphasizes the imperativeness of tenets of a regenerative business atmosphere which aims at reducing waste and increasing the efficiency of resources. By adopting these circular economy practices like recycling, upcycling, and remanufacturing, cities would be able to minimize their environmental footprint and encourage eco-friendly practices. The duo of HCA and Industry 5.0 support the development of resilient cities by improving disaster preparedness and response. By analyzing data on previous events and risks, city managers can discover high-risk areas and execute measures to avoid inherent risks. The same authorities can also leverage technology to enhance early warning systems, emergency response management, as well as post-crisis recovery exercises.

A major global challenge that has often caused an emergency and which the UN captured as one of the targets of the 17 SDGs is irresponsible resource consumption and production. In developing states like Nigeria, Haiti, and Nepal, irresponsible waste disposals have led to blockages that caused several emergencies. SDG 12, which dwells on responsible consumption and production, may be supported by HCA and Industry 5.0. HCA helps organizations in this regard to improve resource allocation and consumption trends by analyzing information concerning energy, water, and raw material usage. With this, organizations are allowed to outline areas of waste and create strategies and tactics that instill more efficient and sustainable resource management. Through the same HCA, organizations would identify opportunities to minimize waste and equally improve the initiative to recycle it. Through the analysis of information on waste generation, disposal, and recycling rates, organizations would be able to make informed decisions to reduce their environmental impacts. The same data can also be used to discover preferences, needs, and behaviors. The information garnered can then be utilized to develop educational campaigns that promote sustainable consumption patterns and increase awareness about the need for responsible production, consumption, and waste management. On the other hand, Industry 5.0 uses advanced technologies to achieve greater transparency and traceability, facilitating responsible sourcing, waste reduction, and circular economy practices. It especially promotes the utilization of smart technologies to survey and track product lifecycles. This is how businesses would be able to assess the effect of their products on the ecosystem all year round.

Climate Action, which is the focus of Goal 13, is enhanced as HCA allows industries to critically study their employees so as to harness their endowed qualities and competencies to address climate-related challenges. The industrial sectors can carry out trainings and workshops to equip their staff members with the necessary knowledge and skills that are required to imbibe responsible habits. With its innovations too, Industry 5.0 can adequately minimize environmental impact through the utilization of data analytics and automation. Equally important to note is the fact that Industry 5.0 can spur the activation and embracement of renewable energy sources and smart grids that are required for ameliorating shifts in weather patterns.

It is noteworthy to observe that HCA can assist SDG 14 in identifying gaps and opportunities for improvement in marine-related sectors [27]. The creation of targeted training exercises for various employee categories can provide them with the skills necessary to address issues such as water pollution and overfishing. In the same manner, Industry 5.0 can ignite innovation in sustainable marine practices within the framework of SDG 14. It can, for instance, allow the creation of automated procedures for sustainable aquaculture, monitoring systems for marine pollution, and effective and environmentally friendly fishing practices. Like SDG 14, the aims of SDG 15 can be more successfully achieved following the character and potentials of HCA and Industry 5.0. Business outfits can find opportunities for capacity building and training programs that align with Goal 15 by evaluating information regarding workers' skills, experience, and development. This allows for the promotion of workers who understand issues that concern environmental sustainability. Hence, a staff that is capable of churning out meaningful inputs that would lead to the conservation of terrestrial natural resources. Industry 5.0 on its own can promote sustainable land use and biodiversity conservation through the implementation of eco-friendly practices like ethical procurement, recycling, waste reduction, and energy efficiency. On the flip side, HCA would assist organizations in tracking and measuring progress by gathering and evaluating crucial insights, which same organizations can utilize to understand their influence on the environment, monitor progress over time, as well as pinpoint domains that require additional attention. With this industries would be able to decipher the best way to implement eco-friendly practices in their outfits.

HCA can support SDG 16 by assisting organizations in evaluating and improving their internal processes, policies, and practices to ensure fairness, transparency, and accountability. Employing data and analytics enables HCA to identify prejudicial arenas in the workplace. Cases such as discrepancies in compensation, uneven prospects for promotion, and/or deficiency in diversity and inclusivity would be promptly discovered and adequately addressed. In consonance with the goals of lowering inequality and fostering social cohesion, the insight gained can be exploited to resolve these anomalies so as to promote organizational equity and inclusivity. For Industry 5.0, its role is basically to promote synergy among key players in the organization which it does by automating managerial functions and encouraging transparency within supply chains. Furthermore, the adoption of innovations that come with the Fifth Industrial Revolution can further increase employees' expertise and open them up to more valuable employment opportunities. It is in this light, for instance, that Industry 5.0 presents telemedicine, robotic surgery, e-teaching, and distance learning programs as job opportunities for both medical practitioners and educationists in the contemporary world. This has not only helped in the achievement of goal 16 but also serves to promote other goals like equality and universal accessibility to health and education.

Finally, SDG 17 is aided toward success by the two innovations being espoused. HCA, for instance, exploits the analysis of personnel data to evolve valuable policies on the allocation of resources aimed at capacity building and realization of all the SDGs. Naturally, this process makes it easier for different employers, educational institutions, and training facilities to collaborate. As a result, resources are more efficiently allocated to address technical deficiencies and promote sustainable development.

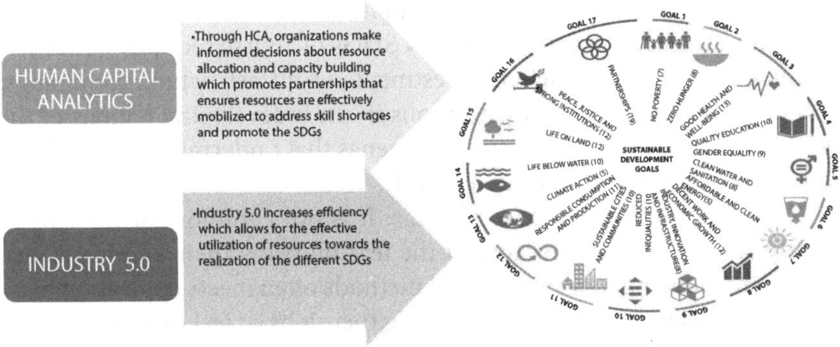

Figure 14.2 Nexuses between HCA, Industry 5.0, and SDGs.

Figure 14.2 illustrates how Human Resource Analytics and Industry 5.0 converge to drive progress towards the Sustainable Development Goals (SDGs). In the same light, Industry 5.0 with its integration of digital technologies can enable more efficient resource mobilization by optimizing supply chains, reducing waste, and improving productivity. This increased efficiency allows for the effective use of resources, thus contributing to SDG 17's objective of mobilizing financial resources for sustainable development.

14.5 Inherent and Emerging Challenges

As learned from the foregoing, both HCA and Industry 5.0 are very recent concepts that aim to promote productivity in the activities of humans which subsequently promotes sustainable development. These two concepts though hold great potential for worldwide objectives for a decent planet, their ability to realize the SDGs would obviously hit brick walls due to a number of issues among which are inadequate knowledge, challenges with execution, phobia and resistance to change, policy bottlenecks, and data security concerns. Taking these challenges one after the other would be apt.

1. Inadequate Knowledge: Since both HCA and Industry 5.0 are very recent trends, many corporate organizations as well as the individuals who work in them are yet to be aware of their importance and benefits. In fact, many countries of the world have yet to internalize the knowledge and needs of the UN SDGs [20]. These shortcomings slow down the adoption and execution of these concepts.

2. Challenges with Execution: The implementation of HCA and Industry 5.0 toward the achievement of the UN SDGs of course requires significant financial commitment such as investments in infrastructure, technology, and personnel trainings. Organizations in most developing regions of the world would face constraints in these arenas that undermine their abilities to fully embrace these innovative trends.

3. Phobia and Resistance to Change: It is not common for humans to swiftly adapt to change because of the fear of losing their existing status. Hence, introducing new systems and methods often meets opposition from workers who would naturally fear losing their jobs or feel overstretched by the need to acquire new techniques. Moreover, employees have different levels of comprehension. Hence, time and energy may be wasted in the effort to internalize new methods of doing things in organizations.

4. Policy Bottlenecks: HCA and Industry 5.0 may suffer setbacks due to state policies and regulations which can either support or limit their integration into existing systems. Where, for instance, the policies and regulations of a state have not been amended to suit the incorporation of practices and technicalities of HCA and Industry 5.0, the realization of the targets of the SDGs may remain a mirage.

5. Data Security Concerns: The challenge and consequent efforts to protect or secure data in this era of Information and Communication Technology (ICT) when hackers operate with impunity can be daunting [18]. The accumulation and analysis of vast data in HCA raise privacy concerns for individuals and organizations alike. A middle ground is necessary to mediate between information-driven decision-making and protecting personal data and of course, this requires a whole lot of cyber-security measures.

6. Loss of Valuable Time and Energy: Organizations and their employees would at the initial stage of their efforts to explore HCA and Industry 5.0 in the realization of the UN SDGs lose valuable time and energy. Training exercises come with great cost not only on finance but also on valuable time and energy which are needed to allow for proper comprehension.

14.5.1 Measures to Address the Challenges which Bedevils HCA and Industry 5.0 from Advancing UN SDGs

Although adopting HCA and Industry 5.0 faces the daunting challenges enumerated above, this subsection proffers valuable admonitions to address some of these challenges. These solutions however require the partnership or collaboration of stakeholders working in various sectors to promote ethical, inclusive, and sustainable practices in leveraging technology and human capital for positive socio-economic outcomes.

1. Education and Sensitization: There is a dire need for the government to educate and/or sensitize stakeholders, especially organizations and their employees about the benevolences of HCA and Industry 5.0 in efforts to attain the various SDGs. In this regard, such supra-national institutions like the United Nations, African Union, European Union, and BRICS must educate stakeholders which includes national policymakers, policy executioners, and the populace about the prospects of these concepts to address socio-economic and environmental problems which the SDGs seek to address.

2. Manpower Trainings: There is also the need to invest in the building of the capacities of employees to increase their knowledge and skills on HCA and Industry 5.0. In this light, training programs, seminars, and workshops should be embarked upon to ensure that skilled employees in various organizations are capable of driving the ideals of HCA and Industry 5.0 effectively.

3. Collaboration and Partnerships: Collaborations among various agencies such as those of public institutions, private sector outfits, academicians, non-profits, and international agencies are very much necessary to collectively address the challenges mentioned earlier. The reason for this is that such collaborations and partnerships would pave the way for easy SWOT analysis in any given situation.

4. Regulatory Policy Frameworks: Policies and other regulatory frameworks that support the adoption and integration of HCA and Industry 5.0 in achieving the SDGs need to be developed and implemented. In enacting and implementing the regulations, organizations must make sure that the rules themselves are sustainable, inclusive, and ethical.

5. Data Security: There is a need for thorough information governance regulation and data privacy protection measures to address issues associated with the acquisition, storage, and utilization of sensitive personal data of employees in HCA. Equally, it is important to promote transparency and accountability in data handling practices. In all of these, the consent of employees must be sought in the ways and manners information concerning them may be used.

6. Funding: It is imperative to note at this juncture that sufficient financial resources must be allocated and invested in research, innovations, trainings, and the infrastructures related to HCA and Industry 5.0. Since sourcing funds is a difficult task, particularly in developing states of the world, it is advisable to encourage public-private partnerships to pave the way for sustainable financing for ideas and projects that are aligned with the SDGs.

7. Equity: Organizational managers must abhor discrimination in the implementation of HCA and Industry 5.0. In other words, they must

ensure inclusiveness and equal opportunity for all individuals. They must address all forms of biases in the collection and analysis of data, human resource planning, and access to scientific discoveries [26].

8. Monitoring and Evaluation: Finally, there is a need to evolve an adequate monitoring and evaluation framework in order to ascertain the effects of HCA and Industry 5.0 on the 17 UN SDGs. It is ultimately required that progress should be regularly assessed, gaps identified, and strategies formulated to guarantee uninterrupted progression.

14.6 Concluding Remarks

From the foregoing discourse, it is obvious that HCA and Industry 5.0 are potentially positioned to promote the realization of the lofty objectives captured in the SDGs. Both HCA and Industry 5.0 promise to turn around global industries, transform existing business models, and enhance decision-making processes that are associated with the objectives of the SDGs. Some of the benefits accruable to organizations that capitalize on HCA, for instance, are that useful ideas about their human resources would be unbridled allowing the organizations to make important decisions concerning the management of talents, development of skills, and the welfare of employees. Of course, this in turn advances several SDGs including SDGs 8 and 10 which are aimed at achieving fair labor and economic development with a commitment to inclusivity.

Industry 5.0 on its path accentuates the collaboration of man and scientific innovations which optimizes resource utilization, waste reduction, and supporting green production techniques as well as thoughtful consumption habits. It aligns with several of the SDGs including numbers 9 and 12 which were formulated to promote industries, innovations, infrastructures, and responsible consumption and production.

It is most important to note in this conclusive remark that both the HCA and Industry 5.0 promote decisions that are inspired and anchored on empirically generated data. This has the benefits of leading to planned or earmarked interventions and improved results in areas like poverty alleviation, healthcare delivery, and education. As discussed earlier, this obviously promotes progress toward the realization of SDGs 1, 3, and 4. In addition, the joint adoption of HCA and Industry 5.0 enhances collaborative partnerships which bring together various stakeholders whether with the government circle or the populace to collectively address complex societal issues. This of course is the thrust of SDG 17 which emphasizes partnerships for the attainment of all the other goals.

References

1. Ody, A.J., Griffin, C.C., Ferranti, D., Jacinto, J., Warren, N., Enhancing Development through Better Use of Public Resources: How Independent Watchdog Groups Can Help. *Brookings*, 157, 1, 2006, September 1, Retrieved November, 2023 from www.brookings.edu.
2. White, J. and Bottorf, C., HR Analytics Definition, Best Practices & Examples. *Forbes Advisor*, July, 2023 edition, 2023, July 18, Retrieved December 26 from www.forbes.com.
3. Lykov, D. and Razumowsky, A., Industry 5.0 and human capital. *E3S Web Conferences*, 376, 05053, 2023.
4. Ghobakhloo, M., Iranmanesh, M., Mubarak, M.F., Mubarik, M., Rejeb, A., Nilashi, M., Identifying industry 5.0 contributions to sustainable development: A strategy roadmap for delivering sustainability values. *Sustain. Prod. Consum.*, 33, 716–737, 2022.
5. Sabbaghi, O., The United Nations Sustainable Development Goals and human capital: the case of Azerbaijan. *Int. J. Soc. Econ.*, 51, 5, 655–668, 2023, https://doi.org/10.1108/IJSE-02-2023-0137.
6. Babasanya, A.O., Oseni, I.O., Subair, A.S., Human Capital Development: A Catalyst for Achieving SDGs in Nigeria. *AUDCE.*, 14, 4, 25–41, 2018.
7. Lalwani, P., What Is HR Analytics? Definition, Importance, Key Metrics, Data Requirements, and Implementation. *Spiceworks*, August, 2023 edition, 2021, March 11, Retrieved March 11, 2024 from https://www.spiceworks.com/hr/hr-analytics/articles/what-is-hr-analytics/#_001.
8. Levenson, A., Using targeted analytics to improve talent decisions. *People Strategy*, 2, 34, 2011.
9. Etukudo, R.U., *Strategies for Using Analytics to Improve Human Resource Management*, Walden University Scholarly Works, Minneapolis, Minnesota, 2019.
10. Cosentino, J., HR Compliance: A Practical Guide for 2025. *AIHR*. November edition, 1–2, Amsterdam, The Netherlands, 2024, Retrieved September 20, 2023 from www.aihr.com.
11. SHRM, *Benchmarking human capital metrics*, Society for Human Resource Management, Alexandria, VA, 2013, March 26, Retrieved December 26, 2023 from http://www.shrm.org/templatestools/toolkits/pages/benchmarkinghumancapitalmetrics.aspx.
12. Andreev, I., Human Resource Analytics. *Velamis*, December, 2020 edition, 2023, March 14, Retrieved March 1, 2024 from https://www.valamis.com/hub/analytics.
13. Sonawawne, N., Industry 5.0: The Fifth Industrial Revolution. *Enterp. Talk*, June edition, 2023, June 30, Retrieved January 30, 2024 from https://enterprisetalk.com/topics/featured.
14. Dharmarajan, S., Industry 5.0: The Next Industrial Revolution, 2023, Retrieved January 10, 2024 from https://in.linkedin.com/in/shankar-dharmarajan-9188376?trk=article-ssr-frontend-pulse_publisher-author-card.

15. United Nations, Resolution adopted by the General Assembly on 25 September 2015, Transforming our world: the 2030 Agenda for Sustainable Development (A/RES/70/1 Archived 28 November 2020 at the Wayback Machine, 2015.
16. United Nations, Resolution adopted by the General Assembly on 6 July 2017, Work of the Statistical Commission pertaining to the 2030 Agenda for Sustainable Development (A/RES/71/313 Archived 28 November 2020 at the Wayback Machine), 2017.
17. The 17 Sustainable Development Goals, 10 August 2022, sdgs.un.org.
18. Enahoro, M.A. and Olawade, D., GSM and the Nigerian Economy: The Journey from 2004 to 2019. *Int. J. Econ. Finance*, 13, 7, 69, 2021.
19. Jaiyeola, T., 75% Internet penetration to generate 44 million jobs in Nigeria, others–Report. *Punch*, 2022, June 12, Retrieved December 24, 2023 from https://punchng.com/75-internet-penetration-to-generate-44-million-jobs-in-nigeria-others-report/.
20. Ugnich, E., Chernokozov, A., Ugnich., M., Human capital in the system of sustainable development goals: significance and prospects. *E3S Web Conferences*, 258, 07053, 2021.
21. Xu, X., Lu, Y., Vogel-Heuser, B., Wang, L., Industry 4.0 and Industry 5.0-Inception, conception and perception. *J. Manuf. Syst.*, 61, 2021, 530–535, 2021, DOI - 10.1016/j.jmsy.2021.10.006.
22. Leus, R., *The Use of Digital Educational Technology Affordances to Develop 21st-Century Skills in Online Learning*, University of Pretoria, South Africa, 2023.
23. Zafar, M.H., Langas, E.F., Sanfilippo, F., Exploring the synergies between collaborative robotics, digital twins, augmentation, and industry 5.0 for smart manufacturing: A state-of-the-art review. *Rob. Comput. Integr. Manuf.*, 2024, 102769, 2024, ISSN 0736-5845.89, doi: 10.1016/j.rcim.2024.102769.
24. Kolia, A., *The Contribution of Shipping to the Achievement of Sustainable Goals of Development*, University of Piraeus, Publication, Piraeus, Athens, 2023.
25. Paschek, D., Caius-Tudor, L., Ocakci, E., Ivascu, Industry 5.0 Challenges and Perspectives for Manufacturing Systems in the Society 5.0, in: *Sustainability and Innovation in Manufacturing Enterprise: Indicators, Models and Assessment for Industry 5.0*, A. Draghici and L. (Eds.), Springer Nature, Singapore, 2022.
26. Goodhart, M., *Human Rights: Politics and Practice*, Oxford University Press, Oxford, England, 2016.
27. Kumari, P., Anand, A., Praveen, P., Verma, A.R., Godiyal, A., Infrastructure Potential and Human-Centric Strategies in the Context of Industry 5.0, in: *Infrastructure Possibilities and Human-Centered Approaches With Industry 5.0*, M.A. Khan, A.R. Verma, M.K. Panda (Eds.), IGI Global, Hershey, Pennsylvania, 2024.
28. Barbier, E.B. and Burgess, J.C., The Sustainable Development Goals and the systems approach to sustainability. Economics. *Open-Access Open-Assessment E-J.*, 11, 2017-28, 1–22, 2017, http://dx.doi.org/10.5018/economics-ejournal.ja.2017-28.

15

Transforming Workplaces with Human-Robot Collaboration

B. Swathi

Department of Commerce, St. Mary's College, Yousufguda, Hyderabad, Telangana, India

Abstract

Industry 5.0 is an idea that goes beyond what is traditionally considered "industry" and applies to all types of businesses and organizations. The implications of Industry 5.0 for business strategy are relevant across industries, unlike Industry 4.0, which was mainly focused on manufacturing and industrial processes. Industry 5.0 has a much broader scope. Cooperative and interactive human-robot relationships are a key component of Industry 5.0. Robocops, or multipurpose robots, are getting easier to get hold of and less expensive thanks to advances in robotics and artificial intelligence (AI). According to this creative strategy, humans and robots will work together closely in the future, utilizing each other's special advantages. In order to foster a symbiotic relationship that maximizes the potential of artificial intelligence and the creativity of human thought, this collaboration involves robots that are not just machines but rather are integrated with the human brain. Humans and robots are interacting more frequently as a result of this trend, both at home and at work. Robotics and AI applications are increasingly integrated into the work environment. Companies are starting to keep personnel records. Companies need to reevaluate how they engage with their employees in light of this human-centered approach. Making sure that technology maximizes human workers' potential rather than taking their place is the central tenet of Industry 5.0. It aims to solve the problem of attaining greater productivity while keeping the indispensable human interaction in the manufacturing sector by enabling cooperation between robots and the human brain. In this concept, humans and technology live in harmony and support each other's skills and abilities to usher in a new

Email: drswathi1973@gmail.com

Deepa Gupta, Mukul Gupta, Pawan Budhwar, Jim Westerman, Rajesh Kumar Dhanaraj and Balamurugan Balusamy (eds.) Human Capital Analytics: Exploring the HR Spectrum in Industry 5.0, (325–336) © 2025 Scrivener Publishing LLC

era of shared goals and accomplishments. This paper investigates novel techniques and methods in human-robot cooperation that support industry sustainability.

***Keywords*:** Industry 5.0, sustainability, coexistence, AI, humans, robots

15.1 Introduction

"Smart Manufacturing for the Future," the Fourth Industrial Revolution's central theme, has garnered interest from people worldwide. The concept of integrating different innovations to accomplish the objective of automated production is covered, along with revolutionary changes. The Fifth Industrial Revolution theme now has a place in this [17]. Industry 5.0 is an idea that goes beyond what is traditionally considered "industry" and applies to all types of businesses and organizations. Industry 5.0 covers a much wider range of topics than Industry 4.0, which was mainly concentrated on smart manufacturing moving forward [14]. This indicates that Industry 5.0 is going to impact company strategy more broadly, not just for one industry in particular [4]. Reviewing how Industry 5.0 impacts corporate strategy calls for a thorough, exhaustive approach that takes into account every industry. Applications for Industry 5.0 can be found in services, healthcare, education, and other sectors in addition to the production and manufacturing industries. This diverse environment means that any discussion about the strategic implications of Industry 5.0 must take this into consideration [19].

15.2 Sustainability and Industry 5.0

The concept of sustainable manufacturing is dynamic. The opportunities and effects are changed based on the environmental concerns and priorities of sustainability. The core of Industry 5.0 is Environmental Sustainability. The focus is on resource efficiency and environmentally conscious practices [31]. The organizations must consider these strategies which complement ecological and social objectives. Industry 5.0 can support achieving sustainability goals through the effective utilization of resources, waste reduction, and usage of eco-friendly technologies [17].

15.2.1 Human-Robot Co-Working (HRC)

Robots and humans collaborate in the workplace today. Robots boost productivity [21]. They allow for flexible automation processes and enhance productivity. They also assist and relieve human operators [15]. The other component that combines human capabilities with the accuracy of machines is human-robot collaboration (HRC) [15].

It is applied in many different situations and domains. This leads to a broad range of tasks and collaborative actions. Robots are able to go to predetermined places, search for objects or people, speak or interact in other ways, and cooperatively fetch, hold, and even support objects carried by humans [28].

15.2.2 Literature Review

Industry 5.0 focuses on the basic principle that innovations in technology must complement human labor rather than replace it [9]. Utilizing the unique skills of each other envisions a future in which humans and robots collaborate closely [37].

Rapid changes in the manufacturing sector make it imperative to increase productivity without substituting human labor [25]. When testing autonomous vehicles in actual traffic situations, this tendency is particularly apparent. Businesses are starting to keep employee records for these reasons since they are growing so accustomed to deploying AI and robots in our workplaces [23]. Although HRC has been extensively studied, most of the research has been on low-level tasks and robot development [26]. However, a significant research gap still exists in the field of organizational issues that arise in cooperative human-robot settings [11].

Businesses may find that implementing Industry 5.0 fosters the creativity and potential of their workforce. In the context of Industry 5.0, the human-centered approach focuses on the necessity of attending to basic human wants and requirements [38]. This strategy looks to improve processes to better meet the needs of laborers rather than assuming that workers will quickly adapt to new innovations [39]. The approach seeks to uphold the rights of workers, encourage independence, and respect human dignity [34].

This means that creating environments at work where employees are valued and given authority should be prioritized [32]. Technology advancements might not be able to completely meet consumers' demands for customization. It implies that production workers are still necessary to achieve this degree of customization because only humans are able to come up with original ideas for developing products that are personalized [25].

The most advanced collaborative robots are typically humanoids—robots that resemble humans in shape. Since they can function in human spaces and be easily integrated into current work environments, they do not require the construction of special facilities [20]. They are helpful for collaborative work with humans because they can move at the same speed as humans and pass objects between humans [14]. Bipedal walking robots, however, require sophisticated motion control and sensing because they are inherently less stable and more prone to fall over than their wheeled counterparts [5]. Furthermore, because batteries move less efficiently over longer periods of time, improved battery performance is needed [41]. Manufacturing, warehousing, and hospitality are just a few of the industries that use industrial robots to supplement human labor. Cobots, or collaborative robots, are becoming more and more popular; they are machines that work alongside humans in the same area. In order to prevent infectious diseases, maintain productivity, and deal with labor shortages, collaborative robots have recently been introduced in a wide range of workplaces [6].

15.2.3 Objectives and Methodology

The present paper examines the new technologies and methods in HRCs that contribute to sustainability in the industries. The study also explores the implications of Industry 5.0 on the workforce, addressing concerns and opportunities. The study highlighted the specific industries and use cases where human-robot teamwork is gaining prominence. The data for the study were collected from various secondary sources and conclusions were drawn.

15.3 Industry 5.0, Human Resources, and Robots

The advent of Industry 5.0 clearly denotes a shift in the role that employees play within companies. Owners of businesses now regard their employees as investments under this new paradigm. Industry 5.0 acknowledges the employer's interest in investing in the skills, capacities, and well-being of employees to achieve shared objectives [22]. The shift demonstrates how businesses are beginning to understand the value of human resources and how it is turning into one of the primary characteristics of Industry 5.0 [14]. This emphasizes the notion that workers are essential to a company's success and that both the business and the employee stand to gain from their development. It also highlights the importance of process adaptation to meet employee needs, respecting workers' rights and dignity, and realizing the worth of investing in human resources to achieve common corporate objectives [16]. The objective of this strategy is to create a more equitable and favorable working relationship between employers and employees.

Humans are inherently social creatures, and they engage in social interactions in various aspects of their lives, including the workplace [12]. Human-robot co-working is anticipated to be a novel experience for the majority of employees in office settings, so the integration of robotics into the workplace is predicted to have an unprecedented impact on social interactions [13]. Although most people's conception of robots comes from movies and books, their actual experience of coexisting with robots may differ from what they had anticipated [32].

15.3.1 Human and Robot Interaction

Employees are likely to have varying views on how to socially interact with robots. Interacting with robots may require employees to learn how to behave and communicate effectively with these machines. While interacting with humans may come naturally, the same may not apply to robots. Employees may need to adjust their behavior to interact successfully with robots. This can create complexities in workplace dynamics as individuals differ in their comfort levels and expectations regarding social interaction with robotic colleagues [11]. Some humans may prefer robots that exhibit social behavior, while others may view such behavior as artificial and "fake," considering it to be a result of computer programming. Non-verbal communication is a significant part of human interaction and robots may or may not understand non-verbal cues and signals, which could lead to challenges in communication. Humans may need to adapt their communication style when working with robots. Due to the growing integration of automation and robots in organizations, human resources (HR) departments will need to comprehend the social dynamics, expectations, and relationships between people and robotics in the workplace [22].

It is expected that humans will need time to learn and adapt to working with robots. Just as with any new technology or work environment, there may be a learning curve as employees become accustomed to the presence and capabilities of robots [24]. Robots can have varying levels of capabilities, from basic to advanced. The passage points out that it might be challenging and confusing for humans to distinguish between robots with different capabilities. This underscores the need for clarity in robot capabilities [40].

There are two main schools of thought on the future of HRC in the workplace [30].

Robots complementing humans: According to this theory, mundane and repetitive jobs will be replaced by robots, freeing up people to concentrate on more creative and strategic work. This would lead to a more efficient and productive workplace, with humans and robots working together to achieve common goals [39].

Robots competing with humans: This view is that robots will eventually become so capable that they will be able to perform most jobs better and more cheaply than humans. This would lead to widespread job displacement and unemployment, as humans are forced to compete with robots for a shrinking number of jobs [2].

Industry 5.0 seeks to enhance human workers' capacities and provide possibilities for skill development, as opposed to replacing them [39]. The following are some thoughts on the potential benefits that affect different facets of industrial operations.

15.3.2 Industry 5.0 - Advantages

Industry 5.0 makes it easier for humans and robots to work together seamlessly, which increases productivity across a range of jobs. Productivity gains in manufacturing and other industries can result from the fusion of machine and human intelligence. Production processes may become more flexible and responsive with the speedy reconfiguration and repurposing of robotic equipment. Cobots, or collaborative robots, can assist people in the production process to guarantee accuracy and precision [8]. Real-time monitoring and quality control are made possible by the integration of sensors and AI, which lowers errors and raises total product quality. Sophisticated automation and intelligent technologies simplify procedures, cutting lead times, and maximizing resource use [10]. Robots are capable of performing labor-intensive, repetitive tasks, allowing human workers to focus on more complex and creative aspects of their jobs. Humans and robots working together promote a culture of continuous improvement and innovation and can help achieve sustainability objectives by cutting waste and improving resource utilization [25]. Integration of environment-friendly practices with manufacturing processes helps in environment preservation [3]. There are concerns about adopting Industry 5.0 and requires resolutions for instance strong cyber security protection, moral concerns, etc. The successful implementation needs proper advanced planning and evaluation [33].

15.3.3 Concerns in Industry 5.0

The major requisite of Industry 5.0 is the availability of a skilled workforce which includes software developers, data analysts, etc., and this requires effective training programs either to upskill the existing or hiring the new [23].

Research shows that transformation from traditional to modern and dealing with automated systems is an arduous task [19]. The risk of augmented cyber warfare, hacks, intrusions, etc. provides unwanted access to the data concerning the privacy and protection of sensitive information [18]. Apart from this, resistance from organizations to change might avert the implementation of Industry 5.0 [7].

Technology may grow more quickly than legislative frameworks, which might lead to confusion and even legal issues, concerns about privacy, responsible AI use, and the abuse of cutting-edge technologies are just a few of the ethical issues that come up [34]. It is also critical to remember that in many domains, robots still lack human capabilities [8]. For instance, robots continue to have difficulty with tasks requiring dexterity, creativity, and social intelligence. This implies that even in a future where robots are extensively employed, humans will probably still have a significant role in the workplace [1].

It is important to note that these are just some potential benefits and drawbacks. Actually, robots will probably have a complex and wide-ranging effect on the workplace [5]. There is evidence to support both of these views.

The possibilities for using robots in the workplace are endless, and these are just a few instances. Robots will likely be utilized in ever-more creative ways to enhance worker safety, productivity, and overall satisfaction as technology develops and they become more intelligent [35].

Robotics will ultimately affect the workplace based on how we choose to use them. Robots can enhance human productivity and quality of life if they are used to complement humans and automate repetitive tasks [9]. But there is a growing fear that using robots to compete with humans and replace workers will result in job losses and unemployment. This is a valid concern, and it is probably going to make some people feel badly about robots.

However, it is important to remember that historical data show that technological advancement frequently leads to the creation of new employment. For example, the vehicle's advancement led to the automotive industry hiring mechanics and workers who assemble cars [28]. Similar to this, the development of the computer resulted in the creation of jobs in the IT sector, including web designers and software developers. It is likely that the same will happen with robots [6]. Humans will be free to concentrate on more fulfilling and creative work as robots replace menial tasks. For example, robots may eventually be able to perform all of the tasks involved in running a hotel or restaurant. Robots will replace menial tasks, freeing up humans to concentrate on more fulfilling and creative work. This would free up people to work in jobs like marketing campaign managers, which demand more creativity and customer interaction [36].

Acceptance, usability, and trust must be recognized as essential requirements for the successful integration of HRC. These components emphasize the human-centered aspect of collaborative robotics [27]. Workers must have a psychologically secure experience when interacting with robots, and this is reflected in their trust. While usability is required for the realistic integration of robotic systems into current workflows, acceptance is the key to the adoption of collaborative technologies as a whole [1]. Humans and robots coexisting in harmony, each enhancing the other's skills and abilities rather than competing with one another or posing a threat to the world economy, is the vision of the concept of human-robot co-working [17].

The following elements contribute to a successful HRC:

- Effective leadership is necessary to guarantee the successful implementation of human-robot co-working and the resolution of related issues.
- Good communication is essential for HRC.
- Establishing ethical guidelines for the use of co-working robots and humans is essential as this trend gains traction.

Numerous scholarly investigations underscore the imperative nature of integrating sustainability and the pivotal role that humans play in shaping the trajectory of forthcoming industries. Social and environmental needs are the foundation of developing new concepts, and economic sustainability is the cornerstone of evolution. The foundation of Industry 5.0 is made up of the three development pillars of human-centric, sustainable, and resilient development [29]. This shift highlights the reality that human capital is becoming an indispensable asset in Industry 5.0 and demonstrates how companies are beginning to realize its significance.

15.4 Conclusion

Industry 5.0 is essentially a collaboration of three segments: ecological, social, and technological. Industry 5.0 recognizes the role that technology plays in the advancement of business and industry. Nevertheless, the accomplishment of business goals is coupled with social goals both within and outside of the workplace such as human-machine relations and social and ecological responsibility.

Human-robot co-working will still be a significant shift for organizations whether or not Industry 5.0 is about it. Actually, the presence of robots in our lives will probably bring about a major shift for humanity. The aim is to create technology that bears many similarities to human beings. This will strike some as exciting and inventive, or dangerous to humankind.

Human perception of robots will probably change as more people interact with them. The way that today's kids react might be different from how our generation does because they will develop alongside these or related technologies. Their offspring will live in a robot-populated society. Taking into account the disparities between the generations, we should begin constructing a robotic society where people maximize the benefits of technology while attempting to limit its negative effects.

References

1. Adadi, A. and Berrada, M., Peeking Inside the Black-Box: A Survey on Explainable Artificial Intelligence (XAI), in: *IEEE Access*, vol. 6, pp. 52138–52160, 2018, doi: 10.1109/ACCESS.2018.2870052.
2. Amr, A., *Future of industry 5.0 in society: human-centric solutions, challenges and prospective research areas*, vol. 11, no. 91, p. 40, Springer Nature - PMC COVID-19 Collection, 2022, doi: 10.1186/s13677-022-00314-5.
3. Aslam, F., Aimin, W., Li, M., Ur Rehman, K., Innovation in the era of IoT and industry 5.0. *Absolute Innov. Manage. (AIM) Framework. Inf.*, 11, 124, 2020, https://doi.org/10.3390/info11020124.
4. Bajic, B., Rikalovic, A., Suzic, N., Piuri, V., Industry 4.0 Implementation Challenges and Opportunities: A Managerial Perspective, in: *IEEE Systems Journal*, vol. 15, no. 1, pp. 546–559, March 2021, doi: 10.1109/JSYST.2020.3023041.
5. Bednar, P.M. and Welch, C., Socio-technical perspectives on smart working: Creating meaningful and sustainable systems. *Inf. Syst. Front.*, 22, 281–298, 2020, https://doi.org/10.1007/s10796-019-09921-1.
6. Bi, Z., Luo, M., Miao, Z., Zhang, B., Zhang, W., Wang, L., Safety assurance mechanisms of collaborative robotic systems in manufacturing. *Rob. Comput. Integr. Manuf.*, 67, 102022, 2021. ISSN 0736-5845, E-ISSN 1879-2537
7. Bonilla, S.H., Silva, H.R.O., Terra, M., da Silva, R., Gonçalves, F., Sacomano, J.B., Industry 4.0 and sustainability implications: A scenario-based analysis of the impacts and challenges. *Sustainability*, 10, 10, 37402020, 2018, https://doi.org/10.3390/su10103740.
8. Brun, L. and Wioland, L., Prevention of occupational risks related to the human-robot collaboration. *Adv. Intell. Syst. Comput.*, 441–446, 2021.
9. Chander, B., Pal, S., De, D., Buyya, R., Artificial intelligence-based internet of things for industry 5.0, in: *Artificial Intelligence-based Internet of Things Systems*, pp. 3–45, Springer, 2022, ISBN: 978-3-030-87058-4. doi: 10.1007/978-3-030-87059-1_1.

10. Deepa, N., Pham, Q.V., Nguyen, D.C., Bhattacharya, S., Prabadevi, B., Gadekallu, T.R., Pathirana, P.N., A survey on blockchain for big data: approaches, opportunities, and future directions. *Future Gener. Comput. Syst.*, 2022.
11. Di Pasquale, V., Miranda, S., Neumann, W.P., Ageing and human-system errors in manufacturing: a scoping review. *Int. J. Prod. Res.*, 58, 15, 4716–4740, 2020, https://doi.org/00207543.2020.1773561.
12. Doyle-Kent, M. and Kopacek, P., Industry 5.0: Is the manufacturing industry on the cusp of a new revolution?, in: *Proceedings of the International Symposium for Production Research*, Springer, 2019.
13. Demir, K.A., Döven, G., Sezen, B., Industry 5.0 and Human-Robot Co-working. *Procedia Comput. Sci.*, 158, 688–695, 2019, https://doi.org/10.1016/j.procs.2019.09.104.
14. Demir, K.A. and Cicibaş, H., The Next Industrial Revolution: Industry 5.0 and Discussions on Industry 4.0, in: *Industry 4.0 From the Management Information Systems Perspectives*, pp. 247–260, Peter Lang Publishing House, 2018. ISSN: 978-3-631-75770-3.
15. Demir, K.A., Research Questions in Roboethics, Mugla. *J. Sci. Technol.*, 3, 2, 160–165, 2017.
16. De Simone, V., Di Pasquale, V., Giubileo, V., Miranda, S., Human-, Robot Collaboration: an analysis of worker's performance. *Procedia Comput. Sci.*, 200, 1540–1549, 2022, https://doi.org/10.1016/j2022.01.355.
17. Felsberger, A. and Reiner, G., Sustainable Industry 4.0 in production and operations management: A systematic literature review. *Sustainability*, 12, 19, 7982, 2020, https://doi.org/10.3390/su12197982.
18. Gajdzik, B., Grabowska, S., Saniuk, S., A theoretical framework for Industry 4.0 and its implementation with selected practical schedules. *Energies*, 2021, 14, 940, 2021, https://doi.org/10.3390/en14040940.
19. Gajdzik, B., Grabowska, S., Saniuk, S., Wieczorek, T., Sustainable development and Industry 4.0: A bibliometric analysis identifying key scientific problems of the sustainable Industry 4.0. *Energies*, 13, 4254, 2020, https://doi.org/10.3390/en13164254.
20. Galin, R. and Meshcheryakov, R., Review on human-robot interaction during collaboration in a shared workspace, in: *Lecture Notes in Computer Science (including subseries Lecture Notes in Artificial Intelligence and Lecture Notes in Bioinformatics)*, pp. 63–74, Springer International Publishing, 2019, Doi: 10.1007/978-3-030-26118-4_7. ISSN: 978-3-030-26117-7.
21. Gervasi, R., Mastrogiacomo, L., Franceschini, F., A conceptual framework to evaluate human-robot collaboration. *Int. J. Adv. Manuf. Technol.*, 108, 2020.
22. Grabowska, S., Saniuk, S., Gajdzik, B., Industry 5.0: improving humanization and sustainability of Industry 4.0. *Scientometrics*, 127, 3117–3144, 2022, https://doi.org/10.1007/s11192-022-04370-1.

23. Gualtieri, L., Rauch, E., Vidoni, R., Emerging research fields in safety and ergonomics in industrial collaborative robotics: A systematic literature review. *Rob. Comput. Integr. Manuf.*, 67, 101998, 2021. ISSN 0736-5845.
24. Gualtieri, L., Rojas, R.A., Ruiz Garcia, M.A., Implementation of a laboratory case study for intuitive collaboration between man and machine in SME assembly, in: *Industry 4.0 for SMEs: Challenges, Opportunities and Requirements*, pp. 335–382, Springer International Publishing, 2020.
25. Javaid, M. and Haleem, A., Critical components of Industry 5.0 towards a successful adoption in the field of manufacturing. *J. Ind. Integr. Manage.*, 5, 327–348, 2020, https://doi.org/10.1142/S2424862220500141.
26. Demir, K.A., Döven, G., Sezen, B., Industry 5.0 and Human-Robot Co-working, Industry 5.0 and Human-Robot Co-working. *Procedia*, 158, 688–695, 2019, https://doi.org/10.1016/j.procs.2019.09.104.
27. Leong, Y.K., Tan, J.H., Chew, K.W., Show, P.L., Significance of industry 5.0, in: *The Prospect of Industry 5.0 in Biomanufacturing*, p. 326, CRC Press, Boca Raton, 2020. eBook ISBN 9781003080671.
28. Liu, H. and Wang, L., Gesture recognition for human-robot collaboration: A review. *Int. J. Ind. Ergon.*, 68, 355–367, 2018.
29. Longo, F., Padovano, A., Umbrella, S., Value-oriented and ethical technology engineering in industry 5.0: a human-centric perspective for the design of the factory of the future. *Appl. Sci.*, 10, 12, 4182, 2020, https://doi.org/10.3390/app10124182.
30. Maddikunta, P.K., Pham, Q.V., Prabadevi, B., Deepa, N., Dev, K., Gadekallu, T.R., Liyanage, M., Industry 5.0: a survey on enabling technologies and potential applications. *J. Ind. Inf. Integr.*, 26, 100257, 2021. ISSN 2452-414X.
31. Madsen, D.O. and Berg, T., an exploratory bibliometric analysis of the birth and emergence of industry 5.0. *Appl. Syst. Innov.*, 4, 4, 87, 2021, https://doi.org/10.3390/asi4040087.
32. Majumdar, A., Garg, H., Jain, R., Managing the barriers of industry 4.0 adoption and implementation in textile and clothing industry: interpretive structural model and triple helix framework. *Comput. Ind.*, 125, 103372, 2021, https://doi.org/10.1016/j.compind.2020.103372.
33. Masood, T. and Sonntag, P., Industry 4.0: adoption challenges and benefits for SMEs. *Comput. Ind.*, 121, 103261, 2020, https://doi.org/10.1016/j.compind.2020.103261.
34. Maurtua, I., Ibarguren, A., Kildal, J., Susperregi, L., Sierra, B., Human-robot collaboration in industrial applications: Safety, interaction and trust. *Int. J. Adv. Rob. Syst.*, 14, 4, 2017, doi:10.1177/1729881417716010.
35. Messeri, C., Zanchettin, A.M., Gianotti, E., Chirico, A., Magoni, S., *et al.*, On the effects of leader-follower roles in dyadic human-robot synchronisation, Transactions on Cognitive and Developmental Systems. *IEEE*, 99, 2991864, 2020.
36. Nahavandi, S., Industry 5.0—A human-centric solution. *Sustainability*, 11, 16, 4371, 2019, https://doi.org/10.3390/su11164371.

37. Robla-Gomez, S., Becerra, V.M., Llata, J.R., Gonzalez-Sarabia, E., Torre-Ferrero, C., Perez-Oria, J., Working Together: A Review on Safe Human-Robot Collaboration in Industrial Environments, in: *IEEE Access,* vol. 5, pp. 26754–26773, 2017, doi: 10.1109/ACCESS.2017.2773127.
38. Saniuk, S., Grabowska, S., Gajdzik, B., Social expectations and market changes in the context of developing the industry 4.0 concept. *Sustainability,* 12, 1362, 2020, https://doi.org/10.3390/su12041362.
39. Villani, V., Pini, F., Leali, F., Secchi, C., Survey on human–robot collaboration in industrial settings: Safety, intuitive interfaces and applications. *Mechatronics,* 55, 248–266, 2018.
40. Vural, O. and Hekim, N., *Birth of Industry 5.0: Making Sense of Big Data with Artificial Intelligence, The Internet of Things and Next-Generation Technology Policy,* 2018, https://doi.org/10.1089/omi.2017.0194.
41. Zhang, C. and Chen, Y.A., A review of research relevant to the emerging industry trends: industry 4.0, IoT, blockchain, and business analytics. *J. Ind. Integr. Manage.,* 5, 165–180, 2020, https://doi.org/10.1142/S2424862219500192.

16

Human Capital Analytics in Industry 5.0 for Sustainable Growth

Channi Sachdeva[1]*, Veena Grover[2] and Veer P. Gangwar[1]

[1]*Mittal School of Business, Lovely Professional University, Phagwara, India*
[2]*Veena Grover, School of Management, NIET, Greater Noida, India*

Abstract

To accomplish the Sustainable Development Goals (SDGs), it is necessary to comprehend the potential of human capital analytics and embrace the ideas of Industry 5.0. In this paper, some crucial points are explored for achieving SDGs. Human capital analytics maximizes the potential and also helps in understanding, that collaboration between humans and machines can be increased from Industry 5.0. It is essential to invest in humans and embrace the technology with both hands for the development of SDGs. In this way, decentralized decision-making takes place and also helps in sustainable value creation. This paper explores how the integration of human capital analytics and Industry 5.0 catalyzes progress toward SDGs. It also opens the door to innovations, creativity, rapid growth, and quick and accurate decision-making. This paper emphasizes the need for policymakers to invest in human priority along with technology for the betterment of the organization. It can create a better future for the organization and SDGs achieved more accurately.

***Keywords*:** Sustainable development, industry 5.0, human capital analytics, innovation, united nations sustainable development goals (UN SDGs)

**Corresponding author*: channikaur105@gmail.com

Deepa Gupta, Mukul Gupta, Pawan Budhwar, Jim Westerman, Rajesh Kumar Dhanaraj and Balamurugan Balusamy (eds.) Human Capital Analytics: Exploring the HR Spectrum in Industry 5.0, (337–346) © 2025 Scrivener Publishing LLC

16.1 Introduction of SDGs and the Role of Humans in Organization

There are 17 Sustainable Development Goals (SDGs) and these SDGs clearly define which serves the needs and profitability of the organization while not affecting the future generation. A strong economy helps society, makes organizations more profitable, and protects the environment too because organizations are facing big challenges without technology in their workings, decision-making, accuracy, etc.

Human capital analysts focus on human resource well-being and support in the organization with SDGs and Industry 5.0. When human capital analytics empire with Industry 5.0, then it affects positively the decision-making process, innovation, creating value in the organization and policy makers' jobs, and overall well-being environment.

Overall, in this introduction, we learned about SDGs and human capital analytics toward Industry 5.0 for the development and growth of the organization in a positive manner.

16.2 Human Capital Analytics: Concepts and Applications

This section explains human capital analytics and the effective utilization of human resources, along with fundamentals and their application.

Key concepts: *Talent acquisition* is the first concept of human capital analytics. It means putting the right person in the right place. *Retention*, in other words, always makes star performers (employees) happy in the organization. *Development*, in another way, uses training and development programs to enhance the skills of employees in the organization. *Performance management* entails understanding and tackling every department that well they are performing their duties in the organization and making adjustments wherever required.

Human capital analytics helps organizations understand their employees by utilizing data to manage productivity and sustainability. The organization needs to create a positive and healthy environment for employees. It helps achieve goals in the organization.

Human capital analytics uses tools and methodologies for data collection, data interpretation, visualization methods, and holistic insights (deeper insights lead to better decisions for a stronger workforce) into the organization's performance of the employees and the organization.

In summary, this section explains concepts, deeper insights, understanding of human capital insights, and practicality in the context of a better organization.

16.3 Literature Review

Michael Rada invented the term "Industry 5.0" [2]. The SDGs are a unified goal that includes social, environmental, and human well-being objectives [10]. The most popular Industry 5.0 technologies for sustainability were the Internet of Things (IoT), intelligent machines, and collaborative robots. This study then examined existing studies in four important research themes: Robot advancement, educational sustainability, human-centeredness, and ecological advancement [3]. Despite technological advancements, inefficient resource utilization and waste management pose significant difficulties for society and the environment [5].

Industry 5.0 shifts the paradigm and delivers resolution by reducing reliance on technology and assuming that growth is built on collaboration between humans and robots [1]. Almost every country in the world today recognizes the importance of sustainable waste management [4]. Automation, artificially intelligent technology (AI), the IoT, analytics for prediction, big data, 3D printing, nanotechnology, fifth-generation wireless technology, and biotechnology have all helped to boost creativity and output in nearly every industry, including agriculture, manufacturing, and offerings [6]. The rise of the Industrial Age resulted in tremendous changes in all aspects of life. However, with the introduction of new social development principles such as sustainability, human-centeredness, and carbon emissions, the production system/paradigm has struggled to meet the needs of a dynamic society [12]. The research's path to Industry 5.0–driven sustainability is aimed at creating an understanding of how the industry may contribute to sustainable development by detailing how the growth of its functions should be controlled to maximize cooperation and contributions to the desired sustainability ideals [8]. Industry 5.0 has arrived and has sounded the alarm, urging businesses to apply it as soon as possible; the advantage is that the industry is still in its early phases [7]. Industry 5.0, also known as neo-industrialization, looks to be a substitute for a group of concerns in today's world [16]. The research findings imply that the successful implementation of I5.0 projects necessitates a systematic measurement tool from which businesses and officials may gain significant insights into understanding and managing such problems [9]. Emphasized stakeholder salience, integration and collaboration as human capital analytics key enablers of Industry 5.0 change [8]. Furthermore, while I5.0 is still in its early stages, many organizations are finding it difficult to implement because of cost constraints, a reluctance to change, an efficient norm for digital-physical systems, and an effective collaboration between human and robot processes [11]. Creating a secure connection between the internet and physical space can promote a focus on human culture that combines economic growth with social challenges [14]. Human-machine collaboration strives to rapidly increase production. Industry 5.0 can increase production quality by outsourcing monotonous and uninteresting activities to robots and leaving creative jobs to humans [13]. This collaboration is one of the foundational ideas of Industry 5.0. Moreover, executives feel that implementing Industry 5.0 may save costs, increase long-term viability assist in the creation of bulk customization, and increase efficiency in operations [15]. The rapid technology breakthroughs of Industry 5.0 have intensified organizational rivalry across all industries and businesses. Given this, technological competitiveness is vital for enterprises to distinguish themselves from competitors, anticipate emerging competitors, develop innovation, and enhance performance in general and sustainability [17]. There is a scarcity of comprehensive conceptualizations of the Construction 5.0 concept from human-centricity, long-term viability, and resiliency perspectives. This study supports the idea of Industry 5.0 from a driven by technology, super-smart society, and a partnership between humans and robots [18].

16.4 Integrating SDGs with Human Capital Strategies

Integrating SDGs with human capital strategies is used to manage organizational development according to SDGs objectives. There are various steps involved in it. Some of them are the following:

i. **Recognizing the Sustainable Development Goals:** Industries need to understand 17 SDGs and their objectives too. If organizational targets are set according to SDGs, then it tackles many issues like economic issues, environmental issues, and social issues. By working together to solve these interconnected challenges, we can build a better future for the organization.
ii. **Determining the Importance:** An organization has to identify which SDGs are important for their organization and how this impacts the working of employees and the

organization's future. Organizations should understand how their strategies contribute to SDGs.

iii. **Monitoring Human Resource Techniques:** Techniques for the development of human resources involve recruitment, the process of selection, development and training, employee engagement, employee retention, performance measurement, and performance management. Organization has to analyze the area in which contributions take place to SDGs.

iv. **Setting Goals and Targets:** The organization strategizes clear objectives according to SDGs and organizations. Objectives decided by the organization must enhance productivity, employee well-being, and lifelong learning for employees.

v. **Execution and Supervision:** After setting the goals, the organization must take the initiative and programs that promote SDGs into human capital plans. This may include training and development of employees, employee skill enhancement programs, employee wellbeing programs, etc. that connect with SDGs and organizational benefits. These new opportunities can take place if continue to monitor it.

vi. **Stakeholder Engagement:** Stakeholder involvement is critical to the attainment of SDGs and organizational goals; they are linked since investment plans are discussed and explained by stakeholders.

By aligning human capital and SDGs, these things are required for enhancing productivity, enhancing the skills of employees, enhancing the profit of the organization, enhancing and developing society, etc.

16.5 Utilizing Data Analysis for Managing Talent and Development

Utilizing the data analysis indulges in data-driven insights used for enhancing the recruitment of employees, development of employees, training of employees, performance measurement of employees, and retention within an organization. With the power of data analysis, organizations can enhance competitiveness and achieve the SDGs goals which are integrated with organizational goals rapidly and with more accuracy. Here are a few points on which data analysis can be utilized:

i. **Recruitment and Selection:** At the time of recruitment and selection if the organization has accurate data, then it can be analyzed through technology, and working with it becomes easier. In this way, recruitment and selection of employees take less time and accuracy will increase.
ii. **Training, Learning, and Development:** Through the analyzed data, ability deficits can be quickly identified and training can become merely effective for employees. Measurement of performance after training can also be analyzed well, and it meets the SDGs and organizational goals too.
iii. **Management of Performance:** Through the data analysis, tracking the employees' performance is easy. After analyzing the performance, an organization can pinpoint areas of improvement and target those weaknesses for improving productivity and reaching goals.
iv. **Planning Succession:** Analyzed data will improve the planning of the organization and enhance the chances to achieve goals appropriately in the context of SDGs. By analyzing the performance of the employees, organizations can set their goals accordingly and improve them if required.
v. **Employee Engagement:** An engagement of employees in working becomes easy, if data are analyzed, identification of skills will become easier and engagement can be done accordingly. This approach improves the loyalty and satisfaction of employees.
vi. **Employee Retention:** By analyzing employee feedback and turnover patterns, exit interviews can be taken and improve/mold the strategies of the organization.

16.6 Industry 5.0 Principles for Sustainable Value Creation

Principles of Industry 5.0 focuses on SDGs with the integration of organizational goals and also focuses on preparing smart business models with advanced technologies and human skills too. A few points that highlight it are the following:

i. **Collaboration of Machine and Human:** Collaboration of human skill sets and machine skill sets, then it will enhance productivity and accuracy. It increases the level of satisfaction and engagement of employees in an organization.

ii. **Customization of Work:** To meet the needs of the customer, an organization can customize the products and services with the help of advanced technologies and also take care of SDGs like reducing wastage, etc.

iii. **Decentralized Decision-Making:** Industry 5.0 gives importance to decision-making which is decentralized because, in this way, work becomes more effective and easier. In this way, productivity can be increased and the possibility of reaching goals with SDGs is increased.

16.7 Challenges and Opportunities for Promoting Sustainable Development via Insights and Industry 5.0

SDGs have both challenges as well as opportunities. Complexities can be increased, enhancement of innovation, and many more things. So, acceptance of challenges and work for the opportunities is essential for an organization, with the involvment of both employees and the principles of Industry 5.0.

Let's discuss the challenges first:

i. **Accessibility and the Quality of the Data:** For every organization, ensuring the quality of data and accessibility poses a big challenge because productivity, planning, decision-making, etc. largely depend on the quality and analysis of data. To address this, modern technologies are constantly used to collect and analyze data.

ii. **The Shortage of Talent in Employees:** There is a lack of talent for particular work in particular employees. It can be important to overcome these situations by providing them with good training and development programs.

iii. **The Skill Gap in Employees:** The shortage of skills in the employee is a big drawback in the organization. To overcome this skill, enhancement programs are important for employees to increase the productivity of the organization.

iv. **Resource and Cost Constraints:** The shortage of resources and cost increase and decrease affect the production of the organization and it also affects the employee engagement in the organization.

Now opportunities:

i. **Engagement of Stakeholders:** Stakeholders will engage in organizational decisions because new opportunities can knock on the door frequently if the productivity of the organization is good and employees are satisfied.
ii. **Collaboration and Innovation:** Promoting innovation and collaboration, combining human skills with advanced technologies can improve the productivity of an organization and also meet out the employee satisfaction, and employee engagement in the industry.
iii. **Optimization of Resources and Efficiency:** Advancements in technologies help in the proper utilization of resources and also increase their efficiency. Reduce wastage of the resources, putting the right people at the right place, accurate decision-making in the organization, accuracy in data analyses will improve the optimization of resources and efficiency.

16.8 Future Directions

Innovation and strategies impact maximum on the organization. These are some key areas where the organization focuses:

i. **Integration of Emerging Technologies:** Organizations can integrate with new and emerging technologies like blockchain, digital twins, and artificial intelligence. This can increase the productivity of employees as well as the profitability of the organization.
ii. **Adaptation and Continuous Learning:** Continuous learning takes place with emerging technologies if adaptability increases then opportunities and productivity in the organization also increase day by day and it is also good for achieving SDGs.
iii. **Partnership Collaboration:** Integration of SDGs and organizational goals increases partnership collaboration and the growth and development of the organization.

References

1. Adel, A., Future of Industry 5.0 in society: human-centric solutions, challenges, and prospective research areas. *J. Cloud Comput.*, 11, 1, 40, 2022.
2. Akundi, A., Euresti, D., Luna, S., Ankobiah, W., Lopes, A.J., Edinbarough, I., State of Industry 5.0—Analysis and Identification of Current Research Trends. *Appl. Syst. Innov.*, 5, 1, 27, 2022.
3. Baig, M. and Yadegaridehkordi, E., Industry 5.0 applications for sustainability: A systematic review and future research directions. *Sustain. Dev.*, 2023.
4. Debnath, B., Mainul Bari, A.B.M., Mithun Ali, S., Ahmed, T., Ali, I., Kabir, G., Modelling the Barriers to Sustainable Waste Management in the Plastic-Manufacturing Industry: An Emerging Economy Perspective. *Sustain. Anal. Model.*, 3, 100017, 2023.
5. Dwivedi, A.N., Agrawal, D., Jha, A., Mathiyazhagan, K., Studying the interactions among Industry 5.0 and circular supply chain: Towards attaining sustainable development. *Comput. Ind. Eng.*, 176, 108927, 2023.
6. Espina-Romero, L.C., Guerrero-Alcedo, J.M., Avila, N.G., Noroño Sánchez, J.G., Gutiérrez Hurtado, H., Quiñones Li, A.E., Industry 5.0: Tracking Scientific Activity on the Most Influential Industries, Associated Topics, and Future Research Agenda. *Sustainability*, 15, 6, 5554, 2023.
7. Ghobakhloo, M., Iranmanesh, M., Faraz Mubarak, M., Mubarik, M., Rejeb, A., Nilashi, M., Identifying industry 5.0 contributions to sustainable development: A strategy roadmap for delivering sustainability values. *Sustain. Prod. Consump.*, 2022.
8. Ghobakhloo, M., Iranmanesh, M., Morales, M.E., Nilashi, M., Amran, A., Actions and approaches for enabling Industry 5.0-driven sustainable industrial transformation: A strategy roadmap. *Corp. Soc. Responsib. Environ. Manage.*, 2022.
9. Karmaker, C.L., Mainul Bari, A.B.M., Anam, Z., Ahmed, T., Mithun Ali, S., de Jesus Pacheco, D.A., Moktadir, A., Industry 5.0 challenges for post-pandemic supply chain sustainability in an emerging economy. *Int. J. Prod. Econ.*, 2023.
10. Kasinathan, P., Pugazhendhi, R., Elavarasan, R.M., Ramachandaramurthy, V.K., Ramanathan, V., Subramanian, S., Kumar, S., Nandhagopal, K., Vijaya Raghavan, R.R., Rangasamy, S., Devendiran, R., Alsharif, M.H., Realization of Sustainable Development Goals with Disruptive Technologies by Integrating Industry 5.0, Society 5.0, Smart Cities and Villages. *Sustainability*, 2022.
11. Kumar, U., Kaswan, M.S., Kumar, R., Chaudhary, R., Garza-Reyes, J.A., Rathi, R., Joshi, R., A systematic review of Industry 5.0 from main aspects to the execution status. *TQM J.*, 2023.
12. Leng, J., Chao Sha, W., Wang, B., Zheng, P., Zhuang, C., Liu, Q., Wuest, T., Mourtzis, D., Wang, L., Industry 5.0: Prospect and retrospect. *J. Manuf. Syst.*, 65, 279–295, 2022.

13. Maddikunta, P.K.R., Quoc Pham, V., Prabadevi, B., Deepa, N., Dev, K., Gadekallu, T.R., Ruby, R., Liyanage, M., Industry 5.0: A survey on enabling technologies and potential applications. *J. Ind. Inf. Integr.*, 26, 100257, 2022.
14. Mishra, P., Thakur, P., Singh, G., Sustainable Smart City to Society 5.0: State-of-the-Art and Research Challenges. *SAIEE Afr. Res. J.*, 2022.
15. Mukherjee, A.A., Raj, A., Aggarwal, S., Identification of barriers and their mitigation strategies for industry 5.0 implementation in emerging economies. *Int. J. Prod. Econ.*, 2023.
16. Pereira, R. and dos Santos, N., Neoindustrialization—Reflections on a New Paradigmatic Approach for the Industry: A Scoping Review on Industry 5.0. *Logistics*, 2023.
17. Rajumesh, S., Promoting sustainable and human-centric industry 5.0: a thematic analysis of emerging research topics and opportunities. *J. Bus. Socio-economic Dev.*, 2023.
18. Yitmen, I., Almusaed, A., Alizadehsalehi, S., Investigating the Causal Relationships among Enablers of the Construction 5.0 Paradigm: Integration of Operator 5.0 and Society 5.0 with Human-Centricity, Sustainability, and Resilience. *Sustainability*, 15, 11, 9105, 2023.

17

HR 5.0 – Demystifying the Way Forward

Ritu Saxena[1]*, Priyanshi Jindal[2] and Harshit Gouri[3]

[1]I.T.S School of Management, Ghaziabad, Uttar Pradesh, India
[2]Shannon Advisors Private Limited, Delhi, India
[3]St. Stephen's College, University of Delhi, Delhi, India

Abstract

The human resources (HR) industry is undergoing a transformation, in the digital age. HR 5.0 represents an approach to HR that uses technology, data, and analytics to drive a more focused and adaptable workforce that puts people first. HR 5.0 seeks to improve employee satisfaction, engagement, and productivity by fostering a culture of creativity, education, and teamwork. However, the implementation of HR 5.0 has some limitations and possibilities. This chapter explores the issues and developments HR professionals face as they embrace HR 5.0 including the impact of intelligence (AI) and automation on future performance and skill development Shift from traditional management systems to connected teams The need for diversity, equity, and inclusion (DEI) A flexible and diverse foster workforce; the strategic role of HR as a driver of change in digital transformation efforts; and ethical considerations in the use of data, for HR decision-making purposes. Additionally, she provides practical advice and tips for HR leaders to succeed in today's digital environment.

***Keywords*:** HR 5.0, machine learning, challenges, opportunities, artificial intelligence, automation

**Corresponding author*: profritusaxena@gmail.com

Deepa Gupta, Mukul Gupta, Pawan Budhwar, Jim Westerman, Rajesh Kumar Dhanaraj and Balamurugan Balusamy (eds.) Human Capital Analytics: Exploring the HR Spectrum in Industry 5.0, (347–358) © 2025 Scrivener Publishing LLC

17.1 Introduction

HR 5.0 is the most advanced generation of HR technology designed to empower employees by delivering an unparalleled experience and amplifying the efficiency of HR processes. This holds great paradigm shifts in the way HR processes are managed and delivered. It can even change the very face of the HR industry [1, 2]. Advanced analytics and AI will be the heart of HR 5.0 since it leverages the tools toward the automation and optimization of most of the HR processes in recruitment, onboarding, performance management, and employee engagement. HR 5.0 will also aim to be a promoter of a culture based on humans, in which diversity, inclusion, well-being, and lifelong learning of employees are valued. The concept of Employee Experience is at the center of HR 5.0.

HR 5.0 systems use powerful technologies such as chatbots and natural language processing to offer more personalized, interactive, and intuitive experiences to employees. The following three demands are placed on on-demand learning and development, real-time feedback, and career growth opportunities [3]:

HR 5.0 features data-driven decision-making. With a large volume of employees' data collection and analysis, the HR 5.0 system offers a real-time insight tool that is able to help in preparing valid decisions for talent management, workforce planning, and other initiatives that are must by the HR fraternity. Another very important characteristic of HR 5.0 is the use of advanced technologies to remove any sort of bias and discrimination from HR in decision-making. The HR 5.0 system, through AI and machine learning, will ensure that no form of unconscious bias in the hiring and performance management process is harbored, hence all decisions made will be flowing out of objective grounds [4].

A dynamic workplace means agility and flexibility are paramount to HR 5.0. The 5.0 systems will need to adapt quickly to changing needs and priorities. This might include integration with other HR and business systems to aid remote and distributed workforces. HR 5.0 is a great movement to how HR processes can be managed and delivered—a revolution that can be experienced in the HR industry [1]. These HR 5.0 systems should be equipped with an advanced technology stack, from AI, machine learning, to natural language processing, to help automate and optimize HR processes for the best employee experience and data-driven decision-making. HR 5.0 has a human focus; it is agile, flexible, and eliminates bias and discrimination. It will be a revolution in the world of work and talent management.

17.2 Literature Review

Fast improvement in technology, coupled with the current momentum of the ever-increasing demand for agile, data-driven, and personalized HR practices, has laid at the heart of driving HR 5.0.

History of HR Evolution 5.0:

HR 1.0: This was considered a very basic version or form of HR management that was focused on basic administrative functions such as payroll, benefits administration, and compliance.

HR 2.0: The arrival of the new information of the '80s with HR 2.0 brought with it HR software, including other tools in the category of applicant tracking systems and e-learning platforms. 0 – HR 0 mainly dealt with the automation and efficiency of HR processes. HR 3.0 – Between the late 1990s and the early years of the 2000s [5], HR 3.0 came across the issue of talent management, enabling efficient recruitment, training, and development of employees. This was also the generation where talent management systems and the use of metrics to measure performance and productivity increased. HR 4.0: The HR 4.0 uses modern and sophisticated technologies. For instance, automation, cloud computing, and mobile gadgets among others. These are used to help optimize the HR processes [5, 6].

Attention shifted to increased efficiency, cost reduction, and improvement in the general effectiveness of HR practices. HR 5.0 - The new generation, powered with state-of-the-art technology such as artificial intelligence, machine learning, and big data analytics, optimizes HR processes for the new, more personalized, agile, and data-driven approach to practice, putting emphasis on employee experience, well-being, and engagement. HR 5.0 represents the human resource (HR) practices in the 4th Industrial Revolution (4IR). "It seeks to leverage digital technologies such as Artificial Intelligence (AI), Big Data, Cloud, and Blockchain to improve and renovate much-needed HR efficiency, effectiveness, and agility".

HR 5.0 strives to create a human-centric culture through a mindset of diversity, inclusion, well-being, and lifelong learning for all employees [1]. However, implementing HR 5.0 is not plain sailing. A few of the key challenges that remain to HR leaders and professionals include the demand for digital skills and competencies both within HR staff and the employees. A Deloitte survey showed that only 17% of HR professionals felt they were prepared or very prepared to tackle the AI impact on the workforce. Further to this, only 38% of the workers agree that their organizations are assisting them in preparation for future work. Some of the stakeholders are resistant to change and innovation [7]. HR 5.0 implementation would mean that it is moving from a way of thinking and acting in HR in conventional methods to increasingly agile, collaborative practices [8]. However, many managers and employees might be generally disfavored to fully embrace these new working mechanisms, and some may also be afraid of losing jobs or status resulting from the fact that automation and digitization are taking place.

Ethical and legal consequences of the implementation of digital technologies in HR processes: For instance, the use of AI in talent acquisition or performance management may bring issues of bias, discrimination, privacy, or accountability. Here, HR leaders and professionals are to employ digital technologies humanely, based on ethical principles and legal regulations.

The problem, however, has also been related to the tremendous challenges in terms of HR 5.0 implementation in organizations. The main challenges include fostering digital thinking and a culture of professionals among HR and employees.

- Ensure the use of data and AI is ethical and responsibly handled in the development of HR decisions and throughout the HR processes.
- Balancing the needs against automation with that of humanization of services and HR interactions.
- The changing nature of the needs and opportunities of the 4IR requires reskilling and upskilling the workforce.
- To create a diversified, inclusive work environment that supports teamwork and creativity in order to pursue human welfare.
- Aligning HR Strategy with Business Strategy and Organizational Culture.
- Develop new computational competencies and skills for HR Managers and employees.
- Managing the ethical, legal, and social implications of data and AI usage in HR.
- The balance between people and technology in HR.
- Creation of an employee-oriented company culture that emphasizes quality, continuous improvement, key values, and achievement of the company's objectives.
- Measure and show the value and impact of HR 5.0 initiatives

17.2.1 Challenges in Implementing in HR 5.0

Data Privacy and Security - HR 5.0 includes large volume data collection and processing involving the organizational employee pool. Hence, data privacy and security assume as much importance in HR 5.0. The data should be secured so that the data is not prone to various risks in cyberspace, such as data breaches, identity theft, ransomware, phishing, or insider attacks [9, 10]. Data privacy and security also deal with compliance with pertinent laws and regulations, such as the General Data Protection Regulation (GDPR), the California Consumer Privacy Act (CCPA), and the Health Insurance Portability and Accountability Act (HIPAA). These laws require organizations to seek the data subject's consent and be transparent and accountable to him, in their processing activities of personal data, by putting in place necessary and appropriate technical and organizational measures to safeguard such personal data, ensuring its integrity and respect for the data subject's rights in regards to access, rectification, erasure, and portability.

Data privacy and security represent an organization's ethical and legal responsibility to the data collected and used by their employee [11, 12]. Respect for privacy and security of employee data will enhance the organization's gain of trust and loyalty from its workforce, improve its reputation and brand image, and lessen legal risks with related penalties, among many others. Further, security of data and privacy are also prime concerns to ensure the quality and accuracy of employee data that improves decision-making, performance management, talent acquisition, and retention and development [13].

It is therefore incumbent for organizations to take a more proactive and all-around approach to data privacy and security in HR 5.0 that would involve all stakeholders, including employees, managers, HR professionals, IT staff, legal counsel, and outside partners.

Resistance to Change: Employees are uncooperative in moving to new technologies or processes and, most particularly, if it is something they are not aware of and if it is going to threaten their job security [14]. Resistance to change can sometimes manifest as failure to engage in the change process, absenteeism, poor performance, or even sabotage.

HR leaders will have to find a way around this by communicating the benefits and rationale for HR 5.0 to all stakeholders, involving them in the process of design and implementation, providing appropriate training and support, and dealing with any arising concerns or feedback promptly and respectfully.

Management Change is one of the most complex aspects associated with the implementation of HR 5.0. HR 5.0 is a monumental change in how HR processes are managed and delivered, moving from the present transactional and reactive mode to the strategic and proactive strategy [15]. This, therefore, calls for HR personnel to take on new competencies, mindsets, and new roles like business partners, data analysts, and change agents. Consequently, this will put demands on employees in terms of adaptation to new ways of using and accessing HR services, which will be self-service platforms, chatbots, and personalized learning paths.

These changes may receive stiff resistance from the employees and human resource personnel who have become accustomed to traditional practices and systems. Hence, the vision and benefits of HR 5.0 should be articulated clearly and repeatedly, and enough training and support given to effect the change.

Talent Acquisition and Learning — HR 5.0 is the new Human Resources paradigm that leverages digital technologies, data analytics, and human-centered design in its operations to make the HR function agile, personalized, and impactful. 5.0, with the ambition of turning HR from a defensive and transactional position into a proactive and strategic partner that works in order to drive business performance and employee engagement. But such lofty ambitions do take work and may encounter every manner of challenge or barrier. One of the major challenges is that HR 5.0 will require management to change [16]. That is to say, HR 5.0 will require HR leaders and professionals to embrace the new mindsets, skills, and behaviors it is demanding.

They are also expected to communicate and collaborate effectively with other stakeholders, such as business leaders, employees, and outside partners, in co-creating and co-delivering value-added HR solutions.

Skills Gap - One of the bottlenecks HR 5.0 would need to jump over pertains to the potential skills gap that may be lying amidst the employees. HR 5.0 is a paradigm shift utilizing technologies in artificial intelligence, big data, cloud computing, and blockchain to revolutionize the function of human resources management.

In this case, equipping the employee with technical skills and digital literacy that would be used in leveraging these technologies is an imperative action to take [17, 18]. However, the market or the organization with regard to talent may be short in terms of the required skills. The above factors may pose a barrier toward implementation and performance and the competitiveness of the Organization. It is, therefore, pertinent to ensure and resolve the skill gap through training, development, and recruitment strategies.

17.2.2 Opportunities in Implementing HR 5.0

Enhanced Employee Experience – Enhanced employee experience is one of the most important benefits of HR 5.0, the latest development in human resource management increasingly underpinned by digital transformation and innovation. HR 5.0 has the power to make organizations build a very personal, engaging, and absolutely seamless employee experience through the use of advanced technologies such as AI and natural language processing in improved communication, learning and development programs, and career growth opportunities [19]. For instance, AI can make it possible for an HR practitioner to analyze issues emanating from employee feedback and improve sentiment, at the same time providing personalized recommendations for intervention. Natural Language Processing can be used by HR to overcome language and cultural barriers in the workplace and effectively communicate with employees, even developing in-house training content that is more immersive and interactive. 5.0 HR can offer employees the ability to access relevant information and resources they need from wherever and whenever they require, even down to mentors and peers who will be able to help the employee in their career development. In other words, HR 5.0 would help organizations to improve in the domain of effective attraction, retention, and motivation of talents that are able to allow for an innovative and collaborative culture.

Data-Driven Decision-Making – One of the key features of HR 5.0, or the latest advancement in the management of human resources, remains that it makes decisions in a data-oriented style.

HR 5.0 gives the organization real-time, data-based insights that aid their decision-making in talent management, workforce planning, and other HR initiatives. The data analytics can [20], for example, be applied to establish the organization's skills gaps in HR 5.0, taking recruitment actions targeting successful candidates or promoting the best talents from inside, establishing the optimal benefit and compensation packages, ensuring effective training and development programs, and establishing the impact of employee engagement and retention on business performance. Data-driven decision-making will, therefore, put HR 5.0 in a strategic position to ensure that the strategies for human capital meet the overall organizational goals and objectives of the business, culminating in a competitive advantage within the market.

Improved HR Processes – The potential of automation and streamlining for HR 5.0 includes recruitment, onboarding, performance management, and employee engagement. With the help of new, advanced technologies like artificial intelligence, cloud computing, and blockchain, HR 5.0 can help avoid human fallibilities [21]. This will save time and cost. The quality and consistency of service receivers will be improved.

For example, HR 5.0 can accelerate and improve intelligence-based hiring decisions through the analysis of a huge volume of data collected from many sources, including resumes, social media profiles, and assessments. Correspondingly, HR 5.0 will improve the employee experience by giving them the opportunity to receive relevant personalized and timely delivery of feedback, recognition, and support that should be relevant to the needs and aspirations of each employee. Thus, HR 5.0 will make it possible to be based on the culture of learning and innovations, through the implementation of continuous learning opportunities, career development paths, and opportunities for employees to collaborate.

Increased Efficiency and Productivity: An advantage of HR automation is increased efficiency and productivity in the human resources department [1]. HR professionals can use their time and resources away from monotonous HR tasks such as payroll, benefits administration, employee onboarding, performance management, and compliance so that they can concentrate on more strategic initiatives for their companies. HR automation allows HR professionals to:

- Improve employee engagement and retention by offering timely recognition, feedback, and development opportunities.
- Get a flexible and fair hiring and development optimization process that will ensure talent attraction and management is enhanced with improved bias reduction and talent sourcing.
- HR Automation allows the HR Professionals to be more focused on added value activities that may enhance the organization's performance and competitiveness.
- Enable the sharing of learning content developed on order, personalized, and tailored through a culture of learning and innovation that facilitates sharing knowledge, collaboration, and creativity.

Support the organization in realizing the change and transformation through aligning HR policies and practices with business goals, facilitating communication and feedback, and measuring and reporting on HR outcomes.

Competitive Advantage - Competitive advantage is that type of advantage edge of an organization over its rivals in the market.

This can be through offering superior products or services, reducing costs, or having a base of loyal customers.

HR 5.0 is a concept that deals with the transformational nature of human resources in the digital age, where data, analytics, automation, and artificial intelligence are implemented to provide an improved experience and performance of the workforce [2].

Which means HR 5.0 adopting organizations can increase their competitive advantage through attracting and retaining top talents of the industry to help be the trendsetters rather than fall back. Therefore, enabling an organization with HR 5.0 would further help in creating a culture of innovation, team collaboration, and agility to empower employees with learning and growth for contributing their best toward organizational goals. HR 5.0 will enable organizations to pre-act and respond to the changes in the needs and expectations of the workforce, just like customers and society.

17.3 Recommendations for Solving the Challenges Faced in HR 5.0

HR professionals can adopt a proactive and strategic approach to address these challenges. There are some possible recommendations that can help to solve the challenges faced in HR 5.0:

- HR professionals should embrace a continuous learning and innovation culture where they can be encouraged to experiment with new tools and methods, learn from failures, and share best practices with peers and stakeholders.
- We align HR strategies and practices with the Organization's vision, mission, values, and external trends and opportunities in the market and society.
- It engages employees in co-creating and co-delivering HR solutions that meet their diverse needs and preferences, such as personalized learning paths, flexible work arrangements, and feedback mechanisms.
- They leverage data and analytics to measure and improve HR performance and impact, using dashboards, surveys, and sentiment analysis to track employee engagement, satisfaction, and productivity.

- They are building partnerships and networks with internal and external stakeholders, such as managers, leaders, customers, suppliers, competitors, regulators, and academia, to exchange insights, resources, and best practices on HR 5.0.
- Investing in continuous learning and development for HR professionals and employees, such as providing online courses, webinars, podcasts, mentoring programs, and certifications on digital transformation, innovation, and HR best practices.
- We are communicating clearly and consistently with all stakeholders about the vision, goals, benefits, and challenges of HR 5.0, such as using various channels and formats such as emails, newsletters, blogs, videos, podcasts, webinars, town halls, and workshops to share information, stories, best practices, and lessons learned.

HR professionals can overcome the challenges faced in HR 5.0 and become catalysts for change and innovation in their organizations.

17.4 Conclusion

HR 5.0 represents a transformative shift in how human resources are managed and delivered in organizations. By adopting advanced technologies like artificial intelligence, machine learning, big data analytics, and automation, HR 5.0 aims to create a more personalized, data-driven, and human-centric employee experience.

While implementing HR 5.0 current challenges such as data privacy and security concerns, resistance to change, skills gaps, and ethical implications of using AI, the potential opportunities are significant. HR 5.0 can enhance employee engagement and productivity through improved processes, data-driven decision-making, increased efficiency, and a competitive edge for organizations.

For a smooth transition to HR 5.0, HR professionals must embrace a culture of continuous learning, build strategic partnerships, engage employees in co-creating solutions, invest in developing digital skills, communicate transparently, and ensure the responsible use of data and technology.

As the workforce and workplace evolve rapidly, HR 5.0 provides a roadmap for HR to become a proactive strategic partner, driving organizational performance and employee well-being. By addressing the challenges proactively and capitalizing on the opportunities, HR leaders can position their organizations for success in the digital age while prioritizing human-centric values of diversity, inclusion, and lifelong learning.

References

1. Ganatra, N.J. and Pandya, J.D., The transformative impact of artificial intelligence on hr practices and employee experience: A review. *J. Manage. Res. Anal.*, 10, 2, 106–111, Jun. 2023, doi: 10.18231/j.jmra.2023.018.
2. Agustono, D.O.S., Nugroho, R., Yanu Alif Fianto, A., Artificial Intelligence in Human Resource Management Practices. *KnE Social Sci.*, 8, 9, 958–970, 2023.
3. Firdausa Nuzula, I. and Miftahul Amri, M., Will ChatGPT bring a New Paradigm to HR World? A Critical Opinion Article. *J. Manage. Stud. Dev.*, 2, 02, 142–161, Apr. 2023, doi: 10.56741/jmsd.v2i02.316.
4. Marinelli, M., From Industry 4.0 to Construction 5.0: Exploring the Path towards Human–Robot Collaboration in Construction. *Systems*, 11, 3, 152, Mar. 2023, doi: 10.3390/systems11030152.
5. Banerjee, P., Towards an Automated, Vigilant, and Strategic HRM Function in Industry 5.0, pp. 97–114, 2023, doi: 10.4018/978-1-6684-6745-9.ch006.
6. Agarwal, A., Mathur, P., Walia, S., *Journey of HR From Industry 1.0 to 5.0 and the Road Ahead*, pp. 172–184, 2023, doi: 10.4018/978-1-6684-6403-8.ch009.
7. Nowak, R.M., How resistance to change impairs innovation. *J. Strategy Manage.*, 16, 4, 609–629, Nov. 2023, doi: 10.1108/JSMA-08-2022-0144.
8. Moraru, G.-M. and Popa, D., Potential Resistance of Employees to Change in the Transition to Industry 5.0. *MATEC Web Conf.*, 343, 07005, Aug. 2021, doi: 10.1051/matecconf/202134307005.
9. Jha, S., Data Privacy and Security Issues in HR Analytics: Challenges and the Road Ahead, pp. 199–206, 2022, doi: 10.1007/978-981-16-2126-0_17.
10. Pooja, P. and Greeshma, B., Human Resource Security in IT Sector. *Int. J. Res. Appl. Sci. Eng. Technol.*, 10, 5, 3190–3194, May 2022, doi: 10.22214/ijraset.2022.42978.
11. Blikhar, M., Organizational and legal mechanism of protection of personal data. *Uzhhorod Natl. Univ. Herald. Series Law*, 2, 77, 31–36, Jul. 2023, doi: 10.24144/2307-3322.2023.77.2.4.
12. McCoy, M.S., *et al.*, Ethical Responsibilities for Companies That Process Personal Data. *Am. J. Bioethics*, 23, 11, 11–23, Nov. 2023, doi: 10.1080/15265161.2023.2209535.
13. Pratomo, A., Santoso, J., Nugroho, A., Fildansyah, R., Vandika, A., Analysis of Data Privacy Policy, Data Processing Ethics, and Technology Ethics Awareness on User Privacy Protection in West Java. *West Sci. Soc. Humanit. Stud.*, 2, 3, 412–422, 2024. 10.58812/wsshs.v2i03.715.

14. Evans, M., II and Britt, D.W., Resistance to Change. *Reprod. Sci.*, 30, 3, 835–853, Mar. 2023, doi: 10.1007/s43032-022-01015-9.
15. Bahl, S., Challenge of Implantation of Change Management Strategies: An Empirical Study. *Psychol. Educ.*, 55, 1, 384–392, 2018, doi: 10.48047/pne.2018.55.1.48.
16. Oueidat, D., The relationship between Talent Acquisition and Organizational Performance. (c2022). *LAU*, 2022, doi: 10.26756/th.2022.499.
17. Juhász, T., Horváth-Csikós, G., Gáspár, T., Gap analysis of future employee and employer on soft skills. *Hum. Syst. Manage.*, 42, 5, 527–542, Sep. 2023, doi: 10.3233/HSM-220161.
18. Trevelin, A.T.C., Neto, A.C., De Freitas Censoni, P.G., Work Disruptions and Skill Shifts: Insights on the Characterization, Importance and Development of Soft Skills. *Eur. J. Dev. Stud.*, 3, 4, 15–23, Jul. 2023, doi: 10.24018/ejdevelop.2023.3.4.275.
19. Giugliano, G., Laudante, E., Formati, F., Buono, M., Approaches and technologies for human-centered Industry 5.0. *Proyecta56 Ind. Des. J.*, 3, 78–90, 2023, https://doi.org/10.25267/P56-IDJ.2023.i3.05.
20. Varsha, P.S. and Nithya Shree, S., Embracing Data-Driven Analytics (DDA) in human resource management to measure the organization performance, in: *Handbook of Big Data Research Methods*, pp. 195–213, Edward Elgar Publishing, 2023, https://www.elgaronline.com/edcollchap/book/9781800888555/book-part-9781800888555-17.xml.
21. Pratap Singh Rathore, S., The Impact of AI on Recruitment and Selection Processes: Analysing the role of AI in automating and enhancing recruitment and selection procedures. *Int. J. Global Acad. Sci. Res.*, 2, 2, 78–93, Jun. 2023, doi: 10.55938/ijgasr.v2i2.50.

18

The Digital Transformation of HRM: Comparing Traditional and Technology-Based Practices

Pardeep Kaur

University School of Applied Management, Punjabi University, Patiala, Punjab, India

Abstract
In traditional times, organizations are doing various administrative tasks manually, which uses a lot of time and paperwork. In today's times, it is not possible to handle everything manually because of complicated business processes. Upgrading technology will bring about a big revolution in every aspect of organizations, including human resource management and its practices. With the advent of digital technologies, organizations gain the potential to enhance the efficiency and effectiveness of various HR practices, with less paperwork, and virtual meetings, which leads to less time wastage and more productivity. This study aims to explore the digital transformation of HRM and compare traditional and modern technology-based HRM practices. Moreover, this study focuses on potential risks, challenges faced by modern technology-based HRM practices, and major concerns related to digital transformation.

Keywords: Technology, digital transformation, HRM practices, administrative tasks

18.1 Introduction

The current period is known as the "digital age," and digital transformation has become a global consensus among enterprises. 5G, cloud computing,

Email: Kpardeepkor@gmail.com

Deepa Gupta, Mukul Gupta, Pawan Budhwar, Jim Westerman, Rajesh Kumar Dhanaraj and Balamurugan Balusamy (eds.) Human Capital Analytics: Exploring the HR Spectrum in Industry 5.0, (359–372) © 2025 Scrivener Publishing LLC

big data, artificial intelligence, IoT, blockchain, and other technologies have become the driving and enabling forces of work [1]. One of the business functions most affected by digital transformation is human resource management, which is a people-oriented approach. With this approach, a transition was made from personnel management to human resource management, and a strategic view was added to this understanding [2].

In this modern business world, the human resource management function has undergone a profound transformation. Basically, human resource management is about how organizations manage their most valuable asset, i.e., human resources. Due to globalization and the need to gain a competitive advantage, every company is pressuring the Human Resource Management department to adopt digital technologies to remain competitive. The intensive use of computers in business life and the increasing changes in technologies have influenced human resource management which gave rise to the ultimate result: digital human resource management. Thus, many firms have established digital human resource management systems to gather, process, and store information about human resources [3]. Human resource department reshapes their functions and processes into technology-based HRM practices, which is termed "Digital Transformation." This transformation replaced the traditional methods and practices with technology-based HRM Practices which leads to more efficiency and productivity, improved decision-making, and organizational outcomes. This digital transformation not only impacts the HR leaders and professionals but also influences the entire organization because it needs a massive change in business models and work designs. HR leaders and professionals also have to develop their skills and abilities to face technology-based challenges. Digital transformation plays a pivotal reshaping company culture, HRM processes, and practices, as well as employees' productivity and engagement. Digital transformation strategies can best be understood from a business-centric perspective. These strategies aim to transform products, processes, and all organizational aspects in response to new technology [4].

With this study, we seek deeper information about the digital transformation of HRM practices and processes. It is drawing a clear comparison between traditional and technology-based practices. It also finds the major challenges and risks associated with digital transformation how HR professionals adapt these technologies and face challenges to transform their departments and how these changes impact employees and overall organizational success.

18.2 Background of HRM and Related Work

The current period is a digital period. Every organization has to change its business models, processes, and practices to adapt to the changing environment.

Rapid developments in Internet technology have also diversified the understanding and operation of human resource management [5]. Professionals and academics need to know what human resource practices are necessary in this Industry 4.0 environment and digital revolution [6]. HR professionals and leaders use technology-based software and virtual platforms to perform their functions like recruitment, job application, attendance, employee profiles, performance evaluation, and payroll. This has reduced the burden of HR professionals because of lesser time consumption and paperless work and they are able to focus on other important functions such as talent management and goal achievement.

Technology has made HRM more efficient. It has expanded the scope of HR professionals. With the help of social media platforms such as LinkedIn, Instagram, and Twitter, it is easy to approach a wider pool of candidates for recruitment. Moreover, at the time of the interview, candidates need not be present in the organization. Virtual interviews are possible with the help of video conferencing tools such as Zoom and Google Meet. Training is provided to the selected candidates virtually through online learning platforms. Flexible work arrangement is a term in which employees are given the option to work remotely. It is also a practice of digital transformation.

During digital transformation, HRM faced many challenges such as data privacy and security.

The HR department must ensure that employee data are kept safe, secure, and protected. HR professional have to upgrade their skill set to effectively use HR tools and software.

18.2.1 Literature Review

S Strohmeier in his study "Digital human resource management: A conceptual clarification" discusses the concept of digital human resource management and its related concepts he uncovers that digital human resource management is an evolutionary advancement of previous conceptualizations of technology-based human resource management. He provides a conceptual basis for future work on digital human resource management [7]. Another study by **J Zhang and Z Chen**, titled "Exploring Human Resource Management Digital Transformation in the Digital Age," points out that digital HRM processes refer to all HRM functions via digital technologies. It is emphasized that although it brings many benefits for business, its negative impact cannot be ignored [8].

E Ertemsir and Y Bal in their study "Digital Transformation of HR: A Must OR Just Cost" discuss the digitalization process via its pros and cons. They also discuss how new applications such as artificial intelligence affect HRM processes and functions [9]. **PM Gilch and J Sieweke** in their study "Recruiting digital talent: The strategic role of recruitment in organizations' digital transformation" examine the role of recruitment in organizations' digital transformation. They found that the recruitment of digital talent as a new target group triggers change within the company in three ways. First, recruiters have realized the need to adapt their measures and processes to the new target group. Second, recruiters have developed a new self-understanding. Third, recruiters have recognized the need to support the organization's digital transformation by taking on a bridging function [10].

A Jani, A Muduli, and K Kishore in their study "Human resource transformation in India: examining the role digital human resource technology and human resource role" discussed that the transformation of HR processes can significantly enhance business outcomes. They also found that just implementation and adoption of digital technology may not guarantee HR transformation unless HR optimizes the specific role as per the need of the hour [11]. **C Bengtsson and M Bloom** in their study "Human Resource Management in a Digital Era" show that the implications of digitalization must be understood from a holistic perspective. The study shows that digitalization does not only reduce and automate administrative tasks but also has many implications for HR managers [12].

M Mosca in his study "Digitalization of HRM: A study of success factors and consequences in the last decade" identifies the factors that determine the success of digitalization of HRM and defines its consequences also. He found that the factors that determine the success of digitalization are limited and can be grouped into three categories: technological, organizational, and people factors, and he also analyzed that there are positive and negative consequences of digitalization [13]. **AP Chytiri** in his study "Human Resource Manager's role in The Digital Era" highlights HRM in the era of digitalization, emphasizes the roles of HR managers in contemporary organizations, and discusses the impact of technological changes on HR practices. The author also emphasizes the new digital role of human resource management [14]. **S Sharma** in his study "Digital Transformation Enhance Employee Performance" shows that with the digitalization of HR, organizations can enhance the performance of and build the talent leaders as per the organizational needs [15].

Another study by **S O'Reilly**, titled "An Examination of the Digital Transformation of Human Resources post Covid-19," suggests that the relationship between HR professionals and employees requires a new dynamic as working from home becomes more predominant in today's world [16]. **R Fenech, P Baguant, and D Ivanov** in their study "The changing role of human resource management in an era of digital transformation" explore the changing role of HRM in the era of digital transformation. They found that while digitalization impacts day-to-day HR practices and procedures, there is less emphasis on the role of HR in contributing to the strategy of digitalization [4]. **Pelin Vardarlier** in his study "Digital Transformation of Human Resource Management: Digital Applications and Strategic Tools in HRM" emphasizes that traditional methods are no longer sufficient for business procedures. The study focuses on the use of digital applications and software in the HRM of enterprises [5].

18.3 Research Methodology

This study focuses on a comparative analysis of traditional HRM practices and technology-based digital HRM.

18.3.1 Research Objectives

1. To identify the key factors of digital transformation in HRM.
2. To compare traditional HR practices and procedures with technology-based HR practices.
3. To identify the pros and cons of both.
4. To provide recommendations for the successful implementation of digital transformation of HRM.

Research Design: This study used a comparative research design that was conducted by selecting different organizations that represent different levels of digital transformation in HRM practices.
Sampling: Participants for the sample were selected with a purposive sampling technique. They were selected from different organizations and enterprises that have adopted technology-based HR practices and those that have not.
Sample Size: The sample size of this study was 60 respondents and determined on the basis of the availability of potential participants in the area.
Data Collection: The primary method of data collection is used. A survey questionnaire is used to collect data.

The questionnaire was distributed to HR professionals, managers, and employees of selected organizations to collect quantitative data on their experiences with both traditional and digital HRM.

18.3.2 Limitations of the Study

1. The sample of the study may not reflect the entire population of whole enterprises. So, the findings may not be generalizable to every industry or organization.
2. Purposive sampling is used which may result in selection bias, as participants who are willing to participate may have different experiences from those who are unwilling or unavailable.
3. There is a lack of control over all variables that are included in the study which may influence the use of traditional and modern technology-based HR practices, such as organizational culture, leadership style, and external factors.
4. The study has limited scope because it may not cover all aspects of digital HRM, such as the use of software artificial intelligence, social media, or mobile apps, and may not capture emerging or innovative practices.
5. The study was conducted in a limited time, which restrict the sample size, data collection methods, or data analysis techniques used.

18.4 Data Analysis and Interpretation

Table 18.1 Key drivers of digital transformation.

Primary drivers of digital transformation in HRM.		
Cost savings	15	25%
Increased efficiency	12	20%
Improved decision-making	16	26%
All of the above	17	28%

Interpretation

Table 18.1 shows the primary drivers of digital transformation in HRM. The majority of the respondents, i.e., 28%, think that all of the abovementioned factors are primary drivers of digital transformation. 26% of the respondents believe that digital transformation leads to better decision-making. 25% of the total respondents select cost saving as a primary driver and the rest of the respondents, i.e., 20% believe that it increased efficiency.

Overall, the above data suggest that it is beneficial to use digital HRM practices.

Interpretation

Table 18.2 suggest that changing employee expectations plays a major role in digital transformation in HRM. The majority of respondents, i.e., 43%, believe that changing employee expectations are driving a demand for a more personalized employee experience. Another 20% of the respondents believe that they require HR to adopt more efficient processes. Another 20% of the respondents believe that they create a need for more diverse HR tools. The remaining 16.6% of the respondents believe that all of the above expectations contribute to digital transformation in HRM.

Table 18.2 Employee expectations to digital transformation.

How do changing employee expectations contribute to digital transformation in HRM?		
They create a need for more diverse HR tools.	12	20%
They demand a more personalized employee experience.	26	43%
They require HR to adopt more efficient processes.	12	20%
All of the above.	10	16.6%

Interpretation

Table 18.3 shows that the majority of respondents, i.e., 41.6%, selected none of the above options indicating that there is no advantage of traditional HR practices over digital HRM. Another 21.6% of the respondents said that they are easier to implement. They believe that traditional HR practices are easier than technology-based HR practices. 18.3% of the respondents believe that traditional HR practices offer a more personalized employee experience. The remaining 15% of the respondents said that these practices are more cost-effective as compared to technology-based HR practices.

Table 18.3 Advantages of traditional HRM.

Which of the following is an advantage of traditional HR practices over technology-based HR practices?		
They are more cost-effective.	9	15%
They are easier to implement.	13	21.6%
They offer a more personalized employee experience.	11	18.3%
None of the above.	25	41.6%

Table 18.4 Disadvantages of technology based HRM.

What is the disadvantage of technology-based HR practices over traditional HR practices in performance management?		
They provide less real-time feedback.	25	41.6%
They can create bias in evaluations.	9	15%
They rely too much on data and analytics.	16	26.6%
None of the above.	10	16.6%

Interpretation

Table 18.4 shows the disadvantage of technology-based HR practices over traditional HR practices in performance management. The majority of respondents, i.e., 41.6%, said that technology-based HR practices provide less real-time feedback. It indicates that some organizations find it challenging to provide real-time and personalized feedback to employees. 26.6% of the respondents believe that technology-based HR practices rely too much on data and analytics. Another 15% of respondents believe that technology-based HR practices can create bias in evaluations. The remaining 16.6% selected none of the above options. They believe that there is no disadvantage to technology-based HR practices in performance management.

Interpretation

Table 18.5 shows that the use of technology impacts the employee experience. The majority of the respondents, i.e., 48.3%, believe that it provides employees with more opportunities for engagement. 25% of the respondents show that it creates more bureaucratic processes. 18.33% of the respondents believe that the use of technology makes the employee experience less.

Overall, the above results show that the use of technology has both positive and negative impacts on employee experience.

Table 18.5 Impact of use of technology on employee experience.

How does the use of technology impact the employee experience?		
It makes the experience less personalized.	11	18.33%
It provides employees with more opportunities for engagement.	29	48.33%
It creates more bureaucratic processes.	15	25%
None of the above.	5	8.3%

Interpretation

Table 18.6 shows the data of how HR manages the data of employees with the use of technology. The majority of the respondents, i.e., 40%, believe that with the use of technology-based HR practices, it is easy to track employee absences. Another 31.6% of the respondents believe that technology is reducing the need for feedback from employees. Another 21.6% of the respondents show that it is decreasing the need for cybersecurity measures. The remaining 6.6% of the respondents choose none of the above options.

Table 18.6 How technology changes the way HR manages employee data.

What is an example of how technology is changing the way HR manages employee data?		
It simplifies tracking employee absences.	24	40%
It reduces the need for employee feedback.	19	31.6%
It decreases the need for cybersecurity measures.	13	21.6%
None of the above.	4	6.6%

Table 18.7 Key strategies for navigating digital transformation.

What is a key strategy for successfully navigating the digital transformation of HRM?		
Adopting technology for technology's sake.	14	23.3%
Engaging employees in the transformation process.	11	18.3%
Ignoring resistance from employees.	25	41.6%
None of the above	10	16.6%

Interpretation

Table 18.7 shows a key strategy for successfully navigating the digital transformation of HRM. The majority of the respondents, i.e., 41.6%, believe that ignoring resistance from employees is a key strategy for successfully navigating the digital transformation of HRM. 23.3% of the respondents believe that Adopting technology for technology's sake is a key strategy for successfully navigating the digital transformation of HRM. 18.3% of the respondents believe that engaging employees in the transformation process is a key strategy for successfully navigating the digital transformation of HRM.

Overall, it indicates that the engagement of employees is a key strategy in the digital transformation of HRM and organizations should involve employees.

Interpretation

Table 18.8 shows an example of how HR can use technology to better support employee development. Almost half of the respondents, i.e., 46.6%, selected that organizations can use technology to provide online training modules to employees. 21.6% of the respondents believe that HR can use technology by reducing opportunities for employee feedback. 25% of the respondents selected the option that HR can use technology by increasing bureaucratic processes.

Overall, the results suggest that these technology-based techniques help HR to better support employee development in many ways.

Table 18.8 Use of technology for better employee development.

What is an example of how HR can use technology to better support employee development?		
By providing online training modules.	28	46.6%
By reducing opportunities for employee feedback.	13	21.6%
By increasing bureaucratic processes.	15	25%
None of the above.	4	6.6%

Table 18.9 Key considerations for organizations while implementing technology based HRM.

What is a key consideration for organizations when implementing new technology-based HR practices?		
Ensuring that the technology is the most expensive on the market.	16	26.60%
Ensuring that the technology meets the specific needs of the organization.	29	48.30%
Focusing only on cost savings.	11	18.30%
None of the above.	4	6.60%

Interpretation

Table 18.9 shows key considerations for organizations when implementing new technology-based HR practices. The majority of the respondents, i.e., 48.3%, believe that a key consideration for organizations when implementing new technology-based HR practices ensures that the technology meets the specific needs of the organization. 26.60% of the respondents believe that the technology is the most expensive on the market. 18.30% of the respondents believe that organizations are focusing only on cost savings when implementing new technology-based HR practices.

Conclusion

In conclusion, the revolution made by the digital transformation of HRM brings new opportunities and challenges for organizations. Technology-based HRM practices have taken the place of traditional HR practices and processes. It brings lots of changes in the business processes such as the use of social media apps, cloud computing, and HR analytics which facilitate performance management, improved decision-making, learning and development, employee growth, and engagement. However, the use of technology also faced challenges such as data privacy, security issues, ethical considerations, too much reliability on tools, etc. So, HR professionals and managers have to balance it. Overall, digital transformation represents an update to traditional methods of HR practices, and organizations should adopt this environment to beat this competitive business environment.

References

1. Yu, Z. and JInajun, N., How to achieve HRM digital transformation, Available at: https://www.sohu.com/a/400600846_343325, 2020.
2. Kirilmaz, S.K., Digital transformation in human resources management: investigation of digital hrm practices of businesses. *Res. J. Bus. Manag.*, 7, 3, 188–200, 2020.
3. Vardarlier, P. and Ozsahin, M., Digital transformation of human resource management: Social media's performance effect. *Int. J. Innov. Technol. Manag.*, 18, 03, 2150005-1–2150005-22, 2021.
4. Fenech, R., Baguant, P., Ivanov, D., The changing role of human resource management in an era of digital transformation. *Int. J. Entrep.*, *22*, 2, 166–175, 2019.
5. Vardarlier, P., Digital transformation of human resource management: digital applications and strategic tools in HRM. *Digital Bus. Strategies Blockchain Ecosyst. Transformational Des. Future Global Bus.*, 239–264, 2020.
6. Nicolás-Agustín, A., Jiménez-Jiménez, D., Maeso-Fernandez, F., The role of human resource practices in the implementation of digital transformation. *Int. J. Manpow.*, *43*, 2, 395–410, 2022.
7. Strohmeier, S., Digital human resource management: A conceptual clarification. *Ger. J. Hum. Resour. Manag.*, 34, 3, 345–365, 2020.
8. Zhang, J. and Chen, Z., Exploring Human Resource Management Digital Transformation in the Digital Age. *J. Knowl. Econ.*, 1–17, 2023.
9. Ertemsir, E. and Bal, Y., Digital Transformation of HR: A Must or Just Cost. *Bus. Manag. Pract.*, 73, 73–86, 2019.
10. Gilch, P.M. and Sieweke, J., Recruiting digital talent: The strategic role of recruitment in organisations' digital transformation. *Ger. J. Hum. Resour. Manag.*, *35*, 1, 53–82, 2021.
11. Jani, A., Muduli, A., Kishore, K., Human resource transformation in India: examining the role digital human resource technology and human resource role. *Int. J. Organ. Anal.*, *31*, 4, 959–972, 2021.
12. Bengtsson, C. and Bloom, M., Human Resource Management in a Digital Era. *LUP Stud. Pap.*, 0–30, 2017.
13. Mosca, M., Digitalization of HRM: A study of success factors and consequences in the last decade, University of Twente, 2020, Master's thesis.
14. Chytiri, A.P., Human Resource Managers' role in the Digital Era. *J. Bus. Econ.*, 62–72, 2019.
15. Sharma, S., Digital Transformation Enhance Employee Performance. *Int'l. JL Mgmt. Human.*, *4*, 3791, 2021.
16. O'Reilly, S., An Examination of the Digital Transformation of Human Resources post Covid-19, Dublin, National College of Ireland, Doctoral dissertation.

19

Technological Implementation of Industry 5.0 at Kinara Capital – A People's Welfare Organization

Kala Raja Mohan[1]*, R. Narmada Devi[2], Nagadevi Bala Nagaram[2], Sathish Kumar Kumaravel[2] and Regan Murugesan[2]

[1]*Department of Mathematics, Panimalar Engineering College, Poonamallee, Chennai, India*

[2]*Department of Mathematics, Vel Tech Rangarajan Dr. Sagunthala R&D Institute of Science and Technology, Avadi, Chennai, India*

Abstract

The role of financial industries in building the growth of various other industries is vital. Most of the entrepreneurs depend on these types of financial industries for their investment. These industries are the basis for bringing up many successful industrialists. These industries also, in turn, lay the foundation for the financial development of many families by providing employment opportunities. Many of these industries also come up with foreign collaboration. This helps the domestic countries to achieve betterment in both the financial and employment sectors.

This chapter aims to bring out a study on one such financial organization. Financial institutions nowadays make use of many technological advancement techniques to make their work easy and to reduce their transaction timings. Kinara Capital is a non-banking financial organization that provides business loans for needy people. It has been started in 2011 in Bangalore. The growth of the company in this short period of time is remarkable. The organization makes use of recent advancements in technology with an aim to benefit both the employees and their customers. The various techniques applied in the organization through which the mentioned financial industry has reached this tremendous growth and the team that acts behind the company for the people's welfare are to be discussed in this chapter.

Keywords: Kinara capital, business loan, Industry 5.0, employee, customer welfare

**Corresponding author*: kalamohan24@yahoo.co.in

Deepa Gupta, Mukul Gupta, Pawan Budhwar, Jim Westerman, Rajesh Kumar Dhanaraj and Balamurugan Balusamy (eds.) Human Capital Analytics: Exploring the HR Spectrum in Industry 5.0, (373–382) © 2025 Scrivener Publishing LLC

19.1 Introduction

The development of each organization depends on the human resource department. Their involvement in various aspects of work is remarkable. They involve themselves in finding solutions to various issues faced by the employees. The only department that has tied up with all other departments is the human resource department. Starting from entry to exit of an employee happens through the HR team. Initially, their work was done manually which took a lot of time and manpower to complete. At a later stage, a systematic approach to their work happened. An advanced internet provided an opportunity to make an easy approach to their work. Industry 5.0 provides a well-improved path to bring good results. The various works done by researchers on Industry 5.0 have been listed herewith as a literature survey.

Barbara Aquilani in the year 2020 investigated the conversion of Industry 4.0 to Industry 5.0 and its various challenges [9]. Ekaterina V. Orlova in 2021 discussed professional development in the society in Industry 5.0 [13]. Susan Tee Suan Chin in 2021 performed a study on emotional intelligence to analyze the workspace environmental change in Industry 5.0 [24].

Alejandro Cortes-Leal *et al.* in the year 2022 employed a smart management system for workers making use of Industry 5.0 [3]. Amir Mehdiabadi *et al.* in 2022 investigated the application of Industry 5.0 in the banking sector [6]. Amr Adel *et al.* in the same year investigated the various challenges and solutions in the research area using Industry 5.0 [7]. Dimitris Mourtzis *et al.* in 2022 presented a study on the advantages of transition from Industry 4.0 to Industry 5.0 and the opportunities from it [11]. Dr. Meenu Sharma in 2022 narrated the transmission of Industry 5.0 after the pandemic environment [12]. Rini Ade Octaviany *et al.* in the year 2022 proposed a strategy to bring a revolution in human resource management in Industry 5.0 [21]. Sandra Grabowska *et al.* in 2022 developed methods in introducing the sustainability of Industry 5.2 [22]. S D Ganer *et al.* in 2022 performed an analytical study in improvising the human resource management techniques applying Industry 5.0 [23]. Zahoor Ahmed Soomro *et al.* in 2022 implemented Industry 5.0 in the banking sector [26].

Abirami Raja Santhi and Padmakumar Muthuswamy have performed a comparative study between Industry 4.0 and Industry 5.0 in the year 2023 [1]. In the same year, Agnieszka Laskowska and Jan Franciszek Laskowski discussed the involvement of capital management in Industry 5.0 with respect to silver generation [2]. Attila Totha *et al.* in 2023 discussed the collaboration of human-centric relations with Industry 5.0 [8].

Dimitris Mourtzis *et al.* in 2023 discussed the interface between machine and human using Industry 5.0 [10]. Erhan Aydin *et al.* in the year 2023 discussed gender inequality in software development in the human resource industry in Industry 5.0 [14]. Hakan Kuru in 2023 presented a diplomatic approach in establishing Industry 5.0 in employee wellness [15]. Jakub Pizo and Arkadiusz Gola in 2023 the relationship between humans and machines in Industry 5.0 [16]. Joaquín Ordieres-Mere *et al.* in the year 2023 explained the paradigm in integrating the value of humans together with machines in Industry 5.0 [17]. Moin Khan *et al.* in 2023 introduced the strategy to overcome the difficulties in Industry 4.0 to develop into Industry 5.0 [18]. Mohammad Syarief Nur Maulana *et al.* in 2023 performed a SWOT analysis to identify the decision related to human resource management in Industry 5.0 [19]. Morteza Ghobakhloo *et al.* in 2023 investigated sustainable management techniques in Industry 5.0 [20]. Tazim Ahmed *et al.* in the year 2023 implemented artificial intelligence in Industry 5.0 from a supply chain perspective [25].

Ali Nauman *et al.* in the year 2024 applied MEC devices in introducing techniques with Industry 5.0 in the process of optimization of the resource [4]. Amberlyn Bonello *et al.* in 2024 discussed the difficult factor of age using workstations with human-centered operations in Industry 5.0 [5]. This chapter brings about a case study on the banking sector of Kinara Capital. The responsibilities of the human resource department in developing the organization in various aspects are discussed.

19.2 Kinara Capital

Kinara Capital formerly known as "Visage Holdings and Finance Private Limited" is a non-banking finance corporation with a motive to help entrepreneurs develop their business in various aspects. Ms. Hardika Shah, the founder and COE together with Mr. Thirunavukarasu, the COO, inaugurated the organization with social responsibility to motivate and support the MSME entrepreneurs who are in need of financial backlog. When an entrepreneur develops their business in a positive direction, it in turn helps the family and the society to develop. Kinara Capital thus aims to provide a helping hand to develop their business. Being a woman, in order to develop women entrepreneurs, separate business loans are also introduced. Loans to support working capital and machinery purchases are given.

Employees are the backbone of the development of every organization. In addition to employee welfare, the organization provides concentration to the members of the family. This provides a positive vibe from the total family which helps in the development of the organization. This care provided by the HR team is possible only with the support of the founder.

With Bangalore as a head office, the organization was inaugurated in the year 2011. The organization has an increased count of more than 125 renowned branches in more than 100 cities all over India. The growth of the organization in more than 2 decades proves the interest and hope of the public toward the organization.

19.3 HR Team Responsibility

The HR team of every organization acts as the heart of it. Their service in all aspects is adorable, which aims at the development of both the employee and the employer. Kinara also has a well-capable HR team. Listing out the bonding between the HR team, employee, and employer gives an understanding of their effort. Making use of various techniques, the bonding is maintained in a better aspect.

19.3.1 Growth of the Organization

The growth of any organization depends on various aspects with the help of the human resource and development team. Kinara Capital implements various innovative ideas in developing the interest of the employees toward the organization. Implementation of Industry 5.0 by the HR team helps the organization's development.

19.3.2 Employee Growth

Industry 5.0 helps the organization to work in a stress-free environment. The human resource and development team takes care of every employee in developing positive thoughts. The HR team's activities in showing interest in the family of the employees too are remarkable. They involve themselves in conducting various activities which aim to enrich the interest of the whole family. This makes the employees more interested in their job. This also helps to make the workers stay back in the organization for a long period with full satisfaction.

19.3.3 Industry 5.0

The manufacturing processes in the fourth-generation revolution, referred to as Industry 4.0, make use of the integration of digital technologies.

Big data, the Internet of Things, artificial intelligence, and automation are applied in the process of creating smart and efficient output. To make more efficient and easy manufacturing, an advanced level of Industry 5.0 is introduced. The advancement has brought about many smart machines like robots to produce better output.

19.3.4 Predix

The software involved in all aspects of the loan is done with the help of Predix software. All transactions are done with the help of this software. All queries, transactions, loan applications, and disbursements are done with this software. This software which is created according to the requirement of the organization is user-friendly and the time taken in each aspect is less. This makes the employees work on the software with full interest.

19.4 Highlights of HR in Employee Welfare

In every organization, the role of HR plays a very important role. They play various roles in bringing up both the employee's and the organization's health. The HR team of Kinara also plays a significant role. A few of them are listed below.

19.4.1 Newsletter

Many organizations have newsletters to show the happenings. Similarly, Kinara also releases a newsletter every month with a view to taking care of the employee's welfare in all aspects. The various aspects of the content as listed underneath.

- **Department Happenings:** The happenings of the organization irrespective of the state are listed in the newsletter. This information all over the organization helps the employees to gain confidence in their work.
- **Work Anniversary:** The employees who cross their work anniversary in the respective month are highlighted in the newsletter. This information makes employees feel safe with their employment.
- **Appreciation for the Month:** With a motive to encourage the employees and to gain mental strength, the appreciation for their work is spotlighted in the newsletter.

- **Stories to Celebrate:** Kinara provides an opportunity to share their feelings and thoughts on their colleagues in the organization under this tile.
- **Top Performing Branches:** In order to encourage team spirit, every month top performing branches are identified and congratulated under this tag and mentioned in the newsletter.
- **Harmony Club:** The club makes a platform to share information related to their field and helps employees to get updated. This information is shared in a newsletter to gain the importance in the field.
- **Learning and Development:** This section of the newsletter covers the information on various learning resources available to keep the employees updated on their organization software. The materials are also shared online with employees for easy access.
- **IJP and Promotions:** Internal Job Postings are conducted whenever needed and whoever gets promoted is congratulated under this section of the newsletter to make other employees feel confident.
- **Puzzle Time:** In order to make the employees engage in active thinking modules, the puzzle time section is included in the newsletter and whoever comes up with a correct answer on a ranking basis are spotlighted.
- **Kids Zone:** The management also likes to engage the kids of the employees in the organizational activities. The section kids zone comes up with a question every month and the kids who give correct answers are identified and spotlighted in the next month's magazine.
- **Knowledge Corner:** This section provides shortcut keys or any related information about the software used by the organization, which helps to reduce the time used by the employees in various aspects.
- **Special News:** General happenings or news happening in the month are highlighted to make the employees know the general information in real-time life.
- **Activity Calendar:** Various activities are conducted by the HR team related to both mental and physical welfare. The information related to those activities is shared under this title.

19.4.2 Mental Wellness Stories

Every employee's stories based on mental and physical health are being shared. These stories are based on natural behavior and the difficulty of overcoming naturally arising difficulties.

19.4.3 Health Tips

Health tips are shared on a daily basis with all the employees of the organization, which shows the concern given by them to the employees. In turn, it also helps the family when needed.

19.4.4 Birthday and Work Anniversary Wishes

As an appreciation of the service done by the employees, their work anniversaries are shared with all the employees through their official mail. The work anniversary wishes are given to all employees irrespective of the postings. This builds confidence for newly joined employees to have thought that they a joined a well-established organization. Taking individual care of the employees, every day, wishes for those who have birthdays have also been shared with all employees. This helps to develop a rapport among all the employees in the organization. This provides a healthy relationship among the employees. This is also remarkable work done by the HR team with the help of automation techniques.

19.4.5 Children's Day Celebration

Most of the industries concentrate on the individual employees only in various aspects. People welfare organizations like Kinara concentrate on the kids of employees also. They conduct competitions for children's day every year. These competitions are conducted online, which helps to connect the kids of the entire state. This helps to build confidence among kids. In education institutions, most of the children get chance to compete among their known class friends only. But Kinara provides a platform for employee's kids also to build their competitive talent. In addition to prizes, they also encourage the kids by providing gifts for all the kids who participated. HR team involves themselves in such a way that the kids eagerly expect the arrival of children's day every year.

19.4.6 Annual Day Celebration

Annual day is celebrated every year at some renowned venue. It starts with a meeting which is aimed to discuss the annual happenings of the year. Employees are given awards based on their performance in the year. The effort made by them throughout the year gets recognized in the meeting. Discussion on the future plan takes place followed by a delicious lunch. The various sports activities are conducted and the winning person gets recognized.

19.5 Kinara and Industry 5.0

Industry 5.0 aims to make use of artificial intelligence, robotics, machine learning, and automation techniques to find out best results. Kinara makes use of artificial intelligence and machine learning to bring the best possibility of work. Eligibility of the loans, automatic update of money transactions, leave and payroll calculations, assessment of employee's queries, and the calculation of EMI deductions and additions are automatically done with the help of these techniques.

Institution could play a significant role in facilitating the transition to Industry 5.0 by providing the necessary funding and support for businesses embracing this paradigm shift. This might involve financing initiatives aimed at developing technologies that enhance human-machine collaboration, promoting ethical AI applications, supporting workforce training programs for the digital age, and investing in sustainable and socially responsible businesses.

Kinara Capital's involvement in Industry 5.0 could also extend to fostering partnerships and collaborations with organizations and start-ups that are pioneering innovative solutions in areas such as augmented reality, human-robot interaction, personalized healthcare, and environmental conservation. By aligning its strategies with the principles of Industry 5.0, Kinara Capital cannot only contribute to economic growth but also help build a more equitable and human-centered future.

19.6 Conclusion

HR teams act as the heart of any organization. Industry 5.0 helps the team to develop their organization in all aspects. Kinara Capital makes use of the techniques of Industry 5.0 for the growth and development of employees, employers, entrepreneurs, society, and many more. This chapter lists the various aspects in which the organization makes use of Industry 5.0 for its positive development.

References

1. Abirami, R.S. and Muthuswamy, P., Industry 5.0 or industry 4.0S? Introduction to industry 4.0 and a peek into the prospective industry 5.0 technologies. *Int. J. Interact. Des. Manuf.*, 17, 947–979, 2023.
2. Laskowska, A. and Laskowski, J.F., "Silver" Generation at Work—Implications for Sustainable Human Capital Management in the Industry 5.0 Era. *Sustainability*, 15, 1–15, 2023.
3. Cortes-Leal, A., Cardenas, C., Del-Valle-Soto, C., Maintenance 5.0: Towards a Worker-in-the-Loop Framework for Resilient Smart Manufacturing. *Appl. Sci.*, 12, 1–34, 2022.
4. Nauman, A., Ullah Khan, W., Aldehim, G., Alqahtani, H., Alruwais, N., Al Duhayyim, M., Devi, K., Min, H., Nkenyereye, L., Communication and computational resource optimization for Industry 5.0 smart devices empowered by MEC. *J. King Saud Univ. Comput. Inf. Sci.*, 36, 1–11, 2024.
5. Bonello, A., Francalanza, E., Refalo, P., Smart and Sustainable Human-Centred Workstations for Operators with Disability in the Age of Industry 5.0: A Systematic Review. *Sustainability*, 16, 1–16, 2024.
6. Mehdiabadi, A., Shahabi, V., Shamsinejad, S., Amiri, M., Spulbar, C., Birau, R., Investigating Industry 5.0 and Its Impact on the Banking Industry: Requirements, Approaches and Communications. *Appl. Sci.*, 12, 2156, 2022.
7. Amr, A., Future of industry 5.0 in society: Human-centric Solutions, Challenges and Prospective Research Areas. *J. Cloud Comput.*, 40, 1–15, 2022.
8. Totha, A., Nagy, L., Kennedy, R., Bohus, B., Abonyi, J., Ruppert, T., The human-centric Industry 5.0 collaboration architecture. *MethodsX*, Article ID 102260, 1–8, 2023.
9. Aquilani, B., Piccarozzi, M., Abbate, T., Codini, A., The Role of Open Innovation and Value Co-creation in the Challenging Transition from Industry 4.0 to Society 5.0: Toward a Theoretical Framework. *Sustainability*, 12, 1–21, 2020.
10. Mourtzis, D., Angelopoulos, J., Panopoulos, N., The Future of the Human-Machine Interface (HMI) in Society 5.0. *Future Internet*, 15, 162, 2023.
11. Mourtzis, D., Angelopoulos, J., Panopoulos, N., A Literature Review of the Challenges and Opportunities of the Transition from Industry 4.0 to Society 5.0, vol. 15, p. 6276, 2022.
12. Sharma, M., Industry 5.0 Post Pandemic Transformation: A Study Of Challenges To Inclusive Work Environment, vol. 5, pp. 633–638, 2022.

13. Orlova, E.V., Design of Personal Trajectories for Employees' Professional Development in the Knowledge Society under Industry 5.0. *Social Sci.*, 10, 1–29, 2021.
14. Aydin, E., Rahman, M., Ozeren, E., Does Industry 5.0 Reproduce Gender (In)equalities at Organisations? Understanding the Interaction of Human Resources and Software Development Teams in Supplying Human Capitals. *Inf. Syst. Front.*, 1–15, 2023.
15. Kuru, H., Understanding employee wellness in industry 5.0: A systematic review. *J. Ekonomi*, 9, 32–34, 2023.
16. Pizo, J. and Gola, A., Human–Machine Relationship—Perspective and Future Roadmap for Industry 5.0 Solutions. *Machines*, 11, 1–22, 2023.
17. Ordieres-Mere, J., Gutierrez, M., Villalba-Díez, J., Toward the industry 5.0 paradigm: Increasing value creation through the robust integration of humans and machines. *Comput. Ind.*, 150, 1–15, 2023.
18. Khan, M., Haleem, A., Javaid, M., Changes and Improvements in Industry 5.0: A strategic approach to overcome the challenges of Industry 4.0. *Green Technol. Sustainability*, 1, 1–9, 2023.
19. Maulana, M.S.N., SWOT Analysis in a Disruptive 5.0 Society on Human Resources Management. *Int. J. Marketing Hum. Resour. Res.*, 4, 2, 80–86, 2023.
20. Ghobakhloo, M., Iranmanesh, M., Foroughi, B., Tirkolaee, E.B., Asadi, S., Amran, A., Industry 5.0 implications for inclusive sustainable manufacturing: An evidence-knowledge-based strategic roadmap. *J. Clean. Prod.*, 417, 1–16, 2023.
21. Octaviany, R.A., Sihotang, W., Simarmata, P.S., Rahman, A., Muliati, A., Human Resource Development Strategy As Preparation For The Industrial Revolution Era 5.0. *Int. J. Educ. Res. Soc. Sci.*, 1157–1164, 2022.
22. Grabowska, S., Saniuk, S., Gajdzik, B., Industry 5.0: improving humanization and sustainability of Industry 4.0. *Scientometrics*, 127, 3117–3144, 2022.
23. Ganer, S.D., Kediya, S.O., Suchak, A.K., Dey, S.K., Band, G., Analytical study of HRM practices in industry 5.0. *International Conference on Advances in Mechanical Engineering*, pp. 1–9, 2022.
24. Tee Suan Chin, S., Influence of Emotional Intelligence on the Workforce for Industry 5.0. *J. Hum. Resour. Manage. Res.*, 2021, 1–7, 2021.
25. Tazim, A., Lekha Karmaker, C., Benta Nasir, S., Moktadir, A., Kumar Paul, S., Modeling the artificial intelligence-based imperatives of industry 5.0 towards resilient supply chains: A post-COVID-19 pandemic perspective, vol. 177, pp. 1–12, 2023.
26. Soomro, Z.A., Ali, Q., Parveen, S., Diffusion of Industry 5.0 in the financial sector: A developmental study. *BAM*, 1, 1–10, 2022.

Index

ADDIE model, 202
Administrative, 103–104
Administrative tasks, 359, 362
Age of information and telecommunication, 67, 68
Agenda 2030, 311
Agile HR practices, 88, 354
AI, 325, 327, 331
Algorithmic bias, 54
All-inclusive view of DEI experience, 300
Analytics, 153–157, 308, 313–315, 317–319, 323
Artificial intelligence (AI), 19–20, 42, 43, 50, 83, 86, 90–93, 94, 114, 309–310, 313, 347, 360, 362, 364
Artificial intelligence of things (AIoT), 84
Augmented reality (AR), 41, 314
Automatic, 326
Automation, 54

Belonging and inclusion, 299
Bias in AI-driven HR, 350
Big data analytics, 352
Blockchain, 20, 42, 353
Business, 373, 375, 380
Business environment, 66, 101–104, 107, 108

Candidate assessment, 222
Career coaching, 245
Career dimensions, 241
Change management, 351
Cloud storage vs. on-premise storage, 200
Cloud-based HR systems, 42
Cobots, 328, 330
Collaborative decision-making, 41
Collaborative robotics, 332
Common data quality issues, 197
Compliance with regulations (GDPR, CCPA), 187
Continuous learning, 39, 41
Co-operative human robot, 327
Cost efficiency, 171
Cross-sectional design, 120
Customization, 327
Cyber warfare, 331
Cyber-physical systems, 33
Cybersecurity in HR, 352

Data analytics, 42, 46, 48
Data cleansing techniques, 199
Data driven, 144, 145, 146, 148, 149
Data management solutions, 132–134
Data privacy, 54
Data privacy & security, 351
Data privacy and compliance considerations, 187
Data quality and safekeeping, 233
Data security, 117
Data-driven culture, 131
Data-driven decision making, 353
Data-driven insights, 180
Data-driven strategies, 284–285
Decision science, 202
Decision-making models, 250

DEI, 286–288
DEI software, 293
Descriptive analysis, 205
Descriptive analytics, 240
Different sectors, 6, 16
Digital data collection, 173
Digital data collection methods, 190
Digital insurgency, 86
Digital revolution, 67
Digital transformation, 37, 91–92, 356, 359–366, 368–371
Digital twins, 309324
Digitalization, 27, 362, 363, 371
Disaster preparedness, 316
Diversification, 159
Diversity, equity, and inclusion (DEI), 356
Domain expertise, 231

Eco friendly, 326
Economic, 104–106
Economic development, 66
Effective leadership, 332
E-HRM, 83
Emerging technologies, 40–42, 84
Emotional diagnostics, 158
Emotional intelligence, 37, 39
Employee, 373–381
Employee engagement, 46, 50, 116, 145, 147, 155, 156, 244, 354
Employee experience, 348
Employee insights, 308
Employee motivation, 246
Employee performance, 115
Employee potential, 249
Employee recognition, 246
Employee retention, 46, 239
Employee surveillance, 352
Employee talent and acquisition, 239
Employee well-being, 43, 54
Enhanced employee development, 171
Enhanced organizational agility, 182
Entrepreneur, 373
Environment, 326, 327, 329, 332
Ethical AI automation, 85, 88, 94, 95
Ethical considerations, 36, 54
Ethical considerations in HR, 350
Ethical issues, 115
Ethical procedures, 132–134
Evaluation of human capital, 264, 276
Evidence-based decision making, 131

Factors of employee potential, 241
Fairness and bias, 117
Fifth industrial development, 65, 67, 69, 70, 72, 75, 76, 77, 78
Fifth industrial revolution, 305–306, 309, 312, 314–315, 318, 323
First industrial revolution, 71
Flexible workforce, 357
Flight risk prediction, 223
Forecasting price, 309, 310
Fourth industrial revolution, 85, 306–307, 309
Fundamental dimensions, 241
Future of work, 357

Gamification, 42
GDPR & HR data protection, 351
Generative design, 309
Growth dimensions, 241

HR analytics, 103
HR 5.0, 101–102, 106, 108, 347
HR analytics, 19–20
HR as a business partner, 356
HR automation, 354
HR chatbots, 348
HR digital literacy, 356
HR employees, 107–108
HR evolution (HR 1.0 to HR 5.0), 349
HR functions, 101–102, 104, 108
HR information, 146
HR innovation, 355
HR leadership in digital age, 355
HR metrics, 240

HR metrics and KPIs, 357
HR professionals, 101–102, 104, 106–107
HR self-service portals, 353
HR spectrum, 101102
HR-driven organizational culture, 355
HRIS, 103
HRM, 101–103, 108
HRM practices, 359, 360, 363, 365, 370, 371
Human capital, 66, 71, 78, 144, 145, 148, 149, 150, 201
Human capital analytics (HCA), 7–8, 32, 45–46, 114, 305–306, 308, 338–339, 347
Human capital analytics in industry 5.0 for sustainable growth, 337
Human capital practices, 269
Human capital return on investment (HCROI), 267
Human capital value added (HCVA), 267
Human centric approach, 67, 73
Human centricity, 310
Human economic value added (HEVA), 267
Human machine collaboration, 84–85
Human resource, 102108
Human resource analytics (HR analytics), 239
Human resource management (HRM), 65, 71, 75, 359–363, 371
Human resource planning, 226
Human resources, 65, 66, 67, 70
Human robot co-working (HRC), 326, 327, 328, 329, 332
Human-centered, 23
Human-centric innovation, 41
Human-machine collaboration, 36–37
Humanoids, 327

Inclusion, 292–293
Industrial environment, 67
Industrial revolution, 65, 66, 68, 69, 71, 72, 73, 262, 326
Industry 1. 0, 68, 77
Industry 2.0, 68
Industry 3.0, 68
Industry 4.0, 14–15, 67, 68, 69, 70, 71, 72
Industry 5.0, 6–7, 13, 33–38, 65, 66, 67, 68, 69, 70, 71, 72, 73, 74, 75, 77, 82–84, 87–89, 91, 94–97, 102–103, 108, 306–310, 312–324, 326, 327, 328, 331, 332, 342–344, 349, 373–377, 380
Information technology (IT), 5
Informed decision-making, 169
Internet of Things (IoT), 21
IoMT, 93
IoT, 90, 92, 94
IoT gadgets, 316
IoT sensors, 91
Irresponsible resource consumption and production, 316
Isomorphism, 207
IT and HR collaboration, 131

K.A.S.H. model, 95
Key HR metrics and KPIs, 204
Kinara capital, 373–376, 380
KPIs, 201

Labour market, 216
Leadership influence, 246
Leadership potential, 241
Learning and development, 227
Learning solutions, 116
Legal and compliance issues, 351
Longitudinal design, 132–134

Machine learning (ML), 42, 43, 114, 348
Manufacturing sector, 325327
Millennium development goals (MDGs), 311
Mobility as a service (MaaS), 93, 94

Natural language processing (NLP), 348
Network analysis, 286
Newsletter, 377, 378

Optimize workforce management, 178
Optimizing workforce size, 227
Organizational climate, 241
Organizational culture, 246
Organizational outcomes, 115
Organizational performance, 246
Overfitting and underfitting, 230

People analytics, 23–24, 308
Performance data, 116
Performance evaluation, 244
Performance management, 46, 43, 226, 247, 348
Performance metrics, 225
Personalized employee development, 181
Personalized interventions, 223
Practical issues, 115
Predictive analysis, 206
Predictive analytics, 42, 46, 206, 220–221, 224, 235, 240
Predictive maintenance, 309
Predix, 377
Prescriptive analysis, 206
Prescriptive analytics, 240
Productiveness 5.0, 82, 97
Productivity and efficiency, 246
Proliferation, 205
Proof-of-concept projects, 132–134

Quantitative study, 120

Recruitment analytics, 222
Remote work, 353
Resilience, 310
Resilient cities, 316
Resistance to change, 356
Resource allocation, 48
Resource-based view (RBV), 117
Retention, 223
Retention rate, 205
Reward management, 246
Robotic process automation (RPA), 116
Robotics, 7, 14, 114, 312, 314, 324, 329, 331

Sampling techniques, 121
Scalability issues, 231
SDGs with human capital strategies, 340–341
Secondary data, 121
Self organizing logistics (SoL), 93, 94
Sentiment analysis, 43, 285
SHRM, 82
Skill assessment, 46
Skill development and upskilling, 350
Smart city technologies, 316
Smart manufacturing, 326
Smart mobility, 93
Social, 105–106
Social dynamics, 329
Social exchange theory, 117
Society, 374, 375, 381
Strategic decision-making, 239
Strategic HR, 350
Strategic planning, 101–110
Strategic workforce planning, 170
Strategies, 148, 149, 153, 154
Stratified sampling, 121
Structural equation modeling (SEM), 115
Succession planning, 46, 225
Supportive bright passage system (S-BPS), 93
Survey methodology, 132–134
Sustainability, 31, 36, 307, 309–310, 314–316, 318, 323–324, 326
Sustainable development, 338, 340
Sustainable development goals (SDGs), 305–306, 319, 323–324
SWOT, 105–106

Talent acquisition, 46, 49, 116, 143, 145, 153, 154, 350
Talent analytics, 308
Talent metrics, 308
Talent recruitment, 131
Talent value model, 211
Technologies, 4
Technology, 101–105

Technology acceptance model (TAM), 117
Technology-based HRM, 359, 360
Traditional HRM, 363
Training and development, 247
Transparent governance, 54
Types of HR data, 183

United Nations (UN), 316, 321, 323–324
Upskilling and reskilling, 36

VIBE, 295–297
Virtual HR practices, 86–88
Virtual reality (VR), 41

Work environment, 246
Workforce, 148, 149–152
Workforce analytics, 308
Workforce management, 43–44
Workforce performance, 114, 131
Workforce planning, 240, 353

Printed in the USA/Agawam, MA
September 16, 2026

910661.125